ART

OR,

SHIFTS AND CONTRIVANCES AVAILABLE IN WILD COUNTRIES.

By FRANCIS GALTON, F.R.S.,

AUTHOR OF TRAVELS IN TROPICAL SOUTH AFRICA; FORMERLY, GOLD MEDALLIST AND
HONORARY SECRETARY OF THE ROYAL GEOGRAPHICAL SOCIETY.

FIFTH EDITION.

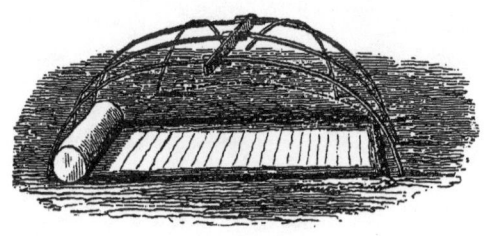

LONDON:

JOHN MURRAY, ALBEMARLE STREET.

1872.

The right of Translation is reserved.

ISBN-13: 978-1535080606
ISBN-10: 1535080604

PREFACE TO THE FIFTH EDITION.

This Edition does not differ materially from the fourth. I have incorporated some new material, including Colomb and Bolton's flashing signals, but in other respects the Work is little altered. I therefore reprint the

PREFACE TO THE FOURTH EDITION.

In publishing a Fourth Edition of the 'Art of Travel,' it is well that I should preface it with a few words of explanation on the origin and intention of the Book and on the difference between this and former Editions.

The idea of the work occurred to me when exploring South-western Africa in 1850-51. I felt acutely at that time the impossibility of obtaining sufficient information on the subjects of which it treats; for though the natives of that country taught me a great deal, it was obvious that their acquaintance with bush lore was exceedingly partial and limited. Then remembering how the traditional maxims and methods of travelling in each country differ from those of others, and how every traveller discovers some useful contrivances for himself, it appeared to me, that I should do welcome service to all who have to rough it,—whether explorers, emigrants, missionaries or soldiers,*—by collecting the scattered expe-

* "... the soldier should be taught all such practical expedients and their philosophy, as are laid down in Mr. Galton's useful little book ..."—'Minute by the late Sir James Outram on Army Management.' *Parliamentary Return*, 330, *of May* 24, 1860, p. 159.

riences of many such persons in various circumstances, collating them, examining into their principles, and deducing from them what might fairly be called an "Art of Travel." To this end, on my return home, I searched through a vast number of geographical works, I sought information from numerous travellers of distinction, and I made a point of re-testing, in every needful case, what I had read or learned by hearsay.

It should be understood that I do not profess to give exhaustive treatises on each of the numerous subjects comprised in this volume, but only such information as is not generally known among travellers. A striking instance of the limited geographical area over which the knowledge of many useful contrivances extends, is that described as a '*Dáterám*,' p. 164, by which tent ropes may be secured in sand of the loosest description. Though tents are used over an enormous extent of sandy country, in all of which this simple contrivance would be of the utmost value on every stormy night, and though the art of pitching tents is studied by the troops of all civilised and partly civilised nations, yet I believe that the use of the dáterám never extended beyond the limits of a comparatively small district in the south of the Sahara, until I had described it in a former Edition; and further, my knowledge of that contrivance was wholly due to a single traveller, the late Dr. Barth.

The first Edition of the 'Art of Travel' was published in 1854: it was far less comprehensive than the later ones; for my materials steadily accumulate, and each successive Edition has shown a marked improvement on its predecessor. Hitherto I have adhered to the original arrangement of the work, but am now obliged to deviate from it, for the contents have outgrown the system of classification I first adopted. Before I could interpolate the new matter prepared for this Edition, I found it necessary to recast the last one, by cutting it into pieces, sorting it into fresh paragraphs and thoroughly revising the writing—disentangling here and consolidating there. The present Edition will consequently be found more conveniently arranged than those that preceded it, and, at the same time, I trust the copiousness of its Index will enable persons to find with readiness any passage they had remarked in a former Edition, and to which they may desire again to refer.

I am still most thankful to strangers as well as to friends for contributions of hints or corrections, having been indebted to many a previously unknown correspondent for valuable information. I beg that such communications may be addressed to me, care of my publisher, Mr. Murray, 50, Albemarle Street, London.

P.S.—A reviewer of my Third Edition accused me of copying largely from an American book, called 'The Prairie Traveller,' by, the then, Capt. Randolph B. Marcy. I therefore think it well to remark that the first Edition of that work was published in 1859 (Harper and Brothers, New York;—by authority of the American War Department), and that the passages in question are all taken from my second Edition published in 1856; part of them are copies of what I had myself written, the rest are reprints of my quotations, as though the Author of the 'Prairie Traveller' had himself originally selected them.

I take this opportunity of remarking that though I have been indebted for information to a very large number of authors and correspondents, yet I am sorry to be unable to make my acknowledgments except in comparatively few instances. The fact is that the passages in this book are seldom traceable to distinctly definite sources: commonly more than one person giving me information that partially covers the same subject, and not unfrequently my own subsequent enquiries modifying or enlarging the hints I had received. Consequently I have given the names of authorities only when my information has been wholly due to them, or when their descriptions are so graphic that I have transferred them without alteration into my pages, or else when their statements require confirmation. It will be easy to see by the context to which of these categories each quotation belongs.

CONTENTS.

Preparatory Enquiries, p. 1. Organising an Expedition, 5. Outfit, 9.

Medicine, 14.

Surveying Instruments, 24. Memoranda and Log-Books, 26. Measurements, 32.

Climbing and Mountaineering, 43.

Cattle, 53. Harness, 65. Carriages, 75.

Swimming, 82. Rafts and Boats, 88. Fords and Bridges, 107.

Clothing, 111.

Bedding, 123. Bivouac, 129. Huts, 141. Sleeping-Bags, 150. Tents, 153. Furniture, 168.

Fire, 171.

Food, 189. Water for Drinking, 211.

Guns and Rifles. 237. Gun-fittings and Ammunition, 244. Shooting, hints on, 250. Game, other means of capturing, 262.

Fishing, 269.

Signals, 273.

Bearings by Compass, Sun, &c., 283. Marks by the way-side, 289. Way, to find, 292.

Caches and Depôts, 300.

Savages, Management of, 308. Hostilities, 310.

Mechanical Appliances, 322. Knots, 325.

Writing Materials, 328.

Timber, 333. Metals, 338. Leather, 341. Cords, String, and Thread, 344. Membrane, Sinew, and Horn, 346. Pottery, 348. Candles and Lamps, 348.

Conclusion of the Journey, 351.

ART OF TRAVEL.

PREPARATORY INQUIRIES.

To those who meditate Travel.—*Qualifications for a Traveller.*—If you have health, a great craving for adventure, at least a moderate fortune, and can set your heart on a definite object, which old travellers do not think impracticable, then—travel by all means. If, in addition to these qualifications, you have scientific taste and knowledge, I believe that no career, in time of peace, can offer to you more advantages than that of a traveller. If you have not independent means, you may still turn travelling to excellent account; for experience shows it often leads to promotion, nay, some men support themselves by travel. They explore pasture land in Australia, they hunt for ivory in Africa, they collect specimens of natural history for sale, or they wander as artists.

Reputed Dangers of Travel.—A young man of good constitution, who is bound on an enterprise sanctioned by experienced travellers, does not run very great risks. Let those who doubt, refer to the history of the various expeditions encouraged by the Royal Geographical Society, and they will see how few deaths have occurred; and of those deaths how small a proportion among young travellers. Savages rarely murder new-comers; they fear their guns, and have a superstitious awe of the white man's power: they require time to discover that he is not very different to themselves, and easily to be made away with. Ordinary fevers are seldom fatal to the sound and elastic constitution of youth, which usually has power to resist the adverse influences of two or three years of wild life.

Advantages of Travel.—It is no slight advantage to a young man, to have the opportunity for distinction which travel affords. If he plans his journey among scenes and places likely to interest the stay-at-home public, he will probably achieve a reputation that might well be envied by wiser men who have not had his opportunities.

The scientific advantages of travel are enormous to a man prepared to profit by them. He sees Nature working by herself, without the interference of human intelligence; and he sees her from new points of view; he has also undisturbed leisure for the problems which perpetually attract his attention by their novelty. The consequence is, that though scientific travellers are comparatively few, yet out of their ranks a large proportion of the leaders in all branches of science has been supplied. It is one of the most grateful results of a journey to the young traveller to find himself admitted, on the ground of his having so much of special interest to relate, into the society of men with whose names he had long been familiar, and whom he had reverenced as his heroes.

To obtain Information.—The centres of information respecting rude and savage countries are the Geographical, Ethnological, and Anthropological Societies at home and abroad. Any one intending to travel should put himself into communication with the Secretary, and become a member of one or more of these Societies; he will not only have access to books and maps, but will be sure to meet with sympathy, encouragement, and intelligent appreciation. If he is about to attempt a really bold exploration under fair conditions of success, he will no doubt be introduced to the best living authorities on the country to which he is bound, and will be provided with letters of introduction to the officials at the port where he is to disembark, that will smooth away many small difficulties and give him a recognised position during his travels.

Information on Scientific Matters.—Owing to the unhappy system of education that has hitherto prevailed, by which boys acquire a very imperfect knowledge of the structure of two dead languages, and none at all of the structure of the living world, most persons preparing to travel are overwhelmed with the consciousness of their incapacity to observe, with intelligence, the country they are about to visit. I have been very frequently begged by such persons to put them in the way of obtaining a rudimentary knowledge of the various branches of science, and have constantly made inquiries; but I regret to say that I have been unable to discover any establishment where suitable instruction in natural science is to be obtained by persons of the age and station of most travellers. Nor do I know of any persons who advertise private tuition in any of its branches whose names I might therefore be at liberty to publish, except Professor Tennant, who gives private lessons in mineralogy at his shop in the Strand, where the learner might easily familiarise himself with the ordinary minerals and fossils, and where collections might be purchased for after reference. An intending traveller could readily find naturalists who would give lessons, in museums and botanical gardens, adapting their instruction to his probable wants, and he would thus obtain some familiarity with the character of the principal plants and animals amongst which he would afterwards be thrown. If he has no private means of learning the names of such persons, I should recommend him to write to some public Professor, stating all particulars, and begging the favour of his advice. The use of the sextant may be learnt at various establishments in the City and East End of London, where the junior officers of merchant vessels receive instruction at small cost. A traveller could learn their addresses from the maker of his sextant. He might also apply at the rooms of the Royal Geographical Society, 1, Savile Row, London, where he would probably receive advice suitable to his particular needs, and possibly some assistance of a superior order to that which the instructors of whom I spoke profess to afford. That well-known volume, 'The Admiralty Manual of Scientific Inquiry,' has been written to meet the wants of uninformed travellers; and a small pamphlet, 'Hints to Travellers,' has been published, with the same object, by the Royal Geographical Society. It is procurable at their rooms. There is, perhaps, no branch of Natural History in which a traveller could do so much, without more information than is to be obtained from a few books, than that of the Science of

Man. He should see the large collection of skulls in the College of Surgeons, and the flint and bone implements in the British Museum, the Christie Museum, and elsewhere, and he should buy the principal modern works on anthropology, to be carefully re-studied on his outward voyage.

Conditions of Success and Failure in Travel.—An exploring expedition is daily exposed to a succession of accidents, any one of which might be fatal to its further progress. The cattle may at any time stray, die, or be stolen; water may not be reached, and they may perish; one or more of the men may become seriously ill, or the party may be attacked by natives. Hence the success of the expedition depends on a chain of eventualities, each link of which must be a success; for if one link fails, at that point, there must be an end of further advance. It is therefore well, especially at the outset of a long journey, not to go hurriedly to work, nor to push forward too thoughtlessly. Give the men and cattle time to become acclimatised, make the bush your home, and avoid unnecessary hardships. Interest yourself chiefly in the progress of your journey, and do not look forward to its end with eagerness. It is better to think of a return to civilisation, not as an end to hardship and a haven from ill, but as a close to an adventurous and pleasant life. In this way, risking little, and insensibly creeping on, you will make connections, and learn the capabilities of the country, as you advance; all which will be found invaluable in the case of a hurried or disastrous return. And thus, when some months have passed by, you will look back with surprise on the great distance travelled over; for, if you average only three miles a day, at the end of the year you will have advanced 1200, which is a very considerable exploration. The fable of the Tortoise and the Hare is peculiarly applicable to travellers over wide and unknown tracts. It is a very high merit to accomplish a long exploration without loss of health, of papers, or even of comfort.

Physical Strength of Leader.—Powerful men do not necessarily make the most eminent travellers; it is rather those who take the most interest in their work that succeed the best; as a huntsman says, " it is the nose that gives speed to the hound." Dr. Kane, who was one of the most adventurous of travellers, was by no means a strong man, either in health or muscle.

Good Temper.—Tedious journeys are apt to make companions irritable one to another; but under hard circumstances, a traveller does his duty best who doubles his kindliness of manner to those about him, and takes harsh words gently, and without retort. He should make it a point of duty to do so. It is at those times very superfluous to show too much punctiliousness about keeping up one's dignity, and so forth; since the difficulty lies not in taking up quarrels, but in avoiding them.

Reluctant Servants.—Great allowance should be made for the reluctant co-operation of servants; they have infinitely less interest in the success of the expedition than their leaders, for they derive but little credit from it. They argue thus:— "Why should we do more than we knowingly undertook, and strain our constitutions and peril our lives in enterprises about which we are indifferent?" It will, perhaps, surprise a leader who, having ascertained to what frugal habits a bush servant is inured, learns on trial, how desperately he clings to those few luxuries which he has always had. Thus, speaking generally, a Cape servant is happy on meat, coffee, and biscuit; but, if the coffee or biscuit has to be stopped for a few days, he is ready for mutiny.

ORGANISING AN EXPEDITION.

Size of Party.—The best size for a party depends on many considerations. It should admit of being divided into two parts, each strong enough to take care of itself, and in each of which is one person at least able to write a letter,—which bush servants, excellent in every other particular, are too often unable to do. In travel through a disorganised country, where there are small chiefs and bands of marauders, a large party is necessary; thus the great success of Livingstone's earlier expeditions was largely due to his being provided with an unusually strong escort of well-armed and warlike, but not too aggressive, Caffres. In other cases small parties succeed better than large ones; they excite less fear, do not eat up the country, and are less delayed by illness. The last fatal expedition of Mungo Park is full of warning to travellers who propose exploring with a large body of Europeans.

Solitary Travellers.—Neither sleepy nor deaf men are fit to travel quite alone. It is remarkable how often the qualities of wakefulness and watchfulness stand every party in good stead.

Servants.—*Nature of Engagements.*—The general duties that a servant should be bound to, independently of those for which he is specially engaged, are—under penalty of his pay being stopped, and, it may be, of dismissal—to maintain discipline, take share of camp-duties and night-watch, and do all in his power to promote the success of the expedition. His wages should not be payable to him in full, till the return of the party to the town from which it started, or to some other civilised place. It is best that all clothing, bedding, &c., that the men may require, should be issued out and given to them as a present, and that none of their own old clothes should be allowed to be taken. They are more careful of what is their own; and, by supplying the things yourself, you can be sure that they are good in quality, uniform in appearance, and equal in weight, while this last is ascertainable.

The following Form of Agreement is abridged from one that was used in Mr. Austin's expedition in Australia. It seems short, explicit, and reasonable :—

"We, the undersigned, forming an expedition about to explore the interior of ——, under Mr. A., consent to place ourselves (horses and equipments) entirely and unreservedly under his orders for the above purpose, from the date hereof until our return to ——, or, on failure in this respect, to abide all consequences that may result. We fully recognise Mr. B. as the second, and Mr. C. as the third in command; and the right of succession to the command and entire charge of the party in the order thus stated.

"We severally undertake to use our best endeavours to promote the harmony of the party, and the success of the expedition.

"In witness whereof we sign our names.

(Here follow the signatures.)

"Read over and signed by the respective parties, in my presence."

(Here follows the signature of some person of importance in the place where the expedition is organised.)

By the words, "abide all consequences," the leader would be justified in leaving a man to shift for himself, and refusing his pay, if the case were a serious one.

Good Interpreters are very important: men who have been used by their chiefs, missionaries, &c., as interpreters, are much to be preferred; for so great is the poverty of thought and language among common people, that you will seldom find a man, taken at hazard, able to render your words with correctness. Recollect to take with you vocabularies of all the tribes whom you are at all likely to visit.

Engaging Natives.—On engaging natives, the people with whom they have lived, and to whom they have become attached and learnt to fear, should impress on them that, unless they bring you back in safety, they must never show their faces again, nor expect the balance of their pay, which will only be delivered to them on your return.

Women.—*Natives' Wives.*—If some of the natives take their wives, it gives great life to the party. They are of very great service, and cause no delay; for the body of a caravan must always travel at a foot's pace, and a woman will endure a long journey nearly as well as a man, and certainly better than a horse or a bullock. They are invaluable in picking up and retailing information and hearsay gossip, which will give clues to much of importance, that, unassisted, you might miss. Mr. Hearne the American traveller of the last century, in his charming book, writes as follows, and I can fully corroborate the faithfulness with which he gives us a savage's view of the matter. After the account of his first attempt, which was unsuccessful, he goes on to say,—" The very plan which, by the desire of the Governor, we pursued, of not taking any women with us on the journey, was, as the chief said, the principal thing that occasioned all our want: 'for,' said he, 'when all the men are heavy laden, they can neither hunt nor travel to any considerable distance; and if they meet with any success in hunting, who is to carry the produce of the labour?' 'Women,' said he, 'were made for labour: one of them can carry or haul as much as two men can do. They also pitch our tents, make and mend our clothing, keep us warm at night; and in fact there is no such thing as travelling any considerable distance, or for any length of time, in this country without their assistance.' 'Women,' said he again, 'though they do everything, are maintained at a trifling expense: for, as they always stand cook, the very licking of their fingers, in scarce times, is sufficient for their subsistence.'"

Strength of Women.—I believe there are few greater popular errors than the idea we have mainly derived from chivalrous times, that woman is a weakly creature. Julius Cæsar, who judged for himself, took a very different view of the powers of certain women of the northern races, about whom he wrote. I suppose, that in the days of baronial castles, when crowds of people herded together like pigs within the narrow enclosures of a fortification, and the ladies did nothing but needlework in their boudoirs, the mode of life was very prejudicial to their nervous system and muscular powers. The women suffered from the effects of ill ventilation and bad drainage, and had none of the counteracting advantages of the military life that was led by the males. Consequently women really became the helpless dolls that they were considered to be, and which it is still the fashion to consider them. It always seems to me that a hard-worked woman is better and happier for her work. It is in the nature of women to be fond of carrying weights; you may see them in omnibuses and carriages, always preferring to hold their baskets or their babies on their knees, to setting them down on the seats by their sides. A woman, whose modern dress includes I know not how many cubic feet of space, has hardly ever pockets of a sufficient size to carry small articles; for she prefers to load her hands with a bag or other weighty object. A nursery-maid, who is on the move all day, seems the happiest specimen of her sex; and, after her, a maid-of-all-work who is treated fairly by her mistress.

OUTFIT.

It is impossible to include lists of outfit, in any reasonable space, that shall suit the various requirements of men engaged in expeditions of different magnitudes, who adopt different modes of locomotion, and who visit different countries and climates. I have therefore thought it best to describe only one outfit as a specimen, selecting for my example the desiderata for South Africa. In that country the traveller has, or had a few years ago, to take everything with him, for there were no civilised settlers, and the natural products of the country are of as little value in supplying his wants as those of any country can be. Again, South African wants are typical of those likely to be felt in every part of a large proportion of the region where rude travel is likely to be experienced, as in North Africa, in Australia, in Southern Siberia, and even in the prairies and pampas of North and South America. To make such an expedition effective all the articles included in the following lists may be considered as essential; I trust, on the other hand, that no article of real importance is omitted.

Stores for general use.—These are to a great degree independent of the duration of the journey.

Small Stores, various :—   lbs.

One or two very small soft-steel axes; a small file to sharpen them; a few additional tools (see chapter on Timber); spare butcher's knives	8
A dozen awls for wood and for leather, two of them in handles; two gimlets; a dozen sail-needles; three palms; a ball of sewing-twine; bit of beeswax; sewing-needles, assorted; a ball of black and white thread; buttons; two tailors' thimbles (see chapter on Cord, String, and Thread)	3
Two penknives; small metal saw; bit of Turkey hone; large scissors; corkscrew	1½
Spring balances, from ¼ lb. to 5 lbs. and from 1 lb. to 50 lbs. (or else a hand steelyard)	1½
Fish-hooks of many sorts; cobbler's wax; black silk; gut; two or more fishing-lines and floats; a large ball of line; thin brass wire, for springes (see chapters on Fishing and Trapping)	2
Ball of wicks, for lamps; candle-mould (see chapter on Candles); a few corks; lump of sulphur; amadou (see chapter on Fire)	1½
Medicines (see chapter on Medicine); a scalpel; a blunt-pointed bistoury; and good forceps for thorns	1
A small iron, and an ironing-flannel; clothes-brush; bottle of Benzine or other scouring drops	3
Carried forward	21½

	lbs.
Brought forward	21¼

Bullet-mould, not a heavy one; bit of iron plate for a ladle; gun-cleaning apparatus; turnscrews; nipple-wrench; bottle of fine oil; spare nipples; spare screw for cock (see chapter on Gun-Fittings) 2¼

Two macintosh water-bags, shaped for the pack saddle, of one gallon each, with funnel-shaped necks, and having a wide mouth (empty) (see chapter on Water for Drinking) 2¼

Composition for mending them, in two small bottles; and a spare piece of macintosh 0¼

Spare leather, canvas, and webbing, for girths; rings and buckles 20

Two small patrol-tents, poles, and pegs (see chapter on Tents) 30

Small inflatable pontoon to hold one, or even two men (see chapter on Rafts and Boats) 10

Small bags for packing the various articles, independently of the saddle-bags 4

Macintosh sheeting overall, to keep the pack dry .. .., 4

Total weight of various small stores 95

Heavy Stores, various:—   lbs.

Pack saddles, spare saddlery (see chapter on Harness); bags for packing Water-vessels (see chapter on Water for Drinking) .. ..

Heavy ammunition for sporting purposes. (1 lb. weight gives 10 shots. Otherwise each armed man is supposed to carry a long double-barrelled rifle of very small bore, say of 70, and ammunition for these is allowed for below) .. ..

Total weight of various heavy stores .. ..

Stationery:—   lbs.

Two ledgers; a dozen note-books (see chapter on Memoranda and Log-Books); paper 9

Ink; pens; pencils; sealing-wax; gum 2¼

Board to write upon 2

Books to read, say equal to six vols. the ordinary size of novels; and maps 7¼

Bags and cases 3

Sketching-books, colours, and pencils 6

Total weight of stationery 30

Mapping:—   lbs.

Two sextants; horizon and roof; lantern; two pints of oil; azimuth compass; small aneroid; thermometers; tin-pot for boiling thermometers; watches (see chapter on Surveying Instruments) 18

Protractors; ruler; compasses; measuring-tape, &c. 3

Raper's Navigation; Nautical Almanac; Carr's Synopsis, published by Weale; small tables, and small almanacs; star maps 4

Bags and baskets, well wadded 6

Total weight of mapping materials 31

Outfit.

Natural History (for an occasional collector):—   lbs.

    Arsenical soap, 2 lbs.; camphor, ¼ lb.; pepper, ¼ lb.; bag of some powder to absorb blood, 2 lbs.; tow and cotton, about 10 lbs.; scalpel, forceps, scissors, &c., ¼ lb.; sheet brass, stamped for labels, ¼ lb. 16

    Pill-boxes; cork; insect-boxes; pins; tin, for catching, and keeping, and killing, animals; nets for butterflies (say bags and all) 10

    Geological hammers, lens, clinometer, &c. 4

    Specimens. (I make no allowance for the weight of these, for they accumulate as stores are used up; and the total weight is seldom increased.)

        Total weight of Natural History materials (for an *occasional* collector) 30

Stores for Individual Use.

For each white man (independently of duration of journey):—   lbs.

    Clothes; macintosh rug; ditto sheet; blanket-bag; spare blanket 30
    Share of plates, knives, forks, spoons, pannikins, or bowls 2
    Share of cooking-things, iron pots, coffee-mill, kettles, &c. 3
    Spare knife, flints, steel, tinder-box, tinder, four pipes 2
    Bags, 6 lbs. 6
    Provisions for emergency—
        Five days of jerked meat, at 3 lbs. a day (on an average) 15
        Two quarts of water (on an average), 4 lbs.; share of kegs, 1¼ lb. ... 8

        Total for each white man 66

For each white man, and for each six months:—   lbs.

    Tea and coffee, 9 lbs.; tobacco, 6 lbs.; salt, 6 lbs.; pepper, 1 lb. 22
    Brandy or rum, occasionally served out 6
    White sugar, 2 lbs.; arrowroot, 1 lb.; dried onions, &c., 3 lbs. 6
    Ammunition for small-bored rifles, with reserve powder and caps 9

        Total for six months 43
        (or at the rate of 7 lbs. per month).

For each black man (independently of duration of journey):—   lbs.

    Bedding, &c. 9
    Meat and water for emergencies, as above (about) 19
    Share of cooking-things 2

        Total for each black man 30

For each black man, and for each six months:—   lbs.

    Tobacco, 6 lbs.; salt, pepper, &c., 5 lbs. 11
    Presents which will have to be made him from time to time 6

        Total for six months 17
        (or at the rate of 3 lbs. per month).

Presents and Articles for Payment.—It is of the utmost importance to a traveller to be well and judiciously supplied with these: they are his money, and without money a person can no more travel in Savagedom than in Christendom. It is a great mistake to suppose that savages will give their labour or cattle in return for anything that is bright or new: they have their real wants and their fashions as much as we have; and, unless what a traveller brings, meets either the one or the other, he can get nothing from them, except through fear or compulsion.

The necessities of a savage are soon satisfied; and, unless he belongs to a nation civilised enough to live in permanent habitations, and secure from plunder, he cannot accumulate, but is only able to keep what he actually is able to carry about his own person. Thus, the chief at Lake Ngami told Mr. Andersson that his beads would be of little use, for the women about the place already "grunted like pigs" under the burdens of those that they wore, and which they had received from previous travellers. These are matters of serious consideration to persons who propose to travel with a large party, and who must have proportionably large wants.

Speaking of presents and articles for payment, as of money, it is essential to have a great quantity and variety of *small change*, wherewith the traveller can pay for small services, for carrying messages, for draughts of milk, pieces of meat, &c. Beads, shells, tobacco, needles, awls, cotton caps, handkerchiefs, clasp-knives, small axes, spear and arrow heads, generally answer this purpose.

There is infinite fastidiousness shown by savages in selecting beads, which, indeed, are their jewellery; so that valuable beads, taken at hap-hazard, are much more likely to prove failures than not. It would always be well to take abundance (40 or 50 lbs. weight goes but a little way) of the following cheap beads, as they are very generally accepted,—dull white, dark blue, and vermilion red, all of a small size.

It is the ignorance of what are the received articles of payment in a distant country, and the using up of those that are taken, which, more than any other cause, limits the journeyings of an explorer: the demands of each fresh chief are an immense drain upon his store.

Summary.—To know the minimum weight for which a proposed expedition must find means of transport, the omitted figures must be supplied in the following schedule, the others must be corrected where required, and the whole must be added together.

Stores for general use:—   lbs.

    Various small stores 95
    Various heavy stores .. ..
    Stationery 30
    Mapping 31
    Natural History (occasional).. 30

Stores for Individual use:—

    For each white man.. 66
      „   „   (at rate of 7 lbs. per month) .. ..
    For each black man.. 30
      „   „   (at rate of 3 lbs. per month) .. ..
    Presents and articles of payment are usually of far greater weight than all the above things put together.

                Total weight to be carried by the expedition.. .. ..

Mem.—If meat and bread, and the like, have to be carried, a very large addition of weight must be made to this list, for the weight of a daily ration varies from 3 lbs., or even 4 lbs., to 2 lbs., according to the concentration of nutriment in the food that is used. Slaughter animals carry themselves; but the cattle-watchers swell the list of those who have to be fed.

Means of Transport.—In order to transport the articles belonging to an expedition across a wild and unknown country, we may estimate as follows:—

Beasts of burthen :—   lbs.

    An ass will not usually carry more than about (*net weight*) 65
    A small mule 90
    A horse 100
    An ox of an average breed 120
    A camel (which rarely can be used by an explorer) 300

It is very inconvenient to take more than six pack-animals in a caravan that has to pass over broken country, for so much time is lost by the whole party in re-adjusting the packs of each member of it, whenever one gets loose, that its progress is seriously retarded.

Carriages.—An animal—camels always excepted—draws upon wheels in a wild country about two and a half times the weight he can carry.

	lbs.
A light cart, exclusive of the driver, should not carry more than ..	800
A light waggon, such as one or two horses would trot away with, along a turnpike road, not more than	1500
A waggon of the strongest construction, not more than	3000

Weight of Rations.—A fair estimate in commissariat matters is as follows:—

A strong waggon full of food carries 1000 full-day rations.
The pack of an ox " 40 "
The pack of a horse " 30 "
A slaughter ox yields, *as fresh meat* 80 "
A fat sheep yields " 10 "
(N.B. Meat when jerked loses about one-half of its nourishing powers.)

MEDICINE.

General Remarks.—Travellers are apt to expect too much from their medicines, and to think that savages will hail them as demigods wherever they go. But their patients are generally cripples who want to be made whole in a moment, and other suchlike impracticable cases. Powerful emetics, purgatives, and eyewashes are the most popular physickings.

The traveller who is sick, away from help, may console himself with the proverb, that "though there is a great difference between a good physician and a bad one, there is very little between a good one and none at all."

Drugs and Instruments.—*Outfit of Medicines.*—A traveller, unless he be a professed physician, has no object in taking a large assortment of drugs. He wants a few powders, ready prepared; which a physician, who knows the diseases of the country in which he is about to travel, will prescribe for him. Those in general use are as follows:—

1. Emetic, mild; 2. ditto, very powerful, for poison (sulpnate of zinc, also used as an eye-wash in Ophthalmia). 3. Aperient, mild; 4. ditto, powerful. 5. Cordial for diarrhœa. 6. Quinine for ague. 7. Sudorific (Dover's powder). 8. Chlorodyne. 9. Camphor. 10. Carbolic acid.

In addition to these powders, the traveller will want Warburg's fever-drops; glycerine or cold cream; mustard-paper for blistering; heartburn lozenges; lint; a small roll of diachylon; lunar-caustic, in a proper holder, to touch old sores with, and for snake-bites; a scalpel and a blunt-pointed bistoury, with which to open abscesses (the blades of these should be waxed, to keep them from rust); a good pair of forceps, to pull out thorns; a couple of needles, to sew up gashes; waxed thread, or better, silver wire. A mild effervescing aperient, like Moxon's, is very convenient. Seidlitz-powders are perhaps a little too strong for frequent use in a tropical climate.

How to carry Medicines.—The medicines should be kept in zinc pill-boxes with a few letters punched both on their tops and bottoms, to indicate what they contain, as Emet., Astr. &c. It is more important that the bottoms of the boxes should be labelled than their tops; because when two of them have been opened at the same time, it often happens that the tops run a risk of being changed.

It will save continual trouble with weights and scales, if the powders be so diluted with flour, that one *Measureful* of each shall be a full average dose for an adult; and if the measure to which they are adopted be cylindrical, and of such a size as just to admit a common lead-pencil, and of a determined length, it can at any time be replaced by twisting up a paper cartridge. I would further suggest that the powders be differently coloured, one colour being used for emetics and another for aperients.

Lint, to make.—Scrape a piece of linen with a knife.

Ointment.—Simple cerate, which is spread on lint as a soothing plaister for sores, consists of equal parts of oil and wax; but lard may be used as a substitute for the wax.

Seidlitz-powders are not often to be procured in the form we are accustomed to take them in, in England; so a recipe for making 12 sets of them, is annexed:—1½ oz. of Carbonate of Soda and 3 oz. of Tartarised Soda, for the blue papers; 7 drachms of Tartaric Acid, for the white papers.

Bush Remedies.—*Emetics.*—For want of proper physic, drink a charge of gunpowder in a tumblerful of warm water or soap-suds, and tickle the throat.

Vapour-baths are used in many countries, and the following plan, used in Russia, is often the most convenient. Heat stones in the fire, and put them on the ground in the middle of the cabin or tent; on these pour a little water, and clouds of vapour are given off. In other parts of the world branches are spread on hot wood-embers, and the patient is placed upon these, wrapped in a large cloth; water is then sprinkled on the embers, and the patient is soon covered with a cloud of vapour. The traveller who is chilled or over-worked, and has a day of rest before him, would do well to practise this simple and pleasant remedy.

Bleeding and Cupping.—Physicians say, now-a-days that bleeding is rarely, if ever, required; and that frequently it does much harm; but they used to bleed for everything. Many savages know how to cup: they commonly use a piece of a horn as the cup, and they either suck at a hole in the top of the horn, to produce the necessary vacuum, or they make a blaze as we do, but with a wisp of grass.

Illnesses.—Fevers of all kinds, diarrhœa, and rheumatism, are the plagues that most afflict travellers; ophthalmia often threatens them. Change of air, from the flat country up into the hills, as soon as the first violence of the illness is past, works wonders in hastening and perfecting a cure.

Fever.—The number of travellers that have fallen victims to fever in certain lands is terrible: it is a matter of serious consideration whether any motives, short of imperious duty, justify a person in braving a fever-stricken country. In the ill-fated Niger expedition, three vessels were employed, of which the 'Albert' stayed the longest time in the river, namely two months and two days. Her English crew consisted of 62 men; of these, 55 caught fever in the river, and 23 died. Of the remaining seven, only two ultimately escaped scot-free; the others suffering, more or less severely, on their return to England. In Dr. McWilliams's Medical History of this expedition, it is laid down that the Niger fever, which may be considered as a type of pestilential fever generally, usually sets in sixteen days after exposure to the malaria; and that one attack, instead of acclimatising the patient, seems to render him all the more liable to a second. Every conceivable precaution known in those days, had been taken to ensure the health of the crew of the 'Albert.' A great discovery of modern days is the power of quinine to *keep off* many types of fever. A person would, now, have little to fear in taking a passage in a Niger steamer; supposing that vessels ran regularly up that river. The quinine he would take, beginning at the coast, would render him proof against fever, until he had passed the delta; but nothing would remove the risk of a long sojourn in the delta itself. However, I should add that Dr. Livingstone's experience on the

Zambesi throws doubt on the power of quinine to keep off the type of fever that prevails upon that river.

Precautions in unhealthy Places.—There are certain precautions which should be borne in mind in unhealthy places, besides that which I have just mentioned of regularly taking small doses of quinine, such as never to encamp to the leeward of a marsh; to sleep close in between large fires, with a handkerchief gathered round your face (natural instinct will teach this); to avoid starting too early in the morning; and to beware of unnecessary hunger, hardship, and exposure. It is a widely-corroborated fact that the banks of a river and adjacent plains are often less affected by malaria than the low hills that overlook them.

Diarrhœa.—With a bad diarrhœa, take nothing but broth, rice water, and it may be rice, in very small quantities at a meal, until you are quite restored. The least piece of bread or meat causes an immediate relapse.

Ophthalmia.—Sulphate of zinc is invaluable as an eyewash: for ophthalmia is a scourge in parts of North and South Africa, in Australia, and in many other countries. The taste of the solution, which should be strongly astringent, is the best guide to its strength.

Tooth-ache.—Tough diet tries the teeth so severely, that a man about to undergo it, should pay a visit to a dentist before he leaves England. An unskilled traveller is very likely to make a bad job of a first attempt at tooth-drawing. By constantly pushing and pulling an aching tooth, it will in time loosen, and perhaps, after some weeks, come out.

Thirst.—Pour water over the clothes of the patient, and keep them constantly wet; restrain his drinking, after the first few minutes, as strictly as you can summon heart to do it. (See "Thirst" in the chapter on "Water.") In less severe cases, drink water with a tea-spoon; it will satisfy a parched palate as much as if you gulped it down in tumblerfuls, and will disorder the digestion very considerably less.

Hunger.—Give two or three mouthfuls, every quarter of an hour, to a man reduced to the last extremity by hunger; strong broth is the best food for him.

Poisoning.—The first thing is to give a powerful emetic, that whatever poison still remains unabsorbed in the stomach, may be thrown up. Use soap-suds or gunpowder (see Emetics) if proper emetics are not at hand. If there be violent pains and gripings, or retchings, give plenty of water to make the vomitings more easy. Next, do your best to combat the symptoms that are caused by the poison which was absorbed before the emetic acted. Thus, if the man's feet are cold and numbed, put hot stones against them, and wrap them up warmly. If he be drowsy, heavy, and stupid, give brandy and strong coffee, and try to rouse him. There is nothing more to be done, save to avoid doing mischief.

Fleas.—" Italian flea-powder," sold in the East, is really efficacious. It is the powdered "Piré oti" (or flea-bane), mentioned in Curzon's 'Armenia' as growing in that country; it has since become an important article of export. A correspondent writes to me, "I have often found a light cotton or linen bag a great safeguard against the attacks of fleas. I used to creep into it, draw the loop tight round my neck, and was thus able to set legions of them at defiance."

Vermin on the Person.—I quote the following extract from Huc's 'Travels in Tartary':—" We had now been travelling for nearly six weeks, and still wore the same clothing we had assumed on our departure. The incessant pricklings with which we were harassed, sufficiently indicated that our attire was peopled with the filthy vermin to which the Chinese and Tartars are familiarly accustomed; but which, with Europeans, are objects of horror and disgust. Before quitting Tchagan-Kouren, we had bought in a chemist's shop a few sapeks'-worth of mercury. We now made with it a prompt and specific remedy against the lice. We had formerly got the receipt from some Chinese; and, as it may be useful to others, we think it right to describe it here. You take half an ounce of mercury, which you mix with old tea-leaves previously reduced to paste by mastication. To render this softer, you generally add saliva; water could not have the same effect. You must afterwards bruise and stir it a while, so that the mercury may be divided into little balls as fine as dust. (I presume the blue pill is a pretty exact equivalent to this preparation.) You infuse this composition into a string of cotton, loosely twisted, which you hang round the neck; the lice are sure to bite at the bait, and they thereupon as surely swell, become red, and die forthwith. In China and in Tartary you have to renew this salutary necklace once a month."

Blistered Feet.—To prevent the feet from blistering, it is a good plan to soap the inside of the stocking before setting out, making a thick lather all over it. A raw egg broken into a boot, before putting it on, greatly softens the leather: of course the boots should be well greased when hard walking is anticipated. After some hours on the road, when the feet are beginning to be chafed, take off the shoes, and change the stockings; putting what was the right stocking on the left foot, and the left stocking on the right foot. Or, if one foot only hurts, take off the boot and turn the stocking inside out. These were the plans adopted by Captain Barclay. When a blister is formed, "rub the feet, on going to bed, with spirits mixed with tallow dropped from a candle into the palm of the hand; on the following morning no blister will exist. The spirits seem to possess the healing power, the tallow serving only to keep the skin soft and pliant. This is Captain Cochrane's advice, and the remedy was used by him in his pedestrian tour." (Murray's 'Handbook of Switzerland.') The recipe is an excellent one; pedestrians and teachers of gymnastics all endorse it.

Rarefied Air, effects of.—On high plateaux or mountains new-comers must expect to suffer. The symptoms are described by many South American travellers; the attack of them is there, among other names, called the *puna*. The disorder is sometimes fatal to stout plethoric people; oddly enough, cats are unable to endure it: at villages 13,000 feet above the sea, Dr. Tschudi says that they cannot live. Numerous trials have been made with these unhappy feline barometers, and the creatures have been found to die in frightful convulsions. The symptoms of the puna are giddiness, dimness of sight and hearing, headache, fainting-fits, blood from mouth, eyes, nose, lips, and a feeling like sea-sickness. Nothing but time cures it. It begins to be felt severely at from 12,000 to 13,000 feet above the sea. M. Hermann Schlagintweit, who has had a great deal of mountain experience in the Alps and in the Himalayas, up to the height of 20,000 feet or more, tells me that he found the headache, &c., come on when there was a breeze, far more than at any other time. His whole party would awake at the same moment, and begin to complain of the symptoms, immediately on the commencement of a breeze. The symptoms of overwork are not wholly unlike those of the puna, and many young travellers who have felt the first, have ascribed them to the second.

Scurvy has attacked travellers even in Australia; and I have myself felt symptoms of it in Africa, when living wholly on meat. Any vegetable diet cures it: lime-juice, treacle, raw potatoes, and acid fruits are especially efficacious. Dr. Kane insists on the value of entirely raw meat as a certain antiscorbutic: this is generally used by the Esquimaux.

Hæmorrhage from a Wound.—When the blood does not pour or trickle in a steady stream from a deep wound, but jets forth in pulses, and is of a bright red colour, all the bandages in the world will not stop it. It is an artery that is wounded; and, unless there be some one accessible, who knows how to take it up and tie it, I suppose that the method of our forefathers is the only one that can be used by an unskilled traveller; it is to burn deeply into the part as you would for a snake-bite (see next paragraph); or else to pour boiling grease into the wound. This is, of course, a barbarous treatment, and its success is uncertain, as the cauterised artery may break out afresh; still, life is in question, and it is the only hope of saving it. After the cautery, the wounded limb should be kept perfectly still, well raised, and cool, until the wound is nearly healed. A *tourniquet*, which will stop the blood for a time, is made by tying a strong thong, string, or handkerchief firmly above the part, putting a stick through, and screwing it tight. If you know whereabouts the artery lies, which it is the object to compress, put a stone over the place under the handkerchief. The main arteries follow pretty much the direction of the inner seams of the sleeves and trousers.

Snake-bites.—Tie a string tight above the part, suck the wound, and caustic it as soon as you can. Or, for want of caustic, explode gunpowder in the wound; or else do what Mr. Mansfield Parkyns well suggests, *i. e.*, cut away with a knife, and afterwards burn out with the end of your iron ramrod, heated as near a white heat as you can readily get it. The arteries lie deep, and as much flesh may, without much danger, be cut or burnt into, as the fingers can pinch up. The next step is to use the utmost energy, and even cruelty, to prevent the patient's giving way to that lethargy and drowsiness which is the usual effect of snake-poison, and too often ends in death.

Wasp and Scorpion-stings.—The oil scraped out of a tobacco-pipe is a good application; should the scorpion be large, his sting must be treated like a snake-bite.

Broken Bones.—It is extremely improbable that a man should die, in consequence of a broken leg or arm, *if the skin be uninjured;* but, if the broken end forces its way through the flesh, the injury is a very serious one. Abscesses form, the parts mortify, and the severest consequences often follow. Hence, when a man breaks a bone, do not convert a simple injury into a severe one, by carrying him carelessly. If possible, move the encampment to the injured man, and not *vice versâ*. Mr. Druitt says:—"When a man has broken his leg, lay him on the other side, put the broken limb exactly on the sound one, with a little straw between, and tie the two legs together with handkerchiefs. Thus the two legs will move as one, and the broken bone will not hurt the flesh so much, nor yet come through the skin."

Drowning.—A half-drowned man must be put to bed in dry, heated clothes, hot stones, &c., placed against his feet, and his head must be raised moderately. Human warmth is excellent, such as that of two big men made to lie close up against him, one on each side. All rough treatment is not only ridiculous but full of harm; such as the fashion —which still exists in some places—of hanging up the body by the feet, that the swallowed water may drain out of the mouth.

I reprint here the instructions circulated by Dr. Marshall Hall:—

"1. Treat the patient instantly, on the spot, in the open air, exposing the face and chest to the breeze (except in severe weather).

"*To Clear the Throat*—2. Place the patient gently on the face, with one wrist under the forehead; all fluids and the tongue itself then fall forwards, leaving the entrance into the windpipe free. If there be breathing—wait and watch; if not, or if it fail,—

"*To Excite Respiration*—3. Turn the patient well and instantly on his side, and—4. Excite the nostrils with snuff, the throat with a feather, &c., dash cold water on the face previously rubbed warm. If there be no success, lose not a moment, but instantly—

"*To Imitate Respiration*—5. Replace the patient on his face, raising and supporting the chest well on a folded coat or other article of dress;—6. Turn the body very gently on the side and a little beyond, and then briskly on the face, alternately; repeating these measures deliberately, efficiently, and perseveringly fifteen times in the minute, occasionally varying the side; when the patient reposes on the chest, this cavity is compressed by the weight of the body, and expiration takes place; when he is turned on the side, this pressure is removed, and inspiration occurs. 7. When the prone position is resumed, make equable but efficient pressure, with brisk movement, along the back of the chest; removing it immediately before rotation on the side: the first measure augments the expiration, the second commences inspiration. The result is—Respiration;—and, if not too late,—Life.

"*To induce Circulation and Warmth*—8. Rub the limbs upwards, with firm grasping pressure and with energy, using handkerchiefs, &c. By this measure the blood is propelled along the veins towards the heart. 9. Let the limbs be thus dried and warmed, and then clothed, the bystanders supplying coats, waistcoats, &c. 10. Avoid the continuous warm-bath, and the position on or inclined to the back."

Medicine.

Litter for the Wounded.—If a man be wounded or sick, and has to be carried upon the shoulders of others, make a litter for him in the Indian fashion; that is to say, cut two stout poles, each 8 feet long, to make its two sides, and three other cross-bars of 2½ feet each, to be lashed to them. Then supporting this ladder-shaped framework *over* the sick man as he lies in his blanket, knot the blanket up well to it, and so carry him off palanquin-fashion. One cross-bar will be just behind his head, another in front of his feet; the middle one will cross his stomach, and keep him from falling out; and there will remain two short handles for the carriers to lay hold of. The American Indians carry their wounded companions by this contrivance after a fight, and during a hurried retreat, for wonderful distances. A kind of waggon-roof top can easily be made to it, with bent boughs and one spare blanket. (See Palanquin.)

SURVEYING INSTRUMENTS.

In previous editions I reprinted here, with a few trifling alterations, part of a paper that I originally communicated to the Royal Geographical Society, and which will be found at the end of their volume for 1854. In addition to it, communications are published there from Lieutenant Raper, Admiral FitzRoy, Admiral Smyth, Admiral Beechey, and Colonel Sykes; the whole of which was collected under the title of 'Hints to Travellers;' they were printed in a separate form and widely circulated. When the edition was exhausted, a fresh Committee was appointed by the Council of the Royal Geographical Society, consisting of Admiral Sir George Back, Admiral R. Collinson, and myself, to revise the pamphlet thoroughly. This process was again gone through in 1871, and now the pamphlet is so much amended and enlarged that I should do no good by making extracts. It is much better that intending travellers should apply for this third edition of the 'Hints to Travellers' at the Society's rooms, 1, Savile Row: for it gives a great deal of information upon instruments that they would find of real value. Its price is 1s.

Porters for delicate Instruments.—Entrust surveying instruments and fragile articles to some respectable old savage, whose infirmities compel him to walk steadily. He will be delighted at the prospect of picking up a living by such easy service.

Measuring low angles by reflexion.—An ordinary artificial horizon is useless for very low angles. They can be measured to within two or three minutes, by means of a vertical point of reference obtained in the following manner:—Tie two pieces of thread, crossing each other at two feet above the ground, put the vessel of mercury underneath it, and look down upon the mercury. When the eye is so placed, that the crossed threads exactly cover their reflexion, the line of sight is truly vertical; and, if the distant object be brought down to them by the sextant, the angle read off will be 90° + altitude. Captain George's arrangement of glass floating on mercury (made by Cary, Fleet Street, London), allows of very low angles being observed, but the use of this instrument requires considerable caution as to the purity of the mercury and the cleanliness of the glass.

Substitute for glass roof to Horizon.—For want of a glass roof to place over the mercury, a piece of gauze stretched over the vessel will answer very tolerably for the purpose of keeping off the wind. The diameter of the pupil of the eye is so large, compared to the thickness of the threads of the gauze, that the latter offer little impediment to a clear view of the image.

Silvering Glasses for Sextants.—" Before taking leave of this subject it may not be unimportant to describe the operation of silvering the glasses of sextants, as those employed on surveying duties very frequently have to perform the operation.

" The *requisites* are clean tinfoil and mercury (a hare's foot is handy)—lay the tinfoil, which should exceed the surface of the glass by a quarter of an inch on each side, on a smooth surface (the back of a book), rub it out smooth with the finger, add a bubble of mercury, about the size of a small shot, which rub gently over the tinfoil until it spreads itself and shows a silvered surface, gently add sufficient mercury to cover the leaf so that its surface is fluid. Prepare a slip of paper the size of the tinfoil. Take the glass in the left hand, previously well cleaned, and the paper in the right. Brush the surface of the mercury gently to free it from dross. Lay the paper on the mercury, and the glass on it. Pressing gently on the glass, withdraw the paper. Turn the glass on its face, and leave it on an inclined plane to allow the mercury to flow off, which is accelerated by laying a strip of tinfoil as a conductor to its lower edge. The edges may, after twelve hours' rest, be removed. In twenty-four hours give it a coat of varnish, made from spirits of wine and red sealing-wax. It may be as well to practise on small bits of common glass, which will soon prove the degree of perfection which the operator has attained." (Admiral Sir E. Belcher.)

MEMORANDA AND LOG-BOOKS.

Best form for Memoranda.—I have remarked that almost every traveller who is distinguished for the copiousness and accuracy of his journals, has written them in a remarkably small but distinct handwriting. *Hard* pencil-marks (HHH pencils) on common paper, or on metallic paper, are very durable. Dr. Barth wrote his numerous observations entirely in Indian-ink. He kept a tiny saucer in his pocket, rubbed with the ink; when he wanted to use it, he rubbed it up with his wetted finger-tip, or resupplied it with fresh ink, and filled his pen and wrote. Captain Burton wrote very much in the dark, when lying awake at night; he used a board with prominent lines of wood, such as is adopted by the blind. It is very important that what is written should be intelligible to a stranger after a long lapse of time. A traveller may die, and his uncompleted work perish with him; or he may return, and years will pass by, and suddenly some observations he had made will be called in question.

Professor J. Forbes says:—"The practice which I have long adopted is this:—to carry a memorandum-book with Harwood's prepared paper" (in this point of detail I do not concur; see next paragraph) "and metallic pencil, in which notes and observations and slight sketches of every description, are made on the spot, and in the exact order in which they occur. These notes are almost ineffaceable, and are preserved for reference. They are then extended, as far as possible, every evening with pen and ink, in a suitable book, in the form of a journal; from which, finally, they may be extracted and modified for any ultimate purpose. The speedy extension of memoranda has several great advantages: it secures a deliberate revision of observations, whether of instruments or of nature, whilst further explanation may be sought, and very often whilst ambiguities or contradictions admit of removal by a fresh appeal to facts. By this precaution, too, the risk of losing all the fruits of some weeks of labour, by the loss of a pocket-book, may be avoided."

It has occurred to me, frequently, to be consulted about the best way of keeping MSS. Captain Blakiston, who surveyed the northern part of the Rocky Mountains, and subsequently received the medal of the Royal Geographical Society, for his exploration and admirable map of the Yang-tse-Kiang, in China, paid great attention to the subject: he was fully in possession of all I had to say on the matter; and I gladly quote the method he adopted in North America, with slight modifications, according to the results of his experience, and with a few trivial additions of my own. For the purposes of memoranda and mapping data, he uses three sets of books, which can be ordered at any lithographer's:—

No. 1. *Pocket Memorandum Book*, measuring three inches and a half by five, made of strong paper. (Captain Blakiston did not use, and I should not advise travellers to use, "prepared" paper, for it soon becomes rotten, and the leaves fall out; besides that, wet makes the paper soppy.) The books are paged with bold numbers printed in the corners; two faint red lines are ruled down the middle of each page, half an inch apart, to enable the book to be used as a field-surveyor's book when required. In this pocket-book, every single thing that is recorded at all, is originally recorded with a hard HHH pencil. Everything is written consecutively, without confusion or attempt to save space. There may easily be 150 pages in each of these books; and a sufficient number should be procured to admit of having at least one per month. Do not stint yourself in these.

No. 2. *Log-Book.*—This is an orderly way of collecting such parts of the surveying material as has been scattered over each day in your note-book. It is to be neatly written out, and will become the standard of future reference. By using a printed form, the labour of drawing up the log on the one hand, and that of consulting it on the other, will be vastly diminished. I give Captain Blakiston's form, in pages 28, 29, and I would urge intending travellers not to depart from it without very valid reasons, for it is the result of considerable care and experience. The *size* in which the form is printed here is not quite accurate, because the pages of this book are not large enough to admit of it, but the *proportion* is kept. The actual size is intended to be five and a half inches high and nine inches wide, so that it should open freely along one of the narrow sides of the page, in the way that all memoranda

PAGE 1 OF DAILY "LOG."—(See description of Log-Book in pp. 27, 30.)

DATE.								
Place.	Local Time.		Course (true).	Geograph. Miles.		Altitude above Sea.	Nature of Country.	Reference.
	From	To		Intervg.	Total.			
		Lat. by Observation. Lat. by Account.						
		Long. by O. ,, ,, Account.						
		Chronometer. No.	Error { at noon on G.M.T. { at on Local M.T. Rate.					
		Variation of Compass.						

Local Time.	Thermometer.		Barometer (or temp. boiling water).			Wind.		Weather.
	Dry.	Wet.	No.	Alt. Ther.	Corrected.	Direction.	Force.	

PAGE 2 OF DAILY "LOG."—(See description of Log-Book in pp. 27, 30.)

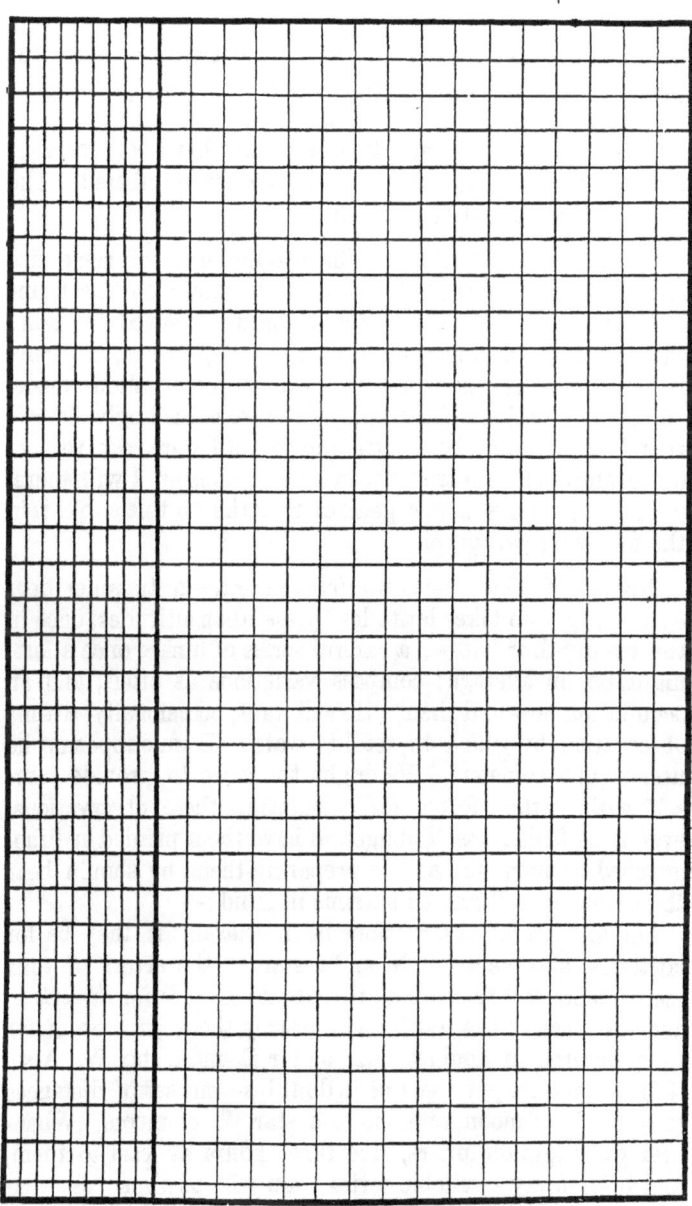

* For "Plan" of Route (usual scale, 4 miles = 1 inch).
† For "Section" of Route (usual vertical scale, 200 feet = 1 inch).

books ought to open. Four pages go to a day; of these the pages 1 and 2 are alone represented in this book, pages 3 and 4 being intended to be left blank.

The bold figures, 17 and 18, in the right-hand corners of the form I give, show how the pages should be numbered. The lines in p. 18 should be faint blue.

No. 3. Calculation Book.—This should be of the same size and shape as the *Log Book*, and should contain outline forms for calculations. The labour and confusion saved by using these, and the accuracy of work that they ensure, are truly remarkable. The instruments used, the observations made, and especially the tables employed, are so exceedingly diverse, that I fear it would be to little purpose if I were to give special examples: each traveller must suit himself. I will, therefore, simply make a few general remarks on this subject, in the following paragraph.

Number of Observations requiring record.—A traveller does excellently, who takes latitudes by meridian altitudes, once in the twenty-four hours; a careful series of lunars once a fortnight, on an average; compass variations as often; and an occultation now and then. He will want, occasionally, a time observation by which to set his watch (I am supposing he uses no chronometer). He ought therefore to provide himself with outline forms for calculating these observations, even if he finds himself obliged to have them printed or lithographed on purpose; and in preparing them, he should bear the following well-known maxims in mind:—

Let all careful observations be in *doubles*. If they be for latitudes, observe a star N. and a star S.; the errors of your instruments will then affect the results in *opposite directions*, and the mean of the results will destroy the error. So, if for time, observe in doubles, viz., a star E. and a star W. Also, if for lunars, let your sets be in doubles—one set of distances to a star E. of moon, and one to a star W. of moon. Whenever you begin on lunars, give three hours at least to them, and bring away a reliable series; you will be thus possessed of a certainty to work upon, instead of the miserably unsatisfactory results obtained from a single set of lunars taken here and another set there, scattered all over the country, and impossible to correlate. A series should consist of six sets, each set including three simple distances. Three of these sets should be to a star or stars E. of moon, and three to a star or stars W. of moon. Lunars not taken on the E. and W. plan are almost worthless, no matter how numerous they may be, for the sextant, &c., might be inaccurate to any amount, and yet no error be manifest in their results. But the E. and W. plan exposes errors mercilessly, and also eliminates them. One of the best authorities on the requirements of sextant observations in rude land travel, the Astronomer Royal of Cape Town, says to this effect:—" Do not observe the altitude of the star in taking lunars, but compute it. The labour requisite for that observation is better bestowed in taking a large number of distances." So much delicacy of hand and of eyesight is requisite in taking lunars that shall give results reliable to seven or eight miles, and so small an exertion or flurry spoils that delicacy, that economy of labour and fidget is a matter to be carefully studied.

These things being premised, it will be readily understood that outline forms sufficient for an entire series of lunars will extend over many pages—they will, in fact, require eighteen pages. There are four sets of observations for time:—one E. and one W., both at beginning and close of the whole; one for latitudes N. and S.; six for six sets of lunars, as described above; six for the corresponding altitudes of the stars, which have to be computed; and, finally, one page for taking means, and recording the observations for adjustment, &c. Each double observation for latitude would take one page; each single time observation one page; and each single compass variation one page. An occultation would require three pages in all; one of which would be for time. At this rate, and taking the observations mentioned above, a book of 500 pages would last half a year. Of course where the means of transport is limited, travellers must content themselves with less. Thus Captain Speke, who started on his great journey amply equipped with log-books and calculation-books, such as I have described, found them too great an incumbrance, and was compelled to abandon them. The result was, that though he brought back a very large number of laborious observations, there was a want of method in them, which made a considerable part of his work of little or no use, while the rest required very careful treatment, in order to give results commensurate with their high intrinsic value.

MEASUREMENTS.

Distance.—*To measure the Length of a Journey by Time.*—The pace of a caravan across average country is 2½ statute, or 2 geographical, miles per hour, as measured with compasses from point to point, and not following the sinuosities of each day's course; but in making this estimate, every minute lost in stoppages by the way is supposed to be subtracted from the whole time spent on the road. A careful traveller will be surprised at the accuracy of the geographical results, obtainable by noting the time he has employed in actual travel. Experience shows that 10 English miles per day, measured along the road—or, what is much the same thing, 7 geographical miles, measured with a pair of compasses from point to point—is, taking one day with another, and including all stoppages of every kind, whatever be their cause,—very fast travelling for a caravan. In estimating the probable duration of a journey in an unknown country, or in arranging an outfit for an exploring expedition, not more than half that speed should be reckoned upon. Indeed, it would be creditable to an explorer to have conducted the same caravan for a distance of 1000 geographical miles, across a rude country, in six months. These data have, of course, no reference to a journey which may be accomplished by a single great effort, nor to one where the watering-places and pasturages are well known; but apply to an exploration of considerable length, in which a traveller must feel his way, and where he must use great caution not to exhaust his cattle, lest some unexpected call for exertion should arise, which they might prove unequal to meet. Persons who have never travelled—and very many of those who have, from neglecting to analyse their own performances—entertain very erroneous views on these matters.

Rate of Movement to measure.—*a. When the length of pace &c., is known before beginning, to observe.*—A man or a horse walking at the rate of one mile per hour, takes 10 paces in some ascertainable number of seconds, dependent upon the length of his step. If the length of his step be 30 inches, he will occupy 17 seconds in making 10 paces. Conversely, if the same person counts his paces for 17 seconds, and finds that he has taken 10 in that time, he will know that he is walking at the rate of exactly 1 mile per hour. If he had taken 40 paces in the same period, he would know that his rate had been 4 miles per hour; if 35 paces, that it had been 3·5, or 3½ miles per hour. Thus it will be easily intelligible, that if a man knows the number of seconds appropriate to the length of his pace, he can learn the rate at which he is walking, by counting his paces during that number of seconds and by dividing the number of his paces so obtained, by 10. In short the number of his paces during the period in question, gives his rate per hour, in miles and decimals of a mile, to one place of decimals. I am indebted to Mr. Archibald Smith for this very ingenious notion, which I have worked into the following Tables. In Table I., I give the appropriate number of seconds corresponding to paces of various lengths. I find, however, that the pace of neither man nor horse is constant in length during all rates of walking; consequently, where precision is sought, it is better to use this Table on a method of approximation. That is to say, the traveller should find his approximate rate by using the number of seconds appropriate to his estimated speed. Then, knowing the length of pace due to that approximate rate, he will proceed afresh by adopting a revised number of seconds, and will obtain a result much nearer to the truth than the first. Table I. could of course be employed for finding the rate of a carriage, when the circumference of one of its wheels was known; but it is troublesome to make such a measurement. I therefore have calculated Table II., in terms of the radius of the wheel. The formulæ by which the two Tables have been calculated are, $m = l \times 0·5682$ for Table I., and $m = r \times 3·570$ for Table II., where m is the appropriate number of seconds; l is the length of the pace, or circumference of the wheel; and r is the radius of the wheel.

The Tables will be found on the next page.

Tables for the easy determination of the Rate of Travel.

TABLE I.—Pace or Stride of Man, Horse, Camel, &c.

Length of pace in inches.	Appropriate number of seconds.	Length of pace in inches.	Appropriate number of seconds.	Length of pace in inches.	Appropriate number of seconds.	Length of pace in inches.	Appropriate number of seconds.	Length of pace in inches.	Appropriate number of seconds.
1	0·57	11	6·2	21	11·9	31	17·6	41	23·3
2	1·13	12	6·8	22	12·5	32	18·2	42	23·9
3	1·70	13	7·4	23	13·1	33	18·4	43	24·4
4	2·27	14	8·0	24	13·7	34	19·3	44	25·0
5	2·84	15	8·4	25	14·3	35	19·9	45	25·6
6	3·41	16	9·1	26	14·8	36	20·5	46	26·1
7	3·98	17	9·7	27	15·4	37	21·1	47	26·7
8	4·55	18	10·2	28	15·9	38	21·6	48	27·3
9	5·11	19	10·8	29	16·4	39	22·2	49	27·8
10	5·68	20	11·4	30	17·0	40	22·8	50	28·4

TABLE II.—Radius of Carriage Wheel.

Length of radius in inches.	Appropriate number of seconds.	Length of radius in inches.	Appropriate number of seconds.	Length of radius in inches.	Appropriate number of seconds.
1	3·57	11	00·0	21	75·0
2	7·14	12	42·8	22	78·5
3	10·71	13	46·4	23	82·1
4	14·28	14	50·0	24	85·7
5	17·85	15	53·6	25	89·2
6	21·42	16	57·1	26	92·8
7	24·99	17	60·7	27	96·4
8	28·56	18	64·3	28	100·0
9	32·13	19	67·8	29	103·5
10	35·70	20	71·4	30	107·1

b. When the length of Pace is unknown *till after observation.*—In this case, the following plan gives the rate of travel per hour, with the smallest amount of arithmetic.

For statute miles per hour—Observe the number of paces (n) taken in 5·7 seconds: let i be the number of inches (to be subsequently determined at leisure) in a single pace; then $\frac{ni}{100}$ is the rate per hour.

For geographical miles per hour—The number of seconds to be employed is 5. This formula is therefore very simple, and it is a useful one. (A statute mile is 1760 yards, and a geographical mile is 2025 yards.)

Measurements. 35

For finding the rate in statute miles per hour in a carriage—Observe the number of revolutions (n) made by the wheel in 18 seconds: let d be the number of inches in the diameter of the wheel; then $\frac{nd}{100}$ is the rate per hour.

The above method is convenient for measuring the rate at which an animal gallops. After counting its paces it may be through a telescope, during the prescribed number of seconds, you walk to the track, and measure the length of its pace. If you have no measuring tape, stride in yards alongside its track, to find the number of yards that are covered by 36 of its paces. This is, of course, identical with the number of inches in one of its paces.

Convenient Equivalents.—The rate of 1 mile per hour, is the equivalent to each of the rates in the following list:—

Yards.	Feet.	Inches.	
29·333,	or 88·000,	or 1056·000,	in 1 minute.
or 0·488,	or 1·466,	or 17·600,	in 1 second.

Measurement of Length.—Actual measurement with the rudest makeshift, is far preferable to an unassisted guess, especially to an unpractised eye.

Natural Units of Length.—A man should ascertain his height; height of his eye above ground; ditto, when kneeling: his fathom; his cubit; his average pace; the span, from ball of thumb to tip of one of his fingers; the length of the foot; the width of two, three, or four fingers; and the distance between his eyes. In all probability, some one of these is an even and a useful number of feet or inches, which he will always be able to recollect, and refer to as a unit of measurement. The distance between the eyes is instantly determined, and, I believe, never varies, while measurements of stature, and certainly those of girth of limb, become very different when a man is exhausted by long travel and bad diet. It is therefore particularly useful for measuring small objects. To find it, hold a stick at arm's-length, at right angles to the line of sight; then, looking past its end to a distant object, shut first one eye and then the other, until you have satisfied yourself of the exact point on the stick that covers the distant object as seen by the one eye, when the end of the stick exactly covers the same object, as seen by the other eye. A stone's throw is a good standard of reference for greater distances. Cricketers estimate distance by the length between wickets. Pacing yards should be practised. It is well to dot or burn with the lens of your opera-glass a scale of inches on the gun-stock and pocket-knife.

Velocity of Sound.—Sound flies at 380 yards or about 1000 feet in a second, speaking in round numbers: it is easy to measure rough distances by the flash of a gun and its report; for even a storm of wind only makes 4 per cent. difference, one way or the other, in the velocity of sound.

Measurement of Angles.—*Rude Measurements.*—I find that a capital substitute for a very rude sextant is afforded by the outstretched hand and arm. The span between the middle finger and the thumb subtends an angle of about 15°, and that between the forefinger and the thumb an angle of 11¼°, or one point of the compass. Just as a person may learn to walk *yards* accurately, so may he learn to span out these angular distances accurately; and the horizon, however broken it may be, is always before his eyes to check him. Thus, if he begins from a tree, or even from a book on his shelves and spans all round until he comes to the tree or book again, he should make twenty-four of the larger spans and thirty-two of the lesser ones. These two angles of 15° and 11¼° are particularly important. The sun travels through 15° in each hour; and therefore, by "spanning" along its course, as estimated, from the place where it would stand at noon (aided in this by the compass), the hour before or after noon, and, similarly, after sunrise or before sunset, can be instantly reckoned. Again, the angles 30°, 45°, 60°, and 90°, all of them simple multiples of 15°, are by far the most useful ones in taking rough measurements of heights and distances, because of the simple relations between the sides of right-angled triangles, one of whose other angles are 30°, 45°, or 60°; and also because 60° is the value of an angle of an equilateral triangle. As regards 11¼°, or one point of the compass, it is perfectly out of the question to trust to bearings taken by the unaided eye, or to steer a steady course by simply watching a star or landmark, when this happens to be much to the right or the left of it. Now, nothing is easier than to span out the bearing from time to time.

Right-angles to lay out.—A triangle whose sides are as 3, 4, and 5, must be a right-angled one, since $5^2 = 3^2 + 4^2$; therefore we can find a right-angle very simply by means of a measuring-tape. We take a length of twelve feet, yards, fathoms, or whatever it may be, and peg its two ends, side by side, to the ground. Peg No. 2 is driven in at the third division, and peg No. 3 is held at the seventh division of the cord, which is stretched out till it becomes taut; then the peg is driven in. These three pegs will form the corners of a right-angled triangle; peg No. 2 being situated at the right-angle.

Proximate Arcs.—

   $1°$ subtends, at a distance of 1 statute mile, 90 feet.
   $1'$ subtends, at a distance of 1 statute mile, 18 inches.
   $1'$ subtends, at a distance of 100 yards, 1 inch.
   $1''$ of latitude on the earth's surface is 100 feet.
   $30'$ is subtended by the diameter of either the sun or the moon.

Angles measured by their Chords.—The number of degrees contained by any given angle, may be ascertained without a protractor or other angular instrument, by means of a Table of Chords. So, also, may any required angle be protracted on paper, through the same simple means. In the first instance, draw a circle on paper with its centre at the apex of the angle and with a radius of 1000, next measure the distance between the points where the circle is cut by the two lines that enclose the angle. Lastly look for that distance (which is the chord of the angle) in the annexed table, where the corresponding number of degrees will be found. If it be desired to protract a given angle, the same operation is to be performed in a converse sense. I need hardly mention that the chord of an angle is the same thing as twice the sine of half that angle; but as tables of natural sines are not now-a-days commonly to be met with, I have thought it well worth while to give a Table of Chords. When a traveller, who is unprovided with regular instruments, wishes to triangulate, or when having taken some bearings but having no protractor, he wishes to lay them down upon his map, this little table will prove of very great service to him. (See "Measurement of distances to inaccessible places.")

TABLE of Chords to Radius of 1000.

Deg.	Chords.	Deg.	Chords.	Deg.	Chords.	Deg.	Chords.
1	017	46	781	91	1427	136	1854
2	035	47	798	92	1439	137	1861
3	052	48	813	93	1451	138	1867
4	070	49	829	94	1463	139	1863
5	087	50	845	95	1475	140	1879
6	105	51	861	96	1486	141	1885
7	122	52	877	97	1498	142	1891
8	139	53	892	98	1509	143	1897
9	157	54	908	99	1521	144	1902
10	174	55	924	100	1532	145	1907
11	192	56	939	101	1543	146	1913
12	209	57	954	102	1554	147	1918
13	226	58	970	103	1565	148	1923
14	244	59	985	104	1576	149	1927
15	261	60	1000	105	1587	150	1932
16	278	61	1015	106	1597	15	1936
17	296	62	1030	107	1608	152	1941
18	313	63	1045	108	1618	153	1945
19	330	64	1060	109	1628	154	1949
20	347	65	1075	110	1638	155	1953
21	364	66	1090	111	1648	156	1956
22	382	67	1104	112	1658	157	1960
23	399	68	1118	113	1668	158	1963
24	416	69	1133	114	1677	159	1967
25	433	70	1147	115	1687	160	1970
26	450	71	1161	116	1696	161	1973
27	467	72	1176	117	1705	162	1975
28	484	73	1190	118	1714	163	1978
29	501	74	1204	119	1723	164	1981
30	518	75	1218	120	1732	165	1983
31	534	76	1231	121	1741	166	1985
32	551	77	1245	122	1749	167	1987
33	568	78	1259	123	1758	168	1989
34	585	79	1272	124	1766	169	1991
35	601	80	1286	125	1774	170	1993
36	618	81	1299	126	1782	171	1994
37	635	82	1312	127	1790	172	1995
38	651	83	1325	128	1798	173	1996
39	668	84	1338	129	1805	174	1997
40	684	85	1351	130	1813	175	1998
41	700	86	1344	131	1820	176	1999
42	717	87	1377	132	1827	177	1999
43	733	88	1389	133	1834	178	2000
44	749	89	1402	134	1841	179	2000
45	765	90	1414	135	1848	180	2000

Triangulation.—*Measurement of distance to an inaccessible* *place—By similar triangles.*—To show how the breadth of a river may be measured without instruments, without any table, and without crossing it, I have taken the following useful problem from the French 'Manuel du Génie.' Those usually given by English writers for the same purpose are, strangely enough, unsatisfactory, for they require the measurement of an angle. This plan requires pacing only. To measure A B, produce it for any distance, as to D; from D, in any convenient direction, take any equal distances, D C, C d; produce B C to b, making C b = C B; join d b, and produce it to a, that is to say, to the point where A C produced intersects it; then the triangles to the left of C, are similar to those on the right of C, and therefore a b is equal to A B. The points D C, &c., may be marked by bushes planted in the ground, or by men standing.

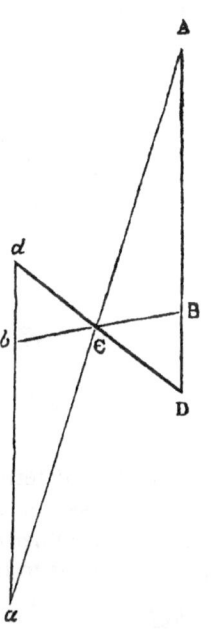

The disadvantages of this plan are its complexity, and the usual difficulty of finding a sufficient space of level ground, for its execution. The method given in the following paragraph is incomparably more facile and generally applicable.

Triangulation by measurement of Chords.—Colonel Everest, the late Surveyor-General of India, pointed out (Journ. Roy. Geograph. Soc. 1860, p. 122) the advantage to travellers, unprovided with angular instruments, of measuring the *chords* of the angles they wish to determine. He showed that a person who desired to make a rude measurement of the angle C A B, in the figure (p. 40), has simply to pace for any convenient length from A towards C, reaching, we will say, the point a', and then to pace an equal distance from A towards B, reaching the point a''. Then it remains for him to pace the distance $a'\ a''$ which is the chord of the angle A to the radius A a'. Knowing this, he can ascertain the value of the angle C A B by reference to a proper table. In the same way the angle C B A can be ascertained. Lastly, by pacing the distance A B, to serve as a base, all the necessary data will have been

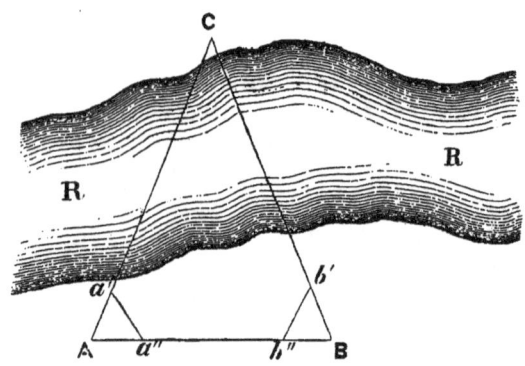

obtained for determining the lines A C and B C. The problem can be worked out, either by calculation or by protraction. I have made numerous measurements in this way, and find the practical error to be within five per cent.

Table for rude triangulation by Chords.—It occurred to me that the plan described in the foregoing paragraph might be exceedingly simplified by a table, such as that which I annex, in which different values of $a'\,a''$ are given for a radius of 10, and in which the calculations are made for a base=100. The units in which A a', A a'', and B b', B b'', are to be measured are intended to be paces, though, of course, any other units would do. The units in which the base is measured may be feet, yards, minutes, or hours' journey, or whatever else is convenient. Any multiple or divisor of 100 may be used for the base, if the tabular number be similarly multiplied. Therefore a traveller may ascertain the breadth of a river, or that of a valley, or the distance of any object on either side of his line of march, by taking not more than some sixty additional paces, and by making a single reference to my table. Particular care must be taken to walk in a straight line from A to B, by sighting some more distant object in a line with B. It will otherwise surprise most people, on looking back at their track, to see how curved it has been and how far their b' B is from being in the right direction.

TABLE FOR ROUGH TRIANGULATION without the usual Instruments, and without Calculation.

Chord of angle situated at the opposite end of base to that from which we desire to learn the distance across the river.

(Chord of angle situated at that end of the base from which we desire to learn the distance across the river — left column)

	5	5½	6	6½	7	7½	8	8½	9	9½	10	10½	11	11½	12	12½	13	13½	14	14½	15	15½	16	16½
5	57	60	64	67	70	73	75	78	81	84	87	89	92	95	98	101	105	109	113	118	123	129	137	146
5½	55	59	62	65	69	72	74	77	81	84	87	90	93	96	100	103	107	112	116	122	128	135	144	155
6	54	57	61	64	68	71	74	77	80	84	87	90	94	97	101	105	110	115	120	126	134	142	153	167
6½	53	56	60	63	67	70	74	77	80	84	87	91	95	99	103	108	113	119	125	132	141	151	164	182
7	52	55	59	63	66	70	73	77	81	85	88	92	96	101	106	111	117	123	130	139	149	161	178	200
7½	51	55	58	62	66	70	73	77	81	85	89	93	98	103	109	118	121	128	136	146	159	174	194	223
8	50	54	58	62	66	70	74	78	82	86	91	95	101	106	112	118	126	134	144	156	170	189	215	253
8½	49	53	57	61	65	70	74	78	83	88	92	97	103	109	116	123	132	141	153	168	185	208	247	294
9	49	53	57	61	66	70	75	79	84	89	94	100	106	113	121	129	139	150	162	181	203	233		
9½	49	53	57	62	66	71	76	81	86	91	97	103	110	118	126	136	147	160	174	194	225	265		
10	48	53	58	62	67	72	77	82	88	94	100	107	113	120	128	138	151	167	191					
10½	48	53	58	63	68	73	78	83	89	94	104	112	120	131	141	155	171	193	223					
11	49	54	58	63	70	74	80	86	92	98	104	110	118	127	135	144	157	173	194					
11½	49	54	59	64	72	76	83	89	96	103	109	115	123	130	138	147	160	175	196	224				
12	50	55	60	65	75	79	85	93	100	105	112	121	127	135	141	151	163	179	199					
12½	50	56	62	67	77	81	89	98	103	110	117	123	133	144	151	163	179	199						
13	52	57	64	70	81	85	93	103	108	117	126	132	139	147	161	171	187	207						
13½	53	59	66	73	85	90	99	109	113	123	134	141	150	160	173	190	211	237						
14	57	62	70	77	99	95	106	118	123	130	144	156	162	174	193	215								
14½	60	65	73	81	102	102	114	129	130	141	153	168	181	194	218	248								
15	60	68	77	87	99	110	126	143	155	164	181	203	225											
15½	64	73	83	95	108	123	141	163	171	191	208	233	265											
16	69	79	90	105	121	140	164	193	215															
16½	76	88	103	120	141	166	199	243	247															

TO USE THE TABLE.

Let AB be the base of 100 feet, yards, minutes' journey, or whatever may be most convenient. C the point on the other side of the river.
$a'a''$ the chord of the angle at A to radius 10.
$b'b''$ the chord of the angle at B to radius 10.
To find AC, enter the Table with $a'a''$ at the top, and with $b'b''$ at the side.
To find BC, enter the Table with $b'b''$ at the side, and with $a'a''$ at the top.

Example: AB = 100 yards; $a'a''$ = 5 paces; $b'b''$ = 10 paces: then AP = 87 yards; BP = 48 yards.

Measurement of Time.—*Sun Dial.*—Plant a stake firmly in the ground in a level open space, and get ready a piece of string, a tent-peg, and a bit of stick a foot long. When the stars begin to appear, and before it is dark, go to the stake, lie down on the ground, and plant the stick, so adjusting it that its top and the point where the string is tied to the stake shall be in a line with the Polar Star, or rather with the Pole (see below); then get up, stretch the string so as just to touch the top of the stick, and stake it down with the tent-peg. Kneel down again, to see that all is right, and in the morning draw out the dial-lines; the string being the gnomon. The true North Pole is distant about 1½ degree, or three suns' (or moons') diameters from the Polar Star, and it lies *between* the Polar Star and the pointers of the Great Bear, or, more truly, between it and ζ Ursæ Majoris.

The one essential point of dial-making is to set the gnomon truly, because it ensures that the shadows shall fall in the same direction at the same hours all the year round. To ascertain where to mark the hour-lines on the ground, or wall, on which the shadow of the gnomon falls, the simplest plan is to use a watch, or whatever makeshift means of reckoning time be at hand. Calculations are troublesome, unless the plate is quite level, or vertical, and exactly facing south or north, or else in the plane of the Equinox.

The figure represents the well-known equinoctial sun-dial. It can easily be cast in lead. The spike points towards the elevated pole, and the rim of the disc is divided into 24 *equal parts* for the hours.

Pendulum.—A traveller, when the last of his watches breaks down, has no need to be disheartened from going on with his longitudinal observations, especially if he observes occultations and eclipses. The object of a watch is to tell the number of seconds that elapse between the instant of occultation, eclipse, &c., and the instant, a minute or two later, when the sextant observation for time is made. All that a watch actually *does* is to beat seconds, and to record the number of beats. Now, a string and stone, swung as a pendulum, will beat time; and a native who is taught to throw a pebble into a bag at each beat, will record it; and, for operations that do not occupy much time, he will be as good as a watch. The rate of the pendulum may be determined by taking two sets of observations, with three or four minutes' interval between them; and, if the distance from the point of suspension to the centre of the stone be thirty-nine inches, and if the string be thin and the stone very heavy, it will beat seconds very nearly indeed. The observations upon which the longitude of the East African lakes depended, after Captain Speke's first journey to them, were lunars, timed with a string and a stone, in default of a watch.

Hour-glass.—Either dry sand or water may be used in an hour-glass; if water be used, the aperture through which it runs must, of course, be smaller.

CLIMBING AND MOUNTAINEERING.

Climbing.—*Climbing trees.*—Colonel Jackson, in his book, 'How to Observe,' gives the following directions for climbing palms and other trees that have very rough barks:—" Take a strip of linen, or two towels or strong handkerchiefs tied together, and form a loop at each end, for the feet to pass tightly into without going through; or, for want of such material, make a rope of grass or straw in the same way. The length should embrace a little more than half of the diameter of the trunk to be climbed. Now, being at the foot of the tree, fix the feet well into the loops, and opening the legs a little, embrace the tree as high up as you can. Raise your legs, and, pressing the cord against the tree with your feet, stand, as it were, in your stirrups, and raise your body and arms higher; hold fast again by the arms, open the legs, and raise them a stage higher, and so on to the top. The descent is effected in the same way, reversing, of course, the order of the movements. The ruggedness of the bark, and the weight of the body pressing diagonally across the trunk of the tree, prevent the rope from slipping. Anything, provided it be strong enough, is better than a round rope, which does not hold so fast." A loop or hoop embracing the body of the climber and the tree, is a helpful addition. Large nails carried in a bag slung round the waist, to be driven into the bare trunk of the tree, will facilitate its ascent. Gimlets may be used for the same purpose. High walls can be climbed by help of this description; a weight attached to one end of a rope, being first thrown over the wall, and the climber assisting himself by holding on to the other end. Trees of soft wood are climbed by cutting notches two feet apart on alternate sides. Also by driving in bamboo pegs, sloping alternately to left or to right; these pegs correspond to the "rungs" of a ladder.

Ladders.—A notched pole or a knotted rope makes a ladder. We hear of people who have tied sheets together to let themselves down high walls, when making an escape. The best way of making a long rope from sheets, is to cut them into strips of about six inches broad, and with these to twist a two-stranded rope, or else to plait a three-stranded one.

Descending cliffs with ropes is an art which naturalists and others have occasion to practise. It has been reduced to a system by the inhabitants of some rocky coasts in the Northern seas, where innumerable sea-birds go for the breeding season, and whose ledges and crevices are crammed with nests full of large eggs, about the end of May and the beginning of June. They are no despicable prize to a hungry native. I am indebted to a most devoted rock-climber, the late Mr. Woolley, for the following facts. It appears that the whole population are rock-climbers, in the following places:—St. Kilda, in the Hebrides; Foula Island, in Shetland; the Faroe Islands generally; and in the Westmaröer Islands off Iceland. Flamborough Head used to be a famous place for this accomplishment, but the birds have become far less numerous; they have been destroyed very wantonly with shot.

In descending a cliff, two ropes are used; one a supple well-made, many-stranded, inch rope (see "Ropes"), to which the climber is attached, and by which he is let down; the other is a much thinner cord, left to dangle over the cliff, and made fast to some stone or stake above. The use of the second rope is for the climber to haul upon, when he wishes to be pulled up. By resting a large part of his weight upon it, he makes the task of pulling him up much more easy. He can also convey signals by jerking it. A usual rock-

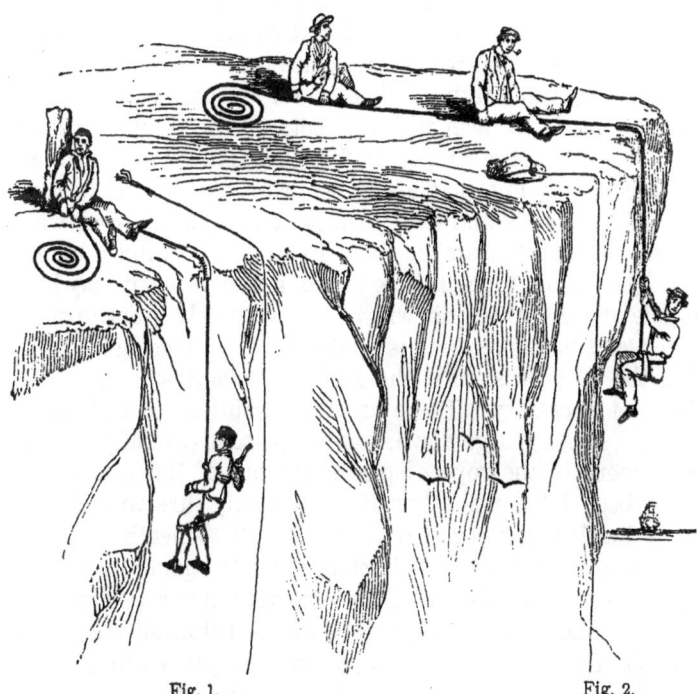

Fig. 1.   Fig. 2.

climbing arrangement is shown in the sketch. One man with a post behind him, as in fig. 1, or two men, as in fig. 2 are entrusted with the letting down of a comrade to the depth of 100 or even 150 feet. They pass the rope either under their thighs or along their sides, as shown in the figures. The climber is attached to the rope, as shown in fig. 2. The band on which he sits is of worsted. A beginner ought to be attached far more securely to the rope.

(I have tried several plans, and find that which is shown in Fig. 1 to be thoroughly comfortable and secure. A stick forms the seat; at either end of it is a short stirrup; garters secure the stirrup leathers to the knees; there is a belt under the arms.)

It is convenient, but not necessary, to have a well-greased leather sheath, a tube of eighteen inches in length, through which the rope runs, as shown in both figures. It lies over the edges of the cliff, and the friction of the rock keeps it steadily in its place.

It is nervous work going over the edge of a cliff for the first time; however, the sensation does *not* include giddiness. Once in the air, and when confidence is acquired, the occupation is very exhilarating. The power of locomotion is marvellous: a slight push with the foot, or a thrust with a stick, will swing the climber twenty feet to a side. Few rocks are so precipitous but that a climber can generally make some use of his hands and feet; enough to cling to the rock when he wishes, and to clamber about its face. The wind is seldom felt by a person touching the face of a precipice: it may blow a gale above, but the air will be comparatively quiet upon its face; and therefore there is no danger of a chance gush dashing the climber against the rocks. A short stick is useful, but not necessary. There are three cautions to be borne in mind. 1. As you go down, test every stone carefully. If the movement of the rope displaces any one of them, after you have been let down below it, it is nearly sure to fall upon your head, because you will be vertically beneath it. Some climbers use a kind of helmet as a shield against these very dangerous accidents. 2. Take care that the rope does not become jammed in a cleft, or you will be helplessly suspended in mid-air. 3. Keep the rope pretty tight when you are clambering about the ledges: else, if you slip, the jerk may break the rope, or cause an overpowering strain upon the men who are holding it above.

Turf and solid rock are much the best substances for the rope to run over. In the Faroes, they tar the ropes excessively; they are absolutely polished with tar. Good ropes are highly valued. In St. Kilda, leather ropes are used: they last a lifetime, and are a dowry for a daughter. A new rope spins terribly.

Leaping Poles.—In France they practise a way of crossing a deep brook by the help of a rope passed round an overhanging branch of a tree growing by its side. They take a run and swing themselves across, pendulum fashion. It is the principle of the leaping-pole, reversed.

The art of climbing difficult places.—Always face difficult places; if you slip, let your first effort be to turn upon your stomach, for in every other position you are helpless. A mountaineer, when he meets with a formidable obstacle, does not hold on the rock by means of his feet and his hands only, but he clings to it like a caterpillar, with every part of his body that can come simultaneously into contact with its roughened surface.

Snow Mountains.—*Precautions.*—The real dangers of the high Alps may be reduced to three:—1. Yielding of snow-bridges over crevices. 2. Slipping on slopes of ice. 3. The fall of ice, or rocks, from above. Absolute security from the first is obtainable by tying the party together at intervals to a rope. If there be only two in company, they should be tied together at eight or ten paces apart. Against the second danger, the rope is usually effective, though frightful accidents have occurred by the fall of one man, dragging along with him the whole chain of his companions. Against the third danger there is no resource but circumspection. Ice falls chiefly in the heat of the day; it is from limestone cliffs that the falling rocks are nearly always detached. When climbing ice of the most moderate slope, nailed boots are an absolute necessity; and for steep slopes of ice, the ice-axe (described below) is equally essential.

Alpine Outfit consists of ropes, ice-axe or alpenstock (there must be at least one ice-axe in the party), nailed boots, coloured spectacles, veil or else a linen mask, muffettees, and gaiters.

I give the following extracts from the Report of a Committee appointed by the Alpine Club in 1864, on Ropes, Axes, and Alpenstocks:—

Ropes.—We have endeavoured to ascertain what ropes will best stand the sharp jerk which would be caused by a man falling suddenly into a crevasse, or down an ice-slope: and on this subject we lay before the Club the result of nearly a hundred experiments, made with various kinds of rope purchased of the best London makers. We considered that the least weight with which it was practically useful to test ropes, was twelve stone, as representing the average weight of a light man with his whole Alpine equipment. In the preliminary experiments, therefore, all ropes were rejected which did not support the strain produced by twelve stone falling five feet. Under this trial, all those plaited ropes which are generally supposed to be so strong, and many most carefully-made twisted ropes, gave way in such a manner as was very startling to some of our number, who had been in the habit of using these treacherous cords with perfect and most unfounded confidence. Only four ropes passed successfully through this trial; these were all made by Messrs. Buckingham and Sons, of 33, Broad-street, Bloomsbury, and can be procured only of them. We confined our further experiments to these ropes, one of which failed under severer tests, while the remaining three, made respectively of Manilla hemp, Italian hemp, and flax, proved so nearly equal in strength that it may fairly be doubted which is on the whole to be preferred. Each of these three ropes will bear twelve stone falling ten feet, and fourteen stone falling eight feet; and it may be useful to say that the strain upon a rope loaded with a weight of fourteen stone, and suddenly checked after a fall of eight feet, is nearly equal to that which is caused by a dead weight of two tons. None of these ropes, however, will bear a weight of fourteen stone falling ten feet; and the result of our experiments is, that no rope can be made, whether of hemp, flax, or silk, which is strong enough to bear that strain, and yet light enough to be portable. We believe that these ropes, which weigh about three-quarters of an ounce to the foot, are the heaviest which can be conveniently carried about in the Alps. We append a statement of the respective merits of the three kinds, all of which are now made by Messrs. Buckingham, expressly for the Club, and marked by a *red* worsted thread twisted in the strands:—

No. 1. MANILLA HEMP. Weight of 20 yards, 48 oz. *Advantages*—Is softer and more pliable than 2. Is more elastic than 2 and 3. When wet, is far more pleasant to handle than 2 and 3. *Disadvantages*—Has a tendency to wear and fray at a knot.

No. 2. ITALIAN HEMP. Weight of 20 yards, 43 oz. *Advantages*—Is less bulky than 1 and 3. Is harder, and will probably wear best, being least likely to cut against rocks. *Disadvantages*—Is much more stiff and difficult to untie than 1 and 3. When wet, is very disagreeable to handle, and is apt to kink.

No. 3. FLAX. Weight of 20 yards, 44 oz. *Advantages*—When dry, is softer, more pliable, and easier to handle than 1 and 2, and will probably wear better than 1. *Disadvantages*—When wet, becomes decidedly somewhat weaker, and is nearly as disagreeable to handle as 2.

Knots.—There can be no doubt that every knot in a rope weakens its power of resisting a sudden jerking strain. How great a loss of strength results from a knot we cannot undertake to estimate, but that the loss is a very serious one the following statement will show: these ropes which we report will resist the strain of fourteen stone falling eight feet, will *not* resist it if there is a knot in any one of them; or even if the knots used in attaching them to the point of support, or to the weights, be roughly or carelessly made. The rope in these cases breaks at the knot, for two reasons; partly because the folds, as they cross in the knot, are strained suddenly across each other, and one of them is cut through; and partly because the rope is so sharply bent that the outer side of each fold in the knot is much more stretched than the inner side, so that the strain comes almost entirely upon one side only of each fold. For the first reason, we found it necessary to put a pad of some kind inside the knot—leather, linen, or a little tow or waste rope will do. For the second reason we preferred knots in which the folds are least sharply bent round each other; that is, in which the curves are large. We therefore conclude that—1st. No knot, which is not absolutely necessary, ought to be allowed to remain on the rope: 2nd. The tighter and harder a knot becomes, the worse it is: 3rd. The more loose and open a knot is made, the better it is:—and we append diagrams of those knots which we found by experiment weaken the rope least. For Alpine ropes, only three sorts of knots are ever required, and we suggest one of each kind:—No. 1 is for the purpose of joining two ends. No. 2 is

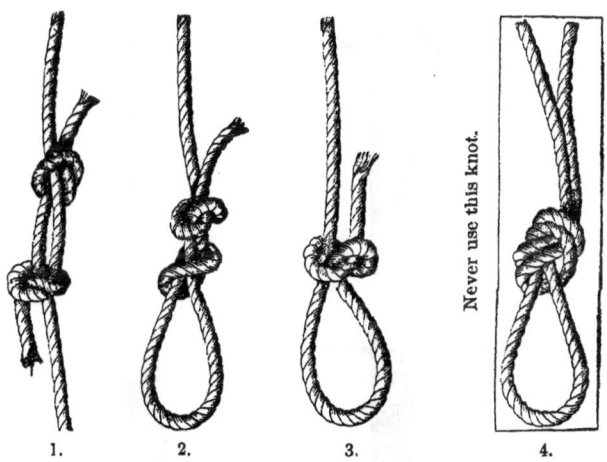

1.   2.   3.   4.

for the purpose of making a loop at one end. No. 3 is for the purpose of making a loop in the middle when the ends are fastened. No. 4 is a knot, of which we give a diagram *in order that no one may imitate it*. It is one of those which most weaken the rope. The only one which seemed to be equally injurious is the common single knot, of which no diagram is necessary. As the ropes which we have recommended are very liable to become untwisted, unless the loose ends are secured, we advise travellers, in order to avoid knots, to have the ends of every piece of rope bound with waxed twine. It should also be known that it is very unsafe to join two pieces of rope by looping one end through the other, so that when the jerk comes, they will be strained across each other as two links of a chain are strained across each other. Unless a pad of some kind divides the loops, one will cut the other through.

Axes.—The axes made in England for the purpose of being taken out to Switzerland, may be divided into two classes, namely: travellers' axes, intended to be used for chipping a few occasional steps, for enlarging and clearing out those imperfectly made, and for holding on to a snow-slope,—and guides' axes, which are the heavier implements required for making long staircases in hard blue ice. We have had three models prepared, of which diagrams are appended; the first two represent the lighter axe, or what we have termed the travellers' axe; and the third, the heavier instrument required for guides' work. Diagram No. 1 represents a light axe or pick, of a kind somewhat similar to that recommended by Mr. Stephen, in a paper published a short time ago in the 'Journal.' It has, in the first place, the great advantage of lightness and handiness, while its single blade, to some extent, combines the step-cutting qualities possessed by the two cutters of the ordinary double-headed axe, though the latter instrument is on the whole decidedly superior. The small hammer-head at the back is added in order to balance the pick, and in some degree to improve the hold when the axe-head comes to be used as a crutch handle. This form, it should be understood, we recommend on account of its lightness and of its convenient shape. Diagram No. 2 represents a travellers' axe, slightly heavier than the first; and as this is the shape which appears to us the best adapted for mountain work of all kinds, we desire shortly to state our reasons for recommending it to members of the Club.

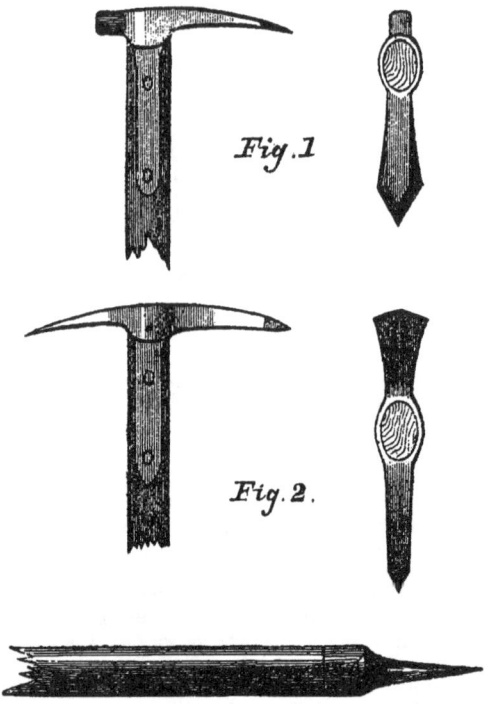

In the first place it is absolutely necessary that one of the cutters should be made in the form of a pick, as this is by far the best instrument for hacking into hard ice, and is also extremely convenient for holding on to a snow-slope, or hooking into crannies, or on to ledges of rock.

For the other cutter we recommend an adze-shaped blade, and we are convinced that this is the form which will be found most generally useful, as being best suited for all the varieties of step-cutting. The hatchet-shaped blade used by the Chamouni guides is no doubt a better implement for making a staircase diagonally up a slope, but on the other hand it is exceedingly difficult to cut steps downwards with a blade set on in this manner; and as mountaineers rarely come down the way by which they went up, if they can help it, it is obvious that this objection to the Chamouni form of axe is conclusive.

We recommend that the edge of the blade should be angular instead of circular, although the latter shape is more common, because it is clear that the angular edge cuts into frozen snow more quickly and easily.

The curve, which is the same in all the axes, approaches to coincidence with the curve described by the axe in making the stroke. A curve is, in our opinion, desirable, in order to bring the point more nearly opposite the centre of percussion, and to make the head more useful for holding on to rocks or a slope.

The axe shown in diagram No. 2, though slightly heavier than No. 1, is not of sufficient weight or strength for cutting a series of steps in hard ice. To those gentlemen, therefore, who do not object to carrying weight, but who desire to have an axe fit for any kind of work, we recommend No. 3. As this is exactly similar in shape to No. 2, differing from it only in size, we have not thought it necessary to give a separate diagram of No. 3.

As to the mode of fastening, which is the same in all the three axes, we should have felt some diffidence in giving an opinion had we not been fortunate enough to obtain the advice of an experienced metal-worker, by whom we were strongly recommended to adopt the fastening shown in the diagrams, as being the method generally considered best in the trade for attaching the heads of hatchets, or large hammers likely to be subjected to very violent strains. It will be seen that the axe-head and fastening are forged in one solid piece, the fastening consisting of two strong braces or straps of steel, which are pressed into the wood about one-eighth of an inch, and are secured by two rivets, passed through the wood and clenched on each side. The braces are put at the side, instead of in front of and behind the axe, because, by this means, the strain which falls on the axe acts against the whole breadth of the steel fastenings, and not against their thickness merely.

We believe that this is the firmest method of fastening which can be adopted, and that so long as the wood is sound, it is scarcely possible for the head of the axe to get loose or to come off; and it has the further advantage of strengthening the wood instead of weakening it, and of distributing the strain produced by step-cutting over a large bearing. It should be added that these axe-heads and fastenings ought to be made entirely of steel.

The dimensions of the axe-heads are as follow :—

No. 1.—Length of blade measured from the wood .. .. 4¼ inches.
        Breadth of blade at widest part.. .. .. 1⅛ ,,
        Weight, including the braces .. .. 13¼ oz.

No. 2.—Length of blade measured from the wood .. .. 3¼ inches.
        Length of pick ,, ,, ,, ... 4¼ ,,
        Breadth of blade at widest part .. .. 1¾ ,,
        Breadth of pick ,, ... 0⅞ ,,
        Weight, including the braces .. .. 15¼ oz.

No. 3.—Length of blade measured from the wood .. .. 4 inches.
        Length of pick ,, ,, ,, ... 5 ,,
        Breadth of blade at widest part.. .. .. 2¼ ,,
        Breadth of pick ,, ... 0⅞ ,,
        Weight, including the braces .. .. 21¼ oz.

We much desired to recommend to the Club some means by which the axe-head might be made moveable, so as to be capable of being put on and taken off the handle quickly and easily. We regret to say, however, that we were unable to discover any plan by which this can be effectually done. We examined very carefully the numerous and formidable weapons which have been sent in by members for exhibition, most of which had elaborate contrivances for fastening on the axe-head. These were all, however, liable to very serious objections. Some were evidently insecure; with others it was necessary that the axe-head should be surmounted by a huge knob, which would prove a most serious impediment in step-cutting; while in the best and firmest which we found, the axe-head was attached to the pole by means of nuts and screws projecting at the side or over the top of the axe. This latter method of fastening seems to us awkward and possibly dangerous, as the nuts, from their position, are very likely to become loose or to get broken off, and cannot, except when dangerously loose, be fastened or unfastened without a key or wrench—a troublesome article, certain to be lost on the first expedition.

The Handle of the Axe should, we think, be made of ash. We recommend this wood in preference to deal, which is lighter and nearly as strong, because in choosing a piece of ash it is easier to select with certainty thoroughly sound and well-seasoned wood; and in preference to hickory and lance-wood, which are stronger, because those woods are extremely heavy.

The handle should, we believe, be of a very slightly oval form, as it is then more convenient to the grasp than if round. As to the thickness of the wood, we are satisfied it ought nowhere to be less than $1\frac{3}{8}$ inch, since a pole of that diameter, made of ordinarily good ash, is the smallest which cannot be permanently bent by a heavy man's most violent effort; although we have seen some pieces of unusually strong ash of a less thickness, which proved inflexible.

We recommend, then, that the oval section of the handle should have a shorter diameter of $1\frac{3}{8}$ inch, and a longer diameter of $1\frac{1}{4}$ inch, and that the thickness should be the same from one end to the other. The length of the handles for Nos. 1 and 2 should be such that they will reach to just under the arm at the shoulder. The handle for No. 3, which is intended to be used exclusively as an axe, should be between $3\frac{1}{2}$ and 4 feet long. The lower end of the handle should be strengthened in the usual way by a ferrule, and armed with a spike.

The spike should be from $3\frac{1}{2}$ to 4 inches long, clear of the end of the handle, and should have a shank of the same length to be screwed into the wood. The screw should be prevented from moving by a slight rivet passed through it near the upper end after it is fastened in. The exact form of the spike and ferrule are represented in the diagram.

We have further to recommend for axe-handles an addition which is liable to suspicion as an entire innovation, but which, we are confident, will be found valuable at those critical moments when the axe is required to hold up two or three men. It has happened that when the axe has been struck into the snow a man has been unable to keep his hold of the handle, which slips out of his hand, and leaves him perfectly helpless. To guard against this mischance, we propose to fasten a band of leather round the handle, at a distance of a foot from the ferrule at the lower end. This leather should be about an eighth of an inch thick, and will be quite sufficient to check the band when it is sliding down the handle. It should be lashed round the wood and strained tight when wet.

Alpenstocks.—What we have said about the handle of the axe applies in all respects to the Alpenstock, except that the length of the latter should be different, and that the leathern ring would of course not be required. It is generally thought most convenient that the Alpenstock should be high enough to touch the chin of its owner, as he stands upright; but this is a matter on which it is scarcely possible, and, were it possible, scarcely necessary to lay down an absolute rule.

Boots.—Several nails are sure to be knocked out after each hard day's work, therefore a reserve supply is necessary in lands where none other are to be found. No makeshift contrivance, so far as I am aware, will replace the iron last used by shoemakers when they hammer nails into the boot. There is a well-known contrivance of screws with jagged heads, for screwing into boots when a little ice has to be crossed. They do excellently for occasional purposes, but not for regular ice-work, as they are easily torn out. Crampons are soles of leather with spikes; they are tied over the shoes, but neither

English mountaineers nor modern guides ever employ them: nailed boots are better.

Snow Spectacles.—The Esquimaux, who have no coloured glass, or any equivalent for it, cut a piece of soft wood to the curvature of the face; it is about two inches thick, and extends horizontally quite across both eyes, resting on the nose, a notch being cut in the wood to answer the purpose of the bridge of a pair of spectacles. It is tied behind the ears; and, so far as I have now described it would exclude every ray of light from the eyes. Next, a long narrow slit, of the thickness of a thin saw-cut, is made along its middle almost from end to end. Through this slit the wearer can see very fairly. As it is narrower than the diameter of the pupil of his eye, the light that reaches his retina is much diminished in quantity. Crape or gauze is a substitute for coloured glass.

Mask.—Is merely a pocket-handkerchief, with strings to tie it over the face; eye-holes are cut in it, also a hole for the nose, over which a protecting triangular piece of linen is thrown, and another hole opposite the mouth, to breathe through; it is drawn below the chin so as to tie firmly in place. The mask prevents the face from being cut to pieces by the cold dry winds, and blistered by the powerful rays of the sun reverberated from the snow.

CATTLE.

Happy is the traveller who has the opportunity of hiring his cattle with their attendants: for his delay and cares are then reduced to those of making a bargain, and of riding what he has hired; and when one set of animals is tired or worn out, he can leave them behind and ride on with others. But, for the most part, explorers must drive their own beasts with them: they must see to their being watered, tended, and run after when astray; help to pack and harness them; fatigue themselves for their benefit; and drudge at the work of a cowherd for some hours a day.

In fitting out a caravan, as few different kinds of animals should be taken as possible, or they will split into separate herds, and require many men to look after them.

The dispositions of the animals that compose a caravan affect, in no small degree, the pleasure of travelling with it. Now, it is to be noticed that men attach themselves to horses and asses, and in a lesser degree to mules and oxen, but they rarely make friends of camels.

Weights carried by Cattle.—The net weights that these different animals carry in trying, long-continued journeys—through stages uncertain in length, sometimes leading to good pasture, sometimes to bad—must not be reckoned higher than the following; and an animal draws about $2\frac{1}{2}$ times as much net weight as he carries:—An ass, 65 lbs.; a small mule, 90 lbs.; a horse, 100 lbs.; an ox, 120 lbs.; a camel, 180 lbs. to 200 lbs.; elephant, 500 lbs. In level countries—where there is grain, and where the road is known and a regularity in the day's work can be ensured—the weights that may be carried are fully double those of the above list. Captain Burton's donkeys, in East Africa, carried immense weights. Dogs will draw a "travail" (which see) of 60 lbs. for a distance of 15 miles a day, upon hard level country.

Theory of Loads and Distances.—How should we load men or animals of transport, and how should we urge them, in order to obtain the largest amount of effective labour? If they carry a mere feather-weight, they may make long days' journeys; but their value, as animals of transport, is almost nothing. Again, on the other hand, if we load them with an excessive weight, they will soon come to a standstill; and in this case, as in the first, their value as beasts of transport is almost *nil*. What, then, is that moderate load by which we shall obtain the largest amount of "useful effect"? This is a problem which many of the ablest engineers and philosophers have endeavoured to solve; and the formulæ—partly based on theory and partly on experiment—which were used by Euler, are generally accepted as a fair approximation. They are very simple, and peculiarly interesting on account of their wide applicability. They are equally true for men, animals, or machines; and are wholly independent of the way in which the power is applied: whether, for instance, a man carries his burden, or draws it, or rows or punts it in a boat, or winds it up with a crank or tread-mill.

Travellers might well turn the theory to account on their own behalf; they are well situated for testing its truthfulness, by observing the practices of the countries in which they are travelling. Reliable facts upon the extreme distances that can be travelled over, day after day, by people carrying different loads, but equally circumstanced in every other respect, would be very acceptable to me.

The formulæ are as follow:—

Let b be the burden which would just suffice to prevent an animal from moving a step; d the distance he could travel daily if unloaded. Also, let b' be some burden less than b; and let d' be the distance to which he could travel daily when carrying b'.

$$b' d^2 = b(d - d')^2. \qquad (1)$$

Again, the "useful effect" is a maximum, if $b' d'$ is a maximum. When this is the case, then

$$b' = \tfrac{4}{9}b. \qquad (2)$$

And

$$3d' = d. \qquad (3)$$

In other words, an animal gets through most work in the day if he carries $\tfrac{4}{9}$ of the greatest load he could just stagger under; in which case he will be able to travel $\tfrac{1}{3}$ of the distance he could walk if he carried no load at all. (Machinery requires no repose; and therefore d, the distance per day, is convertible into v, the velocity of movement.)

As an example:—Suppose a man is able to walk 10 miles a day, with a load of 130 lbs., and 33 miles a day when he carries nothing. Then, from equation (1), the value of b (the burden under which he would be brought to a standstill) would be about 267½; and the best load for him, from equation (2), would be 119 lbs., which he would be able to carry, according to equation (3), 11 miles a day.

Horses.—The mode of taking wild horses is by throwing the lasso, whilst pursuing them at full speed, and dropping a noose over their necks, by which their speed is soon checked, and they are choked down.

Mr. Rarey's sixpenny book tells all that can be told on the subject of horse-breaking; but far more lies in the skill and horse-knowledge of the operator, than in the mere theory. His way of mastering a vicious horse is by taking up one forefoot, bending the knee, slipping a loop over the knee until it comes to the pastern-joint, and then fixing it tight. The loop must be caused to embrace the part between the hoof and the pastern-joint firmly, by the help of a strap of some kind, lest it should slip. The horse is now on three legs, and he feels conquered. If he gets very mad, wait leisurely till he becomes quiet, then caress him, and let the leg down and allow him to rest; then repeat the process. If the horse kicks in harness, drive him slowly on three legs.

In breaking-in a stubborn beast, it is convenient to physic him until he is sick and out of spirits, or to starve him into submission.

Salt keeps horses from straying, if they are accustomed to come up to the camp and get it. But it is a bad plan, as they are apt to hang about, instead of going off to feed. They are so fond of salt, that they have been known to stray back to a distant house where they had been allowed to lick it.

Shooting Horse.—Spur him as much as you will, but never use a whip; else, whenever you raise your gun to fire, he will fool a dread that it may be the whip, and will be unsteady.

Horse neighing.—Mungo Park tells how he clutched his horse's muzzle with both hands to prevent his neighing, when he was in concealment and horsemen were passing near.

Addenda.—In climbing a steep hill hang on to the tail of your horse as you walk behind him. Horses are easily driven in file by securing the halter of each horse to the tail of the one before him. To swim horses across a river, to sleep by their side when there is danger, to tether them, and to water them from wells, are all described elsewhere. (See " Horses " in index.)

Mules.—Mules require men who know their habits; they are powerful beasts, and can only be mastered with skill and address. A savage will not assist in packing them, for he fears their heels: the Swiss say mules have always an *arrière-pensée*. They have odd secret ways, strange fancies, and lurking vice. When they stray, they go immense distances;

and it is almost beyond the power of a man on foot to tend them in a wild country: he can neither overtake them easily, nor, when overtaken, catch them. The female is, in most breeds, much the more docile. They suffer from African distemper, but in a less degree than horses. The following descriptions of mule caravans are exceedingly graphic and instructive:—" The madrina (or godmother) is a most important personage. She is an old steady mare, with a little bell round her neck, and wheresoever she goes the mules, like good children, follow her. If several large troops are turned into one field to graze in the morning, the muleteer has only to lead the madrinas a little apart and tinkle their bells, and, although there may be 200 or 300 mules together, each immediately knows its own bell, and separates itself from the rest. The affection of these animals for their madrina saves infinite trouble. It is nearly impossible to lose an old mule: for, if detained several hours by force, she will, by the power of smell, like a dog, track out her companions, or rather the madrina; for, according to the muleteer, she is the chief object of affection. The feeling, however, is not of an individual nature; for I believe I am right in saying that any animal with a bell will serve as a madrina." (Charles Darwin.)

" After travelling about 14 miles, we were joined by three miners; and our mules, taking a sudden liking for their horses, jogged on at a more brisk rate. The instincts of the mulish heart form an interesting study to the traveller in the mountains. I would (were the comparison not too ungallant) liken it to a woman's; for it is quite as uncertain in its sympathies, bestowing its affections when least expected, and, when bestowed, quite as constant, so long as the object s not taken away. Sometimes a horse, sometimes an ass, captivates the fancy of a whole drove of mules, but often an animal nowise akin. Lieutenant Beale told me that his whole train of mules once galloped off suddenly, on the plains of the Cimarone, and ran half a mile, when they halted in apparent satisfaction. The cause of their freak was found to be a buffalo-calf, which had strayed from the herd. They were frisking around it in the greatest delight, rubbing their noses against it, throwing up their heels, and making themselves ridiculous by abortive attempts to neigh and bray; while the poor calf, unconscious of its attractive qualities, stood trembling in their midst. It is customary to have a horse in the mule-trains of the traders of North Mexico, as a sort of magnet to keep together the separate atoms of the train, for, whatever the temptation, they will never stray from him." (Taylor's 'Eldorado.')

Asses.—Notwithstanding his inveterate obstinacy, the ass is an excellent and sober little beast, far too much despised by us. He is not only the most enduring, but also one of the quickest walkers among cattle, being usually promoted to the leadership of a caravan. He is nearly equal to the camel in enduring thirst, and thrives on the poorest pasture, suffers from few diseases, and is unscathed by African distemper. The long desert-roads and pilgrim-tracts of North Africa are largely travelled over by means of asses.

Asses taught not to kick.—Mungo Park says that the negroes, where he travelled, taught their asses as follows:—They cut a forked stick, and put the forked part into the ass's mouth, like the bit of a bridle; they then tied the two smaller parts together above his head, leaving the lower part of sufficient length to strike against the ground if the ass should attempt to put his head down. It always proved effectual.

Not to bray.—Messrs. Huc and Gabet, who were distracted by the continual braying of one of their asses throughout the night, appealed to their muleteer: he put a speedy close to the nuisance by what appears to be a customary contrivance in China, viz., by lashing a heavy stone to the beast's tail. It appears that when an ass wants to bray he elevates his tail, and, if his tail be weighted down, he has not the heart to bray. In hostile neighbourhoods, where silence and concealment are sought, it might be well to adopt this rather absurd treatment. An ass who was being schooled according to the method of this and the preceding paragraph, both at the same time, would be worthy of an artist's sketch.

Oxen.—Though oxen are coarse, gross, and phlegmatic beasts, they have these merits: they are eminently gregarious, and they ruminate their food. The consequence is, first, that one, two, or more, are very seldom missing out of a drove; and, secondly, that they pick up what they require, in a much shorter time than horses, mules, &c., who have to chew as they eat. Oxen require less tending than any other beasts of burden.

To train a Pack-ox.—An ox of any age, however wild he may be, can be broken in, in three or four days, so as to carry a pack of about 70 lbs.; though it is true that he will frequently kick it off during the journey, and give excessive trouble. It would be scarcely possible to drive more than three of these newly-taught oxen at a time, on account of the frequent delays caused by the unruliness of one or other of them. Much depends on the natural aptitude of the animal in estimating the time required for making a steady pack-ox; some will carry a good weight and go steadily after only a fortnight's travel; some will never learn. But in all cases they prove unruly at the beginning of a journey.

To break-in an ox, take a long thong or cord, make a noose at one end of it, and let two or three men lay hold of the other; then, driving all the herd together in a clump, go in among them, and, aided by a long stick, push or slip the noose round the hind leg of the ox that you want, and draw tight. He will pull and struggle with all his might, and the other oxen will disperse, leaving him alone dragging the men about after him. Next, let another man throw a noose round his horns, and the beast is, comparatively speaking, secured. It is now convenient to throw the animal down on his side, which is easily done by judicious tugging at his tail and at the thongs. To keep him on the ground, let one man take the tail, and, passing it round one thigh, hold him down by that, while one or two men force the horns down against the ground. His nose has next to be pierced. A stick, shaped like a Y, eight inches long, is cut of some tough wood; and the foot of it, being first sharpened, is forcibly poked through the wall that divides the nostrils, and a thin thong is tied firmly to either end of this nose-stick. The thong is gathered together, and wound in a figure of 8 round the two horns, where it henceforward remains while the animal feeds, and by clutching at which, he is at any time caught.

Next for the packing: as the ox lies on the ground, scrape a hole in the sand under his belly, and then, having laid a few skins on his back, pass a thong round him and them, several times; tie the ends fast, and, taking a stick, pass it through and twist it round, until the lashings are extremely tight, then let it be secured. Now let the ox go, and get quickly out of his way, in case he should be savage. When the ox gets up, he is sulky and ferocious by turns; and kicks, jumps, and bellows, but at last joins his companions.

If he has been well packed, the skins will keep in place and not fall off; but whether they do or not, he must be re-caught and re-packed every day. A young ox is generally more difficult to break-in than an old one: I do not know why. An ox requires no pack-saddle; his back is too round to carry one with advantage. It is therefore usual to lay spare skins, &c., upon him, and over these the bags that have to be packed. A great length of thong is required to lash them. It is convenient to make a pair of very large saddle-bags out of skin or canvas, which require simply to be placed on the ox's back and there girthed.

To train an Ox to carry a Rider.—It takes a very long time to train an ox to carry a riding-saddle well and steadily: indeed, very few oxen can be taught to go wherever they may be guided by the rider; they are of so gregarious a nature, that, for the most part, they will not move a step without companions. Hence, those oxen only are thought worth breaking-in which are observed to take the part of leaders of the drove when pasturing, and which are therefore supposed to have some independence of disposition. The first time of mounting an ox to break him in, is a work of almost certain mischance: for the long horns of the ox will often reach the rider, however far back he may sit, and the animal kicks and bucks in a way that severely tries the best of seats. All riding-oxen's horns should have the tips sawn off. After being mounted a very few times, the ox goes pretty steadily; but it is long before he learns to carry a rider with ease to himself. I should like to hear if Rarey's plan of tying up the foreleg would influence them. Their character is so wholly unlike that of a horse, that I doubt if it would.

In riding, it must be recollected that the temper of an ox is far less quick, though his sensations may be as acute as those of a horse: thus, he does not start forwards on receiving a cut with the whip, even though he shrink with the pain; but he thinks about it, shakes his head, waits a while, and then breaks gradually into a faster pace. An ox will trot well enough with a light weight; and, though riding myself upwards of 13 stone, I once took an ox 60 miles in a day and a half: this is, perhaps, as much as an ox could, in fairness, be made to do. A ride-ox can be tied up by his nose-bridle; but, if wild or frightened, he will assuredly struggle till the nose-stick be torn out of his nose, and he becomes free. It is, therefore, better to tie the bridle to a tuft of grass, or a slender twig, rather than to a tree or to the saddle-bags. Mounting an ox is usually a troublesome business, on account of his horns. To make ride-oxen quiet and tame, scratch their backs and tails—they dearly love it—and hold salt in your hands for them to lick. They soon learn their names, and come to be caressed when called.

Cows.—Most breeds of cows, out of Europe, cease to give milk after their calf dies; and the only way of making them continue their yield, is to spread out the calf's hide for them to lick, some time before milking them; it retains its effect for a week or more. Messrs. Huc and Gabet give the following graphic account of this contrivance, as applied to restive cows:—" These long-tailed cows are so restive and difficult to milk, that, to keep them at all quiet, the herdsman has to give them a calf to lick meanwhile. But for this device, not a single drop of milk could be obtained from them. One day a Lama herdsman, who lived in the same house with ourselves, came, with a long dismal face, to announce that his cow had calved during the night, and that unfortunately the calf was dying. It died in the course of the day. The Lama forthwith skinned the poor beast, and stuffed it with hay. This proceeding surprised us at first, for the Lama had by no means the air of a man likely to give himself the luxury of a cabinet of natural history. When the operation was completed, we observed that the hay-calf had neither feet nor head; whereupon it occurred to us that, after all, it was perhaps a pillow that the Lama contemplated. We were in error; but the error was not dissipated till the next morning, when our herdsman went to milk his cow. Seeing him issue forth—the pail in one hand, the hay-calf under the other arm—the fancy occurred to us to follow him. His first proceeding was to put the hay-calf down before the cow. He then turned to milk the cow herself. The mamma at first opened enormous eyes at her beloved infant; by degrees she stooped her head towards it, then smelt at it, sneezed three or four times, and at last proceeded to lick it with the most delightful tenderness. This spectacle grated against our sensibilities: it seemed to us that he who first invented this parody upon one of the most touching incidents in nature must have been a man without a heart. A somewhat burlesque circumstance occurred one day, to modify the indignation with which this treachery inspired us. By dint of caressing and licking her little calf, the tender parent one fine morning unripped it: the hay issued from within; and the cow, manifesting not the slightest surprise nor agitation, proceeded tranquilly to devour the unexpected provender."

The Highlanders used this contrivance, and called it a "Tulchan": hence King James's bishops were nicknamed "Tulchan bishops," to imply that they were officials of straw, merely set up as a means of milking the Scotch people of their money, in the form of church-dues.

Camels.—Camels are only fit for a few countries, and require practised attendants; thorns and rocks lame them, hills sadly impede them, and a wet slippery soil entirely stops them.

Elephants.—They are expensive and delicate, but excellent beasts of burden, in rainy tropical countries. The traveller should make friends with the one he regularly rides, by giving it a piece of sugar-cane or banana before mounting. A sore back is a certain obstacle to a continuance of travel; there is no remedy for it but rest. The average burden, furniture included, but excluding the driver, is 500 lbs., and the full average day's journey 15 miles.

Dogs.—Dogs will draw a "travail" (which see) of 60 lbs. for 15 miles a day, over hard, level country, for days together; frequently they will accomplish much more than that. For Arctic travel, they are used in journeys after they are three years old; each dog requires eight or ten herrings per day, or an equivalent to them. A sledge of 12 dogs carries 900 lbs.; it travels on smooth ice seven or eight miles an hour; and in 36 days, 22 sledges and 240 dogs travelled 800 miles—1210 versts. (Admiral Wrangel.) Dogs are used by the Patagonian fishermen to drive fish into their nets, and to prevent them from breaking through the nets when they are inside them. (See next paragraph for "Sheep-dogs.")

Goats and Sheep.—Goats are much more troublesome to drive than sheep, neither are they such enduring walkers, nor do they give as much meat; but their skins are of such great use to furnish strong leather, that it is seldom convenient to make up a caravan without them. She-goats give some milk, even when travelling fast, and in dry countries; but a ewe-sheep is not worth milking under those circumstances, as her yield is a mere nothing. Goats are very mischievous—they make their way out of all enclosures, and trespass everywhere. They butt at whatever is bright or new, or strange to them; and would drive an observer, who employed astronomical instruments on stands, to distraction. In an open country, where there are no bushes for a kraal, nets must be taken, and stakes cut, to make enclosures for the sheep. If they stray at all, the least thing scares them, and they will wander very far, and scatter. Goats are far more social and intelligent. If one, two, or three sheep only be driven, long thongs must be tied to their legs, and allowed to trail along the ground, by which they may be re-caught if they gallop off. When the Messrs. Schlagintweit were encamped at vast heights, among the snows of the Himalaya, they always found it practicable to drive sheep to their stations. When sheep, &c., are long hurdled at night, near the same encampment, the nuisance of flies and ticks becomes intolerable. Sheep-dogs seem to prove of less use to travellers than might have been expected; perhaps the other dogs corrupt them.

Management of Cattle generally.—To make an animal rise

when he throws himself on the ground with his pack, and will not get up, it is not of much use to flog him; twisting or biting his tail is the usual way, or making a blaze with grass and a few sticks under his nostrils. The stubbornness of a half-broken ox is sometimes beyond conception.

Cattle Bells, in countries where they can be used without danger, should always be taken; it adds greatly to the cheerfulness and gregariousness of the animals—mules positively require them. Hard wood is sonorous enough for bells.

Brands and Cattle-marks.—In buying oxen out of the herds of pastoral people, it is very difficult to remember each animal so as to recognise it again if it strays back to its former home; it requires quite a peculiar talent to do so. Therefore it is advisable that the traveller's cattle should be marked or branded. A trader in Namaqua Land, took red paint, and tied a brush on to a long stick; with this he made a daub on the hind quarters of the freshly-bought and half-wild cattle, as they pushed through the door of his kraal. It naturally excites great ridicule among natives, to paint an ox that he may be known again; but, for all that, I think the trader's plan well worth adopting. The same might be done to sheep, as a slit ear is not half conspicuous enough. A good way of marking a sheep's ear is to cut a wad out of the middle of it, with a gun-punch; but it will sometimes tear this hole into a slit, by scratching with its foot.

Chaff, to cut.—Tie a sickle against a tree, with its blade projecting; then, standing in front of the blade, hold a handful of reeds across it with both hands, one hand on either side of the blade; pull it towards you, and the reeds will be cut through; drop the cut end, seize the bundle afresh, and repeat the process. In this way, after a little practice, chaff is cut with great ease and quickness. A broken sickle does as well as a whole one, and a knife may be used, but the curve of its edge is ill adapted for the work.

Cattle will eat many sorts of herbage, as reeds and gorse, if cut small; but will not touch them, if uncut.

Occasional Food for Cattle.—They will also eat seaweed and leaves, especially birch and poplar leaves, and even thrive upon them.

Pulling Cattle out of Holes.—The bight of a cord, or of some substitute for one, may be thrown over a horse's head, and he can be dragged out by a team of cattle with but very little danger to his neck. A crupper under his tail, or a thong as a breeching may be used. In Canada and the United States, a noose of rope is often run round the horse's neck, and hauled tight—thus temporarily choking the animal and making him still; he is then pulled as quickly as possible out of the hole, and no time is lost in slackening the rope.

HARNESS.

Saddles for riding.— Good saddles for riding, and, I may add, especially for packing, are of nearly as great importance as the goodness of the animal who carries them. English saddlers never, I believe, can be induced to stuff a saddle sufficiently; because they have no opportunity of seeing the miserable, scraggy condition of a travelled horse's back, to which it is destined to fit. But an English saddle, restuffed at a bush frontier town, is excellent.

Three rings, and nine of what saddlers call "D's," should be fixed to the saddle, not simply into the leather-work, but firmly riveted or secured into the tree itself. This must be especially insisted on, or frequent disasters will occur. The three rings are to be fixed to the pommel—one on the top, and one on each side of it; the nine "D's" are placed as follows:—three along the back of the saddle, two more on each side of the seat, and two in front, for the breastplate.

Fittings.—To these may be tied a light valise in front; a gun-holster on the right of the pommel; and a small bag—containing odds and ends, gunpowder, spare bullets, a few presents, &c.—on its left. On the right of the seat, a sabre-tasch, or thin leather portfolio-shaped pocket, for paper and writing materials; on the left, the water-canteen and hobbles; behind, the crupper and small saddle-bags. A breastplate is not worth having, except in a very hilly country. This description of a saddle, of course, applies to that of the travelling-horse. For the saddle of the shooting-horse the arrangement is different; only the gun-holster, and perhaps the water-canteen can then be taken. An ox carries a saddle precisely like a horse. I rode mine nearly 1600 miles, in South Africa, with a common hunting-saddle and its ordinary girths.

In default of riding-saddles, a pack-saddle must be cushioned to form a comfortable seat (see "Pack-saddles").

Saddle-bags are so troublesome to open, and require so many straps, that I believe it is best to use a bag of macintosh or canvas, rolled up and tied behind the saddle, where it should rest on a pad. The pad is made of two cushions, each 9 inches long and 4 broad, sewn on a piece of leather, lying parallel to one another, and 4 inches apart. The space between the cushions corresponds to the backbone of the horse. To keep the whole in shape, it is usual to stitch four or five laths of wood lengthways to the upper surface of the pad; upon these laths the bag will rest. If there be occasion to carry a bag on horseback for a short distance, pass one of the stirrup-leathers through its string; then throw the bag over to the other side of the saddle: it will lie behind the rider's leg, and be out of his way and he will sit upon part of its string.

Australians, as is well known, insist on the merits of a "swag," or a long package formed by rolling all their possessions into their blanket. They carry it over the saddle-bows.

Sore backs.—Sore backs are the plague of beasts of burden; for, if the skin be once broken, it will never heal thoroughly again during the whole journey. Every precaution should, therefore, be taken at first starting: the saddles should be well-stuffed; the saddle-cloths ample, and without hem or edging (blankets are as good as any); the journeys should be short; the packs light and carefully balanced; rests of a day or two should frequently be given, and salt-water should be rubbed on the back. Travelling in the very early morning is found to be bad for animals' backs; but travelling late at night is not so. An Australian correspondent remarks, that a party of travellers or explorers in Australia, on leaving their camp, invariably saddle their horses with ample saddle-cloths below the saddle, and assist each other by turns, to fold the cloths in various ways. For instance, if the ridge of the back, or wither, should be found galled, the cloth would be folded up, so that the saddle should rest entirely on the two folded pads, as in the figure.—Other modes of folding will suggest themselves, according to the way in which the back may be rubbed.

The first appearance of a sore back is a small hardish swelling or *warble*: this must at once be attended to, either by folding the saddle-cloth in some appropriate way, or by picking out the saddle-stuffing, so as to ease all pressure from off it; otherwise, it will get larger and larger, and a single day will convert what might have been easily cured, into a serious and irremediable gall. Girth-galls, on their first appearance, may be relieved, if not cured, by sewing two rolls of soft woollen material on to the girth. The hair from the animal's mane or tail has been used on an emergency to stuff a saddle.

Pack-Saddles.—*To make when Travelling.*—Cut four bent

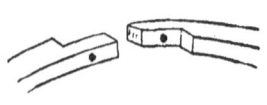

Fig. 1.

Fig. 2.

pieces of tough wood, and two small planks; season them as well as you can (see "Wood, to season"), and join them together, as in figs. 1 and 2, using raw hide in addition to nails or pegs. Stuffed cushions must be secured inside the planks by tying or otherwise. With a saw and a mortise-chisel, a saddle of the pattern shown in fig. 3 would be easy to make. It is stronger than the one just described, and the notched cross-bar is very convenient for the pack-ropes.

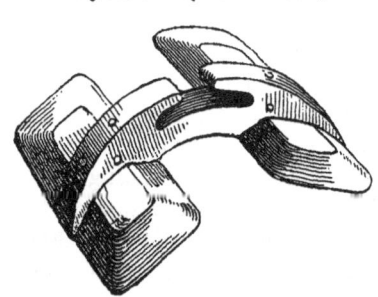

Fig. 3.

Pack-Saddles made by Saddlers.—There has been, perhaps, no journey in which pack-horses worked so effectively as during the exploration of North Australia under Mr. Gregory. I am much indebted to Mr. Baines, the artist of the expedition, who has subsequently travelled extensively, for the following very interesting account:—

"The pack-saddles were made after a model by Mr. Gregory, and are the best I have yet seen. Two boards of light wood are connected by bows of iron, 1½ inch wide and ¼ inch thick, with hooks inserted in either side, for the pack-bags to hook on to. The straps for the breastings, breechings, and girths, were screwed to the boards; the crupper passed through a ring on the after bow; and a light pad, which could easily be taken out to be re-stuffed, was secured by small thongs, passed through holes in the ends of the boards.

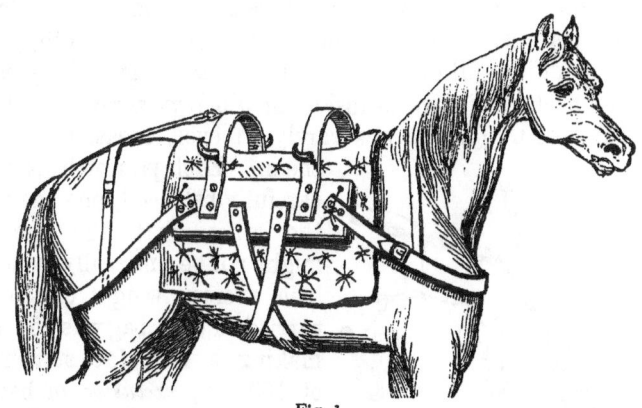

Fig. 1.

We had two girths, which crossed each other under the horse. (In unloading, the neck-strap is unbuckled on the near side, also the breasting and girths; and the whole is drawn off behind.)

"The pack-bags were made of one width of canvas, turned up so as to have no seam in the bottom. Pear-shaped pieces were sewn in to form the ends, and rope was stitched along the seams, having eyes above, by which the bag was hung upon the hooks (fig. 2). The flour-bags were made of canvas, of the usual width, with a round bottom stitched into them. The mouth was sewn up when full, and an oiled bag of the same size drawn over it.

Fig. 2.

"When all our horses were saddled up, the word 'on packs' was given. Dr. Mueller and I used to work together, and had our packs laid out in pairs; so that when each horse was

led between his bags, we hooked them on at the same moment. When we halted, we laid our bags on a couple of poles, to keep them from the ground, as in the drawing.

"The bags sometimes came off when we were travelling; but it was generally easy to catch the horse and reload him. When a horse rolled over, or fell in a river, it was rather an advantage than otherwise to get clear of them. Our waterproof bags were of leather, lined with waterproof cloth, just large enough to fill one of the canvas pack-bags. They had a brass neck with a worm inside, in which we screwed a plug of soft wood. (There was rarely, if ever, occasion to use them.)

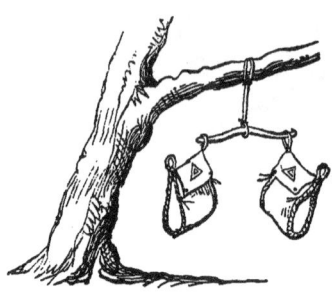

Each pair of bags was carefully balanced, one against the other, that the horses might not be unequally loaded. The average weight of stores carried in each bag was 75 lbs., making a load (at starting) of 150 lbs., *exclusive* of bags, packages, or saddlery. Bells were attached to the necks of the horses most apt to stray; but the clappers were tied up with a piece of thong, to keep them quiet on the march; and were loosened at night, so that the sound might guide us in searching for them next morning.

"We watched two hours each during night; the morning watch boiled the water, and woke the rest at four. We made our breakfast of tea or coffee, damper, and pork, which we ate raw, and went out for the horses; which were generally saddled up, and on the move, before sunrise. We travelled till one or two, when we led the horses to water, looked to any sores that might be caused by the pressure of their saddles, dressed them and altered the stuffing of the saddle to give them relief, and, after dinner, which was rather a brief ceremony, had the rest of the day for scientific or artistic pursuits, —that is, if something else did not require immediate attention. We could never trust to our guns for provision, as game was very scarce, and we had no opportunity of seeking it."

Sir Samuel Baker gave considerable attention to the subject of pack-saddles. The following is his account of the method he adopted in Africa :—" I had arranged their (the donkeys') packs so well, that they carried their loads with the greatest comfort. Each animal had an immense pad, well stuffed with goats' hair; this rested from the shoulder to the hip bones; upon this rested a simple form of saddle made of two forks of boughs inverted, and fastened together with rails; there were no nails in these saddles, all the fastenings being secured with thongs of raw hide. The great pad projecting before and behind, and also below the side of the saddle, prevented the loads from chafing the animal. Every donkey carried two large bags made from the hides of antelopes that I had formerly shot on the frontier of Abyssinia, and these were arranged with taggles on the one to fit into loops on the other, so that the loading and unloading was exceedingly simple. The success of an expedition depends mainly upon the perfection of the details, and, where animals are employed for transport, the first consideration should be bestowed upon saddle-packs. The facility of loading is all-important, and I now had an exemplification of its effect upon both animals and men; the latter began to abuse the camels and to curse the father of this, and the mother of that, because they had the trouble of unloading them for the descent into the river's bed, while the donkeys were blessed with the endearing name of 'my brother,' and alternately whacked with the stick."

The art of packing.—The art of good packing is to balance the packs accurately, and to lash tightly to the saddle, so that they will never slip. The entire load is then secured to the animal's back, by moderate girthing. It is going on a false principle, to wind one long cord round the horse, saddle, and packs; making, as it were, a great faggot of them.

To tighten the lashings of a pack, thrust a stick through them, twist it forcibly round and round, till the lashings are screwed tight enough, and then secure the stick.

Half-filled sacks require to have laths of wood, or a handful of twigs, put between them and the packing-cord, to equalise its pressure; otherwise, they are strangled out of shape and never lie firmly against the saddle.

Other Harness.—*Cruppers.*—A crupper rope should be passed through a leather tube, fitting it loosely. Cruppers for pack-saddles, adapted to very mountainous countries, like those used in Norway, can readily be made by travellers. Instead of employing a ring to enclose the tail of the beast (which is sure to fret its sides), he should pass a curved bar of wood, a foot long, underneath the tail, and tie a cord to the pack-saddle, from either end of the bar.

Girths.—A roll of spare webbing should be taken to patch up torn girths; but a good substitute for a girth is made by cutting a band of tanned, or even of dressed, leather, to within four inches of its end, into seven or nine bands, and plaiting these together. But it takes a beginner just ten times as long to plait a girth as to weave it, and, therefore, for making more than one girth, it is well worth while to set up a rude loom. Do this as though you were making a mat. (See "Mat.") Girths need not be buckled; they may be laced.

Stirrups must be very roomy, enough to admit clumsily-shaped shoes, such as are made in the bush; they must be broad under the sole of the foot, and also at the place which rubs against the little toe. Unless they are heavy, it is not easy to find them with the foot; travellers in South Africa cut them out from any thick raw hide—that of giraffe, rhinoceros, or sea-cow does admirably. A wooden stirrup may be cut or burnt out of a block. It should have lead melted into it to give it sufficient weight.

A stick and a thong, as shown in the figure, is a poor makeshift. Willow, or any other lithe wood, is easily bent into the required shape, especially if its outer edge be nicked with a knife; otherwise it would be a mere loop of wood, such as is represented in the next figure but two, in the paragraph on Rings.

Bridles and Bits.—Leave behind all English notions of snaffles and double reins, and ride with nothing but an easy curb. The horse must also carry a headstall and a halter; I like one with plenty of tassels, to keep off the flies. A temporary substitute for a curb is made by noosing a string, and putting the noose round the horse's lower jaw. If the string be long enough, it can be doubled back again, and tied to the other side of the noose, so as to make a complete bridle. The groom's fashion of giving the halter a hitch, and putting it round the jaw, is well known.

Buckles.—A contrivance like this will often be found useful to replace a buckle and strap; by twisting the lower thong more tightly, its length can be shortened as much as may be required. If the tongue  of a buckle breaks, a nail or a peg, pushed through the buckle-hole, as in the figure below, will replace it.

To Padlock a Bag.—A padlock, passed through the next buckle-hole, as is also shown in the same figure, prevents pilferers from unbuckling and opening the package. It is well to learn some artful sailor's-knot for tying up bags, with which other people cannot meddle without your finding it out.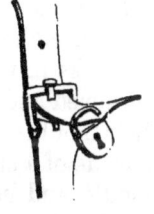

Rings.—In packing-gear and other harness, use is frequently made of rings. Iron ones may be replaced by a loop of tough wood, such as the peasants of the Campagna commonly employ: a piece of the thickness of a small walking-stick, and eight inches long, is bent (see " Wood, to bend "); its arms are notched when they cross, and are firmly nailed or lashed.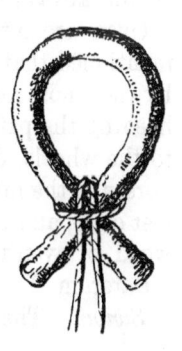

Tethers, Hobbles, and Knee-halters.—Cattle may be secured at night by being tethered, hobbled, knee-haltered, or driven into an enclosure made of bushes. The nature of the country, and what dangers are apprehended, determine which plan is most advisable. A knee-haltered horse has a good chance of escape if he scents a wild beast that is creeping up to him; for he can gallop, though with labour, to a short distance. A hobbled horse has no chance at all; though, indeed, they have been known to fight desperately with their teeth and feet, and learn to be cunning and watchful. If the hobbles are of iron, and made like handcuffs, it is hardly possible for robbers—at all events for savages—to unlock or cut them. A horse that is hobbled or knee-haltered, can graze during the night; but if tied up or pounded, his grass must be cut for him. A horse may be successfully hobbled with a stirrup-leather, by putting its middle round one fetlock, then twisting it half-a-dozen times, and, lastly, buckling it round the other fetlock. The hobble used by Mr. Gregory takes into five separate pieces, viz.,

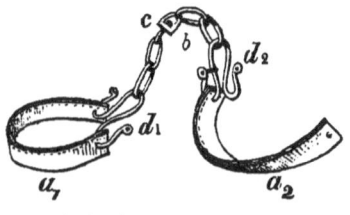

two fetlock straps, a_1, a_2; a chain, b, having a swivel point, c, in the middle; and two double pot-hooks, d_1, d_2, which pass through eyes in the fetlock straps, and also through the end links in the chain. The two ends of both, d_1 and d_2, are thickened and pierced, so as to admit of tying a thong across their mouths, as shown on one side of d_2. The fetlock strap is made of a strip of thick leather, folded lengthways down its middle, and having its edges sewn together. The sewn edge should always be the uppermost, when on the horse's legs.

Oxen are often picketed to their yokes; I have already mentioned that it is hazardous to secure ride and pack oxen by their nose reams, as they will tear themselves loose without heeding the pain, if really frightened. Horses are often tied to the wheels, &c., of the wagon. When you wish to picket horses in the middle of a sandy plain, dig a hole two or three feet deep, and tying your rope to a faggot of sticks or brushwood, or even to a bag filled with sand, bury this in it. (See "Dateram.")

Swivel.—The woodcut shows how a makeshift swivel can

be fitted to a tether rope. Without one, the rope will be twisted almost up to a knot by the horse walking round and round his picket peg; with one, the rope will turn freely in the hole, through which its large knotted head prevents it from being drawn.

The figure below is a better sort of swivel. It must be made of hard tough wood, like oak: it is six inches in length. It has, I presume, some advantages over those of iron, because 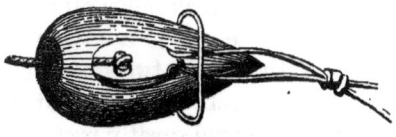 in countries where iron abounds, as in Piedmont, it holds its ground against them. The ropes have been drawn thinner than their just proportion, for the sake of distinctness.

I give a drawing of yet another description of swivel; it is a trifle more complicated than the first, but I am assured that 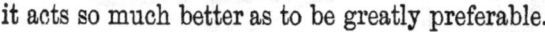 it acts so much better as to be greatly preferable.

Horse-collar.—This, in its simplest form, consists of two stout bars that are a little bent or shaped with a knife; they go one on either side of the animal's neck, and are tied together both above and below it. To these bars, which are very thickly padded, the traces are fastened.

Traces and Trektows can be made of raw hide, cut into a long thong, then bent into three parts, and twisted and laid together, as is done in rope-making; the whole is then stretched tight between two trees to dry. An ox-hide will make a trektow for four pairs of oxen. Poles of wood are very generally used as traces; a thong, or a few links of chain, being fastened at either end, by which to attach them.

Greasing Harness.—In dry climates take frequent opportunities of greasing every part of the harness. (See "Hides; Leather, to grease.")

CARRIAGES.

Wagons.—A traveller's wagon should be of the simplest possible construction, and not too heavy. The Cape wagons, or, at all events, those of a few years back, undoubtedly shared the ponderousness of all Dutch workmanship. Weight is required only when crashing through a bushy country, where a wagon must break down all before it: in every other case it is objectionable. It is a saving of labour to have one large wagon, rather than two small ones, because a driver and a leader are thereby spared. But if a very light wagon has to be taken, I should greatly prefer its being made on the Swiss and German fashion, with a shifting perch, as in the figure.

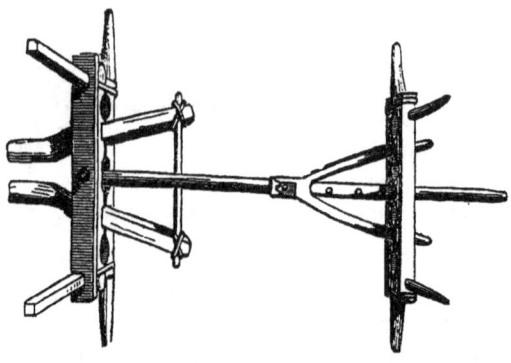

These are the simplest of affairs, and will split up into two carts—the pole and the fore-wheels forming one, and the perch and the hind-wheels another: now, should a great loss occur among the traveller's cattle, or should he break a wheel, or even strain an axle-tree, in a timberless country, it may be very convenient to him to abandon part of his stores, and to build up a cart for carrying on the remainder. Lady Vavasour describes one of these wagons in the following graphic manner:—"The perch is moveable, and they can make it any length they please; it is of so simple a construction that every farmer can repair his own, and make anything of it. If he has a perch, a pole, and four wheels, that is enough; with a little ingenuity, he makes it carry stones, hay, earth, or anything he wants, by putting a plank at each side. When he wants a carriage for pleasure, he fits it up for that purpose; his moveable perch allows him to make it anything. I counted seventeen grown persons sitting side by side, looking most happy, in one of them, drawn only by a pair of small horses, and in this hilly country."

Drays.—Two-wheeled drays, and not wagons, are used very

generally in Australia. A long bar is crossed by a short one near one of its ends,—this latter forms the axletree; the body of the dray is built where the two cross; and the cattle are yoked or harnessed to the long end of the bar, which acts as a pole.

Tarring Wheels.—Tar is absolutely essential in a hot country, to mix with the grease that is used for the wagon-wheels. Grease, alone, melts and runs away like water: the object of the tar is to give consistency to the grease: a very small proportion of tar suffices, but without any at all, a wagon is soon brought to a standstill. It is, therefore, most essential to explorers to have a sufficient quantity in reserve. Tar is also of very great use in hot dry countries for daubing over the wheels, and the woodwork generally, of wagons. During extreme heat, when the wood is ready to crack, all the paint should be scraped off it, and the tar applied plentifully. It will soak in deeply, and preserve the wood in excellent condition, both during the drought and the ensuing wet season. (See "Tar, to make.") It is not necessary to take off the wheels in order to grease the axles. It is sufficient to bore an auger-hole right through the substance of the nave, between the feet of two of the spokes, and to keep a plug in the hole. Then, when you want to tar a wheel, turn it till the hole is uppermost, take the plug out, and pour in the tar.

Breaks and Drags.—*Breaks.*—Every cart and wagon in Switzerland, and, indeed, in most parts of the Continent, has a break attached to it: the simplest kind of break is shown in fig. 2, which represents a cart tilted upwards. Fig. 1 shows the break itself; fig. 2 explains how it is fitted on to the cart. It will easily be understood how, by tightening the free end of the cord, the break is pressed against the wheels. The bent piece of iron shown in fig. 2, by which the bar of the break is kept in its place, may

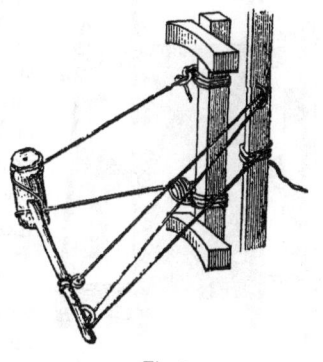

Fig. 1.

be replaced by a piece of wood, or even by a thong of leather. Every explorer's wagon should be furnished with a break.

Fig. 2.

A simple break, used in Italy, in some parts of England, and probably elsewhere, is shown in fig. 3. A rail is lashed to the body of the cart, both before and behind the wheel, and is made to press against the wheel. Either both lashings can be tightened at the same time, as at A, A; or only one of them, as at B. When the lashings are loose, the rail rests partly on the nave of the wheel and does not sensibly interfere with its movement.

Fig. 3.

Other Means of Checking a Wagon on a Hill-side.—In going down a steep hill a middling-sized tree may be felled, and its root tied to the hind axletree, while its branchy top sweeps along the ground, as is seen in the lowermost wagon in the sketch. In the south-west of France the leaders of the team are unharnessed and taken to the back of the wagon, to

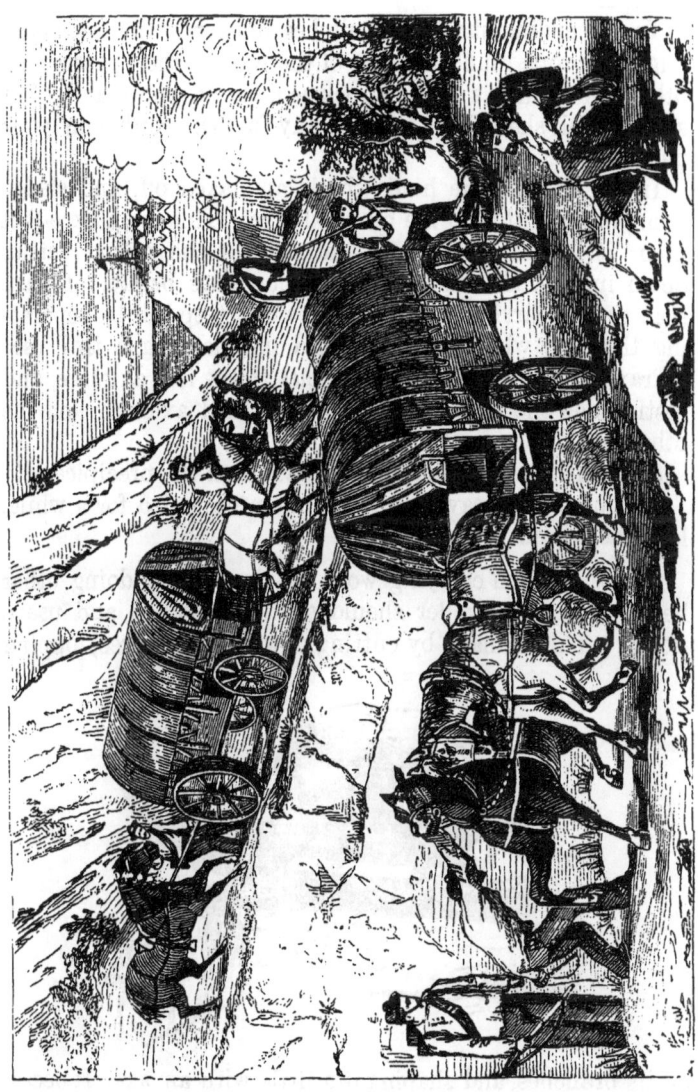

which the collar of the front horse is made fast; in this way they can aid the horses in the shafts. This same plan may be seen practised hourly in the Strand in London, whence heavy wagons are taken down a very steep and narrow lane to the Adelphi.

In descending short steep pitches, unharness the cattle, and "fasten a rope round the axle of the wagon; then passing the other end round a tree or rock as a check, you may let her slide, which she will do without any further trouble on your part." (F. Marryat.)

In some places the hind wheels are taken off, and sledge runners are fitted to the hind axletree. This is an excellent plan; it has the further advantage that the wagon settles down into a more horizontal position than before. I have seen timber carried on a wagon down a steep hill by separating the front wheels from the hind ones, lashing a trail (see "Travail" below) of two short poles to the fore axletree, and resting one end of the timber on the hind axletree, and the other end on the trail.

Shoe the wheel on the side *furthest* from the precipice.

If you have to leave a cart or wagon untended for a while, lock the wheel.

Sledges.—When carrying wood or stones, and doing other heavy work, a traveller should spare his wagon and use a sledge. This is made by cutting down a forked tree, lopping

off its branches, and shaping it a little with an axe. If necessary, a few bars may be fixed across the fork so as to make a stage. Great distances may be traversed by one of these rude affairs, if the country is not very stony. Should it capsize, no great harm is done; and if it breaks down, or is found to have been badly made, an hour's labour will suffice to construct another. Sledges are very useful where there is an abundance of horse or ox power, but no wagon or packing-gear.

North American Travail.—In a North American Indian horse "travail," the crossing of the poles (they are the poles of the wigwams) usually rests on a rough pack-saddle or pad, which a breast-strap keeps from slipping backwards. In a dog travail the cross of the poles rests on the back of the neck, and is kept in place by a breast or rather a neck strap; the poles are wrapped with pieces of buffalo robe where they press

against the dog. Captain Blakiston—a very accurate authority—considers that a horse will travel 30 miles in the day, dragging on the travail a weight of about 200 lbs., including a child, whose mother sits on the horse's back; and that a dog, the size of an average retriever, will draw about 80 lbs. for the same distance. (N.B. The North American plains are perfectly level.)

Palanquins, carried like sedan-chairs, between two animals —one going before the other in shafts—are in use in various countries; but I am not aware that explorers have ever properly tried them. Their advantage would lie in combining the convenience of a cart with much of the independence of pack-horses. For whatever is lashed on a pack-saddle must be securely tied up; it is therefore severely compressed, and cannot be taken out *en route*. But with a cart or a palanquin there is no such inconvenience: things may be quickly thrown into them or taken out; pockets and drawers may be fitted up; and the palanquin would afford some shelter in rain. I should think it would be well worth while to try one of these contrivances. It might be made *en route*; first accustoming the animals, when carrying their packs, to walk between long shafts, then, after some days, taking the load off their saddles, and lashing them on to the shafts. If all went well, a regular palanquin might be constructed with legs, to be let down when the animals are off-packed, and on which it might stand until ready to be again carried onwards. Half-a-dozen palanquins in file would make a pretty, and, I should think, a manageable and effective caravan. Asses ought to be able to carry them well; a couple of asses would probably carry a greater weight than a single pack-horse, and would give no greater trouble: if so, their hardiness would be invaluable.

SWIMMING.

General Remarks.—*Rate of Swimming.*—People swim much more slowly than is commonly supposed. In races between first-rate swimmers, for distances of 300 yards and upwards, the average pace of two miles an hour is barely, if at all, exceeded.

Learning to Swim.—A good way of teaching a person to swim, is a modification of that adopted at Eton. The teacher may sit in a punt or on a rock, with a stout stick of 6 or 10 feet in length, at the end of which is a cord of 4 feet or so, with loops. The learner puts himself into the loops; and the teacher plays him, as a fisherman would play a fish, in water that is well out of his depth: he gives him just enough support to keep him from drowning. After six or a dozen lessons, many boys require no support at all, but swim about with the rope dangling slack about them. When a boy does this, he can be left to shift for himself. The art of swimming *far* is acquired, like the art of running far, by a determination to go on, without resting a moment, until utterly unable to make a stroke further, and then to stop altogether. Each succeeding day, the distance travelled is marvellously increased, until the natural limit of the man's powers is attained. The chilliness consequent on staying long in water is retarded by rubbing all over the body, before entering it, about twice as much oil or bear's-grease as a person uses for his hair.

To support those who cannot Swim.—If a person cannot swim a stroke, he should be buoyed up with floats under his arms, and lashed quite securely, to his own satisfaction; then he can be towed across the river with a string. If he lose courage halfway, it cannot be helped: it will do him no harm, and his swimming friend is in no danger of being grappled with and drowned. For very short distances, a usual way is for the man who cannot swim to hold his friend by the hips. A very little floating power is enough to buoy a man's head, above still water. (See "African Swimming Ferry," below.)

Landing through Breakers.—In landing through a heavy surf, wait for a large wave, and come in on the crest of it; then make every possible exertion to scramble up to some firm holding-place, whence its indraught, when it returns, can be resisted. If drawn back, you will be heavily battered, perhaps maimed, certainly far more exhausted than before, and not a whit nearer to safety. Avoid receiving a breaker in the attitude of scrambling away from it on hands and knees: from such a position, the wave projects a man headforemost with fearful force, and rolls him over and over in its surge. He ought to turn on his back the instant before the breaker is upon him; and then all will go well, and he will be helped on, and not half-killed by it. Men on shore can rescue a man who is being washed to and fro in the surf, by holding together, *very* firmly, hand-in-hand, and forming a line down to the sea: the foremost man clutches the swimmer as soon as he is washed up to him, and holds him firmly while the wave is retiring. The force of the indraught is enormous, and none but strong men can withstand it.

Floats.—If a traveller can swim pretty well, it is a good plan to make a float when he wishes to cross a river, and to lay his breast upon it, while his clothes and valuables are enclosed in a huge turban on his head. In this way, he may cross the broadest streams and float great distances down a river. He may tie paddles to his hands. His float may consist of a faggot of rushes, a log of wood, or any one of his empty water-vessels, whether barrels or bags; for whatever will keep water in, will also keep it out. The small quantity of air, which might escape through the sides of a bag, should be restored by blowing afresh into it, during the voyage. A few yards of intestine blown out and tied here and there, so as to form so many watertight compartments, makes a capital swimming-belt: it may be wound in a figure of 8 round the neck and under the armpits. When employing empty bottles, they should be well corked and made fast under the armpits, or be stuffed within the shirt or jersey, and a belt tied round the waist below them, to keep them in place.

African Swimming Ferry.—The people of Yariba have a singular mode of transporting passengers across rivers and streams, when the violence and rapidity of their currents prevent them from using canoes with safety. The passenger

grasps the float (see fig.), on the top of which his luggage is lashed; and a perfect equilibrium is preserved, by the ferry-man placing himself opposite the passenger, and laying hold of both his arms. They being thus face to face, the owner of the float propels it by striking with his legs. The natives use as their float two of their largest calabashes, cutting off their small ends, and joining the openings face to face, so as to form a large, hollow, watertight vessel.

Makeshift Life-belt.—A moderately effective life-belt may be made of holland, ticking, canvas, or similar materials, in the following manner, and might be used with advantage by the crew of a vessel aground some way from the mainland, who are about to swim for their lives:—Cut out two complete rings, of 16 inches outer diameter and 8 inches inner diameter; sew these together along both edges, with as fine a needle as possible and with double thread: add strong shoulder-straps, so that it shall not, by any possibility, slip down over the hips; and, lastly, sew into it a long narrow tube, made out of a strip, a foot long and two inches wide, of the same material as the belt. At the mouth of this, a bit of wood, an inch long, with a hole bored down its middle, should be inserted as a mouthpiece. Through this tube the belt can be re-inflated by the swimmer while in the water, as often as may be necessary; and, by simply twisting the tube and tucking its end in the belt, its vent can always be closed. After a canvas belt is *thoroughly* drenched, it will hold the air very fairly: the seams are its weakest parts. For supporting a swimmer in calm water, a collar is as good as a belt.

Transport on Water.—*Parcels*.—The swimmer's valuables may as well be put inside the empty vessel that acts as his float, as in the turban on his head (see "Floats"). A goatskin is often filled half full of the things he wants to carry, and is then blown out and its mouth secured. A very good life-belt may be bought, which admits of this arrangement: it has a large opening at one end, which is closed by a brass door that shuts like the top of an inkstand, and is then quite air-tight.

A small parcel, if tightly wrapped up in many folds, will keep dry for a long time, though partly immersed in water: the outside of it may be greased, oiled, or waxed, for additional security. If deeply immersed, the water is sure to get in.

Swimming with Horses.—In crossing a deep river, with a horse or other large animal, drive him in: or even lead him along a steep bank, and push him sideways, suddenly into the water: having fairly started him, jump in yourself, seize his tail, and let him tow you across. If he turns his head with the intention of changing his course, splash water in his face with your right or left hand, as the case may be, holding the tail with one hand and splashing with the other; and you will, in this way, direct him just as you like. This is by far the best way of swimming a horse: all others are objectionable and even dangerous with animals new to the work,—

such as to swim alongside the horse, with one hand on his shoulder; or, worst of all, to retain your seat on his back. If this last method be persisted in, at least let the rider take his feet out of the stirrups, before entering the water.

To float a Wagon across a River.—It must be well ballasted, or it will assuredly capsize: the heavy contents should be stowed at the bottom; the planking lashed to the axletrees, or it will float away from them; great bundles of reeds and the empty water-vessels should be made fast high above all, and then the wagon will cross without danger. When it is fairly under weigh, the oxen will swim it across, pulling in their yokes.

Water Spectacles.—When a man opens his eyes under water, he can see nothing distinctly; but everything is as much out of focus, as if he looked, in air, through a pair of powerful spectacles that were utterly unsuited to him. He cannot distinguish the letters of the largest print in a newspaper advertisement; he cannot see the spaces between the outstretched fingers, at arm's length, in clear water; nor at a few inches' distance, in water that is somewhat opaque. I read a short paper on this subject, at the British Association in 1865, in which I showed the precise cause of this imperfection of vision and how it might be remedied. If the front of our eyeballs had been flat, we should have had the power of seeing under water as clearly as in air; but instead of being flat, they are very convex, consequently our eye stamps a concave lens of high power into the water, and it is the seeing through this concave eyeglass which our eyeball makes for itself, that causes the indistinctness of our vision. Knowing the curvature of the eyeball, it is easy to calculate (as I did in the memoir mentioned above) the curvature of a convex lens of flint-glass that should, when plunged into water, produce effects of an exactly equal and contrary value, exactly neutralizing the effects of the concave eyeglass of water, if it were held immediately in front of the pupil of the eye. I have made several experiments with a view to obtaining serviceable spectacles, for seeing under water. The result is as follows:—experience has shown the distance from the eyeball at which spectacle-glasses can be most conveniently placed; now at that distance, the joint effect of the concave water-lens and the convex glass spectacle-lens, is to produce an opera-glass of exceedingly low magnifying power, that requires a small adjustment for accurate definition at different distances.

If the spectacle-lens be of flint-glass and doubly convex, each of its faces should have a curvature of not greater than 6½ tenths of an inch, nor more than 8½ tenths of an inch in radius: within these limits, it is practicable to obtain perfectly distinct vision under water by pressing the spectacles forwards or backwards to a moderate degree. Lenses of these high magnifying powers are sometimes sold by spectacle-makers, for persons who have undergone an operation for cataract. I have tried, but hitherto without much success, to arrange the fittings by which the lenses are secured so that by a movement of the jaw or by an elevation of the eyebrows, I could give the necessary adjustment of the glasses, leaving my hands free for the purpose of swimming. (See also, under " Fishing;" ' To see Things deep under Water.')

RAFTS AND BOATS.

Rafts.—*Rafts of Wood.*—Rafts are made of logs of wood, held together by pairs of cross-bars, one of each pair lying above the raft and the other below; then, the whole may be made quite firm by a little judicious notching where the logs cross, and a few pegs and lashings. Briers, woodbines, &c.,

will do for these. If the logs are large, they should be separately launched into the river, and towed into their proper places. Outriggers vastly increase the stability of a raft.

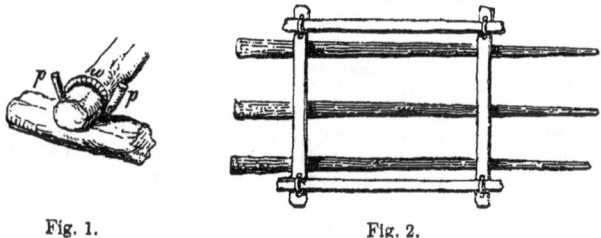

Fig. 1.   Fig. 2.

The raft-fastening in common use, is shown in fig. 1: it is a stout, lithe wand, bent over the cross piece, and wedged into holes in the framework.

The rafts of European rivers are usually built on shore, and launched into the water: three slides are laid for the purpose, on the sloping bank of the river; upon these are laid the four poles, secured together by their ends, which are to form the framework of the raft (fig. 2). Other poles are put in between, until the whole is complete.

Bamboo rafts.—Where bamboo is plentiful, it is preferable to any other material for rafts. A few bamboos lashed into the shape of an ordinary field gate, but with two diagonals, and with handfuls of grass thrown on to make a platform, is very buoyant and serviceable.

Floating power of various Woods.—The floating power of a raft depends on the buoyancy of the wood of which it is made. I give, in a Table (p. 90), a list of the specific gravities of a few well-known woods; and have annexed to them a column of what may be called their "specific floating powers."* Hence, to find the actual floating power of a raft, it is simply necessary to multiply its weight into the specific floating power of the wood of which it is made.

---

* Specific floating power $= \frac{1}{\text{Spec. Gr.}} - 1$. (*Mem.*, the Table of these, in previous editions is incorrect.) Burden $=$ weight of raft $\times$ spec. floating power. Weight of wood required to support a given burden $=$ Burden $\times \frac{\text{Spec. Gr.}}{1 - \text{Spec. Gr.}}$; the last column gives the latter factor.

Thus, a raft of 12 logs of larch, averaging 30 lbs. each, weighs 360 lbs.; this multiplied by ·47, is equal to 169 lbs. very nearly, which is the weight the raft will support without sinking. Poplar is the lightest on the list.

	Specific Gravities.	Specific Floating Powers.	Factors to be multiplied into burden to find weight of raft just able to support it.
Alder	·80	·25	4·0
Ash	·85	·18	5·7
Beech	·85	·18	5·7
Elm	·59 to ·80	·70 to ·25	1·4 to 4·0
Fir	·47 to ·60	1·13 to ·66	0·9 to 1·5
Larch	·53	·89	1·1
Oak	·75	·33	3·0
„ heart of	1·17	sinks	cannot be used
Pine	·40 to ·63	1·50 to ·60	0·7 to 1·7
Poplar	·33	1·63	0·6
Willow	·59	·70	1·4

Examples:—A raft of alder, weighing 200 lbs., would just support 200 × ·25 or 50 lbs.

A burden of 100 lbs. would require a raft of alder, weighing not less than 100 × 4·0, or 400 lbs. to support it.

Burning down Trees.—Where there are no means at hand to fell trees, they should be burnt down; two men may attend to the burning of twenty trees at one and the same time. When felled, their tops and branches, also, are to be trimmed by fire. (See " Hutting Palisades.")

Reed Rafts.—Mr. Andersson, in exploring the Tioughe River, in South Africa, met with two very simple forms of rafts: the one was a vast quantity of reeds cut down, heaped into a stack of from 30 to 50 feet in diameter, pushed out into the water, and allowed to float down stream: each day, as the reeds became water-logged, more were cut and thrown on the stack: its great bulk made it sure of passing over shallow places; and when it struck against "snags," the force of the water soon slewed it round and started it afresh. On an affair of this description, Mr. Andersson, with seven attendants, and two canoes hauled up upon it, descended the river for five days. The second reed raft was a small and neat one, and used for ferries; it was a mattress of reeds, 5 feet long, 3 broad, and some 8 inches thick, tied together with strips of the reeds themselves; to each of its four corners was fixed a post, made of an upright faggot of reeds, 18 inches high; other faggots connected the tops of the posts horizontally, in the place of rails: this was all; it held one or two men, and nothing but reeds or rushes were used in its construction.

Rafts of distended Hides.—"A single ox-hide may be made into a float capable of sustaining about 300 lbs.; the skin is to be cut to the largest possible circle, then gathered together round a short tube, to the inner end of which a valve, like that of a common pair of bellows, has been applied: it is inflated with bellows, and, as the air escapes by degrees, it may be refilled every ten or twelve hours." ('Handbook for Field Service.')

We read of the skins of animals, stuffed with hay to keep them distended, having been used by Alexander the Great, and by others.

Goatskin rafts are extensively used on the Tigris and elsewhere. These are inflated through one of the legs: they are generally lashed to a framework of wood, branches, and reeds, in such a way that the leg is accessible to a person sitting on the raft: when the air has in part escaped, he creeps round to the skins, one after the other, untying and re-inflating them in succession.

African Gourd Raft.—Over a large part of Bornu, especially on its Komádugu—the so-called River Yeou of Central Africa—no boat is used, except the following ingenious contrivance. It is called a "mákara," or boat *par éminence*.

Two large open gourds are nicely balanced, and fixed, bottom downwards, on a bar or yoke of light wood, 4 feet long, 4½ inches wide, and ¾ or 1 inch thick. The fisherman, or traveller, packs his gear into the gourds; launches the *mákara* into the river, and seats himself astride the bar. He then paddles off, with help of his hands (fig. 1). When he leaves the river, he carries the mákara on his back (fig. 2). The late Dr. Barth wrote

Fig. 2.   Fig. 1.

to me, "A person accustomed to such sort of voyage, sits very comfortably; a stranger holds on to one of the calabashes. There is no fear of capsizing, as the calabashes go under water, according to the weight put upon them, from ten to sixteen inches. The yoke is firmly fastened to the two calabashes, for it is never taken off. I am scarcely able, at present, to say how it is fastened. As far as I remember, it is fixed by a very firm lashing, which forms a sort of network over the calabash, and at the same time serves to strengthen the latter and guard it against an accident." It is obvious that the gourds might be replaced by inflated bags or baskets, covered with leather, or by copper or tin vessels, or by any other equivalent. I quite agree with Dr. Barth, that a mákara would be particularly suitable for a traveller. In Bornu, they make large rafts, by putting a frame over several of these mákara, placed side by side.

Rude Boats.—*Brazilian Sailing-boat.*—A simpler sailing-boat or raft could hardly be imagined than that shown in the figure; it is used by fishermen in Brazil.

Rafts and Boats.

Log Canoes are made by hollowing out a long tree by axe and by fire, and fastening an outrigger to one side of it, to give steadiness in the water. Recollect Robinson Crusoe's difficulty in launching his canoe after he had made it. (See "Rafts of Wood.") It is not a difficult, though a tedious operation, to burn out hollows in wood; the fire is confined by wet earth, that it may not extend too far to either side, and the charred matter is from time to time scraped away, and fresh fire raked back on the newly-exposed surface. A lazy savage will be months in making a single canoe in this way.

Canoe of Three Planks.—A swift, safe, and graceful little boat, with a sharp stem and stern, and with a bottom that curves upwards at both ends, can be made out of three planks. The sketch, fig. 1, is a foreshortened view of the boat, and the diagram, fig. 2, shows the shape of the planks from which it is made. The thwart or seat shown in fig. 1 is important in giving the proper inclination to the sides of the boat, for, without it, they would tend to collapse; and the bottom would be less curved at either end. If the reader will take the trouble to trace fig. 2 on a stout card, to cut it out in a single

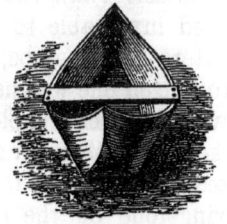

Fig. 1.

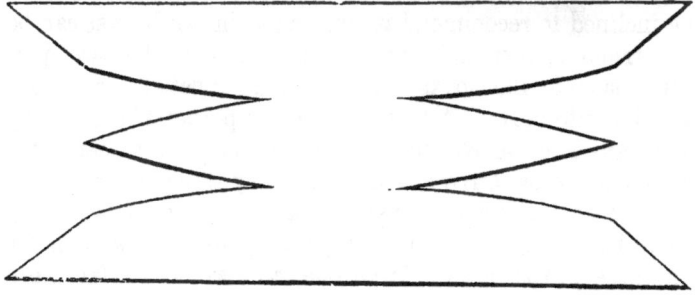

Fig. 2.

piece (cutting only half through the cardboard, where the planks touch), and to fasten it into shape with pieces of gummed paper, he will understand the architecture of the boat more easily than from any description. If he wishes to build a boat he had best proceed to make as large a model in pasteboard as his materials admit, and to cut the planks to scale, according to the pattern of his model. The grace of the boat depends on the cut of its planks, just as much as the elegance of a dress does on that of its cloth. These three-plank canoes are in frequent use in Norway. Bark may be used instead of planks. If the canoe be built of five planks instead of three, a second narrow side-plank being added above each gunwale, the section of the canoe is decidedly improved.

Inflatable India-rubber Boats are an invention that has proved invaluable to travellers: they have been used in all quarters of the globe, and are found to stand every climate. A full-sized one weighs only 40 lbs. They have done especial service in Arctic exploration; the waters of the Great Salt Lake, in the Mormon country, were first explored and navigated with one by Fremont; they were also employed by Dr. Livingstone on the rivers of South Africa. They stand a wonderful amount of wear and tear; but, as boats, they are inferior to native canoes, as they are very slow in the water: it is, indeed, impossible to paddle them against a moderate head-wind. For the general purposes of travellers, I should be inclined to recommend as small a macintosh-boat as can be constructed; just sufficient for one, or at most for two, persons; such as the cloaks that are made inflatable, and convertible into boats. A traveller wants a portable boat, chiefly as means to cross over to a village for help, or to carry his valuables across a river, while the heavy things are risked at a ford; or for shooting, fishing, or surveying. Now a very small boat, weighing about ten pounds, would do as well for all these purposes as a large one, and would be far more portable.

It is perfectly easy to get into a macintosh-boat, after having been capsized out of it into deep water.

Basket-boat with Canvas Sides.—FitzRoy gives an account of a party of his sailors, whose boat had been stolen while they were encamped, putting out to sea in a large basket, woven with such boughs as were at hand, and covered with their canvas tent—the inside of which they had puddled with clay, to keep the water from oozing through too fast. They were eighteen hours afloat in this crazy craft. I mention this instance, to show how almost anything will make a boat. Canvas saturated with grease or oil is waterproof, and painted canvas is at first an excellent covering for a boat, but it soon becomes rotten.

Canoe of Reeds or Vegetable Fibre.—A canoe may be made of reeds, rushes, or the light inner bark of trees. Either of these materials is bound into three long faggots, pointed at one end: these are placed side by side and lashed together,

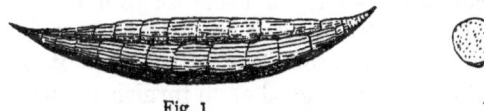

Fig. 1.   Fig. 2.

and the result is a serviceable vessel, of the appearance fig. 1, and section as fig. 2. The Lake Titicaca, which lies far above the limit of trees, is navigated by boats made of rushes, and carrying sails woven of rushes also. Little boats are sometimes made of twigs, and are then plastered both inside and outside with clay, but they are very leaky.

Hide Tray.—This is a good contrivance; and if the hide be smoked (see "Hides") after it is set, it is vastly improved. In its simplest form, Peruvian travellers describe it as a dish or tray, consisting of a dry hide pinched up at the four corners, and each corner secured with a thorn. The preferable plan is to make eyelet-holes round its rim, and pass a thong through, drawing it pretty close: the tray is kept in shape, by sticks put inside and athwart its bottom.

Coracle and Skin Punt.—If a traveller has one hide only at his disposal he should make a coracle, if he has two, a punt. This last is a really useful boat; one in which very great distances of river may be descended with safety, and much luggage taken. Hide boats are very light, since the weight of a bullock's skin only averages 45 lbs.; but, unless well greased, they soon rot. When taken out of the water, they should be laid bottom upwards to dry. To make a proper and substantial coracle, a dozen or more osier or other wands must be cut; these are to be bent, and have both ends stuck in the ground, in such a way as to form the framework of the required boat, bottom upwards, much like half a walnut-shell in shape, but flatter. Where these wands cross, they should be lashed; and sticks should be wattled in, to fill up gaps. A raw hide is then thrown over the framework, sewn in place, and left to dry. Finally, the projecting ends of the osiers have to be cut off. Should this boat, by any chance, prove a failure, the hide is not wasted, but can be removed, soaked till soft, and used again.

A skin punt requires two bullocks' or other hides, and also about ten small willow-trees, or other tough flexible wood, 14 feet long. Captain Palliser says that a couple of days is sufficient for two people to complete an entire punt of this description. He has been so good as to furnish me with the following minute description of the way of making this very useful boat.

1. The keel, stem, and stern might be in one; but, because the stem and stern ought to be strong, this whole line is made of two small trees lashed together with the thick ends outwards, as in fig. 1,

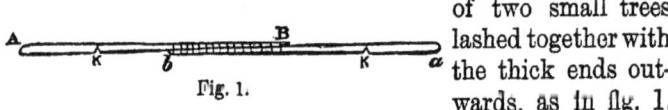
Fig. 1.

where A B is a lithe clean little willow-tree, and *a b* another similar one. They are lashed together at their taper ends.

2. Cut notches half-way through K K, at about 20 to 25 inches from each end; then turn up the notched portions, and you have stem, keel and stern, all in one piece, as in fig. 2.

Fig. 2.

3. Stake out the ground, according to the size your boat will cover, by driving eight strong pointed stakes of wood into the ground; to these lash four cross (willow-tree) sticks, notched in two places, so that each of these four willows shall form two knees, as well as run across the bottom of the boat.

4. Bend two more main willows for gunwales for the boat, and two more for bottom rails. Each separate stick, as will be perceived by fig. 3, is lashed in five different places, and the keel in eight places.

Rafts and Boats.

The main framework being now completed, loosen it from the stakes driven into the ground.

5. Fasten a large number of little slender willow-twigs between each of the main cross-knees, as shown by the thin lines in fig. 3. It is then fit for covering. Lift it up like a basket, and turn it topsy-turvy.

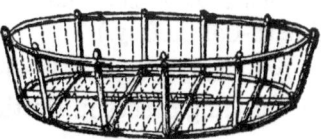

Fig. 3.

6. Kill *two* bulls, skin them, and in skinning, be careful to make your cuts in the skin down the rump to the hock of the animal, and down the brisket in front of the fore-leg to the knee, so as to have your skins as square as possible (fig. 4). Cut off the heads, and sew the skins together at the nape of

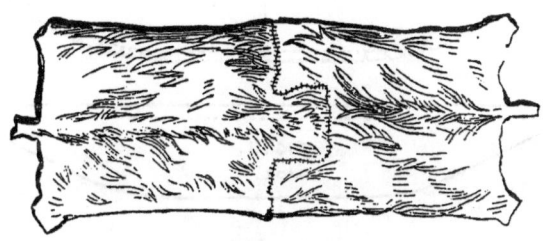

Fig. 4.

the necks; and, while reeking, cover the wicker-work, turning them over it, the hairy side inwards, and fasten it all round by means of skin-cords. Cut holes with a knife round the edges, to pass the cords through, as you lash up to the top-rails of the boat.

7. Leave it 24 hours in the sun; cover the seam where the skins are sewn together, with melted fat, and the boat is fit for use.

Bark Boats.—"From a pine, or other tree, take off with care the longest possible entire portion of the bark; while fresh and flexible, spread it flat as a long rectangular sheet; then turn it carefully up at the sides, the smooth side outwards; *sew* the ends together, and caulk them well. A few cross-sticks for thwarts complete this contrivance, which is made by an American Indian in a few hours, and in which the rapid waters of the Mackenzie are navigated for hundreds

98 *Art of Travel.*

of miles. Ways of strengthening the structure will readily suggest themselves. The native material for sewing is the fibrous root of the pine." ("Handbook for Field Service;" Lieut.-Col. Lefroy.)

Birch-bark Canoes.—Birch bark, as is well known, is used for building canoes in North America, and the bark of many

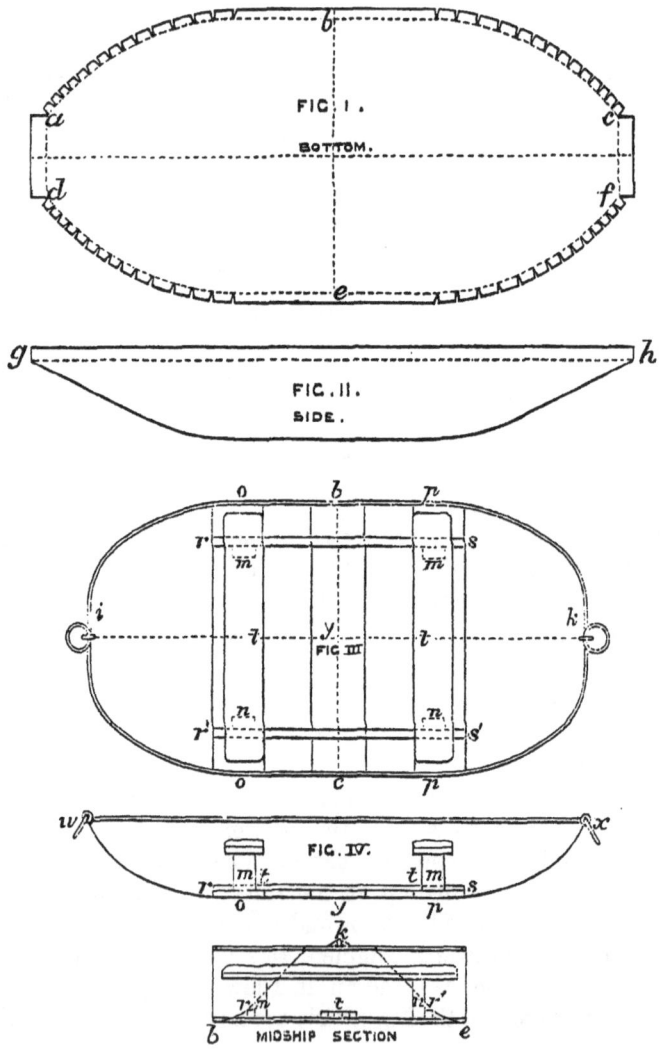

other trees would do for covering the framework of a boat, in default of leather. But it is useless to give a detailed account of birch canoes, as great skill and neat execution are required both in making and in using them.

Boats of Sheet-tin, covered with Pitched Canvas.—These might be made at any of the outposts of civilization. I am indebted to a correspondent, whose name I regret exceedingly to be unable to insert, having unfortunately mislaid it, for the following full description of his shooting-punt. It will be obvious that his methods are applicable not only to their professed object, but also to tin boats of any shape whatever.

" Form the bottom, fig. I., as follows:—Select the thickest sheets of tin and solder them together by their narrowest sides, until as many lengths are made as, when laid side by side, will be sufficient for the whole length and breadth of the figure. The soldering should be by a joint of this kind. These lengths must then be soldered side by side by a similar joint, and the whole sheet thus made, trimmed to the shape of fig. I., care being taken that no two joints in the lengths should be exactly opposite each other. Form two other sheets in a similar manner for the two sides, and of the shape of fig. II. The dotted lines $a\ b\ c\ d\ e\ f$, fig. I., show the portions of the tin round the edges, 1 inch wide, which must be turned up at right angles with the bottom, and to which the sides are to be soldered on the inside; they should have triangular pieces clipped out of them, as shown in the fig., where the bends of the boat begin, to make them take the curve required. The two extra pieces at the ends $a\ d$, $e\ f$, 2 inches wide, are for turning down over an iron rod, which is to pass round the gunwale, to give stiffness to the boat; $g\ h$, fig. II., is a breadth of 2 inches of extra tin, for the same purpose of turning down over the iron rod.

" Each side is now to be soldered to the bottom piece, beginning with the centre, and working in to each end.

" The soldering of the turned-up edges to the bottom, on the outside, may then be done. Separate slips of tin 2 inches wide should then be bent up longitudinally in halves, like angle-iron, and fitted along the joining of the bottom and sides, on the inside, and soldered; these slips may also be clipped on either side, when necessary, to make them take the curves.

"The measure round the gunwale may now be taken within the edge of the tin, and an iron rod $\frac{3}{8}$ of an inch thick, to go round this gunwale, bent to the form of the outline of fig. III., $i\,b\,k\,c$, which will now be that of the boat, and the ends welded at their meeting. Sufficient iron rod must be taken to form eyes at i and k to receive rings of 3 or 4 inches diameter, through which a pole is to be passed, for carrying the boat, and for their welding at the meeting of the ends.

"The iron-rod gunwale may now be put in, and the 2 inches width of tin, allowed in excess on the sides and ends of the bottom, turned down closely over the rod, all round and soldered on the inside. The side elevation of the boat will now be as $w\,x\,y$, fig. IV.

"The boat should be proved as to being water-tight by filling it with water, any leak being stopped by more solder.

"The outside must now be covered with pitched canvas, thus:—

"Turn it upside down, in a sheltered spot exposed to the sun, or warm it by other means, and have a caldron of boiling pitch on a fire at hand, also have sufficient canvas sewn together in breadths as will quite cover the boat, bottom and sides; then, beginning across the middle of the bottom, brush on a layer 3 or 4 inches wide of the boiling pitch, and quickly press down the corresponding central portion of the canvas upon it; work on thus, from the centre of the bottom to the ends, laying on a breadth of pitch, and then pressing down and stretching a portion of canvas over it; then turn down the canvas over each side, and pitch in the same way, cutting out the parts of the canvas that would overlap too much at the bends, but leaving no tin uncovered; the boat may then be righted, the excess of canvas cut off, and the edge laid down with pitch, a little short of the gunwale.

"The bottom may then be pitched over the canvas for 6 inches up, and the rest of the outside, with the inside, be painted with two or three coats.

"A flooring of thin planking for $3\frac{1}{2}$ feet of the central portion of the boat must now be made as follows:—Make five planks, between 8 and 9 inches wide, to fit across the beam of the boat, and in each of the outer planks, $o\,o$, $p\,p$, fig. III., fix uprights $m\,n$, 6 inches high, to support a seat, mortised on the pair of uprights in each board; the ends of each seat should be short of the breadth of the boat by an inch or so, so as not to bear against the sides; then lay down two ribs of tough wood, fitted to bear equally across the planking, on each side, as rs, $r's'$, and screw each end of them down to the outer planks only.

"Wooden cleats can be fixed on each board at $t\,t$, each to receive the butts of two guns, while their barrels lie in hollows formed in the cushions of the seat opposite them, so that the rower can put down his paddles and take up his gun instantly; steps for a mast can be also contrived at the same points. This woodwork is to be also well painted; it can be taken out with ease, as it is nowhere connected with the tin of the boat. Care should be taken that no projections in this woodwork, such as screw-heads, &c., should chafe the tin, and that it should be always kept well painted.

"The boat, of which this is a description, drew $2\tfrac{1}{2}$ inches water with one person in, with two guns and ammunition, &c.; it was furnished with two short paddles, which were tied by a short length of string to the sides, so as to be dropped without loss of time on taking up the gun to fire; the boat turned with the greatest ease, by one backing and pulling stroke of the two paddles, and was very stiff in the water.

"Iron rowlocks were fitted to it, on the outside at b, e, fig. 1. [I do not give the diagram by which the author illustrated his description; the rowlocks were applied to the sides of the boat, and each rowlock was secured to the side by three bolts.] The two upper bolts had claw-heads to seize the iron-rod gunwale on the inside, and a piece of wood was fitted on the inside, through which the three bolts passed, to give substance for their hold, their nuts were on the outside. With these rowlocks two oars of 7 feet long were used. The breadth between the horns should be only just enough to admit the oars.

"This boat could be carried on the shoulders of two persons, when suspended on a pole passed through the end rings, for a distance of twelve or fifteen miles daily, with guns and ammunition stowed in it. It could be fired from, standing, without risk, and be poled over marshy ground barely covered with water, or dragged with ease by the person seated in it, through high reeds, by grasping a handful on each side and hauling on them. A rudder was unnecessary. It was in use for more than three years, and, with due care in getting in and out, on a rough shore, and by keeping it well painted and pitched, it never leaked or became impaired in any way."

Boats.—*Of Wood.*—English-made boats have been carried by explorers for great distances on wheels, but seldom seem to have done much useful service. They would travel easiest if slung and made fast in a strong wooden crate or framework, to be fixed on the body of the carriage. A white covering is necessary for a wooden boat, on account of the sun: both boat and covering should be frequently examined. Mr. Richardson and his party took a boat, divided in four quarters, on camel-back across the Sahara, all the way from the Mediterranean to Lake Tchad. A portable framework of metal tubes, to be covered with india-rubber sheeting on arrival, was suggested to me by a very competent authority, the late Mr. M'Gregor Laird.

Copper boats have been much recommended, because an accidental dent, however severe it may be, can be beaten back again without doing injury to the metal. One of the boats in Mr. Lynch's expedition down the Jordan was made of copper.

Corrugated Iron makes excellent boats for travellers; they are stamped by machinery: Burton took one of them to Zanzibar. They were widely advertised some ten years ago, but they never came into general use, and I do not know where they can now be procured.

Canoes.—The earlier exploits of the 'Rob Roy' canoe justly attracted much attention, and numerous canoe voyages have subsequently been made. The Canoe Club is now a considerable institution, many of whose members make yearly improvements in the designs of their crafts. Although canoes are delicately built and apparently fragile, experience has amply proved that they can stand an extraordinary amount of hard usage in the hands of careful travellers. As a general rule, it is by no means the heaviest and most solid things that endure the best. If a lightly-made apparatus can be secured from the risk of heavy things falling upon it, it will outlast a heavy apparatus that shakes to pieces under the jar of its own weight.

A hole cut in the square sail enables the voyager to see ahead.

To carry on Horseback.—Mr. Macgregor, when in Syria, took two strong poles, each 16 feet long, and about 3 inches thick at the larger end. These were placed on the ground 2 feet apart, and across them, at 3 feet from each end, he lashed two stout staves, about 4 feet long. Then a "leading" horse was selected, that is, one used to lead caravans, and on his back a large bag of straw was well girthed and flattened down. The frame was firmly tied on this, and the canoe, wrapped in carpets, was placed on the frame. This simple method was used for three months over sand and snow, rock and jungle, mud and marsh—anywhere indeed that a horse could go. The frame was elevated in front, so as to allow the horse's head some room under the boat's keel. Two girth-straps kept the canoe firmly in position above, and carpets were used as cushions under its bilge. A boy led the horse, and a strong man was told off to hold fast to the canoe in every difficulty. It will be seen, that in the event of a fall, the corners of the framework would receive the shock, not the canoe.

Boating Gear.—*Anchors* may be made of wood weighted with

Fig. 1.

stones. Fig. 1 shows the anchor used by Brazilian fishermen

with their rude boat or sailing-raft already described. Fig. 2 shows another sort of anchor that is in common use in Norway.

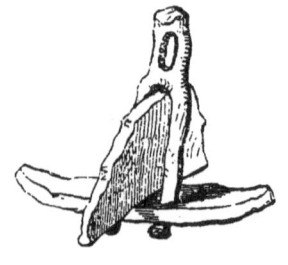

Fig. 2.

Mast.—Where there is difficulty in "stepping" a mast, use a bar across the thwarts and two poles, one lashed at either end of it, and coming together to a point above. This triangle takes the place of the masts, and is secured by shrouds fore and aft. It is a very convenient rig for a boat with an outrigger: the Sooloo pirates use it.

Outrigger Irons.—Mr. Gilby informs me that he has travelled with a pair of light sculls and outrigger irons, which he was able to adapt to many kinds of rude boats. He found them of much service in Egypt.

Keels are troublesome to make: lee-boards are effective substitutes, and are easily added to a rude boat or punt when it is desired to rig her as a sailing-craft.

Rudder.—A rude oar makes the most powerful, though not the most convenient rudder. In the lakes of North Italy, where the winds are steady, the heavy boats have a bar upon which the tiller of the rudder rests: this bar is full of small notches; and the bottom of the tiller, at the place where it rests on the bar, is furnished with a blunt knife-edge; the tiller is not stiffly joined to the rudder, but admits of a little play up and down. When the boatman finds that the boat steers steadily, he simply drops the tiller, which forthwith falls into the notch below it, where it is held tight until the steersman cares to take the tiller into his hand again.

Buoys.—An excellent buoy to mark out a passage is simply a small pole anchored by a rope at the end. It is very readily seen, and exposes so little surface to the wind and water, that it is not easily washed away. A pole of the thickness of a walking-stick is much used in Sweden. Such a buoy costs only a rope, a stick, and a stone. A tuft of the small branches may be left on the top of the pole.

Log.—For a log use a conical canvas bag thus—

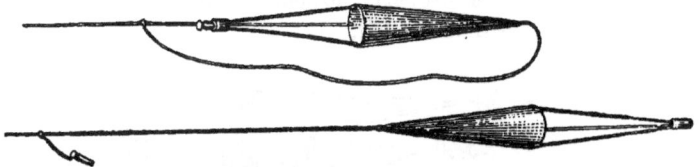

When the peg is drawn out by the usual jerk, the bag no longer presents its mouth to the water, but is easily drawn in by the line attached to its point.

Boat Building.—*Caulking.*—Almost anything that is fibrous does for caulking the seams of a boat. The inner bark of trees is one of the readiest materials.

Securing Planks.—In default of nails, it is possible to drill or to burn holes in the planks and to sew them together with strips of hide, woodbine, or string made from the inner bark of fibrous trees. Holes may be drilled on precisely the same principle as that which I have described in making fire by friction.

Lengthening Boats.—If you have an ordinary boat, and wish to make it of greater burden, saw it in half and lengthen it. Comparatively coarse carpentering is good enough for this purpose.

Boat Management.—*Hauling boats on Shore.*—To haul up a boat on a barren shore, with but a few hands, lay out the anchor ahead of her to make fast your purchase to; or back the body of a wagon underneath the boat as she floats, and so draw her out upon wheels. A make-shift framework, on small solid wheels, has been used and recommended.

Towing.—A good way of fastening a tow-rope to a boat that has no mast is shown in the diagram, which, however, is very coarsely drawn. A curved pole is lashed alongside one of the knees of the boat, and the tow-rope, passing with a turn or two round its end, is carried on to the stern of the boat. By taking a few turns, more or less, with the rope round the stick, the line of action of the tow-rope on the boat's axis may be properly adjusted. When all is right the boat ought to steer herself.

When Caught by a Gale recollect that a boat will lie-to and live through almost any weather, if you can make a bundle of a few spare spars, oars, &c., and secure them to the boat's head, so as to float in front of and across the bow. They will act very sensibly as a breakwater, and will always keep the boat's head towards the wind. Kroomen rig out three oars in a triangle, lash the boat's sail to it, throw overboard, after making fast, and pay out as much line as they can muster. By making a canvas half-deck to an open boat, you much increase its safety in broken water; and if it be made to lace down the centre, it can be rolled up on the gunwale, and be out of the way in fine weather.

In Floating down a Stream when the wind blows right against you (and on rivers the wind nearly always blows right up or right down), a plan generally employed is to cut large branches, to make them fast to the front of the boat, weight them that they may sink low in the water, and throw them overboard. The force of the stream acting on these branches will more than counterbalance that of the wind upon the boat. For want of branches, a kind of water-sail is sometimes made of canvas.

Steering in the Dark.—In dark nights, when on a river running through pine forests, the mid stream can be kept by occasionally striking the water sharply with the blade of the oar, and listening to the echoes. They should reach the ear simultaneously, or nearly so, from either bank. On the same principle, vessels have been steered out of danger when caught by a dense fog close to a rocky coast.

Awning.—The best is a wagon-roof awning, made simply of a couple of parallel poles, into which the ends of the bent ribs of the roof are set, without any other cross-pieces. This roof should be of two feet larger span than the width of the boat, and should rest upon prolongations of the thwarts, or else upon crooked knees of wood. One arm of each of the knees is upright, and is made fast to the inside of the boat, while the other is horizontal and projects outside it: it is on these horizontal and projecting arms that the roof rests, and to which it is lashed. Such an awning is airy, roomy, and does not interfere with rowing, if the rowlocks are fixed to the poles. It also makes an excellent cabin for sleeping in at night.

Sail Tent.—A boat's sail is turned into a tent by erecting a gable-shaped framework: the mast or other spar being the ridge-pole, and a pair of crossed oars lashed together supporting it at either end; and the whole is made stable by a couple of ropes and pegs. Then the sail is thrown across  the ridge-pole (not over the crossed tops of the oars, for they would fret it), and is pegged out below. The natural fall of the canvas tends to close the two ends, as with curtains.

Tree-snakes.—Where these abound, travellers on rivers with overhanging branches should beware of keeping too near inshore, lest the rigging of the boat should brush down the snakes.

FORDS AND BRIDGES.

Fords.—In fording a swift stream, carry heavy stones in your hand, for you require weight to resist the force of the current: indeed, the deeper you wade, the more weight you require; though you have so much the less at command, on account of the water buoying you up.

Rivers cannot be forded if their depth exceeds 3 feet for men or 4 feet for horses. Fords are easily discovered by tying a sounding-pole to the stern of a boat rowing down the middle of the stream, and searching those places where the pole touches the bottom. When no boat is to be had, fords should be tried for where the river is broad rather than where it is narrow, and especially at those places where there are bends in its course. In these the line of shallow water does not run straight across, but follows the direction of a line connecting a promontory on one side to the nearest promontory on the other, as in the drawing; that is to say, from A to B, or from B to C, and *not* right across from B to *b*, from A to *a*, or from C to *c*. Along hollow curves, as at *a*, *b*, *c*, the stream runs deep, and usually beneath overhanging banks; whilst in front of promontories, as at A, B, and C, the water is invariably shoal, unless it be a jutting rock that makes the promontory. Therefore, by entering the stream at one promontory, with the intention of leaving it at another, you ensure that at all events the beginning and end of your course shall be in shallow water, which you cannot do by attempting any other line of passage.

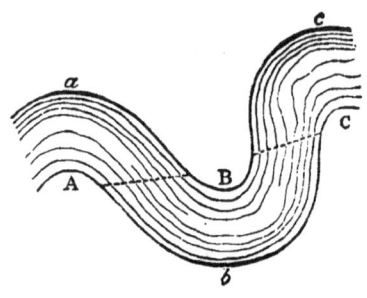

To Cross Boggy and Uncertain Ground.—*Swamps.*—When you wish to take a wagon across a deep, miry, and reedy swamp, outspan and let the cattle feed. Then cut faggots of reeds, and strew them thickly over the line of intended passage. When plenty are laid down, drive the cattle backwards and forwards, and they will trample them in. Repeat the process two or three times, till the causeway is firm enough to bear the weight of the wagon. Or, in default of reeds, cut long poles and several short cross-bars, say of two feet long; join these as best you can, so as to make a couple of ladder-shaped frames. Place these across the mud, one under the intended track of each wheel. Faggots strewn between each round of the ladder will make the causeway more sound. A succession of logs, laid crosswise with faggots between them, will also do, but not so well.

Passing from Hand to Hand.—When many things have to be conveyed across a piece of abominably bad road—as over sand-dunes, heavy shingle, mud of two feet deep, a morass, a jagged mountain tract, or over stepping-stones in the bed of a rushing torrent—it is a great waste of labour to make laden men travel to and fro with loads on their backs. It is a severe exertion to walk at all under these circumstances, letting alone the labour of also carrying a burden. The men should be stationed in a line, each at a distance of six or seven feet from his neighbour, and should pass the things from hand to hand, as they stand.

Plank Roads.—" Miry, boggy lines of road, along which people had been seen for months crawling like flies across a plate of treacle, are suddenly, and I may almost say magically, converted into a road as hard and good as Regent Street by the following simple process, which is usually adopted as soon as the feeble funds of the young colony can purchase the blessing. A small gang of men, with spades and rammers, quickly level one end of the earth road. As fast as they proceed, four or five rows of strong beams or sleepers, which have been brought in the light wagons of the country, are laid down longitudinally, four or five feet asunder; and no sooner are they in position than from other wagons stout planks, touching each other, are transversely laid upon them. From a third series of wagons, a thin layer of sand or grit is thrown upon the planks, which instantly assume the appearance of a more level McAdam road than in practice can ever be obtained. Upon this new-born road the wagons carrying the sleepers, planks, and sand, convey, with perfect ease, these three descriptions of materials for its continuance. The work advances literally about as fast as an old gouty gentleman can walk; and as soon as it is completed, there can scarcely exist a more striking contrast than between the two tenses of what it was and what it is. This 'plank road,' as it is termed in America, usually lasts from eight to twelve years; and as it is found quite unnecessary to spike the planks to the sleepers, the arrangement admits of easy repair, which, however, is but seldom required." (Sir Francis Head, in *Times*, Jan. 2, 1855.)

Snow.—Sir R. Dalyell tells me that it is the practice of muleteers in the neighbourhood of Erzeroum, when their animals lose their way and flounder in the deep snow, to spread a horse-cloth or other thick rug from off their packs upon the snow in front of them. The animals step upon it and extricate themselves easily. I have practised walking across deep snow-drifts on this principle, with perfect success.

Weak Ice.—Water that is slightly frozen is made to bear a heavy wagon, by cutting reeds, strewing them thickly on the ice, and pouring water upon them; when the whole is frozen into a firm mass the process must be repeated.

Bridges.—*Flying Bridges* are well known: a long cord or chain of poles is made fast to a rock or an anchor in the middle of a river. The other end is attached to the ferry-boat, which being so slewed as to receive the force of the current obliquely, traverses the river from side to side.

Bridges of Felled Trees.—If you are at the side of a narrow but deep and rapid river, on the banks of which trees grow long enough to reach across, one or more may be felled, confining the trunk to its own bank, and letting the current force the head round to the opposite side; but if "the river be too wide to be spanned by one tree—and if two or three men can in any manner be got across—let a large tree be felled into the water on each side, and placed close to the banks opposite to each other, with their heads lying up-streamwards. Fasten a rope to the head of each tree, confine the trunks, shove the head off to receive the force of the current, and ease off the ropes, so that the branches may meet in the middle of the river at an angle pointing upwards. The branches of the trees will be jammed together by the force of the current, and so be sufficiently united as to form a tolerable communication, especially when a few of the upper branches have been cleared away. If insufficient, towards the middle of the river, to bear the weight of men crossing, a few stakes with forks left near their heads, may be thrust down through the branches of the trees to support them." (Sir H. Douglas.)

CLOTHING.

General Remarks.—There are such infinite varieties of dress, that I shall only attempt a few general remarks and give a single costume, that a traveller of great experience had used to his complete satisfaction. The military authorities of different nations have long made it their study, to combine in the best manner the requirements of handsome effect, of cheapness, and of serviceability in all climates, but I fear their results will not greatly help the traveller, who looks more to serviceability than to anything else. Of late years, even Garibaldi with his red-shirted volunteers, and Alpine men with their simple outfit, have approached more nearly to a traveller's ideal.

Materials for Clothes.—*Flannel.*—The importance of flannel next the skin can hardly be overrated: it is now a matter of statistics; for, during the progress of expeditions, notes have been made of the number of names of those in them who had provided themselves with flannel, and of those who had not. The list of sick and dead always included names from the latter list in a very great proportion.

Cotton is preferable to flannel for a sedentary life, in hot damp countries, or where flannel irritates the skin. Persons who are resident in the tropics, and dress in civilised costume, mostly wear cotton shirts.

Linen by universal consent is a dangerous dress wherever there is a chance of much perspiration, for it strikes cold upon the skin when it is wet. The terror of Swiss guides of the old school at a *coup d'air* on the mountain top, and of Italians at the chill of sundown, is largely due to their wearing linen shirts. Those who are dressed in flannel are far less sensitive to these influences.

Leather is the only safeguard against the stronger kinds of thorns. In pastoral and in hunting countries it is always easy to procure skins of a tough quality that have been neatly dressed by hand. Also it will be easy to find persons capable of sewing them together very neatly, after you have cut them out to the pattern of your old clothes.

Bark Cloth is used in several parts of the work. It is simply a piece of some kind of peculiarly fibrous bark; in Unyoro, Sir S. Baker says, the natives use the bark of a species of fig-tree. They soak it in water and then beat it with a mallet, to get rid of all the harder parts;—much as hemp is prepared. "In appearance it much resembles corduroy, and is the colour of tanned leather: the finer qualities are peculiarly soft to the touch, as though of woven cotton."

Effect of colour on warmth of clothing.—Dark colours become hotter than light colours in the sunshine, but they are not hotter under any other circumstances. Consequently a person who aims at equable temperature, should wear light colours. Light colours are far the best for sporting purposes, as they are usually much less conspicuous than black or rifle-green. Almost all wild beasts are tawny or fawn-coloured, or tabby, or of some nondescript hue and pattern: if an animal were born with a more decided colour, he would soon perish for want of ability to conceal himself.

Warmth of different Materials.—"The indefatigable Rumford made an elaborate series of experiments on the conductivity of the substances used in clothing. His method was this:—A mercurial thermometer was suspended in the axis of a cylindrical glass tube ending with a globe, in such a manner that the centre of the bulb of the thermometer occupied the centre of the globe; the space between the internal surface of the globe and the bulb was filled with the substance whose conductive power was to be determined; the instrument was then heated in boiling water, and afterwards, being plunged into a freezing mixture of pounded ice and salt, the times of cooling down 135° Fahr. were noted. They are recorded in the following table:—

Surrounded with—	Seconds.
Twisted silk	917
Fine lint	1032
Cotton wool	1046
Sheep's wool	1118
Taffety	1169
Raw silk	1264
Beaver's fur	1296
Eider down	1305

Surrounded with—	Seconds.
Hare's fur	1312
Wood ashes	927
Charcoal	937
Lamp-black	1117

Among the substances here examined, hare's fur offered the greatest impediment to the transmission of the heat. The transmission of heat is powerfully influenced by the mechanical state of the body through which it passes. The raw and twisted silk of Rumford's table illustrate this" (Prof. Tyndall on Heat.)

Waterproof Cloth.—Cloth is made partly waterproof by rubbing soap-suds into it (on the wrong side), and working them well in: and when dry, doing the same with a solution of alum; the soap is by this means decomposed, and the oily part of it distributed among the fibres of the cloth. (See "Tarpaulins.")

Incombustible Stuffs.—I extract the following paragraph from a newspaper. Persons who make much use of musquito curtains, will be glad to read it. "The *Répertoire de Chimie Pure et Appliquée* publishes the following remarks by the celebrated chemists, MM. Dœbereiner and Œlsner, on the various methods for rendering stuffs incombustible, or at least less inflammable than they naturally are. The substances employed for this purpose are borax, alum, soluble glass, and phosphate of ammonia. For wood and common stuffs, any one of these salts will do; but fine and light tissues, which are just those most liable to catching fire, cannot be treated in the same way. Borax renders fine textile fabrics stiff; it causes dust, and will swell out under the smoothing-iron; so does alum, besides weakening the fibres of the stuff, so as to make it tear easily. Soluble glass both stiffens and weakens the stuff, depriving it both of elasticity and tenacity. Phosphate of ammonia alone has none of these inconveniences. It may be mixed with a certain quantity of sal-ammoniac, and then introduced into the starch prepared for stiffening the linen; or else it may be dissolved in 20 parts of water, in weight, to one of phosphate, and the stuff steeped into the solution, then allowed to dry, and ironed as usual.

Phosphate of ammonia is cheap enough to allow of its introduction into common use, so that it may be employed at each wash. Phosphate of ammonia is obtained by saturating the biphosphate of lime with liquid ammonia."

Sewing Materials.—An outfit of sewing materials consists of needles and thread; scissors; tailor's thimble; wax; canvas needles, including the smaller sizes which are identical with glove needles and are used for sewing leather; twine; a palm; awls for cobbling, both straight and curved; cobbler's wax; and, possibly, bristles. The needles and awls in use are conveniently carried in some kind of metal tube, with wads of cork at either end, to preserve their points. (See also the chapter on "Thread, for stitches," &c.)

Articles of Dress.—*Hats and Caps.*—There is no perfect head-dress; but I notice that old travellers in both hot and temperate countries have generally adopted a scanty "wide-awake." Mr. Oswell, the South African sportsman and traveller, used for years, and strongly recommended to me, a brimless hat of fine Panama grass, which he had sewn as a lining to an ordinary wide-awake. I regret I have had no opportunity of trying this combination, but can easily believe that the touch of the cool, smooth grass, to the wet brow, would be more agreeable than that of any other material. I need hardly mention Pith hats (to be bought under the Opera Colonnade, Pall Mall), Indian topees, and English hunting-caps, as having severally many merits. A muslin turban twisted into a rope and rolled round the hat is a common plan to keep the sun from the head and *spine*: it can also be used as a rope on an emergency.

Coat.—In nine cases out of ten, a strong but not too thick tweed coat is the best for rough work. In a very thorny country, a leather coat is almost essential. A blouse, cut short so as to clear the saddle, is neat, cool, and easy, whether as a riding or walking costume. Generally speaking, the traveller will chiefly spend his life in his shirt-sleeves, and will only use his coat when he wants extra warmth.

To carry a Coat.—There are two ways. The first is to fold it small and strap it to the belt. If the coat be a light one it can be carried very neatly and comfortably in this way, lying in the small of the back. The second is the contrivance of a friend of mine, an eminent scholar and divine, who always employs it in his vacation rambles. It is to pass an ordinary strap, once round the middle of the coat and a second time round both the coat and the left arm just above the elbow, and then to buckle it. The coat hangs very comfortably in its place and does not hamper the movements of the left arm. It requires no further care, except that after a few minutes it will generally be found advisable to buckle the strap one hole tighter. A coat carried in this way will be found to attract no attention from passers by.

Waistcoats are more convenient for their pockets than for their warmth. When travelling in countries where papers have to be carried, an inside pocket between the lining and the waistcoat, with a button to close it, is extremely useful. Letters of credit and paper money can be carried in it more safely than in any other pocket.

Trousers.—If you are likely to have much riding, take extra leather or moleskin trousers, or tweed covered down the inside of the legs with leather, such as cavalry soldiers generally wear. Leather is a better protection than moleskin against thorns; but not so serviceable against wet: it will far outlast moleskin. There should be no hem to the legs of trousers, as it retains the wet.

Watch-pocket.—Have it made of macintosh, to save the watch from perspiration. The astronomer-royal of Cape Town, Sir T. Maclear, who had considerable experience of the bush when measuring an arc of the meridian, justly remarked to me on the advantage of frequently turning the watch-pocket inside out, to get rid of the fluff and dust that collects in it and is otherwise sure to enter the watch-case.

Socks.—The hotter the ground on which you have to walk, the thicker should be your socks. These should be of woollen, wherever you expect to have much walking; and plenty of them will be required.

Substitute for Socks.—For want of socks, pieces of linen may be used; and, when these are properly put on they are said to be even better than socks. They should be a foot square, be made of soft worn linen, be washed once a-day, and be smeared with tallow. They can be put on so dexterously as to stand several hours' marching without making a single wrinkle, and are much used by soldiers in Germany. To put them on, the naked foot is placed crosswise; the corners on the right and on the left are then folded over, then the corner which lies in front of the toes. Now the art consists in so drawing up these ends, that the foot can be placed in the shoe or boot without any wrinkles appearing in the bandage. One wrinkle is sure to make a blister, and therefore persons who have to use them should practise frequently how to put them on. Socks similar to these, but made of thick blanket, and called "Blanket Wrappers," are in use at Hudson's Bay instead of shoes.

Shirt-sleeves.—When you have occasion to tuck up your shirt-sleeves, recollect that the way of doing so is, not to begin by turning the cuffs inside out, but outside in—the sleeves must be rolled up inwards, towards the arm, and not the reverse way. In the one case, the sleeves will remain tucked up for hours without being touched; in the other, they become loose every five minutes.

Gloves, Mits, and Muffs.—In cold dry weather, a pair of old soft kid gloves, with large woollen gloves drawn over them, is the warmest combination. Mits and muffetees merely require mention. To keep the hands warm in very severe weather, a small fur muff may be slung from the neck, in which the hands may rest till wanted.

Braces.—Do not forget to take them, unless you have had abundant experience of belts; for belts do not suit every shape, neither are English trousers cut with the intention of being worn with them. But trousers made abroad, are shaped at the waist, especially for the purpose of being worn without braces; if desired. If you use braces, take two pairs, for when they are drenched with perspiration, they dry slowly. Some people do not care to use a belt, even with trousers of an ordinary cut, but find that a tape run through a hem along the upper edge of the trousers acts sufficiently well. Capt. Speke told me he always used this plan.

Boots.—Boots of tanned leather such as civilised people wear, are incomparably better for hard usage, especially in wet countries, than those of hand-dressed skins. If travelling in a hot, dry country, grease plentifully both your shoes and all other leather. " La graisse est la conservation du cuir," as I recollect a Chamouni guide enunciating with profound emphasis. The soles of plaited cord used in parts of the Pyrenees, are durable and excellent for clambering over smooth rock. They have a far better hold upon it than any other sole of which I have knowledge. Sandals are better than nothing at all. So are cloths wound round the feet and ankles and tied there: the peasants of the remarkable hilly place where I am writing these lines, namely Amalfi, use them much. They are an untidy chaussure, but never seem to require to be tied afresh. In the old days of Rome this sort of foot-gear was common. Haybands wound round the feet are a common makeshift by soldiers who are cut off from their supplies. It takes some months to harden the feet sufficiently to be able to walk without shoes at all. Slippers are great luxuries to footsore men. They should of course be of soft material, but the soles should not be too thin or they will be too cold for comfort in camp life.

Leggings.—Macintosh leggings to go over the trousers are a great comfort in heavy showers, especially when riding.

Gaiters.—If the country be full of briars and thorns, the insteps suffer cruelly when riding through bushes. It is easy to make gaiters either with buttons or buckles. A strip of wood is wanted, either behind or else on each side of them, to keep them from slipping down to the ankle.

Dressing Gown.—Persons who travel, even with the smallest quantity of luggage, would do wisely to take a thick dressing-gown. It is a relief to put it on in the evening, and is a warm extra dress for sleeping in. It is eminently useful, comfortable and durable.

Poncho.—A poncho is useful, for it is a sheet as well as a cloak; being simply a blanket with a slit in the middle to admit the wearer's head. A sheet of strong calico, saturated with oil, makes a waterproof poncho.

Complete Bush-costume.—Mr. Gordon Cumming describes his bush-costume as follows :—" My own personal appointments consisted of a wide-awake hat, secured under my chin by 'rheimpys' or strips of dressed skin, a coarse linen shirt, sometimes a kilt, and sometimes a pair of buckskin knee-breeches, and a pair of 'veldtschoens,' or home-made shoes. I entirely discarded coat, waistcoat, and neckcloth; and I always hunted with my arms bare; my heels were armed with a pair of powerful persuaders, and from my left wrist depended, by a double rheimpy (thong), an equally persuasive sea-cow jambok (whip of solid leather). Around my waist I wore two leathern belts or girdles. The smaller did the duty of suspender, and from it on my left side depended a plaited rheimpy, eight inches in length, forming a loop, in which dangled my powerful loading-rod, formed of a solid piece of horn of the rhinoceros. The larger girdle was my shooting-belt; this was a broad leather belt, on which were fastened four separate compartments, made of otterskin, with flaps to button over, of the same material. The first of these held my percussion-caps; the second, a large powder-flask; the third and fourth, which had divisions in them, contained balls and patches, two sharp clasp-knives, a compass, flint and steel. In this belt I also carried a loading-mallet, formed from the horn of the rhinoceros; this and the powder-flask were each secured to the belt by long rheimpys, to prevent my losing them. Last, but not least, in my right hand I usually carried my double-barrelled two-grooved rifle, which was my favourite weapon. This, however, I subsequently made up my mind was not the tool for a mounted man, especially when quick loading is required."

Wet Clothes, to dry.—*Fire for drying Clothes.*—To dry clothes it is a very convenient plan to make a dome-shaped framework of twigs over a smouldering fire; by bending each twig or wand into a half-circle, and planting both ends of it in the ground, one on each side of the fire. The wet clothes are laid on this framework, and receive the full benefit of the heat. Their steam passes readily upwards.

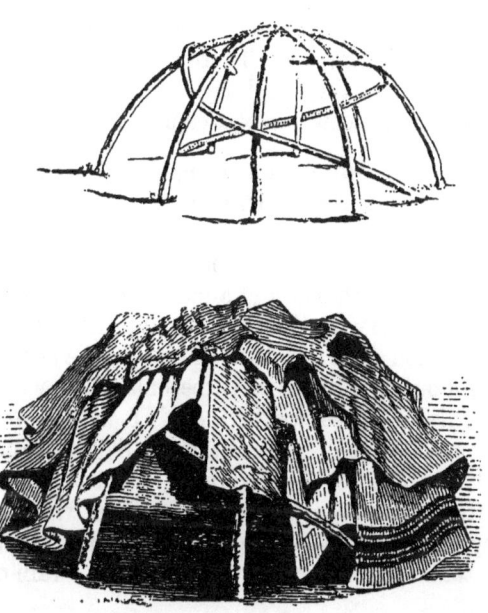

To keep Clothes from the wet.—Mr. Parkyns says, " I may as well tell, also, how we managed to keep our clothes dry when travelling in the rain: this was rather an important consideration, seeing that each man's wardrobe consisted of what he carried on his back. Our method was at once effective and simple: if halting, we took off our clothes and sat on them; if riding, they were placed under the leathern shabraque of the mule's saddle, or under any article of similar material, bed or bag, that lay on the camel's pack. A good shower-bath did none of us any harm; and as soon as the rain was over, and the moisture on our skins had evaporated, we had our garments as warm, dry, and comfortable, as if they had been before a fire. In populous districts, we kept on our drawers, or supplied their place with a piece of rag, or a skin; and then, when the rain was over, we wrapped ourselves up in our 'quarry,' and taking off the wetted articles, hung them over the animal's cruppers to dry." Another traveller writes:—

"The only means we had of preserving our sole suit of clothes dry from the drenching showers of rain, was by taking them off and stuffing them into the hollow of a tree, which, in the darkness of the night, we could do with propriety."

Mr. Palliser's boatmen at Chagre took each a small piece of cloth, under which they laid their clothes every time that they stripped in expectation of a coming storm.

Dipping clothes wetted with rain, in Sea-water.—Captain Bligh, who was turned adrift in an open boat after the mutiny of the 'Bounty,' writes thus about his experience:—
"With respect to the preservation of our health, during a course of 16 days of heavy and almost continual rain, I would recommend to every one in a similar situation the method we practised, which is to dip their clothes in the salt water and wring them out as often as they become filled with rain: it was the only resource we had, and I believe was of the greatest service to us, for it felt more like a change of dry clothes than could well be imagined. We had occasion to do this so often, that at length our clothes were wrung to pieces; for except the few days we passed on the coast of New Holland, we were continually wet, either with rain or sea."

Washing Clothes.—*Substitute for Soap.*—The lye of ashes and the gall of animals are the readiest substitutes for soap. The sailor's recipe for washing clothes is well known, but it is too dirty to describe. Bran, and the meal of many seeds, is good for scouring: also some earths, like fuller's-earth. Many countries possess plants that will make a lather with water. Dr. Rae says that in a very cold climate, when fire, water, and the means of drying are scarce, it will be found that rubbing and beating in snow cleanses all clothing remarkably well, particularly woollens. When preparing for a regular day's washing, it is a good plan to boil an abundance of ashes in water, strain off the lye, adding the gall of any animal you may have killed, and let the clothes soak in it. Next morning, take them to the water-side, and wash and beat them with a flat piece of wood, or lay them on a broad stone and knead and wring them with the hands.

Lye of Ashes.—In choosing plants to burn for ashes (whence the lye is to be made by pouring hot water on them), it must be recollected that all plants are not equally efficacious: those that contain the most alkali (either potash or soda) are the best. On this account, the stalks of succulent plants, as reeds, maize, broom, heath, and furze, are very much better than the wood of any trees; and twigs are better than timber. Pine and fir-trees are the worst of woods. The ashes of most kinds of seaweed yield abundance of alkali. Potash is the alkali that is obtained from the ashes of land plants, and soda from those of marine plants.

10,000 parts of pine or fur	contain	4	parts of alkali.
,, poplar	,,	7	,,
,, beech-wood	,,	14	,,
,, oak	,,	15	,,
,, willow	,,	28	,,
,, elm, maple, and wheat straw	,,	39	,,
,, thistles, flax-stems, and small rushes	,,	50	,,
,, large rushes	,,	72	,,
,, stalk of maize	,,	175	,,
,, bean-stalks	,,	200	,,

Soap is made by keeping fat constantly simmering in lye of ashes (see preceding paragraphs) for some days; adding fresh lye as fast as the water boils away, or is sucked up by the fat. After one or two trials, the knack of soap-making is easily caught. The presence of salt makes the soap hard; its absence, soft; now many ashes contain a good deal of salt, and these may make the soap too hard, and will have to be mixed with other sorts of ashes before being used: experience must guide the traveller in this. A native woman will probably be found without difficulty, who will attend night and day to the pot-boiling for a small payment. Inferior soap may be made by simply putting some grease into a tub of very strong lye, and letting it remain for two or three weeks, without any boiling, but stirring it every day.

Marine Soap is made of soda lye (the lye of seaweeds) and cocoa-nut oil; it makes a lather with salt water, but it has the defect of being very bulky.

To wash Flannels.—Make a lather of soap on a small piece of flannel, and rub with it those parts that require the most cleansing, such as the neck and wristbands of a shirt; then plunge the shirt in water as hot as you can bear it, rinsing it and wringing it out very thoroughly, and hang it up to dry as quickly as possible. Soda should not be used with coloured flannels.

Washing Oneself.—*Warmth of Dirt.*—There is no denying the fact, though it be not agreeable to confess it, that dirt and grease are great protectors of the skin against inclement weather, and that therefore the leader of a party should not be too exacting about the appearance of his less warmly-clad followers. Daily washing, if not followed by oiling, must be compensated by wearing clothes. Take the instance of a dog. He will sleep out under any bush, and thrive there, so long as he is not washed, groomed, and kept clean; but if he be, he must have a kennel to lie in. The same is the case with a horse; he catches cold if he is groomed in the day, and turned out at nights; but he never catches cold when left wholly to himself. A savage will never wash unless he can grease himself afterwards—grease takes the place of clothing to him. There must be a balance between the activity of the skin and the calls upon it; and where the exposure is greater, there must the pores be more defended. In Europe, we pass our lives in a strangely artificial state; our whole body swathed in many folds of dress, excepting the hands and face —the first of which are frequently gloved. We can afford to wash, but naked men cannot.

Best Times for Washing.—The most convenient time for a traveller to make his toilet, in rough travel, is after the early morning's ride, a bath being now and then taken in the afternoon. It is trying work to wash in ice-cold water, in the dark and blowing morning; besides which, when the sun rises up, its scorching heat tells severely on a face that has been washed.

Toilet made overnight.—During the harassing duties of active warfare, officers who aim at appearing in a decorous dress, in whatever emergency their presence may be required, make their toilet overnight before going to sleep.

Economising Water in Washing.—Where water has to be

economised, by far the best way of using it is after the Mahomedan fashion. An attendant pours a slender stream from a jug, which the man who washes himself receives in his hands and distributes over his person.

Bath-glove.—Fold a piece of very coarse towel in two parts: lay your hand upon it, and mark its outline rudely; then guided by the outline, cut it out: sew the two pieces together, along their edges, and the glove is made. It is inexpensive, and portable, and as good a detergent as horsehair gloves or flesh-brushes.

Brushes.—It is well to know how to make a brush, whether for clothes, boots, or hair, and the accompanying section of one will explain itself. Bristles are usually employed, but fibres of various kinds may be used.

BEDDING.

General Remarks.—The most bulky, and often the heaviest, parts of a traveller's equipment are his clothes, sleeping-mat, and blankets: nor is it at all desirable that these should be stinted in quantity; for the hardship that most tries a man's constitution and lays the seeds of rheumatism, dysentery, and fever, is that of enduring the bitter cold of a stormy night, which may happen to follow an exhausting day of extreme heat or drenching wet. After many months' travel and camping, the constitution becomes far less susceptible of injury from cold and damp, but in no case is it ever proof against their influence. Indeed, the oldest travellers are ever those who go the most systematically to work, in making their sleeping-places dry and warm. Unless a traveller makes himself at home and comfortable in the bush, he will never be quite contented with his lot; but will fall into the bad habit of looking forwards to the end of his journey, and to his return to civilisation, instead of complacently interesting himself in its continuance. This is a frame of mind in which few great journeys have been successfully accomplished; and an explorer who cannot divest himself of it, may suspect that he has mistaken his vocation.

It is a common idea among men who are preparing to travel for the first time, that all the bed-clothing about which they need concern themselves, is a sufficiency to cover them, forgetting that a man has an under as well as an upper side to keep warm, and must therefore have clothing between him and the earth, as well as between him and the air. Indeed, on trying the experiment, and rolling oneself up in a single blanket, the undermost side in a cold night is found to be by far the colder of the two. The substance of the blanket is compressed by the weight of the sleeper; the interstices between its fibres cease to exist; and the air which they contained and which is a powerful non-conductor of heat, is squeezed out. Consequently wherever the blanket is compressed, its power of retaining the heat of the sleeper is diminished. Soft fleecy substances, like eider-down quilts, which are extremely warm as coverlets, are well-nigh useless as mattresses. There is another cause why a sleeper requires more protection from below, than from above: it is that if the ground be at all wet, its damp will penetrate through very thick substances laid upon it. It will therefore be clearly understood that the object of a mattress is not alone to give softness to the bed, but also to give warmth; and that if a man lies in a hammock, with only the hammock below, and blankets above, he will be fully as much chilled as if the arrangement had been reversed, and he had lain upon blankets, with only the hammock as a sheet to cover him.

Vital Heat.—The vital heat of a man, either in an active or a latent form, is equal to that which is given out by two ordinary candles: I judge so from the following reasons. All our vital heat is produced by the combustion—for it is simple combustion—of the carbon in our food. Now the quantity of carbon consumed by a man in full diet, in 24 hours, is about 22 oz. in weight. On the other hand, I find that ordinary candles, which mainly consist of carbon, burn at the rate of 11 oz. in 24 hours. Therefore the heat given out by two candles is just about the same as that given out by one man, either in a sensible form, or else under a latent form by the vapour of the breath. Secondly, I have frequently heard it estimated, as the result of the ordinary experience of social life, that a saloon is warmed by each couple of candles somewhat more than it is by the presence of a single guest. Where I write these lines, I have not an opportunity of verifying my rough estimate, by reference to physiological works, but accuracy is of little consequence to my present purpose, which is to give a general idea of the magnitude of the problem to be solved by clothes and tenting. Their joint office is to retain the heat of a mass of flesh and blood, the size and shape of a man, warmed by two candles burning within it, at a temperature of not less than 96° in its inward parts.

Mattresses and their Substitutes.—*A Strip of Macintosh.*—If a traveller can do so, he should make a point of having a strip of macintosh sheeting 7 feet by 4, certainly not less than 6 feet by 3, to lay on the ground below his bedding. Every white servant in the expedition ought to be furnished with a strip of macintosh sheeting, or, failing that, with a strip of painted canvas. However, painted cloth is much inferior to macintosh, as it will not fold up without cracking: it also tears easily, and is heavy. Macintosh, of the sort that suits all climates, and made of linen, not of silk, is invaluable to an explorer, whether in the form of sheeting, coats, water-bags, swimming-belts, or inflatable boats. A little box full of the composition for mending it, and a spare bit of macintosh, should always be taken.

Mattress.—Making a mattress is indeed a very simple affair. A bag of canvas, or other cloth, is made of the size wanted. It is then stuffed full of hair, wool, dry leaves, or cotton, and a strong stitch is put through it every few inches. The use of the stitching is to prevent the stuffing from being displaced, and forming lumps in different parts of the bag.

Palliasse.—Straw, well knitted or plaited together, forms a good mattress, commonly called a palliasse.

Shavings of Wood.—Eight pounds' weight of shavings make an excellent bed, and I find I can cut them with a common spokeshave, in 3½ hours, out of a log of deal. It is practicable to make an efficient spokeshave, by tying a large clasp-knife on a common stick which has been cut into a proper shape to receive it.

Oakum.—Old cord, picked into oakum, will also make a bed.

Various Makeshifts.—If a traveller, as is very commonly the case, should have no mattress, he should strew his sleeping-place with dry grass, plucked up from the ground, or with other things warm to the touch, imitating the structure of a bird's-nest as far as he has skill and materials to do so. Leaves, fern, feathers, heather, rushes, flags of reeds and of maize, wood-shavings, bundles of faggots, and such like materials as chance may afford, should be looked for and appropriated; a pile of stones, or even two trunks of trees rolled close together, may make a dry bedstead in a marshy land. Over these, let him lay whatever empty bags, skins, saddle-cloths, or spare clothes he may have, which from their shape or smallness cannot be turned to account as coverings, and the lower part of his bed is complete.

If a night of unusual cold be expected, the best use to make of spare wearing-apparel, is to put it on over that which is already on the person. With two or three shirts, stockings, and trousers, though severally of thin materials, a man may get through a night of very trying weather.

Preparing the Ground for a Bed.—Travellers should always root up the stones and sticks that might interfere with the smoothness of the place where they intend to sleep. This is a matter worth taking a great deal of pains about; the oldest campaigners are the most particular in making themselves comfortable at night. They should also scrape a hollow in the ground, of the shape shown in fig. 2 (next page), before spreading their sleeping-rugs. It is disagreeable enough to lie on a perfectly level surface, like that of a floor, but the acme of discomfort is to lie upon a convexity. Persons who have omitted to make a shapely lair for themselves, should at least scrape a hollow in the ground, just where the hip-bone would otherwise press.

The annexed sketch (fig. 1) represents a man sleeping in a natural attitude. It will be observed that he fits into a con-

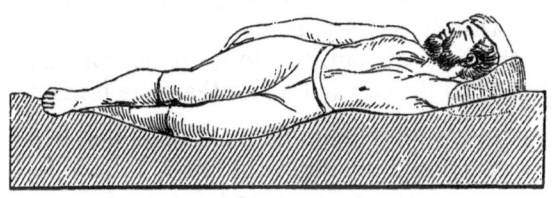

Fig. 1.

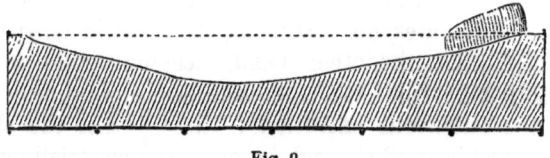

Fig. 2.

cavity of about 6 inches in greatest depth. (The scale on which he is drawn is 6 feet long and 1 foot high.)

Hammocks.—See section on "Furniture."

Coverlets.—*General Remarks.*—For an upper cover, it is of importance to an otherwise unsheltered person, that its texture should be such as to prevent the wind blowing through. If it does so, no thickness is of any avail in keeping out the cold; hence the advantage of skin carosses, buffalo robes, leather sheets, and macintosh rugs. All cloths lose much of their closeness of texture in a hot, dry climate; the fibres shrink extremely, and the wind blows through the tissue as through network. It is in order to make their coverings wind-proof, that shepherd-lads on the hills in Scotland, when the nights are cold, dip their plaids in water, before sitting or lying down in them. The wet swells up the fibres of the plaid, and makes the texture of it perfectly dense and close. It is also of importance that the outer covering should have a certain weight, so as not to be too easily displaced, either by the person fidgeting in his sleep or by the blowing of the wind. In dry weather there is nothing like furs; but in a rainy country I prefer a thick blanket bag (see "Sleeping Bags"), a large spare blanket, and a macintosh sheet and counterpane. It may be objected that the bag and macintosh would be close and stuffy, but be assured that the difficulty when sleeping on mother earth, on a bitter night, is to keep the fresh air out, not to let it in. On fine nights I should sleep on the bag and under the spare blanket.

Stuffy Bedding.—It must be understood that while recommending coverlets that resist the wind, I am very far from advocating extreme stuffiness, and for the following reason. Though a free passage of the wind abstracts an excessive amount of animal heat from the sleeper, yet the freshness of pure air stimulates his body to give it out in an increased proportion. On the other hand, sleeping-clothes that are absolutely impervious to the passage of the wind, necessarily retain the cutaneous excretions: these poison the sleeper, acting upon his blood through his skin, and materially weaken his power of emitting vital heat: the fire of his life burns more languidly. I therefore suspect it would be more dangerous to pass a very cold night enclosed tightly in thin macintosh buttoned up to the chin, than without it. Much less heat would be robbed from the sleeper in the first case, but he would have very much less heat to spare. There is, therefore, an intermediate arrangement of sleeping-gear, neither too stuffy on the one hand nor too open on the other, by which the maximum power of resisting the chill of the night is obtainable.

Sleeping Clothes.—Some travellers prefer to have their blanket at once made up into a loose coat, trousers, and cap, pockets *ad libitum*, and a tape in the trouser band. An extra suit is thus always at hand, the sleeper loses little of the advantages of comfortable bedding, and is always, in some sense, dressed for any emergency.

Feathers.—When you collect bed feathers for coverlets, recollect that if they are cleanly plucked, they will require no dressing of any kind, save drying and beating.

Brown Paper.—Brown paper is an excellent non-conductor

of heat and excluder of draughts: English cottagers often enclose sheets of it within their quilted counterpanes. If thoroughly soaked and then dried, it will not crackle.

Extra Clothes.—If a man be destitute of proper wraps, he cannot do better than put on all the spare clothes he possesses. The additional warmth of a single extra shirt is remarkable.

Dry Clothes.—However wet the weather may be during the day, the traveller should never relax his endeavours to keep a dry and warm change of clothes for his bivouac at night. Hardships in rude weather matter little to a healthy man, when he is awake and moving, and while the sun is above the horizon; but let him never forget the deplorable results that may follow a single night's exposure to cold, malaria, and damp.

Pillows.—A mound of sand or earth, scraped together for a pillow, is ground down into flatness, after a few minutes. A bag filled with earth, or it may be with grass, keeps its shape. Many people use their saddles as pillows; they roll up the flaps and stirrups, and place the saddle on the ground with a stone underneath, at its hindmost end, to keep it level and steady, and then lay their heads on the seat. I prefer using anything else; as, for instance, the stone without the saddle: but I generally secure some bag or other for the purpose, as, without a pillow, it is difficult to sleep in comfort. A bag shaped like a pillow-case, and stuffed with spare clothes, is very convenient. Some people advocate air-cushions.

Mr. Mansfield Parkyns' excellent plan, of sleeping on the side, with the stock of the gun between the head and the arm, and the barrel between the legs, will be described when I speak of "Guns."

BIVOUAC.

There are four ways in which travellers who are thrown upon their own resources may house themselves. They may bivouac, that is to say, they may erect a temporary shelter of a makeshift character, partly from materials found on the spot, and partly from the cloths they may happen to possess; they may build a substantial hut, which of course takes a good deal of labour to complete; they may use sleeping-bags; or they may pitch a regular tent. I will speak of these four methods of encamping,—the bivouac, the hut, the sleeping-bag, and the tent, in that order.

General Remarks.—Bivouacking is miserable work in a wet or unhealthy climate; but in a dry and healthy one, there is no question of its superiority over tenting. Men who sleep habitually in the open, breathe fresher air and are far more imbued with the spirit of wild life, than those who pass the night within the stuffy enclosure of a tent. It is an endless pleasure to lie half awake watching the stars above, and the picturesque groupings of the encampment round about, and to hear on all sides the stirrings of animal life. And later in the night, when the fire is low, and servants and cattle are asleep, and there is no sound but of the wind and an occasional plaintive cry of wild animals, the traveller finds himself in that close communion with nature which is the true charm of wild travel. Now all this pleasure is lost by sleeping in a tent. Tent life is semi-civilization, and perpetuates its habits. This may be illustrated by a simple trait; a man who has lived much in bivouacs, if there be a night alarm, runs naturally into the dark for safety, just as a wild animal would; but a man who travels with tents becomes frightened when away from its lights, or from the fancied security of its walls.

In a dangerous country there can be no comparison between the hazard of a tent and that of a bivouac. In the former a man's sleep is heavy; he cannot hear nearly so well; he can see nothing; his cattle may all decamp; while marauders know exactly where he is lying, and may make their plans accordingly. They may creep up unobserved and spear him through the canvas. The first Napoleon had a great opinion of the advantages of bivouacking over those of tenting. He said it was the healthier of the two for soldiers. (See p. 153.)

Shelter from the Wind.—Study the *form* of a hare! In the flattest and most unpromising of fields, the creature will have availed herself of some little hollow to the lee of an insignificant tuft of grass, and there she will have nestled and fidgeted about till she has made a smooth, round, grassy bed, compact and fitted to her shape, where she may curl herself snugly up, and cower down below the level of the cutting night wind. Follow her example. A man, as he lies upon his mother earth, is an object so small and low that a screen of eighteen inches high will guard him securely from the strength of a storm. A common mistake of a novice lies in selecting a tree for his camping-place, which spreads out nobly above, but affords no other shelter from the wind than

that of its bare stem below. It may be, that as he walks about in search of shelter, a mass of foliage at the level of his eye, with its broad shadow, attracts him, and as he *stands* to the leeward of it it seems snug, and, therefore, without further reflection, he orders his bed to be spread at the foot of some tree. But as soon as he lies down on the ground the tree proves worthless as a screen against the wind; it is a roof, but it is not a wall. The real want in blowy weather is a dense low screen, perfectly wind-tight, as high as the knee above the ground. Thus, if a traveller has to encamp on a bare turf plain, he need only turn up a sod seven feet long by two feet wide, and if he succeeds in propping it on its edge, it will form a sufficient shield against the wind.

In heavy gales, the neighbourhood of a solitary tree is a positive nuisance. It creates a violent eddy of wind, that leaves palpable evidence of its existence. Thus, in corn-fields, it is a common result of a storm to batter the corn quite flat in circles round each tree that stands in the field, while elsewhere no injury takes place. This very morning that I am writing these remarks, November 15, 1858, I was forcibly struck by the appearance of Kensington Gardens, after last night's gale, which had covered the ground with an extraordinary amount of dead leaves. They lay in a remarkably uniform layer, of from three to five inches in depth, except that round each and every tree the ground was absolutely bare of leaves for a radius of about a yard. The effect was as though circular discs had been cut out, leaving the edges of the layer of leaves perfectly sharp and vertical. It would have been a dangerous mistake to have slept that night at the foot of any one of those trees.

Again, in selecting a place for bivouac, we must bear in mind that a gale never blows in level currents, but in all kinds of curls and eddies, as the driving of a dust-storm, or the vagaries of bits of straw caught up by the wind, unmistakably show us. Little hillocks or undulations, combined with the general lay of the ground, are a chief cause of these eddies; they entirely divert the current of the wind from particular spots. Such spots should be looked for; they are discovered by watching the grass or the sand that lies on the ground. If the surface be quiet in one place, while all around it is agitated by the wind, we shall not be far wrong in selecting that place for our bed, however unprotected it may seem in other respects. It is constantly remarked, that a very slight mound or ridge will shelter the ground for many feet behind it; and an old campaigner will accept such shelter gladly, notwithstanding the apparent insignificance of its cause.

Shelter from the Sky.—The shelter of a *wall* is only sufficient against wind or driving rain ; we require a *roof* to shield us against vertical rain, and against dew, or what is much the same thing, against the cold of a clear blue sky on a still night. The temperature of the heavens is known pretty accurately, by more than one method of calculation: it is $-239°$ Fahr.; the greatest cold felt in the Arctic regions being about $-40°$ Fahr. If the night be cloudy, each cloud is a roof to keep off the cold; if it be clear, we are exposed to the full chill of the blue sky, with only such alleviation as the warming and the non-conducting powers of the atmosphere may afford. The effect is greater than most people would credit. The uppermost layer of the earth, or whatever may be lying exposed upon it, is called upon to part with a great quantity of heat. If it so happen that the uppermost layer is of a non-conducting nature, the heat abstracted from it will be poorly resupplied by communication from the lower ones. Again, if the night be a very calm one, there will be no supply of warmth from fresh currents of air falling down upon it. Hence, in the treble event of a clear blue sky, a non-conducting soil, and a perfectly still night, we are liable to have great cold on the surface of the ground. This is shared by a thin layer of air that immediately rests upon it; while at each successive inch in height, the air becomes more nearly of its proper temperature. A vast number of experiments have been made by Mr. Glaisher on this subject ('Phil. Trans.' 1847), the upshot of which is that a thermometer laid on *grass*, under a blue sky on a calm night, marks on an average $8°$ Fahr. colder than one 4 feet above it; 1 inch above grass, $5\frac{1}{2}°$; 1 foot, $1°$; 4 feet, $\frac{1}{2}°$; on gravel and sand the differences are only about one-third as much. Sheep have a practical knowledge of these differences. Often, in an early walk on dewy mornings, I see all the sheep in Hyde Park bivouacked on the gravel walks or Rotten Row. The above figures are the results of experiments made in England, where the air is always moist, and the formation of dew, while it testifies to the cold of the night, assists largely to moderate it. In arid climates the chill would be far greater; such would also be the case at high elevations. One of Mr. Glaisher's experiments showed a difference of no less than 28° between the cold on the ground and that at 8 feet high. This might often be rivalled in an elevated desert, as in that of Mongolia. Hence the value of the protection of a roof and of a raised sleeping-place, to a man sleeping under a blue sky in still weather, admits of easy interpretation.

Various Methods of Bivouacking.—*Unprotected.*—Mr. Shaw, the traveller in Thibet, says:—" My companion and I walked on to keep ourselves warm, but halting at sunset, had to sit and freeze several hours before the things came up. The best way of keeping warm on such an occasion, is to squat down, kneeling against a bank, resting your head on the bank, and nearly between your knees. Then tuck your overcoat in, all round you, over head and all; and if you are lucky, and there is not too much wind, you will make a little atmosphere of your own inside the covering, which will be snug in comparison with the outside air. Your feet suffer chiefly, but you learn to tie yourself into a kind of knot, bringing as many surfaces of your body together as possible. I have passed whole nights in this kneeling position, and slept well; whereas I should not have got a wink had I been stretched at full length with such a scanty covering as a great-coat."

Bushes.—I have shown that the main object before sleeping out at night is to secure a long wind-tight wall, and that the next is to obtain a roof. Both these objects may be attained by pleaching two or three small neighbouring bushes into one; or branches may be torn off elsewhere and interwoven between the bushes. A few leafy boughs, cut and stuck into the ground, with their tops leaning over the bed, and secured in that position by other boughs, wattled-in horizontally, give great protection. Long grass, &c., should be plucked and strewn against them to make them as wind-tight as possible.

Walls.—A pile of saddle-bags and other travelling gear may be made into a good screen against the wind; and travellers usually arrange them with that intention. Walls of stone may be built as a support to cloths, whose office it is to render the walls wind-tight, and also by lapping over their top, to form a partial roof. We have already spoken of a broad sod of turf propped up on edge.

" The Thibetan traveller cares for no roof overhead if he can shelter himself from the wind behind a three-foot wall. Hence the numerous little enclosures clustered together like cells of a honeycomb at every halting-place, with one side always raised against the prevailing wind. (*Shaw.*) These walls are built round shallow pits, each with its rough fire-place in the middle.

Cloths.—Any cloth may be made to give shelter by an arrangement like that in the sketch. The corners of the cloth

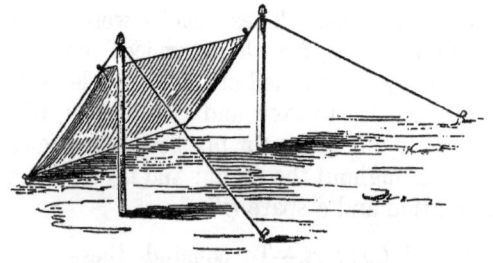

should be secured by simple hitches in the rope, and never by knots. The former are sufficient for all purposes of security, but the latter will jam, and you may have to injure both cloth and string to get them loose again. It is convenient to pin the sides of the cloth with a skewer round the ropes. Any strip of wood makes a skewer. Earth should be banked against the lowest edge of the cloth, to keep out the wind, and to prevent its flapping. The sticks may, on an emergency, be replaced by faggots of brushwood, by guns, or by ropes carried down from the overhanging branches of a large tree. (For a sail supported by oars, see "Sail Tent," p. 108.)

Fremont, the American traveller, bivouacked as follows:—His rifles were tied together near the muzzles, the butts resting on the ground widely apart ; a knife was laid on the rope that tied them together, to cut it in case of an alarm; over this extempore framework was thrown a large india-rubber cloth, with which he covered his packs when on the road; it made a cover sufficiently large to receive about half of his bed, and was a place of shelter for his instruments.

Gordon Cumming.—The following extract is from Mr. Gordon Cumming's book on Africa: it describes the preparations of a practised traveller for a short excursion from his wagons away into the bush. "I had at length got into the way of making myself tolerably comfortable in the field, and from this date I seldom went in quest of elephants without the following *impedimenta, i. e.* a large blanket, which I folded and secured before my saddle as a dragoon does his cloak, and two leather sacks, containing a flannel shirt, warm trousers, and a woollen night-cap, spare ammunition, washing-rod, coffee, bread, sugar, pepper and salt, dried meat, a wooden bowl, and a tea-spoon. These sacks were carried on the shoulders of the natives, for which service I remunerated them with beads. They also carried my coffee-kettle, two calabashes of water, two American axes, and two sickles, which I used every evening to cut grass for my bed, and likewise for my horses to eat throughout the night; and my after-rider carried extra ammunition and a spare rifle."

Importance of Comfort.—To conclude these general hints, let the traveller, when out in trying weather, work hard at making his sleeping-place perfectly dry and comfortable; he should not cease until he is convinced that it will withstand the chill of the early morning, when the heat of the yesterday's sun is exhausted, and that of the coming sun has not begun to be felt. It is wretched beyond expression for a man to lie shivering beneath a scanty covering and to feel the night air become hourly more raw, while his life-blood has less power to withstand it; and to think, self-reproachfully, how different would have been his situation if he had simply had forethought and energy enough to cut and draw twice the quantity of firewood, and to spend an extra half-hour in labouring to make himself a snugger berth. The omission once made becomes irreparable; for in the cold of a pitiless night he has hardly sufficient stamina to rise and face the weather, and the darkness makes him unable to cope with his difficulties.

Bivouac in Special Localities.—*Encampment in Forests.*—A clump of trees yields wonderful shelter. The Swedes have a proverb that "the forest is the poor man's jacket." In fir-woods there is great facility in making warm encampments; for a young tree, when it is felled, yields both poles to support branches for shields against weather, and finer cuttings

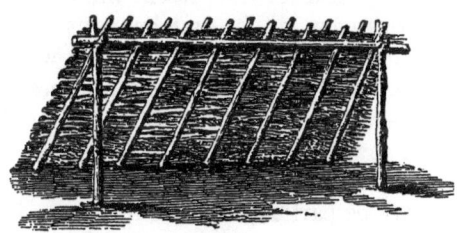

for flooring above the snow or damp. A common plan is to support a cross-bar by two uprights, as shown in the figure; against this cross-bar a number of poles are made to lean; on the back of the poles abundance of fir branches are laid horizontally; and lastly, on the back of these are another set of leaning poles, in order to secure them by their weight.

On Bare Plains.—Avoid sleeping in slight hollows during clear still weather. The cold stratum of air, of which I spoke in the section of "Shelter from the Sky," pours down into them, like water from the surrounding plain, and stagnates. Spring frosts are always more severely felt in hollows. Therefore, in a broad level plain, especially if the night be clear and calm, look out for some slightly rising ground for an encampment. The chilled stratum of air drains from off it, and is replaced by warmer air. Horses and cattle, as the night sets in, always draw up to these higher grounds, which rise like islands through the sea of mist that covers the plain.

Walls have been built for shelter against the wind, on a bare sandy plain, by taking empty bags, filling them with sand, and then building them up as if they had been stones.

Buried, or in Holes.—A European can live through a bitter night, on a perfectly dry sandy plain, without any clothes besides what he has on, if he buries his body pretty deeply in the sand, keeping only his head above ground. It is a usual habit of the naked natives in Australia to do so, and not an unfrequent one of the Hottentots of South Africa. Mr. Moffat records with grateful surprise how he passed a night, of which he had gloomy forebodings, in real comfort, even luxury, by adopting this method. A man may be as comfortable in a burrow as in a den. I shall speak of underground houses under "Hutting;" and for the present will only mention that, in arid countries, dry wells, dug by natives and partially choked by drifted sand, are often to be met with. They are generally found near existing watering-places, where they have been superseded by others, better placed and deeper. Now, there are few warmer sleeping-places than one of these dry wells; a small fire is easily kept burning at the bottom, and the top may be partially roofed over.

In Ashes of Camp Fire.—A few chill hours may be got over, in a plain that affords no other shelter, by nestling among the ashes of a recently burnt-out camp fire.

Warm Carcases.—In Napoleon's retreat, after his campaign in Russia, many a soldier saved or prolonged his life by creeping within the warm and reeking carcase of a horse that had died by the way.

By the water-side.—A stony beach makes a fine dry encamping-place, and has this advantage, that it makes it impossible for marauders to creep up unheard. But the immediate neighbourhood of fresh water is objectionable, for, besides being exposed to malaria and mosquitoes, the night air is more cold and penetrating by its side, than at one or two hundred yards' distance from it. (I will speak of walls of rushes and reeds, under "Huts.")

By Rocks.—In the cruel climate of Thibet, Dr. Hooker tells us that it is the habit to encamp close to some large rock, because a rock absorbs heat all day, and parts with it but slowly during the night-time. It is, therefore, a reservoir of warmth when the sun is down, and its neighbourhood is coveted in the night-time. Owing to the same cause, acting in the opposite direction, the shadow of a broad rock is peculiarly cool and grateful, during the heat of the day, in a thirsty land.

On Heather.—Mr. St. John tells us of an excellent way in which Highland poachers, when in a party, usually pass frosty nights on the moor-side. They cut quantities of heather, and strew part of it as a bed on the ground; then all the party lie down, side by side, excepting one man, whose place among the rest is kept vacant for him. His business is to spread

plaids upon them as they lie, and to heap up the remainder of the heather upon the plaids. This being accomplished, the man wriggles and works himself into the gap that has been left for him in the midst of his comrades.

On Snow.—I shall have to describe snow-houses and snow-walls covered with sail-cloth, under " Huts." Here I will speak of more simple arrangements. Dr. Kane says:—" We afterwards learnt to modify and reduce our travelling-gear, and found that in direct proportion to its simplicity and to our apparent privation of articles of supposed necessity, were our actual comfort and practical efficiency. Step by step, as long as our Arctic service continued, we went on reducing our sledging outfit, until we at last came to the Esquimaux ultimatum of simplicity—raw meat and a fur bag." Lieut. Cresswell, R.N., who, having been detached from Captain McClure's ship in 1853, was the first officer who ever accomplished the famous North-West passage, gave the following graphic account of the routine of his journeying, in a speech at Lynn:—" You must be aware that in Arctic travelling you must depend entirely on your own resources. You have not a single thing else to depend on except snow-water: no produce of the country, nor firewood, or coals, or anything of the sort; and whatever you have to take, to sustain you for the journey, you must carry or drag. It is found by experience more easy to drag it on sledges than to carry it. The plan we adopt is this:—we have a sledge generally manned by about six or ten men, which we load with provisions, with tents, and all requisites for travelling, simple cooking utensils, spirits-of-wine for cooking, &c., and start off. The quantity people can generally drag over the ice is forty days' provisions; that gives about 200 lbs. weight to each. After starting from the ship, and having travelled a certain number of hours—generally ten or eleven—we encamp for the night, or rather for the day, because it is considered better to travel at night and sleep at day, on account of the glare of the sun on the snow. We used to travel journeys of about ten hours, and then encamp, light our spirits-of-wine, put our kettle on it to thaw our snow-water, and after we had had our supper—just a piece of pemmican and a glass of water—we were glad to smoke our pipes and turn into bed. The first thing we did, after pitching the tent, was to lay a sort of macintosh covering over the snow; on this a piece of buffalo robe was stretched. Each man and officer had a blanket sewn up in the form of a bag; and into these we used to jump, much in the same way as you may see a boy do in a sack. We lay down head and feet, the next person to me having his head to my feet, and his feet to my head, so that we lay like herrings in a barrel. After this, we covered ourselves with skin, spreading them over the whole of us; and the closer we got, the better, as there was more warmth. We lay till the morning, and then the process was the same again." It appears that people may bury themselves in snow, and want neither air nor warmth. I have never made the experiment; but have read of numerous instances of people falling into snow-drifts, and not being extricated for many days, and when at length they were taken out, they never seem to have complained of cold, or any other sufferings than those of hunger and of anxiety.

HUTS.

Huts and Snow-Houses.—In making a depôt, it is usual to build a house; often the men must pass weeks in inactivity, and they had better spend their time in making their quarters comfortable than in idleness. Whatever huts are used by the natives are sure, if made with extra care, to be good enough for European travellers.

Log-huts.—In building log-huts, four poles are planted in the ground, to correspond to the four corners; against these, logs are piled one above another, as in the drawing below; they are so deeply notched where their ends are crossed, that the adjacent sides are firmly dovetailed. When the walls are entirely completed, the door and windows are chopped out. The

spaces between the logs must be caulked with moss, &c., or the log-cabin will be little better than a log-cage. It requires a great many logs to make a hut; for, supposing the walls to be 8 feet high, and the trees to average 8 inches in diameter, twelve trees would be required to build up one side, or forty-eight for all four walls. Other timber would also be wanted for the roof.

Underground Huts are used in all quarters of the globe. The experience of our troops when encamped before Sebastopol during an inclement season told strongly in their favour. Their timely adoption was the salvation of the British army. They are, essentially, nothing else than holes in the ground,

Fig. 1.   Fig. 2.

roofed over, fig. 1. The shape and size of the hole corresponds to that of the roof it may be possible to procure for it; its depth is no greater than requisite for sitting or standing. If the roof has a pitch of 2 feet in the middle, the depth of the hole need not exceed 1½ feet. In the Crimea, the holes were rectangular, and were roofed like huts.

Where there is a steep hillside, $a\ a'$, fig. 2, an underground hut, b, is easily contrived; because branches laid over its top, along the surface of the ground, have sufficient pitch to throw off the rain. Of course the earth must be removed from a', at the place intended for the doorway.

Reed Huts.—The reed huts of the Affej Arabs, and other inhabitants of the Chaldean marshes, are shaped like wagon-roofs, and are constructed of semicircular ribs of reeds, planted in the ground, one behind the other, at equal distances apart; each rib being a faggot of reeds of 2 feet in diameter. For strength, they are bound round every yard with twisted bands of reeds. When this framework has been erected, it is covered with two or three sheets of fine reed matting (see "Matting"), which forms a dwelling impervious to rain. Some of the chiefs' huts are as much as 40 feet long, and 12 high; the other huts are considerably smaller. Many of these reed dwellings are contained in compounds enclosed by lofty reed fences; the reeds being planted upright, and simply strung together by a thread run through them, as they stand side by side. (See "Straw and Reed Walls.")

Snow-houses.—Few travellers have habitually made snow-houses, except Sir J. Franklin's party and that of Dr. Rae. Great praises are bestowed on their comfort by all travellers, but skill and practice are required in building them. The mode of erection of these dome-shaped buildings is as follows:—It is to be understood that compact, underlying snow is necessary for the floor of the hut; and that the looser textured, upper layer of snow, is used to build the house. First, select and mark out the circular plot on which the hut is to be raised. Then, cut out of that plot, with knives, deep slices of snow, 6 inches wide, 3 feet long, and of a depth equal to that of the layer of loose snow, say one or two feet. These slices are to be of a curved shape, so as to form a circular ring when placed on their edges, and of a suitable radius for the first row of snow-bricks. Other slices are cut on the same principle for the succeeding rows; but when the domed roof has to be made, the snow-bricks must be cut with the necessary double curvature. A conical plug fills up the centre of the dome. Loose snow is next heaped over the house, to fill up crevices. Lastly, a doorway is cut out with knives; also a window, which is glazed with a sheet of the purest ice at hand. For inside accommodation there should be a pillar or two of snow to support the lamps.

Snow Walls with Tenting for their Roofs.—Sir L. McClintock says:—"We travelled each day until dusk, and then were occupied for a couple of hours in building our snow-hut. The four walls were run up until 5½ feet high, inclining inwards as much as possible, over these our tent was laid to form a roof. We could not afford the time necessary to construct a dome of snow. Our equipment consisted of a very small brown-holland tent, macintosh floor-cloth and felt robes; besides this, each man had a bag of double blanketing, and a pair of fur boots, to sleep in. We wore mocassins over the pieces of blanketing in which our feet were wrapped up, and, with the exception of a change of this foot-gear, carried no spare clothes.

"When we halted for the night, Thompson and I usually sawed out the blocks of compact snow, and carried them to Petersen, who acted as the master-mason in building the hut. The hour-and-a-half or two hours usually employed in erecting the edifice was the most disagreeable part of the day's labour; for, in addition to being already well tired and desiring repose, we became thoroughly chilled while standing about. The dogs were then fed, then the sledge unpacked, and everything carried into it. The door was now blocked up with snow, the cooking-lamp lighted, foot-gear changed, diary written up, watches wound, sleeping-bags wriggled into, pipes lighted, and the merits of the various dogs discussed, until supper was ready; the supper swallowed, the upper robe or coverlet pulled over, and then to sleep. Next morning came breakfast, a struggle to get into frozen mocassins, after which the sledges were packed, and another day's march commenced. In these little huts we usually slept warm enough, although latterly, when our blankets and clothes became loaded with ice, we felt the cold severely. When our low doorway was carefully blocked up with snow, and the cooking-lamp alight, the temperature quickly rose, so that the walls became glazed and our bedding thawed; but the cooking over, or the doorway partially opened, it as quickly fell again, so that it was impossible to sleep, or even to hold one's pannikin of tea without putting mits on, so intense was the cold."—Sir L. McClintock is here speaking of a temperature of $-39°$ Fahr.

Materials for Building Huts.—The materials whence the walls and roofs of huts may be constructed are very numerous: there is hardly any place which does not furnish one or other of them. Those principally in use are as follows:—

Wattle-and-daub, to be executed neatly, requires well-shaped and flexible sticks; but a hut may be constructed much like the sketch (see p. 120) of the way of "Drying Clothes." It is made by planting in the ground a number of bare sticks, 4 feet long, and 1 foot apart, bending their tops together, lashing them fast with string or strips of bark, and wattling them judiciously here and there, by means of other boughs, laid horizontally. Then, by heaping leaves—and especially broad pieces of bark, if you can get them—over all, and banking up the earth on either side, pretty high, an excellent kennel is made. If daubed over with mud, clay, or cattle-dung, the hut becomes more secure against the weather. To proceed a step further:—as many poles may be planted in the ground as sticks have been employed in making the roof; and then the roof may be lifted bodily in the air, and lashed to the top of the poles, each stick to its corresponding pole. This sort of structure is very common among savages.

For methods of digging holes in which to plant the hut-poles, see the chapter on "Wells." The holes made in the way I have there explained are far better than those dug with spades; for they disturb no more of the hardened ground than is necessary for the insertion of the palisades. To jam a pole tightly in its place, wedges of wood should be driven in at its side, and earth rammed down between the wedges.

Palisades are excellent as walls or as enclosures. They are erected of vast lengths, by savages wholly destitute of tools, both for the purposes of fortification and also for completing lines of pitfalls across wide valleys. The pitfalls occupy gaps left in the palisading. The savages burn down the trees in the following manner:—a party of men go to the forest, and light small fires round the roots of the trees they propose to fell. The fires are prevented from flaming upwards by the judicious application of leaves, &c. When the fire has eaten a little way into the tree, the man who watches it scrapes the fire aside and knocks away the charred wood, exposing a fresh surface for fire to act upon, and then replaces the burning embers. A single man may easily attend to a dozen trees, and, indeed, to many more, if the night be calm. Some hours elapse before the trees actually fall. Their tops and branches are burnt off as they lie on the ground. The poles being thus procured for the palisading, they are carried to the required place, where holes are dug for their reception, on the principle described in "Wells," to which I have just alluded.

Straw or Reed Walls of the following kind are very effective, and they have the advantage of requiring a minimum of string (or substitute for string) in their manufacture. The straw,

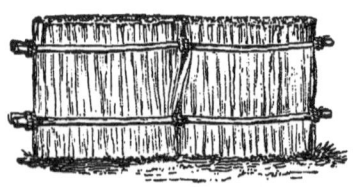

reeds, or herbage, of almost any description, is simply nipped between two pairs of long sticks, which are respectively tied together at their ends, and at a sufficient number of intermediate places. The whole is neatly squared and trimmed. A few of these would give good help in finishing the roof or walls of a house. They can be made moveable, so as to suit the wind, shade, and aspect. Even the hut door can be made on this principle. In reedy countries where there are no sticks, thin faggots of reeds are used in their place.

Bark.—Bark is universally used in Australia for roofs of huts and temporary buildings; the colonists learnt the use of it from the natives, and some trees, at least, in every forest-country might very probably be found as well fitted for that purpose as those in Australia. The bark may be easily removed, only when the sap is well up in the tree, but a skilful person will manage to procure bark at all seasons of the year, except in the coldest winter months; and even then he will light on some tree, from the sunny side of which he can strip broad pieces. The process of bark-stripping is simply to cut two rings right round the tree (usually from 6 to 9 feet apart), and one vertical slit to join them; starting from the slit, and chipping away step by step on either side, the whole cylinder of bark is removed. The larger the tree, the better; for if the tree is less than 18 inches, or so, in diameter, the bark is apt to break when flattened out. When stripped for huts, it is laid on the ground for some days to dry, being flattened out on its face, and a few stones or logs put on it. The ordinary bark of gum-trees is about half an inch to three-eighths thick, so that a large sheet is very heavy. Most exploring expeditions are accompanied by a black, whose dexterity in stripping bark for a wet night is invaluable, as if the bark will " come off " well, he can procure enough of it in an hour's time to make a shelter for a large party.

Huts. 147

Mats can be woven with ease when there is abundance of string, or some equivalent for it (see "String"), in the following manner:—

A, B, are two pegs driven into the ground and standing about a foot out of it. A stake, A B, is lashed across them; a row of pegs, E, are driven into the ground, parallel to A B, and about 6 inches apart. Two sets of strings are then tied to A B; one set are fastened by their loose ends into clefts, in the pegs E, and the other set are fastened to the stick, C D. If there be ten strings in all, then 1, 3, 5, 7, 9, are tied to C D, and 2, 4, 6, 8, 10, to A B. By alternately raising and depressing C D, and by pushing in a handful of rushes between the two sets of strings after each of its movements, and, finally, by patting them home with a flat stick, this rough sort of weaving is carried on very successfully. Mats are also plaited in breadths, and the breadths are stitched together, side by side. Or a thicker kind of mat may be made by taking a wisp of straw and working it in the same way in which straw beehives are constructed. Straw is worked more easily after being damped and beaten with a mallet.

Malay hitch.—I know no better name for the wonderfully simple way (shown in the figure) of attaching together wisps of straw, rods, laths, reeds, planks, poles, or anything of the kind, into a secure and flexible mat; the sails used in the far East are made in this way, and the moveable decks of vessels are made of bamboos, joined together with a similar but rather more complicated stitch. I may remark that soldiers

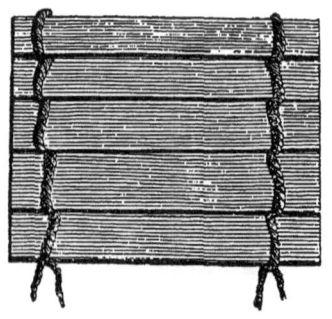

might be trained to a great deal of hutting practice in a very inexpensive way, if they were drilled at putting together huts, whose roofs and walls were made of planks lashed together by this simple hitch, and whose supports were short scaffolding poles planted in deep holes, dug, as explained in the chapter on "Wells," with the hand and a small stick. The poles, planks, and cords might be used over and over again for an indefinite time. Further, bedsteads could be made in a similar way, by short cross-planks lashed together, and resting on a framework of horizontal poles, lashed to uprights planted in the ground. The soldier's bedding would not be injured by being used on these bedsteads, as much as if it were laid on the bare ground. Many kinds of designs and experiments in hutting could be practised without expense in this simple way.

Tarpaulings are very suitable for roofs. Those made after the method used by sailors are much superior to others in softness and durability. The plan is as follows:—As soon as the canvas has been sewn together, it is thoroughly wetted with sea-water; and, while still wet, it is smeared over on one of its sides with tar and grease, boiled together—about two parts tar and one of grease. After being hung up till it is dry, it is turned; and the other side, being a second time well wetted, is at once painted over with the tar and grease, just as the first side had been before. The sailors say that "the tar dries in, as the water dries out;" a saying which I confess I cannot understand.

Other Materials.— I will merely mention these by name, for they require no explanation. They are fascines or faggots;

Huts.

bricks, sun-dried or baked in the oven; turf; stones; and bags or mats, filled with sand or shingle.

Whitewash is lime and water. Lime is made by burning limestone, chalk, shells, or coral in a simple furnace.

Roofs.—*Thatching.*—After the framework of the roof has been made, the thatcher begins at the bottom, and ties a row of bundles of straw, side by side, on to the framework. Then he begins a second row, allowing the ends of the bundles composing it to overlap the heads of those in the first row.

Wood-shingles are tile-shaped slices of wood, easily cut from fir-trees. They are used for roofing, on the same principle as tiles or slates.

Floors.—Concrete for floors, is made of eight parts large pebbles, four parts river-sand, and one part lime (to make lime, see "Whitewash"). Cow-dung and ashes make a hard, dry, and clean floor; such as is used for a threshing-floor. Ox blood and fine clay kneaded together are excellent. Both these latter compositions are in use in all hot dry countries.

Windows.—A window, or rather a hole in the wall, may be rudely shuttered by a stick run through loops made out of wisps of grass. In hot weather, the windows of the hut may be loosely stuffed with grass, which, when watered, makes the hut cooler.

Glass, to cut.—Glass cannot be cut with any certainty, without a diamond; but it may be shaped and reduced to any size by gradually chipping, or rather biting, away at its edges with a key, if the slit between the wards of the key be just large enough to admit the pane of glass easily.

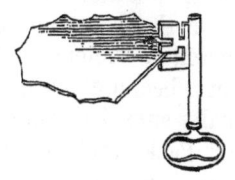

Substitutes for glass.—These are waxed or oiled paper or cloth, bladder, fish-membranes, talc, and horn. (*See* "Horn.")

SLEEPING-BAGS.

Sleeping-bags.—*Knapsack Bags.* — These have been used for the last twenty-five years by the French *douaniers*, who watch the mountain-passes of the Pyrenean frontier. The bags are made of sheepskin, with the wool inside. When not in use they are folded up and buckled with five buckles into the shape of a somewhat bulky knapsack (p. 152), which the recent occupant may shoulder and walk away with.

The accompanying sketches are drawn to scale. They were made from the sleeping-bag belonging to a man 5 feet 6 inches in height; the scale should therefore be lengthened for a taller person, but the breadth seems ample. Its weight was exactly seven pounds. The *douaniers* post themselves on watch more or less immersed in these bags. They lie out in wet and snow, and find them impervious to both. When they sleep, they get quite inside them, stuff their cloaks between their throats and the bag, and let its flap cover their faces. It is easy enough for them to extricate themselves; they can do so almost with a bound. The Spanish Custom-house officers who watch the same frontier, use their cloaks and other wraps, which are far more weighty, and far inferior in warmth and protection to the bags. I described these knapsack bags in 'Vacation Tourists for 1860,' p. 449, and I subsequently had a macintosh bag lined with drugget, made on the same principle. I had a hood to it, and also the means of buttoning it loosely under my chin, to make myself watertight during heavy rain. In that bag I passed many nights of very trying weather. On one instance, I selected a hilltop in Switzerland, on the way from Chambery to the Dent du Midi, during a violent and long-continued thunderstorm. The storm began above my head, then slowly sank to my level, and finally subsided below me. Many Alpine travellers, notably Mr. Packe and Mr. Tuckett, have adopted these bags, and used them continually. Macintosh is certainly oppressive to sleep in, though less so than might have been expected, as the half-unconscious fidgeting of the sleeper changes the air. A man in travelling "condition" would probably find a drugget-bag more healthy than macintosh, even though he became somewhat wet inside it. Beds used to be almost unknown in some parts of the Pyrenees. Sheepskin sleeping-bags were employed instead. Thus, I am assured, that at the beginning of this century, there was hardly a bed in the whole of the little republic of Andorre. The way of arranging them as knapsacks is, as I have said, a recent invention.

In fig. 1 the wide opening to the mouth of the bag is shown; also the ends of the buckles and straps that are sewn (on patches of leather, for additional strength) to the lower side of the bag, as seen in fig. 2. It must be understood that

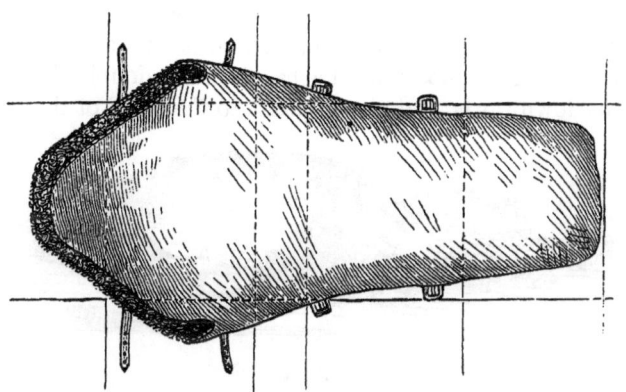

Fig. 1.

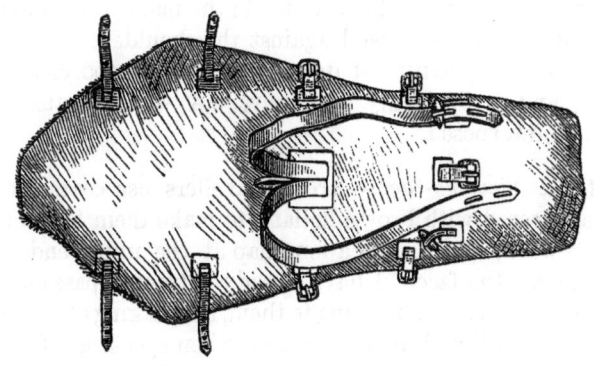

Fig. 2.

the woolly sides of the skins are inwards. The straps that hold the knapsack to the shoulders are secured by a simple fastening, shown in figs. 2 and 3. But the ordinary knapsack hooks and rings, if procurable, would answer the purpose better. The straight lines in fig. 1 show the way in which the bag is to be folded into the shape of fig. 3. Fig. 4 shows the sleeper inside his bag, in which he fits very like a grub in its cocoon, There is no waste of space. For the sake of warmth, the bag is made double from the knees downwards, and also opposite to the small of the back.

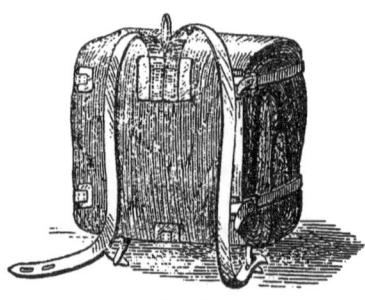

Fig. 3.

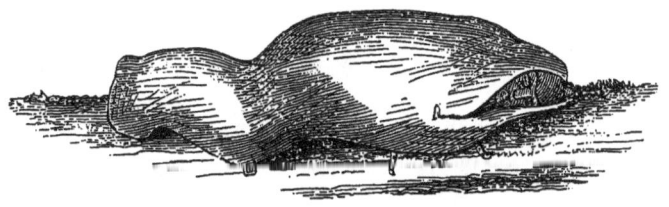

Fig. 4.

During the daytime, when the weather is wet or cold, the bags are of much use, for the *douaniers* sit with them pulled up to their waist. When carried in the manner of a knapsack the bag sits perfectly well against the shoulders; but, owing to the yielding nature of its substance, it lies too close to the back, and is decidedly oppressive. A wicker frame might well be interposed.

Arctic Sleeping-bags.—Arctic travellers use coarse drugget bags, covered with brown holland to make them less pervious to the wind, and having a long flap at the upper end to fold down over the face. I have already extracted passages from travellers' accounts relating to them, in speaking of " Encamping on Snow," p. 140, and another ,when speaking of " Snow-walls with Tenting for their Roofs," p. 143.

Macintosh Sack.—Mr. Falconer writes to me as follows:—
" I travelled in 1841 from Austin in Texas to Mexico through New Mexico. I left Austin in June, and reached Zacateras on Christmas Day. During nearly the whole period we travelled from Austin to New Mexico, I camped without any covering at night for myself, except a large macintosh, made up as a sack, with a piece so laid as a continuation of one side, as to be used as a coverlet, sufficient in length to be brought from the back, over the head, and down on the breast. Inside I placed my blankets. I slept under this covering during many a heavy storm at night, and got out of my soft-coated shell dry in the morning. My opinion is, that every traveller who works his way with a horse should fix on his own saddle the said macintosh sack, two blankets, a tin cup, and a frying-pan. It is amazing, when you get into real working order, how few things are sufficient."

Peasants' Sack.—The peasants in the northern parts of Germany use a strong linen sack, made to draw at one end. This they stuff with straw, hay, dry leaves, &c.; and, putting their feet into it, pull its mouth up to their armpits. They use them when driving their wagons in winter, and when lodging at their wretched roadside inns. (See a letter in the *Times*, February 12, 1855.)

Bag, combined with Tent.—I should think that a combination of a sleeping bag with a very small tent, just large enough to enclose the man's head and shoulders, so as to permit him to eat or write when lying in his bag without fear of the wet would be the smallest and lightest arrangement, compatible with efficiency, in a stormy climate.

TENTS.

General Remarks.—Although tents are not worth the trouble of pitching, on dry nights, in a healthy climate, they are invaluable protectors to a well-equipped traveller against rain, dew, and malaria. But a man who is not so equipped, who has no change of clothes, and no bedstead to sleep on, will do better to sleep in the open air, in front of a good camp fire. Napoleon I., speaking of soldiers, says ('Maximes de Guerre') :—"Tents are not healthy; it is better for the soldier to bivouac, because he sleeps with his feet to the fire, whose neighbourhood quickly dries the ground on which he lies; some planks or a little straw shelter him from the wind. Nevertheless a tent is necessary for superior officers, who have need to write and to consult a map." To a party encamped for a few days, tents are of great use as storehouses for property, which otherwise becomes scattered about, at the risk of being lost or pilfered.

Materials for Tenting.—Light canvas is usually employed, and is, to all intents and purposes, waterproof. Silk, of equal strength with the canvas, is very far lighter: its only disadvantage is its expense. Calico, or cotton canvas, is very generally used for small tents. Leather and felt are warm, but exceedingly heavy; and would only be used in very inclement climates, or where canvas could not be met with. Light matting is not to be despised: it is warm and pretty durable, and makes excellent awning or covering to a framework.

Diagonal Bracing.—A worn-out tent may be strengthened by sewing bands of canvas, which cross each other, and make a kind of net-work: old sails are strengthened in this way.

Tent Pegs should be of galvanized iron; they are well worth the weight of carriage, for not only do wooden ones often fail on an emergency, but cooks habitually purloin them when firewood is scarce.

Tents.—*Large Tents.*—The art of tent-making has greatly advanced since the days of the old-fashioned bell-tent, which is so peculiarly objectionable, as to make it a matter of surprise that it was ever invented and used. It is difficult to pitch; it requires many tent-pegs; it has ropes radiating all round it, over which men and horses stumble; and it is incommodious and ugly.

In choosing a tent, select one that will stand in some sort of shape with only four pegs, or with six at the very utmost; it should admit of being pegged close to the ground without any intervening 'fly;' it is no objection that it should require more than one pole; and, when considering how much weight it will be possible to carry, it must be borne in mind that the tent will become far heavier than it is found to be in the peculiarly dry atmosphere of a tent-maker's show-room. It is very convenient that a tent should admit of being pitched in more than one form: for instance, that one side should open and form an awning in hot weather; also, that it should be easy to attach flys or awning to the tent to increase its available size during the daytime. All tents should be provided with strong covers, for pack-ropes are sure to fray whatever they press against; and it is better that the cover should suffer than the tent itself.

Comparative Size of Tents.—The annexed diagram will show the points on which the *roominess* of a tent mainly depends.

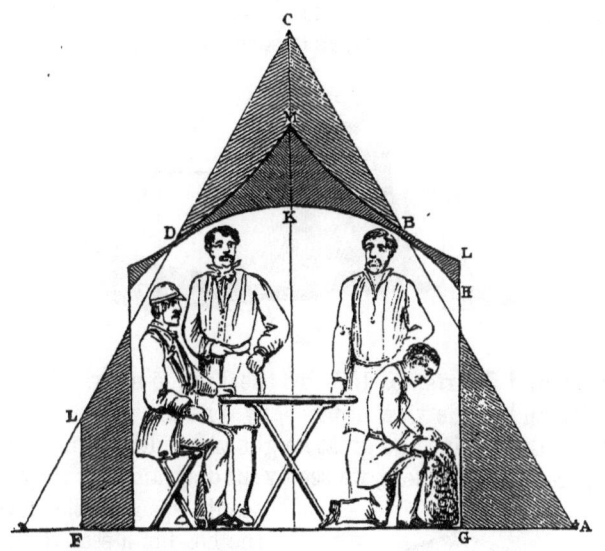

A man wants space to sit at a table, and also to get at his luggage in order either to pack it or to unpack it; lastly, he wants a reasonable amount of standing room. A fair-sized tent ought to include the figures drawn in the diagram; and I have indicated, by lines and shaded spaces, the section of various descriptions of tents that would be just sufficient to embrace them.

One side of the ordinary conical tents (fig. 1), of a front view of fig. 5, and of pyramidal tents (fig. 6), are represented

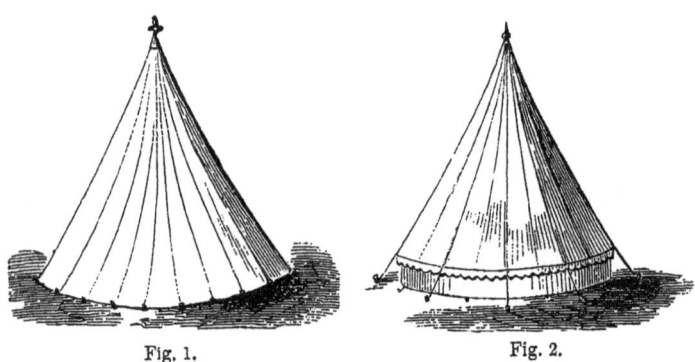

Fig. 1.   Fig. 2.

by the line A B C. Those that have a " fall " (fig. 2), by the lines C D L F. Gipsy-tents, as described p. 161, umbrella-tents

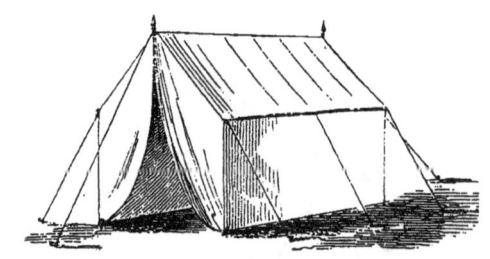

Fig. 3.

(fig. 4), and Jourts, p. 157, by the lines G H B K. Marquees (fig. 3), and a side view of fig. 5, by G L B M.

Notwithstanding the great height and width of conical tents, compared to the others, we see by the diagram that they afford scanty space at the level of the head of a seated person. There is a recent contrivance by Major Rhodes, to be seen at Silver and Co.'s, that is a modification of the gipsy-tent. Among ordinary, well-known tents, I believe none will satisfy the varied wants of a traveller so well as

Fig. 4.

Edgington's three-poled tents (fig. 5). After these I should choose a small marquee (fig. 3); but it is less secure in wind, and the pitch of its roof is bad for rain, and the numerous straggling tent-ropes are objectionable.

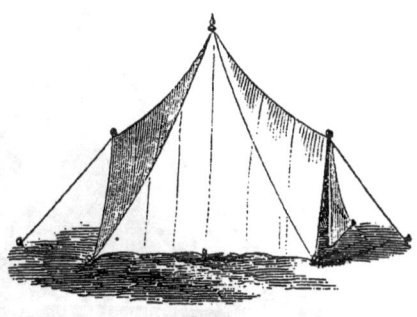

Fig. 5.

A pyramidal tent (fig. 6), of seven or nine feet in the side, is remarkable for its sturdiness: it will stand any weather, will hold two people and a fair quantity of luggage besides; it weighs from 25 to 40 lbs. It is not a good tent for hot weather, for it is far too stuffy,

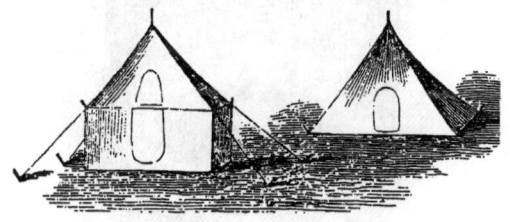

Fig. 7. Fig. 6.

though by taking an additional joint to the tent-pole, and using tent-ropes (as may also be done with any other kind of tent), it may be made more airy by being raised up, and by having walls added to it (fig. 7). In default of canvas, the walls may be constructed of other materials. (See "Materials for Huts.")

Tent Pitched over an Excavation.—A hole may be dug deeply beneath the tent floor, partly for the purpose of a store-room, and partly for that of a living-room when the weather is very inclement. This was practised before Sebastopol in the manner shown in the fig. p. 158. The notched pole acts as a ladder for ascending from below.

Jourts.—The Kirghis-jourt is a capacious, solid, warm, and fireproof structure, that admits of being pitched or taken to pieces in an hour, and withstands the cold and violent winds of the steppes of Central Asia, in a way that no tent or combination of tents could pretend to effect. A jourt of from 20

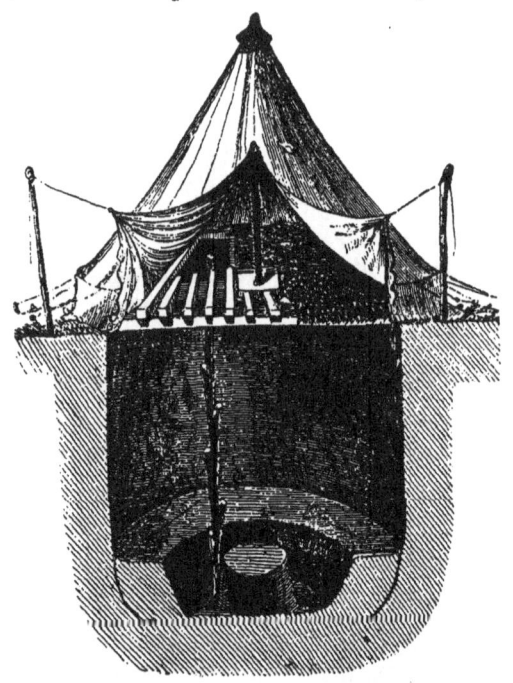

Fig. 8 (relates to p. 157).

to 25, or even 30 feet in diameter, forms two camel-loads, or about half a ton in weight. One camel carries the felt, the other the wood-work. Fig. 9 shows the jourt half-covered; and fig. 10 gives an enlarged view of a portion of its side. There are four separate parts in its structure:—1. The *doorway*, a solid piece of ornamental carpentering, that takes to pieces instantly. 2. The *sides*, which consist of lengths of wood-work, that shut up on the principle of the contrivance known sometimes as "lazy-tongs," and sometimes as "easy-back scissors:" they tie together and make a circle, beginning and ending with the doorway; a tape is wound round them, as shown in fig. 9, about one-third from their tops. 3. The *roof-ribs*. The bottom of each of these is tied to the sides of the jourt (A, fig. 10), and its top fits into a socket in—4, the *roof-ring*, which is a hoop of wood strengthened by transverse bars.

Over this framework broad sheets of felt are thrown: their own weight makes them lie steadily, for they are quite an inch in thickness; however, in very stormy weather, if I recollect aright, they are weighted with stones, or they are stitched together. There is no metal in the structure: the laths of willow-wood that form the sides are united, where they cross, by pieces of sinew knotted at either end; these act as pivots when the sides are shut up. I am indebted to the late Mr. Atkinson for my information on these interesting structures. Further particulars about them, the native way of making

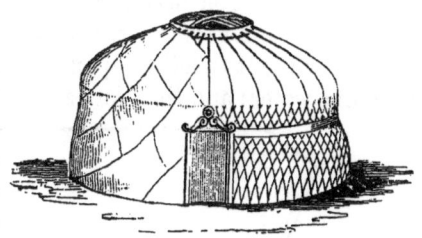

Fig. 9.

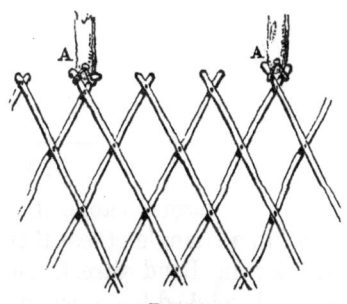

Fig. 10.

the felt, by continually rolling sheepskins with the wool between them, and numerous pictures, in which jourts form a striking feature, will be found in his beautifully illustrated work on Siberia.

Small Tents.—For tents of the smallest size and least pretensions, nothing can be better than the one represented in

Fig. 1.

fig. 1: the ends are slit down their middles, and are laced or buttoned together, so that, by unfastening these, the tent spreads out to a flat sheet of the form of fig. 2, well adapted for an awning, or else it can be simply unrolled and used with the bedding. It is necessary that a tent should be roomy enough to admit of a man undressing himself, when wet through, without treading upon his bed and drenching it with mud and water; and therefore a tent of the above description

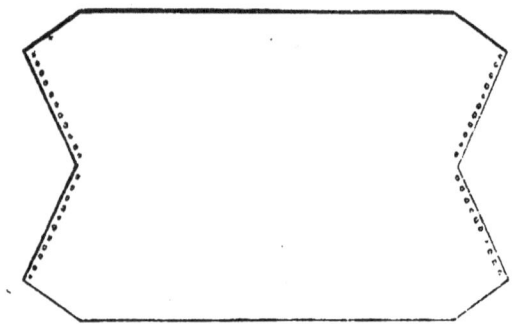

Fig. 2.

is found to be unserviceable, if less than about 7 feet long, or ending in a triangle of less than 5½ feet in the side. Peat, the saddler in Bond Street, once made them; [they cost 2*l*. 10*s*., and weighed 9 lbs. when dry. They are liable to bag in the side when the wind is high : a cross-pole or two sticks, following the seams of the canvas in the above sketch, would make them tauter.

Alpine Tent.—Mr. Whymper contrived a tent for his alpine explorations, which he found eminently successful. It has a waterproof floor, continuous with the sides: it is supported by poles, that slip into hems of the cloth — two poles at either end. These tents have been used on various occasions by Mr. Whymper's brother in Alaska, and by Mr. Freshfield in the Caucasus, and were highly approved of, but I do not know whether these tents would be altogether suitable for more comfortable travel. I myself had a tent made on this principle some years ago, but disliked it, for I found the continuity of the floor with the sides to act unsatisfactorily; the tent retained the damp, and the weight of the body, acting on the floor of the tent, was apt to disturb its walls. Mr. Whymper's tent is procurable at Carter's, Alpine Outfitter, 295, Oxford Street, London.

Boating Tent.—Further on, in the chapter on "Boats," the way is shown by which sailors make a tent out of their lugsail, throwing it over a framework of oars.

Gipsy Tent.—A traveller who has only a blanket, a plaid, or broad piece of material of any kind, with which he wishes to improvise a tent, may make a framework of long wands, planting their ends in the ground, bending their tops together, and lashing or wattling them securely; over this the blanket is thrown (fig. 3). If the sticks are sufficiently long and pliant, their ends should be bent over the roof half-way down the opposite side, as in fig. 1. This adds considerably to the strength of the arrangement.

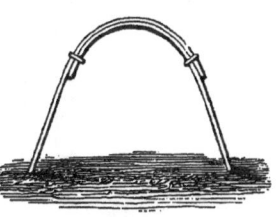

Fig. 1.

The gipsies in England use the following excellent contrivance to save the trouble of tying the sticks together.

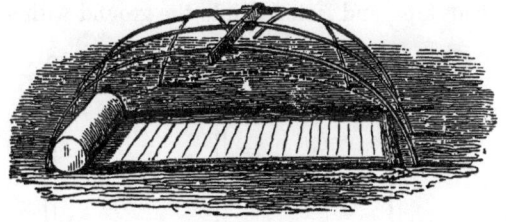

Fig. 2.

They carry a light bar of wood, 2½ feet long, bound with string here and there to keep it from splitting; through this, six holes, each big enough to admit the tip of the little finger, are bored or burnt; they also carry eight hazel rods with them, each six feet long, and arrange their framework as in fig. 2. It will be observed that the two rods which are planted

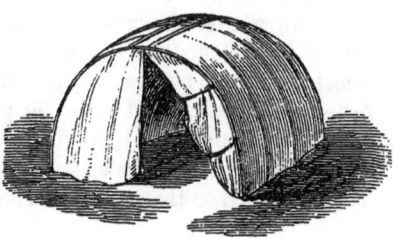

Fig. 3.

behind give additional roominess and stability to the affair. The rug and pillow show the position in which the occupants sleep. Blankets, not sheeting, pinned together with wooden pegs, are thrown over the whole, as in fig. 3.

Tente d'abri.—The French " tente d'abri " has not, so far as I know, been adopted by travellers: it seems hardly suitable, except for soldiers. Each man carries a square of canvas (fig. 1), with buttons and button-holes all round it, by which it can be doubly attached to other similar squares of canvas, and thus, from several separate pieces, one large cloth can be made. The square carried by the French soldier measures 5 feet 4½ inches in the side, reckoning along the buttons; of these there are nine along each edge, including the corner ones. Each soldier has also to carry a tent-staff, or else a proportion of the pegs and cord. When six men club together they proceed as follows:—Three tent-sticks are fixed into the ground, whose tops are notched; a light cord is then passed round their tops, and fastened into the ground with a peg at

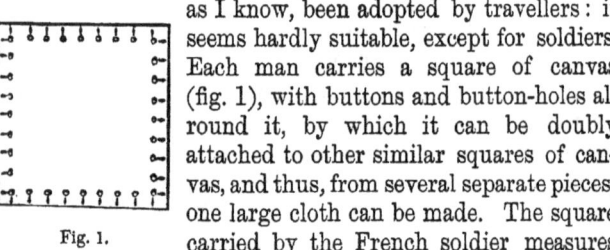

Fig. 1.

Fig. 2.

each end (fig. 2). Two sheets, A and B, are buttoned together and thrown over the cord, and then two other sheets, C and D; and C is buttoned to A, and D to B (fig. 3). Lastly another sheet is thrown over each of the slanting cords, the one buttoned to A and B, and the other to C and D; and thus a sort of dog-kennel is formed, in which six men—the bearers of the six pieces of canvas—sleep. The sides of the tent are of course pegged to the ground. There are many modifications

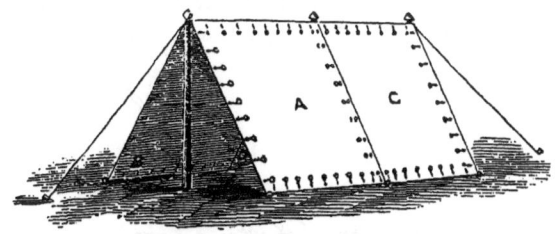

Fig. 3.

in the way of pitching these tents. Should the sticks be wanting, faggots or muskets can be used in their place.

Tent of Mosquito-netting.—I have been informed of a sportsman in Ceylon, who took with him into the woods a cot with mosquito-curtains, as a protection not only against insects, but against malaria. He also had a blanket rolled at his feet: at 3 in the morning, when the chill arose in the woods, he pulled his blanket over him.

Pitching a Tent.—It is quite an art, so to pitch a tent as to let in or exclude the air, to take advantage of sun and shade, &c. &c. Every available cloth or sheet may be pressed into service, to make awnings and screens, as we see among the gipsies. There is a great deal of character shown in each different person's encampment. A tent should never be pitched in a slovenly way: it is so far more roomy, secure and pretty, when tightly stretched out, that no pains should be spared in drilling the men to do it well. I like to use a piece of string, marked with knots, by which I can measure the exact places in which the tent-pegs should be struck, for the eye is a deceitful guide in estimating squareness. (See "Squaring.") It is wonderful how men will bungle with a tent, when they are not properly drilled to pitch it.

To secure Tent-ropes.—When the soil is loose, scrape away the surface sand, before driving the tent-pegs. Loose mould is made more tenacious by pouring water upon it. When one peg is insufficient, it may be backed by another. (See fig.) The outermost peg must be altogether buried in the earth. Heavy saddle-bags are often of use to secure the tent-ropes; and, in rocky ground, heavy piles of stones may be made to answer the same purpose. The tent-ropes may

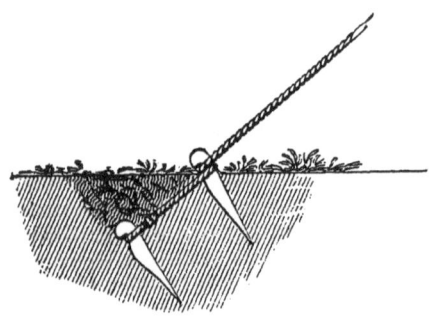

also be knotted to a cloth, on which stones are afterwards piled.

"*Dáterám*" is, as the late Dr. Barth informed me, the Bornu name for a most excellent African contrivance, used in some parts of the Sahara desert, by means of which tent-ropes may be secured, or horses picketed in sand of the driest description, as in that of a sand dune, whence a tent-peg would be drawn out by a strain so slight as to be almost imperceptible. I have made many experiments upon it, and find its efficiency to be truly wonderful. The plan is to tie to the end of the tent-rope, a small object of any description, by its middle, as a short stick, a stone, a bundle of twigs, or a bag of sand; and to bury it from 1 to 2 feet in the loose sand. It will be found, if it has been buried 1 foot deep, that a strain equal to about 50 lbs. weight, is necessary to draw it up; if 1½ feet deep, that a much more considerable strain is necessary; and that, if 2 feet deep, it is quite impossible for a single man to pull it up. In the following theoretical case, the resistance would be as the cube of the depth; but in sand or shingle, the increase is less rapid. It varies under different circumstances; but it is no exaggeration to estimate its increase as seldom less than as the square of the depth. The theoretical case of which I spoke, is this:—Let x be part of a layer of shingle of wide extent: the shingle is supposed to consist of smooth hard spherical balls, all of the same size.

Tents.   165

Let s be a dáterám buried in x; and T the string to which it is tied. Now, on considering fig. 2, where a series of balls

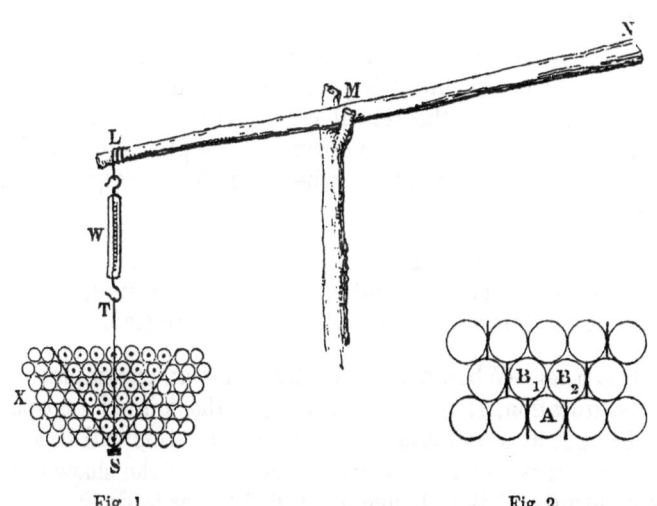

Fig. 1.   Fig. 2.

are drawn on a larger scale and on a plane surface, it is clear that the ball A cannot move in any degree to the right or the left without disturbing the entire layer of balls on the same plane as itself: its only possible movement is vertically upwards. In this case, it disturbs B_1 and B_2. These, for the same reason as A, can only move vertically upwards, and, in doing so, they must disturb the three balls above them, and so on. Consequently, the uplifting of a single ball in fig. 2, necessitates the uplifting of the triangle of balls of which it forms the apex; and it obviously follows from the same principle, that the uplifting of s, in the depth of x, in fig. 1, necessitates the uplifting of a cone of balls whose apex is at s. But the weight of a cone is as the cube of its height and, therefore, the resistance to the uplifting of the dáterám, is as the cube of the depth at which it has been buried. In practice, the grains of sand are capable of a small but variable amount of lateral displacement, which gives relief to the movement of sand caused by the dáterám, for we may observe the surface of the ground to work very irregularly, although extensively, when the dáterám begins to stir. On the other hand, the friction of the grains of sand tends to increase the difficulty of movement. The arrangement shown in the diagram, of a spring weighing-machine tied to the end of a lever, is that which I have used in testing the strain the dáterám will resist, under different circumstances. The size of the dáterám is not of much importance, it would be of still less importance in the theoretical case. Anything that is more than 4 inches long seems to answer. The plan succeeds in a dry soil of any description, whether it be shingly beach or sand.

Bushing a Tent means the burying of bushes in the soil, so far as to leave only their cut ends above the ground, to which a corresponding number of the tent-ropes are tied.

Tent-poles.—When a tent is pitched for an encampment of some duration, it is well to lay aside the jointed tent-pole, and to cut a stout young tree to replace it: this will be found far more trustworthy in stormy weather. If the shape of the tent admits of the change, it is still better to do away with the centre pole altogether; and, in the place of it, to erect a substantial framework of poles, which are to be planted just within the rim of the tent, and to converge to a point, under its peak. A tent-pole can be lengthened temporarily, by lashing it to a log, with the help of a Toggle and strop (which see). A broken tent-pole can be mended permanently, by placing a splint of wood on either side of the fracture, and by whipping the whole together, with soft cord or with the untwisted strand of a piece of rope.

To prevent Tent-poles from slipping.—When the tent is pitched in the ordinary way on a smooth rocky surface, there is considerable danger that the foot of the pole may slip whenever a gust of wind or other sudden impulse sways the tent. This danger is to be obviated on precisely the same principle as that by which builders secure their scaffolding-poles upon the smooth footways of a street: they put the foot of each pole into a bucket, filled with sand. As the base of the bucket is broad, the scaffolding is much less liable to slip, than if the narrow bases of the poles had rested directly upon the pavement.

To tie Things to Tent-poles.—To hang clothes, or anything else, upon a smooth tent-pole, see "Clove-hitch." A strap with hooks attached to it, buckled round the pole, is very convenient. The method shown in the sketch suffices, if the pole be notched, or jointed, or in any way slightly uneven.  Bags, &c., are supposed to be hung upon the bit of wood that is secured to the free end. Convenient pegs, made of bits of wood roughly sharpened, may be driven into the tree, if any, when the encampment is made.

Preparations for a Storm.—Before a storm, dig a ditch as deep as you can round the outside of the tent, to divert the coming sheet of surface-water, and see that the ditch has a good outfall. The ditch will also drain the floor of the tent, if the rain should soak in. Even a furrow scratched with a tent-peg, is better than no ditch at all. Fasten guy-ropes to the spike of the tent-pole; and be careful that the tent is not too much on the strain, else the further shrinking of the materials, under the influence of the wet, will certainly tear up the pegs. Earth, banked up round the bottom of the tent, will prevent gusts of wind from finding their way beneath. It is also a good plan to prepare a small hole near the foot of the tent-pole, with a stone firmly rammed into the bottom, into which the tent-pole may be shifted, as soon as the strain of the tent, under the influence of the wet, becomes dangerous to its safety.

To warm Tents.—"When living in a tent in Otago (New Zealand) during a severe winter, we were perfectly numb with cold at nights, until we adopted the Maori plan, which is to dig a hole about a foot square in the clear, to cover the bottom with a stone or stones, and to fill it at night with red-hot cinders from the camp fire, and lastly, to close the tent excepting a small opening near the top. The cinders are not nearly burnt out by morning. They diffused a pleasant warmth through the tent, and rendered us comfortable all night. There is no danger of suffocation, unless the tent be closed up very tight indeed."—(W. M. Cooper.)

Permanent Camp.—The accompanying sketch shows a tent pitched for a lengthened habitation. It has a deep drain, a

seat and table dug out, and a fireplace. (See the following paragraphs.)

Lost Articles.—Small articles are constantly mislaid and trampled in the sand of the floor of the tent. In searching for them, the ground should be disturbed as little as possible: it is a usual plan to score its surface in parallel lines, with a thin wand. It would be well worth while to make a small light rake to use for this purpose.

Precautions against Thieves.—Natives are apt to creep up to tents, and, putting their hands under the bottom of them, to steal whatever they can: a hedge of thorn-bushes is a protection against this kind of thieving. In some countries a net, with three or four bells attached to it, is thrown over the packages inside a tent. Strings tied horizontally, a foot above the ground, from package to package, are found effective in tripping intruders, See also " Guns set as Spring-guns."

FURNITURE.

Furniture.—The luxuries and elegances practicable in tent-life, are only limited by the means of transport. Julius Cæsar, who was a great campaigner, carried parquets of wooden mosaic for his floors! The articles that make the most show for their weight, are handsome rugs, and skins, and pillows; canteens of dinner and coffee services; and candles, with screens of glass, or other arrangements to prevent them from flickering. The art of luxurious tenting is better understood in Persia than in any other country, even than in India.

Bedsteads.—A portable bedstead, with mosquito-curtains, is a very great luxury, raising the sleeper above the damp soil, and the attacks of most creatures that creep on it; in

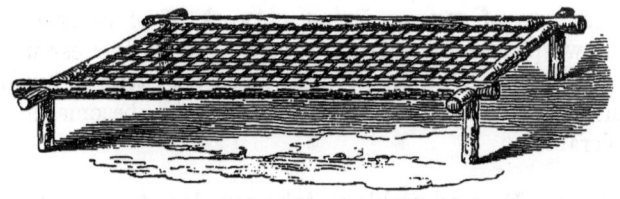

tours where a few luxuries can be carried, it is a very proper article of baggage. It is essential where white ants are numerous. A very luxurious bed is made on the principle of a tennis-player's raquet; being a framework of wood, with strips of raw hide lashed across it from side to side, and from end to end. It is the "angareb" of Upper Egypt.

Hammocks and Cots.—I stated in previous editions of this book, that hammocks and cots had few advocates, owing to the difficulty of suspending them; but Captain M'Gwire's recent ingenious invention quite alters the case. His method will be easily understood by the annexed sketch. The appa-

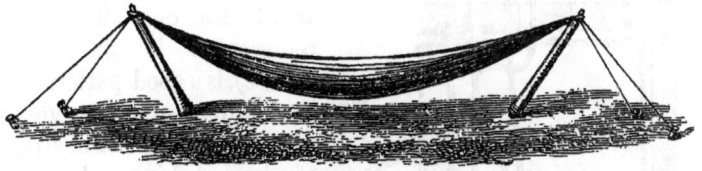

ratus is adapted for use on the wooden floors of houses or ships, by the employment of eyelet-bolts or screw rings instead of pegs, and by putting wooden shoes below the staves to prevent their slipping inwards: the shoes are tied to the eyelet-bolts by a cord.

The complete apparatus, in a very portable form, can be bought at Messrs. Brown's, 165, Piccadilly.

Mosquito Nets and their Substitutes.—A mosquito-curtain may be taken for suspension over the bed, or place where you sit; but it is dangerous to read in them by candle-light, for they catch fire very easily. (See "Incombustible Stuffs.") It is very pleasant, in hot, mosquito-plagued countries, to take the glass sash entirely out of the window-frame, and replace it with one of gauze. Broad network, if of fluffy thread, keeps wasps out. The darker a house is kept, the less willing are flies, &c., to flock in. If sheep and other cattle be hurdled-in near the house, the nuisance of flies, &c., becomes almost intolerable.

Chairs.—It is advisable to take very *low* strong and *roomy* camp-stools, with tables to correspond in height, as a chamber is much less choked up when the seats are low, or when people sit, as in the East, on the ground. The seats should not be more than 1 foot high, though as wide and deep as an ordinary footstool. Habit very soon reconciles travellers to this; but without a seat at all, a man can never write, draw, nor calculate as well as if he had one. The stool represented in the figure (above), is a good pattern: it has a full-sized seat made of canvas or leather, or of strips of dressed hide. A milkman's stool, supported by only one peg, is quickly made in the bush, and is not very inconvenient. The common rush-bottomed chair can be

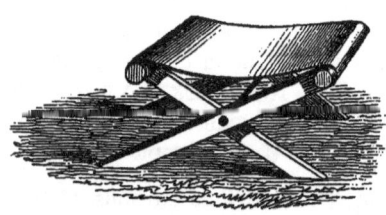
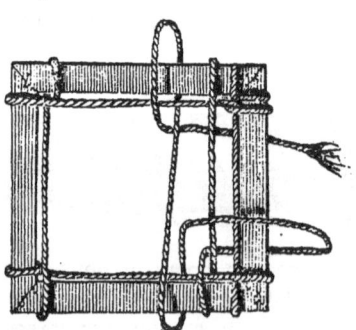

easily made, if proper materials are accessible. The annexed diagram explains clearly the method of their construction.

Table.—The table may consist of a couple of boards, not less than 2 feet long, by 9 inches broad, hinged lengthwise, for the convenience of carriage, and resting on a stand, which should be made on the same principle as the framework of the chair described above. It is well to have the table made of mahogany, for deal warps and cracks excessively. There is no difficulty in carrying furniture like the above, on a packhorse.

Makeshift Chair and Table.—For want of a chair, it is convenient to dig a hole or a trench in the ground, and to sit on one side of it, with the feet resting on its bottom: the opposite side of the trench serves as a table, on which things may be put, within easy reach.

"In a box 2 feet long and 1 foot square at the ends, the lid and its bottom, of course, both measure 2 feet by 1 foot. Now, if the bottom opens on hinges, just like the lid, and if the hinges of both lid and bottom are fixed to the hindmost side of the box, then when the box is laid face downwards, and both the lid and the bottom are opened out and secured in the same horizontal plane with the side to which they are hinged, a table of 3 feet by 2 feet is made. The lid and bottom form the two leaves of the table, and what was the hindmost side, when the box stood on its bottom, is now uppermost, and forms the middle of the table. Such a box would hold, during travel, the things wanted when encamping."—(Peal.)

Hooks.—I have spoken of the way of hanging articles in tents, under "Tent Poles." In a permanent bivouac or in a hut, it is convenient to fix hooked sticks or the horns of animals, against the walls, as pegs.

FIRE.

General Remarks.—Although, in the teeth of every precaution, fires constantly break out, yet when a traveller wants a light and does not happen to have any of his ingenious fire-making contrivances at hand, it is very difficult for him to obtain it. And further, though sparks, of their own accord and in the most unlikely places, too often give rise to conflagrations, yet it requires much skill and practice to succeed without fail, in coaxing a small spark into a serviceable camp fire. Therefore every traveller should carry on his person the means of procuring a light, under ordinary circumstances of wind and weather; that is to say, he should have in his pocket, a light handy steel, a flint or an agate, and amadou or other tinder. I also strongly recommend that he should carry a bundle of half-a-dozen fine splinters of wood, like miniature tooth-picks, thinner and shorter than lucifer-matches, whose points he has had dipped in melted sulphur; also a small spare lump of sulphur of the size of a pea or bean, in reserve. The cook should have a regular tinder-box, such as he happens to have been used to, and an abundance of wax lucifers. Paper fusees are not worth taking in travel, as wet entirely spoils them.

There are usually three separate agents in making a fire, each of which may be varied in many ways and requires separate description. 1. The Spark or other light to start with. 2. The Tinder; that is, some easily ignited and smouldering substance. 3. Fuel, judiciously applied to the burning tinder, or other feeble light, so as to develope it into a serviceable fire.

To obtain Fire from the Sun.—*Burning-glasses.*—The object-glass, and every other convex glass of a telescope, *is* a burning-glass, and has only to be unscrewed to be fit for use. The object lenses of an opera-glass are very efficient. The larger the glass and the shorter its focus, the greater is its heating power. Convex spectacle glasses and eye glasses are too small and of too long a focus to be used with effect, except when the sun is very hot. An old-fashioned watch-glass, filled with water, and having the rays of a powerful sun glittered down upon it vertically by help of a mirror, will give a light. Dr. Kane and other arctic travellers have made burning-glasses of ice.

Reflectors.—The inside of the polished metal cover of a hunting-watch will sometimes converge a sufficiency of rays, to burn. The vestal fire of Rome and the sacred fire of the Mexicans were obtained by means of reflectors. If I understand aright, they consisted of a stone with a conical hollow, carefully polished, the apex of the hollow cone was a right angle: the tinder was held in the axis of the cone. See Tylor's 'Early History of Mankind.'

Black Tinder.—Tinder that is black by previous charring, or from any other cause, ignites in the sun far sooner than light-coloured tinder.

Fire by conversion of motion into heat.—*General Remarks.*— When a moving body is arrested, heat is given out; the quantity of heat being in exact proportion to the mass, multiplied into the square of its velocity. Thus if a cannon ball be fired at an iron target, both it and the ball become exceedingly hot. There is even a flash of light when the velocity of the ball is very high. When bullets are fired with heavy charges at a target, the lead is just melted by the heat of impact, and it "splashes," to use a common phrase. It is obvious from these two examples, that no velocity which the hand of man is able to give to a steel, when striking a flint, or to one stick rubbing against another stick, will be competent to afford a red-hot temperature unless the surface against which impact or friction is made be very small, or unless great care be taken to avoid the wasteful dissipation of heat. The spark made by a flint and steel, consists of a thin shaving of steel, scraped off by the flint and heated by the arrested motion. When well struck, the spark is white-hot and at that temperature it burns with bright scintillations in the air, just as iron that is merely red-hot burns in pure oxygen. This is the theory :. now for the practice.

Flints.—If we may rely on a well-known passage in Virgil, concerning Æneas and his comrades, fire was sometimes made in ancient days by striking together two flints, but I confess myself wholly unable to light tinder with flints alone, and I am equally at a loss to understand what were the "dry leaves" that they are said in the same passage to have used for tinder. Neither can I obtain fire except with a flint and *steel*, or, at least, hardened iron; a flint and ordinary iron will not give an available spark. Flints may be replaced by any siliceous stone, as agate, rock-crystal, or quartz. Agate is preferred to flint, for it gives a hotter spark: it is sold by tobacconists. A partly siliceous stone, such as granite, will answer in default of one that is wholly siliceous. I have been surprised at finding that crockery and porcelain of all kinds will make a spark, and sometimes a very good one. There are cases where a broken teacup might be the salvation of many lives in a shipwrecked party. On coral-reefs, and other coasts destitute of flinty stones, search should be made for drift-wood and drifted sea-weed. In the roots of these, the pebbles of other shores are not unfrequently entangled, and flint may be found among them. The joints of bamboos occasionally contain enough silex to give a spark.

Steels.—The possession of a really good steel is a matter of great comfort in rough travel, for, as I have just said, common iron is incompetent to afford a useful spark, and hardened iron or soft steel is barely sufficient to do so. Any blacksmith will make a good steel out of an old file, if he has nothing more appropriate at hand. A substitute for a steel can be made, even by an ordinary traveller, out of common iron, by means of "casehardening" (which *see*). The link of a chain, or the iron heel of a boot, or a broken horse-shoe, is of a convenient shape for the purpose.

Pyrites are, and have been, widely used for striking sparks. Two pieces struck together, or one piece struck with a steel, gives a good spark; but it is a very friable mineral, and therefore not nearly so convenient as flint.

Guns.—If you wish to get a light by means of a flint-and-steel gun, the touch-hole may be stuffed up, and a piece of tinder put among the priming powder: a light can be obtained in that way without firing the gun. With a percussion-cap gun, a light may be obtained by putting powder and tinder outside the nipple and round the cap; it will, though not with certainty, catch fire on exploding the cap. But the common way with a gun is to pour in a quarter of a charge of powder, and above it, quite loosely, a quantity of rag or tinder. On firing the gun straight up in the air, the rag will be shot out lighted; you must then run after it as it falls, and pick it quickly up. With percussion-caps, gunpowder, and tinder, and without a gun, a light may sometimes be had on an emergency, by scratching and boring with a knife, awl, or nail, at the fulminating composition in the cap, till it explodes; but a cap is a somewhat dangerous thing to meddle with, as it often flies with violence, and wounds. Crushing gunpowder with hard stones may possibly make it explode.

Lucifers.—An inexperienced hand will waste an entire boxful of them, and yet will fail in lighting a fire in the open air, on a windy day. The convenience of lucifers in obtaining a light is very great, but they have two disadvantages: they require that the air should be perfectly still, while the burning sulphur is struggling to ignite the stick; and, again, when the match is thrust among the wood, the sticks upon which it has to act, have not been previously warmed, and consequently, though one or two of them may become lighted, the further progress of the fire is liable to cease. On the other hand, in methods where the traveller begins with tinder, and blows its spark into a flame, the adjacent wood becomes thoroughly heated by the process, and the flame, once started, is almost certain to maintain itself. Consequently, in lighting a fire with lucifers, be careful to shield the match from wind, by throwing a cloak or saddle-cloth, or something else over the head, whilst you operate; and secondly, to have abundance of twigs of the smaller sizes, that there may be no uncertainty of the lucifer-match being able to light them, and set the fire a-going. In a steady downfall of rain, you may light a match for a pipe under your horse's belly. If you have paper to spare, it is a good plan to twist it into a hollow cone; to turn the cone with its apex to the wind; and immediately after rubbing the match, to hold it inside the cone. The paper will become quickly heated by the struggling flame and will burst into a miniature conflagration, too strong to be puffed out by a single blast of air. Wax lucifers are undoubtedly better than wooden ones, for in damp weather, wooden ones will hardly burn; but wax is waterproof, and independent of wet or dry. When there is nothing dry, at hand, to rub the lucifer-match against, scratch the composition on its head with the edge of a knife or with the finger-nail. It is a sure way of lighting it; and with care, there is no need of burning the fingers.

Fire-sticks.—In every country without exception, where inquiry has been made, the method of obtaining fire by rubbing one stick against another, has been employed. In savage countries the method still remains in present use; in nearly all the more civilised ones, it has been superseded within historic periods by flints and steels and the like, and within this present generation by lucifer-matches. The only instance I know in which flints are said to have preceded fire-sticks, is in the quotation below from Pliny. A light has also been obtained in pre-historic times, as I have already mentioned, by reflecting the sun from a hollow surface; but this method required costly apparatus, and could never have been in common use. Hence, although so far as I am aware, the Bible, and Homer, and other records of great antiquity, are absolutely silent on the contemporary methods of procuring fire; and although Pliny says the reverse,—I think we are justified in believing that the plan of rubbing sticks together was absolutely universal in the barbaric infancy of the human race. In later Greek history, Prometheus is accredited with the invention of fire-sticks. Among the Romans both Seneca and Pliny write about them. Pliny says (Nat. Hist. xvi. 76, 77), " There is heat in the mulberry, in the bay-laurel, in ivy, and in all plants whence fire-sticks are made. The experience of soldiers reconnoitring for encamping-grounds, and that of shepherds, made this discovery; for a stone is not always at hand whence a spark might be struck. One piece of wood, therefore, is rubbed by another, and it catches fire through the friction, while a dry tindery substance—fungus and leaves are the most easily attainable—is used to perpetuate the fire. Nothing is better than ivy used as the stick to be rubbed, and bay-laurel as the stick to rub with. Wild vine—not the 'labrusca'—is also found good."

I have made a great many experiments with different kinds of wood, having procured an assortment of those used by the fancy toy-makers of Tunbridge Wells, and the chippings from botanical gardens. I find what I have heard from savages to be quite true; viz., that it is much more difficult to procure good wood for the "fire-block" than for the drill-stick; any tough, hard, and dry stick will do for the latter, but the fire-block must be of wood with little grain; of a middle degree of softness; readily inflammable; and, I presume, a good non-conductor of heat; but I do not know if there be much difference, in this latter respect, between woods of the same quality. If it be too hard, the action of the drill-stick will merely dent and polish it; if very soft, it will be worn away before the friction has time to heat it sufficiently: ivy is excellent. I find it not at all difficult to produce smoke (it is much more difficult to produce fire) with a broken fishing-rod, or ramrod, as a drill-stick, and a common wooden pill-box, or tooth-powder box, as a fire-block. Walnut, also, does as a fire-block, and the stock of a gun is of walnut. Deal and mahogany are both worthless for fire-sticks.

It is well so to notch the fire-block, that the wood-dust, as it is formed by the rubbing, should all run into one place: it will then glow with a smouldering heat, ready to burst out into an available flame with a very little fanning, as soon as a degree of heat sufficient to ignite tinder has been attained. Tinder is a great convenience, in ensuring that the fire, once obtained, shall not be lost again; but it is not essential to have it.

There are many ways of rubbing the sticks together, in use among different nations. Those curious in the matter should consult Tylor's 'Early History of Mankind.' But the traveller will not obtain much assistance from these descriptions, as it will be out of his power to obtain fire by any but the simplest of them, on a first trial. He is only likely to succeed at first by working at leisure, with perfectly dry wood. Even savages, who practise the art all their lives, fail to procure fire in very wet weather, when the shelter is bad. Of the plans employed by savages, the simplest is that in use both in South Africa and in Australia.

The Australian blacks use the flower-stem of the grass-tree, which is of a tough pithy nature, and about one inch in diameter. The operation of making the fire is assisted by the use of a little charcoal-powder, which, in Australia, is found on the bark of almost every tree, from the constant passage of grass-fires over the ground. The process is as follows:

Fig. 1.

—One piece of the stick is notched in the middle, fig. 1, and the notch slightly hollowed out; another is roundly pointed at one end. The black fellow, being seated on the ground,

Fig. 2.

holds down one end of the notched stick with each foot, fig. 2, and placing the point of the other stick into the notch, twirls it rapidly and forcibly between the palms of his hands. In doing this his hands gradually slip down the stick, and he has to shift them rapidly up again, which loses time: but two people, seated opposite, can alternately take up the rubbing, and more easily produce fire. A little of the above-mentioned powdered charcoal is dropped into the notch during the operation. In a very few minutes red-hot powdery ashes commence to work up out of the notch, which falling on a small heap of tow, or of dry tow-like bark, or lint, or cotton stuff, is quickly blown into a flame. The Africans carry the drill-stick, which in shape and size is like an arrow, in a quiver with their arrows, and the fire-block—a stick three inches long and one in diameter, of a different wood—as a pendant to their necklace.

A plan more practicable to an unpractised hand is that in use among some of the North American Indians. I copy the illustration of it from Schoolcraft's work upon those people.

One person works the "drill-stick" with a rude bow, and with his other hand holds a piece of stone or of wood above it, both to steady it and to give the requisite pressure—gentle at first, and increasing judiciously up to the critical moment when the fire is on the point of bursting out. Another man puts his hands on the lower piece of wood, the "fire-block," to steady it, and holds a piece of tinder ready to light it as soon as fire is produced. If a serious emergency should occur, it is by no means hopeless to obtain fire after this method. A large party have considerable advantages over only one or two men, because as the work is fatiguing, the men can undertake it in turns; and, again, as considerable knack is required for success, it is much more probable that one man out of many should succeed, than that only one man, taken at hazard, should do so. But the best plan of all for a party of three or more men is for one of them to hold the upper block, another to hold the lower block and the tinder, should there be any, and the third man to cause the drill-stick to rotate. He will effect this best by dispensing with the "bow," and by simply using a string or thong of a yard or four feet long. He makes one or two turns with the string round the drill-stick, and then holding one end of the string in either hand, he saws away with all his force. I believe that a party of three men, furnished with dry wood of an appropriate quality and plenty of string, would surely produce

smoke on the first few trials, but that they would fail in producing fire. If, however, they had a couple of hours' leisure to master the knack of working these sticks, I think they would succeed in producing fire before the end of that time. The period of time necessary for a successful operation is from one to three minutes. It is of little use fatiguing yourself with sustaining the exertion for a longer period at a time, unless the wood becomes continuously hotter. As soon as the temperature remains uniform it shows that you have let the opportunity slip; it is then the best economy of effort to desist at once, to rest, to take breath, and recommence with fresh vigour.

Fire by Chemical Means.—It is not in the province of this book to describe the various matches that take fire by dipping them into compositions; and I have already spoken of lucifer-matches in the last section. Only one source of fire remains to be noticed, it is—

Spontaneous Combustion.—It is conceivable that the property which masses of greasy rags, and such-like matter, possess of igniting when left to themselves, might, under some circumstances, be the only means available to procure fire. It is at all events well that this property should be borne in mind when warehousing stores, in order to avoid the risk of their taking fire. Any oil mixed with a hatful of shavings, tow, cotton, wool, or rags, heaped together, will become very hot in one, two, or more days, and will ultimately burst into flame. The rapidity of the process is increased by warmth.

Tinder.—*General Remarks.*—There are two divisions of tinder: those that are of a sufficiently strong texture to admit of being grasped in the hand, and those that are so friable as to require a box to hold them. In the first division (a) are the following:—amadou, a roll of rag, a cotton lamp-wick, a roll of touch-paper, a mass of hair of certain plants, and a long string of pith sewed up in a sheath. To ignite these, we must hold them as in fig. 1, and use the steel to strike downwards upon the flint. In the second division (b) are:—tinder of burnt rags, tinder of any kind with grains of gunpowder strewed over it, and touch-wood. All these require tinder-boxes, as explained below. There are also many other substances belonging to both divisions of tinder, in use. A traveller should inform himself about those peculiar to the country that he visits.

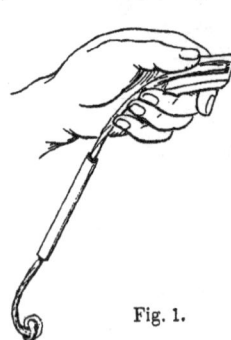
Fig. 1.

a. *Amadou*, punk, or German tinder, is made from a kind of fungus or mushroom that grows on the trunks of old oaks, ashes, beeches, &c.; many other kinds of fungus, and, I believe, all kinds of puff-balls, will also make tinder. "It should be gathered in August or September, and is prepared by removing the outer bark with a knife, and separating carefully the spongy yellowish mass that lies within it. This is cut into thin slices, and beaten with a mallet to soften it, till it can easily be pulled asunder between the fingers. It is then boiled in a strong solution of saltpetre."

A Roll of Rag.—Cotton rag will easily take fire from the spark from a flint, in a very dry climate, if well struck. It must be rolled up moderately tight, so as to have the end of the roll fluffy; the rag having been *torn*, not cut. A rag rolled in this way is not bad tinder, if the sparks are 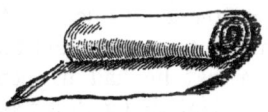 strong, and one commences to blow it the instant one of the fibres is seen to be alight. If its fluffy end be rubbed into a little dry gunpowder, its property as tinder is greatly improved.

Cotton Lamp-wick.—A piece of it drawn through a tin tube, to shield the previously charred part from being rubbed off, is excellent in dry climates. (See fig. 1, p. 180.)

Touch-paper is merely paper dipped in a solution of saltpetre, or what comes to nearly the same thing and is somewhat better, paper smeared with damp gunpowder until it is blackened. Some grains of uncrushed gunpowder should be left adhering to the paper, and a few more should be allowed to lie loosely upon it. Unsized paper, like that out of a blotting-book, is the best suited for making into touch-paper; paper is rendered unsized by being well soaked and washed in water. (See next paragraph.)

Saltpetre for Tinder.—In all cases the presence of saltpetre makes tinder burn more hotly and more fiercely; and saltpetre exists in such great quantities in the ashes of many plants (as tobacco, dill, maize, sunflower), that these can be used, just as they are, in the place of it. Thus, if the ashes of a cigar be well rubbed into a bit of paper, they convert it into touch-paper. So will gunpowder, for out of four parts of it, three are saltpetre; damaged gunpowder may be used for making touch-paper. If it be an object to prepare a store of tinder, a strong solution of saltpetre in water should be obtained, and the paper, or rags, or fungus, dipped into it and hung to dry. This solution may be made by pouring a little water on a charge of gunpowder, or on the ashes above-mentioned, which will dissolve the saltpetre out of them. Boiling water makes a solution forty-fold stronger than ice-cold water, and about eight times stronger than water at 60° Fahr.

Hair of Plants.—The silky down of a particular willow (*S. lanata*) was used by the Esquimaux, with whom Dr. Kane had intercourse; and the botanist Dr. Lindley once informed me that he had happened to receive a piece of peculiarly excellent tinder that was simply the hair of a tree-fern. The Gomuti tinder of the Eastern Archipelago is the hair of a palm.

Pith.—Many kinds of pith are remarkable as tinders; that whence the well-known pith hats are made, is used as tinder in India. Pieces of pith are often sewn round with thin cotton or silk, so as to form a long cord, like the cotton lamp-wick I have described above, and they are carried in tubes for the same reason.

b. We now come to the different kinds of tinder that fall into our second division, namely, those that are too friable to bear handling.

Rags.—Charred linen rags make the tinder that catches fire most easily, that burns most hotly when blown upon, and smoulders most slowly when left to itself, of any kind of tinder that is generally to be obtained. In making it the rags are lighted, and when in a blaze and before they are burnt to white ashes, the flame is stifled out. It is usual to make this kind of tinder in the box intended to hold it; but it can easily be made on the ground in the open air, by setting light to the rag, and dropping pinches of sand upon the flaming parts as soon as it is desired to quench them. The sand is afterwards brushed away, and the tinder gently extricated.

Touch-wood is an inferior sort of tinder, but is always to be met with in woody countries.

Fire. 183

Dry Dung.—Dry and powdered cattle dung—especially horse-dung—will take a spark, but with trouble. After it is lighted it can be kept burning with little difficulty.

Tinder-boxes.—There are three ways of striking a flint, which are best explained by sketches. Fig. 1, p. 180, shows how tinder that is tough enough to bear handling, is grasped together with the flint. When no tinder-box is at hand the more friable kinds of tinder, as touch-wood, may be enveloped

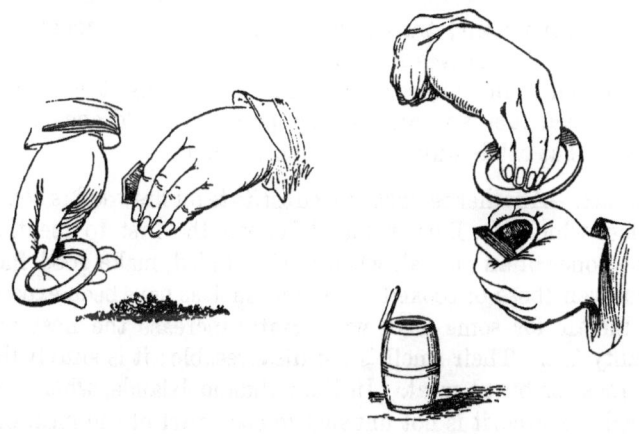

Fig. 2. Fig. 3.

in a roll of rag and be used either as in fig. 1 or in fig. 3. Fig. 2 shows how tinder may be laid on the ground, and how sparks may be struck upon it. The household tinder-boxes of thirty years ago, before lucifers were invented, were for use in this way. Fig. 3 shows how sparks may be struck into a small tinder-box. It is the method most commonly adopted by travellers: for instance, it is universally used in South Africa and in North America. A hollow cylinder of wood or metal, about three inches long, and corked up at one end, is all that is essential. If it be barrel-shaped the flint lies against its sides, at the most convenient angle for striking sparks into the box, as is shown by the bottom drawing of fig. 3.

Wet Weather.—In long-continued soaking weather, the best way of keeping a tinder-box dry is to put it into a small pocket hung close under the armpit.

Fuel.—*Firewood.*—There is a knack in finding firewood. It should be looked for under bushes; the stump of a tree that is rotted nearly to the ground has often a magnificent root, fit to blaze throughout the night,

Dry Cattle-dung.—The dry dung of cattle and other animals, as found on the ground, is very generally used throughout the world, in default of better fuel, and there is nothing whatever objectionable in employing it. The Canadians call it by the apt name of " Bois de Vache." In North and South Africa it is frequently used; throughout a large part of Armenia and of Thibet the natives rely entirely upon it. There is a great convenience in this sort of fuel; because, as it is only in camps that fuel is wanted, so it is precisely at old encamping-places that cattle-dung is abundantly found.

Bones.—Another remarkable substitute for firewood is bones; a fact which Mr. Darwin was, I believe, the first to mention. The bones of an animal, when freshly killed, make good fuel; and even those of cooked meat, and such as have been exposed to the air for some days, will greatly increase the heat of a scanty fire. Their smell is not disagreeable: it is simply that of roast or burnt meat. In the Falkland Islands, where firewood is scarce, it is not unusual to cook part of the meat of a slaughtered bull with its own bones. When the fire is once started with a few sticks, it burns well and hotly. The flame of course depends on the fat within the bones, and therefore the fatter the animal the better the fire. During the Russian campaign in 1829, the troops suffered so severely from cold at Adrianople, that the cemeteries were ransacked for bones for fuel. (Moltke, in the Appendix.)

Sea-weed makes a hot though not a cheerful fire. It is largely used. The vraic or sea-weed gatherers of the Channel Islands are represented in many picturesque sketches. The weed is carted home, spread out, and dried.

Peat.—Travellers must bear in mind that peat will burn, especially as the countries in which it is found are commonly destitute of firewood; and, besides that, are marshy, cold, and aguish.

Charcoal is frequently carried by travellers in sacks; they use a prepared charcoal in the East, which is made in the form of very large buttons, that are carried strung together on a string. An Indian correspondent informs me that they are made by mixing powdered charcoal with molasses, in the proportion of ten to one, or thereabouts, rolling the mass into balls, and drying them in the sun. A single ball is called a "*gul.*" They are used for igniting *hookhas*: they are also burnt inside the smoothing-iron used by washermen in order to heat it. The juice or sap of many plants would probably answer the purpose of molasses in their preparation.

Small Fuel for lighting the Fire.—*Shreds and Fibres.*—The live spark has to be received, and partly enclosed, in a loose heap or nest of finely-shredded fuel. The substances for making such a nest, are one or other of the following list:—

Dry grass of the finest kinds; leaves; moss; lichen, and wild cotton; stalks or bark, broken up and rubbed small between the fingers; peat or cattle-dung pulverised; paper that has been doubled up in many folds and then cut with a sharp knife into the finest possible shavings; tow, or what is the same thing, oakum, made by unravelling rope or string; and scrapings and fine shavings from a log of wood. The shreds that are intended to touch the live spark should be reduced to the finest fibre; the outside of the nest may be of coarser, but still of somewhat delicate material.

Cook should collect them.— It is the duty of a cook, when the time of encamping draws near, to get down from his horse, and to pick up, as he walks along, a sufficiency of dry grass, little bits of wood, and the like, to start a fire; which he should begin to make as soon as ever the caravan stops. The fire ought to be burning, and the kettle standing by its side, by the time that the animals are caught and are ready to be off-packed.

Small Sticks.—There should be abundance of small sticks, and if neither these nor any equivalent for them are to be picked up, the traveller should split up his larger firewood with his knife, in order to make them. It is a wise economy of time and patience to prepare plenty of these; otherwise it will occasionally happen that the whole stock will be consumed and no fire made. Then the traveller must recommence the work from the very beginning, under the disadvantage of increasing darkness. I have made many experiments myself, and have seen many novices as well as old campaigners try to make fires; and have concluded that, to ensure success, the traveller should be provided with small bundles of sticks of each of the following sizes:—1st, size of lucifer-match; 2nd, of lead pencil; 3rd, smaller than little finger; 4th, size of fore-finger; 5th, stout stakes.

In wet Weather, the most likely places to find wherewithal to light a fire, are under large stones and other shelter; but in soaking wet weather, little chips of dry wood can hardly be procured except by cutting them with an axe out of the middle of a log. The fire may then be begun, as the late Admiral the Hon. C. Murray well recommended in his travels in North America, in the frying-pan itself, for want of a dry piece of ground.

To kindle a Spark into a Flame.—*By whirling.*—1st. Arrange the fuel into logs; into small fuel, assorted as described above, and into shreds and fibres. 2nd. Make a loose *nest* of the fibre, just like a sparrow's nest in shape and size, and let the finer part of the fibres be inwards. 3rd. Drop the lighted

tinder in the nest. 4th. Holding the "nest" quite loosely in the half-closed hand, whirl the outstretched arm in vertical circles round the shoulder-joint, as indicated by the dotted line in the diagram. In 30 seconds, or about 40 revolutions, it will begin to glow, and will shortly after burst out in a grand flame. 5th. Drop it, and pile small twigs round it, and nurse the young fire carefully, bearing in mind the proverb that "small sticks kindle a flame, but large ones put it out."

By blowing.—Savages usually kindle the flame by blowing at the live spark and feeding it with little bits of stick, just so much as is necessary. But it is difficult to acquire the art of doing this well, and I decidedly recommend the plan I have described in the foregoing paragraph, in preference to it. When the wind blows steadily and freshly, it suffices to hold up the "nest" against the wind.

Fire.

Sulphur matches are so very useful to convert a spark into a flame, and they are so easily made, in any quantity, out of split wood, straws, &c., if the traveller will only take the trouble of carrying a small lump of sulphur in his baggage, that they always ought to be at hand. The sulphur is melted on a heated stone, or in an old spoon, bit of crockery, bit of tin with a dent made in it, or even a piece of paper, and the points of the pieces of wood dipped in the molten mass. A small chip of sulphur pushed into the cleft end of a splinter of wood makes a fair substitute for a match. (See " Lucifer-matches.")

Camp Fires.—*Large Logs*.—The principle of making large logs to burn brightly, is to allow air to reach them on all sides, and yet to place them so closely together, that each supports the combustion of the rest. A common plan is to make the fire with three logs, whose ends cross each other, as in the diagram. The dots represent the extent of the fire. As the ends burn away, the logs are pushed closer together. Another plan is to lay the logs parallel with the burning ends to the windward, then they continue burning together.

In the pine-forests of the North, at winter time, it is usual to fell a large tree, and, cutting a piece six or eight feet long off the large end, to lay the thick short piece upon the long one, which is left lying on the ground; having previously cut flat with the axe the sides that come in contact, and notched them so as to make the upper log lie steady. The chips are then heaped in between the logs, and are set fire to; the flame runs in between them, and the heat of each log helps the other to burn. It is the work of nearly an hour to prepare such a fire; but when made, it lasts throughout the night. In all cases, one or two great logs are far better than many small ones, as these burn fast away and require constant looking after. Many serious accidents occur from a large log burning away and toppling over with a crash, sending a volley of blazing cinders among the sleeping party. Savages are always getting burnt, and we should take warning from their carelessness: sometimes they find a single scathed tree without branches, which they have no means of felling; this they set fire to as it stands, and when all have fallen off to sleep, the tree tumbles down upon them. Indeed, savages are seldom free from scars or severe burns; they are so cold during the night that they cannot endure to be an inch further from the fire than necessary, and consequently, as they turn about in their sleep, often roll into it.

Logs to cut up, with a small axe or knife.

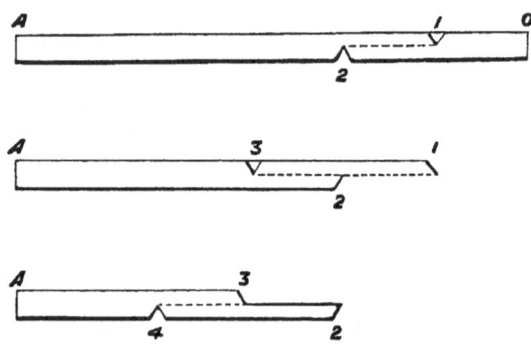

Let A O be the log. Cut two notches (1), (2), on opposite sides. Hold the log by the end A, and strike the end violently against the ground; the piece o, 1, 2, will fly off. Then make the cut (3) on the side opposite to (2), and again strike, and the piece 1, 2, 3, will fly off. So again with cut (4), &c. (Peal.)

Brushwood.—If in a country where only a number of small sticks and no large logs can be collected as firewood, the best plan is to encamp after the manner of the Ovampos. These, as they travel, collect sticks, each man his own faggot, and when they stop, each takes eight or nine stones as large as bricks, or larger, and sets them in a circle; and within these he lights up his little fire. Now the party make their fireplaces close together, in two or more parallel lines, and sleep in between them; the stones prevent the embers from flying about and doing mischief, and also, after the fires have quite burnt out, they continue to radiate heat.

Charcoal.—If charcoal be carried, a small chafing-dish, or other substitute for a fireplace, ought also to be taken, together with a set of tin cooking-utensils.

Fireplaces in Boats.—In boating excursions, daub a lump of clay on the bottom of the boat, beneath the fireplace—it will secure the timbers from fire. "Our primitive kitchen was a square wooden box, lined with clay and filled with sand, upon which three or four large stones were placed to form a hearth." (Burton's 'Medinah.')

Fireplaces on Snow.—On very deep snow, a hearth has to be made of a number of green logs, upon which the fire may be made. (See " Esquimaux Cooking Lamp.")

Cooking-fires.—See chapter on "Cooking."

Fires in the early Morning.—Should your stock of fuel consist of large logs and but little brushwood, keep all you can spare of the latter to make a blaze, when you get up to catch and pack the cattle in the dark and early morning. As you travel on, if it be bitter cold, carry a firebrand in your hand, near your mouth, as a respirator—it is very comforting; then, when the fire of it burns dull, thrust the brand for a few moments in any tuft of dry grass you may happen to pass by, which will blaze up and give a new life to the brand.

FOOD.

The nutritive Elements of Food.—Many chemists have applied themselves in recent years, to discover the exact percentage of nutriment contained in different substances, and to determine the minimum nutriment on which human life can be supported. The results are not very accordant, but nevertheless a considerable approximation to truth has been arrived at. It is now possible to tell whether a proposed diet has any great faults of excess or deficiency, and how to remedy those faults. But it also must be recollected that the stomach is an assimilating machine of limited performance, and must be fed with food that it can digest; it is not enough that the food should contain nutritious matter, if that matter should be in an indigestible form. Burke and Wills perished from sheer inability to digest the seeds upon which the Australian savages lived; and Gardiner's party died of starvation in Tierra del Fuego, because they could not digest the shell-fish which form a common article of diet of the natives of that country. The question of diet must then be limited to food that is perfectly digestible by the traveller. It remains to learn how much nourishment is contained in different kinds of digestible food. Dr. Smith has recently written an elaborate essay on this subject, applying his inquiries chiefly to the food of the poor in England; but for my more general purpose, as it is impossible to do justice to a large and imperfectly understood subject, in the small space I can give to it, it will be better that I should reprint the results given in my previous edition. These are principally extracted from a remarkable paper by Dr. Christison, inserted in the Bluebook Report of the Commission of Inquiry on Crimean matters, in which the then faulty dietary of our soldiers was discussed. It appears 1st, that a man of sedentary life can exist in health on seventeen ounces per day of *real nutriment*; that a man engaged in active life requires fully twenty-eight ounces per day; and, during severe labour, he requires thirty ounces, or even more. 2ndly, that this nutriment must consist of three-quarters, by weight, of one class of nutritive principles, (C), and one quarter of another class of nutritive principles, (N); 3rdly, that all the articles of common food admit of being placed, as below, in a Table, by which we see at a glance how much nutriment of class C, and how much of class N, is found in 100 parts, gross weight, of any of them. Thus, by a simple computation, the effective value of a dietary may be ascertained. Class C, are the carboniferous principles, that maintain respiration; Class N, are the nitrogenous principles, that repair waste of tissue. N will partly replace C, but at a great waste: C will not replace N.

A large number of diets such as those of various armies and navies, of prisons and infirmaries, and of the ordinary diets of different classes of people, have been examined by the

TABLE showing the quantity of Nutriment contained in different articles of Diet.

Articles of Diet.	C. (Carboniferous.)	N. (Nitrogenous.)	Total real Nutriment per cent. of gross weight.
Wheat Flour	71·25	16·25	87·5
Bread	51·5	10·5	62·0
Oatmeal	65·75	16·25	82·0
Pearl Barley	67·0	15·0	82·0
Peas	55·5	24·5	80·0
Potatoes (preserved potatoes are thoroughly dry)	24·5	2·5	27·0
Carrots	8·5	1·5	10·0
Turnips	5·7	0·3	6·0
Cabbage	6·7	0·3	7·0
Lean of Beef and Mutton		27·0	27·0
Fat of meat	100·0		100·0
Average Beef and Mutton	15·0	20·25	35·25
Bacon	62·5	8·36	70·86
Skimmed-milk Cheese	0·4	64·6	65·0
White Fish		21·0	21·0
New Milk	8·0	4·5	12·5
Skimmed Milk	5·5	4·5	10·0
Butter-milk	1·0	6·0	7·0
Beef Tea, strong		1·44	1·44
Beef Tea and Meat decoction of Broth		0·72	0·72
Sugar	100·0		100·0
Butter	100·0		100·0
Total Nutriment required. in Sedentary life	12·57	4·25	17 ounces.
in Active life	21·00	7·00	28 ,,
in Severe labour	22·50	7·50	30 ,,

aid of this Table, with surprisingly uniform results. But these diets chiefly refer to temperate climates; it would therefore be a matter of great interest if travellers in distant lands would accurately observe and note down the weight of their own rations and those of the natives. It is a great desideratum to know the lightest portable food suitable to different countries. Any such reports, if carefully made and extending over a period of not less than two months, would be very acceptable to me. To make them of any use, it is necessary that *every* article consumed should be noted down; and that the weight and state of health, at the beginning and at the end of the period, should be compared.

As examples of the way in which the above Tables should be applied, I will now give three dietaries, in which the quantity of real nutriment has been calculated.

I.—British Navy Allowances. (Admiralty Order, 1824.)

	Gross weight in ounces.		Real Nutriment.		
			C.	N.	Total.
Bread	20·0		10·3	2·1	12·4
or Biscuit		16·0	11·4	2·6	14·0
Oatmeal	1·5	1·5	1·96	0·48	2·44
Cocoa	1·0		0·5		0·5
or Cheese		2·0		1·33	1·33
Sugar	1·5		1·5		1·5
or Butter		1·5	1·5		1·5
Meat	16·0		2·4	3·24	5·64
or Salt Meat		12·0	2·4	3·24	5·64
Vegetables	8·0		0·9	0·15	1·05
or Flour		12·0	8·95	1·95	10·9
Tea	0·25				
or Coffee		1·0			
Total			41·81	15·09	57·0
Daily average			20·9	7·54	28·5

N.B.—Besides this, is beer (in harbour only) sixteen ounces, or spirits four ounces.

Table II. shows the daily food actually consumed by probably the most energetic travelling and exploring party on record. It was during Dr. Rae's spring journey to the Arctic shores of America. He issued, in addition, four ounces of grease or alcohol a day, as fuel for cooking. He found that it required nearly as much fuel to melt the snow, as it did to boil it afterwards. This allowance was found quite sufficient, but there was nothing to spare.

II.—Dr. Rae's Allowances in Arctic America.

	Gross Weight in ounces.	Real Nutriment.		
		C.	N.	Total.
Pemmican ($\frac{1}{3}$ dry meat, $\frac{2}{3}$ fat)	20·0	13·3	6·6	19·9
Biscuit	4·0	2·9	0·6	3·5
Edwards's preserved potatoes	1·6	1·4	0·1	1·5
Flour	5·3	3·8	0·8	4·6
Tea	0·6	?	?	?
Sugar	2·3	2·3		2·3
	33·8	23·7	8·1	31·8

III.—Mr. Austin's Allowances in Western Australia.

	Gross Weight in ounces.	Real Nutriment.		
		C.	N.	Total.
Flour	18·0	12·8	2·9	15·7
Boned salt pork (say a little more lean than fat)	8·0	1·9	2·1	4·0?
Sugar	3·0	3·0	..	3·0
Tea	0·75	..	..	..
	29·75	17·7	5·0	22·7

IV.—A Sepoy's Full Rations are :—

	Gross Weight in ounces.	Real Nutriment.		
		C.	N.	Total.
Wheaten Flour	32	22·8	5·2	29·0
Pulse	4	2·2	1·0	3·2
Butter	1	1·0	0·0	1·0
	37	26·0	6·2	33·3

Game was occasionally shot, by which the serious deficiency in Class N must have been supplied. At the same time, I must say that Australian explorers seem to travel exceedingly well on unusually scanty diets.

Food Suitable for the Stores of Travellers.—The most portable kind of food is, unquestionably, the flesh of cattle; for the beasts carry themselves. The draught oxen used in African and Australian explorations serve as a last resource, when all other food is wanting.

It has been truly remarked with reference to Australian exploring expeditions, that if an exploring party would make up their minds to eat horseflesh, stores of provisions might be largely dispensed with. A few extra horses could be taken; and one shot occasionally, and its flesh dried and slightly salted, sufficiently to preserve it from becoming tainted before the men could consume it.

Portable Food.—The kinds of food that are the most portable in the ordinary sense of the term are:—Pemmican; meat-biscuit; dried meat; dried fish; wheat flour; biscuit; oatmeal; barley; peas; cheese; sugar; preserved potatoes; and Chollet's compressed vegetables. Extract of meat, as I am assured by the highest physiological authors, is not a portable food but a portable savour. It is quite impossible that life should be maintained on any minute amount of material, because so many grains of carbon and so many of nitrogen are daily consumed, and an equivalent *weight* of those elements must, of course, be replaced. Salt meat is not to be depended upon, for it is liable to become hard and worthless, by long keeping.

Pemmican; general remarks.—Of all food usually carried on expeditions, none is so complete in itself, nor contains so large a proportion of nutriment as pemmican. It is especially useful to those who undergo severe work, in cold and rainy climates. It is the mainstay of Arctic expeditions, whether on water, by sledge, or on foot. But, though excellent to men who are working laboriously, it is distasteful to others.

Pemmican is a mixture of about five-ninths of pounded dry meat to four-ninths of melted or boiled grease; it is put into a skin bag or tin can whilst warm and soft. The grease ought not to be very warm, when poured on the dry meat. Wild berries are sometimes added. The skin bags for the pemmican should be shaped like pillow (not bolster) cases, for the convenience of packing on horseback. The pemmican is chopped out with an axe, when required.

I do not know if it can be bought anywhere in England. It was usually prepared in the government yards at Deptford, when made for the Arctic Expeditions. It is largely used in the Hudson's Bay territory. A traveller who desired to furnish himself with pemmican might procure his supplies from thence.

Pemmican, as made in England.—Sir John Richardson describes, in his Narrative, the preparation of the pemmican that he took with him in his last journey. The following is a *résumé* of what he says:—The meat used was round of beef; the fat and membranous parts were pared away; it was then cut into thin slices, which were dried in a malt-kiln, over an oak-wood fire, till they were quite dry and friable. Then they were ground in a malt-mill; after this process the powder resembled finely-grated meal. It was next mixed with nearly an equal weight of melted beef, suet, or lard; and the plain pemmican was made. Part of the pemmican was mixed with Zante currants, and another part with sugar. Both of these mixtures were much liked, especially the latter. The pemmican, when complete, cost at the rate of 1s. 7½d. per pound, but then the meat was only 6¾d. per pound; it is dearer now. The meat lost more than three-quarters of its weight in drying. He had 17,424 lbs. of pemmican in all; it was made from—fresh beef, 35,641 lbs.; lard, 7549 lbs.; currants, 1008 lbs.; and sugar, 280 lbs.

Pemmican, as made in the Prairie.—Mr. Ballantyne, who was in the service of the Hudson's Bay Company, gives the following account:—" Having shot a buffalo, the hunters cut lumps of his flesh, and slitting it up into flakes or layers, hang it up in the sun, or before a slow fire, to dry; *and the fat can be dried as well as the lean.* In this state, it is often made into packs, and sent about the country, to be consumed as dried meat (it is often best relished raw, for, when grilled without fat, it burns and becomes ashy); but when pemmican is wanted, it has to go through another process. When dry, the meat is pounded between two stones till it is broken into small pieces: these are put into a bag made of the animal's hide, with the hair on the outside, and well mixed with melted grease; the top of the bag is then sewn up, and the pemmican allowed to cool. In this state it may be eaten uncooked; but the men who subsist on it when travelling, mix it with a little flour and water, and then boil it—in which state it is known throughout the country by the elegant name of *robbiboo*. Pemmican is good wholesome food; will keep fresh for a great length of time; and, were it not for its unprepossessing appearance, and a good many buffalo hairs mixed with it, through the carelessness of the hunters, would be very palatable. After a time, however, one becomes accustomed to these little peculiarities."

Meat-biscuit.—Meat-biscuit, which is used in American ships, is stated to be a thick soup, evaporated down to a syrup, kneaded with flour, and made into biscuits: these are pricked with holes, dried and baked. They can be eaten just as they are, or made into a porridge, with from twenty to thirty times their weight of water. They were to be bought at Gamble's, 137, Leadenhall Street.

Dried Meat.—When more game is shot than can be eaten before the party travel onwards, it is usual to jerk a part of it. It is cut in long strips, and festooned about the bushes, under the full sun, in order to dry it. After it has been sun-dried it will keep for long, before it becomes wholly putrid. Dried meat is a poor substitute for fresh meat; it requires long steeping in water, to make it tender, and then it is tasteless, and comparatively innutritious. "Four expert men slice up a full-grown buffalo in four hours and a-half." (Leichhardt.) The American buccaneers acquired their name from *boucan*—which means jerked meat, in an Indian dialect; for they provisioned their ships with the dried flesh of the wild cattle that they hunted down and killed.

Dried Fish.—Fish may be pounded entire, just as they come from the river, dried in the sun in large lumps, and kept: the negroes about the Niger do this.

Flour travels conveniently in strong canvas bags, each holding 50 lbs., and long enough to be lashed on to a pack-saddle. (See "Pack-bags," p. 71.)

Chollet's preserved Vegetables relieve agreeably the monotony of a bush diet. A single ration weighs less than an ounce, and a cubic yard contains 16,000 of these rations. They are now to be bought at all provision merchants'—as at Fortnum and Mason's, &c.

Salted Meat.—I have already said (see "Portable Food") that salt meat cannot be depended upon to retain its nutritious qualities for a length of time. When freshly made, it is sure to be good. It is well to recollect that, for want of a salting-tub, animals can be salted in their own hide. A hollow is scraped in the ground, the hide is laid over it and pegged down, and the meat, salt, and water put into it. I know of an instance where this was done on a very large scale.

Condiments.—The most portable and useful condiments for a traveller are—salt, red pepper, Harvey's sauce, lime-juice, dried onions, and curry-powder. They should be bought at a first-rate shop; for red pepper, lime-juice, and curry-powder are often atrociously adulterated.

Salt.—The craving for salt (chloride of sodium) is somewhat satisfied by the potash salts, and, perhaps, by other minerals: thus we often hear of people reduced to the mixing of gunpowder with their food, on account of the saltpetre that it contains. An impure salt is made widely in North Africa, from wood-ashes. They are put into a pot, hot water is poured over them and allowed to stand and dissolve out the salts they contain; the ley is then decanted into another pot, where it is evaporated. The plants in use, are those of which the wetted ashes have a saline and not an alkaline taste, nor a soapy feel. As a general rule, trees that make good soap (p. 122), yield little saltpetre or other good equivalent for salt. Salt caravans are the chief sustainers of the lines of commerce in North Africa. In countries where salt is never used, as I myself have witnessed in South Africa, and among the Mandan North-American Indian tribes (Catlin, vol. i. p. 124), the soil and springs are "brack." Four Russian sailors who were wrecked on Spitzbergen, and whose well-known adventures are to be found in Pinkerton's 'Voyages and Travels,' had nothing whatever for six years to subsist on—save only the animals they killed, a little moss, and melted snow-water. One of them died; the others enjoyed robust health. People who eat nothing but meat, feel the craving for salt far less strongly than those who live wholly on vegetables.

Butcher.—One man in every party should have learnt from a professed butcher, how to cut up a carcase to the best advantage.

Store-keeping.—All stores should be packed and securely lashed, that it may be impossible to pilfer from them. The packages of those that are in use, should be carried in one pair of saddle-bags, to be devoted to that purpose. These should stand at the storekeeper's bivouac, and nobody else should be allowed to touch them, when there. He should have every facility for weighing and measuring. Lastly, it should be his duty to furnish a weekly account, specifying what stores remain in hand.

Wholesome Food, procurable in the Bush.—*Game and Fish.*—See sections upon "Hints on Shooting;" "Other means of capturing Game;" and upon "Fishing;" and note the paragraph on "Nocturnal Animals."

Milk, to keep.—Put it in a bottle, and place it in a pot of water, over a slow fire, till the water boils; let the bottle remain half an hour in the boiling water, and then cork it tightly. Milk with one's tea is a great luxury; it is worth taking some pains to keep it fresh. A traveller is generally glutted with milk when near native encampments, and at other times has none at all. Milk dried into cakes, intended to be grated into boiling water for use, was formerly procurable: it was very good; but I cannot hear of it now in the shops. Milk preserved in tins is excellent, but it is too bulky for the convenience of most travellers. Dried breadcrumb, mixed with fresh cream, is said to make a cake that will keep for some days. I have not succeeded, to my satisfaction, with this recipe.

Butter, to preserve.—Boil it in a large vessel till the scum rises. Skim this off as fast as it appears on the surface, until the butter remains quite clear, like oil. It should then be carefully poured off, that the impurities which settle at the bottom of the vessel may be separated. The clarified butter is to be put aside to be kept, the settlings must be used for common and immediate purposes. Butter is churned, in many countries, by twirling a forked stick, held between the two hands, in a vessel full of cream; or even by shaking the cream in a bottle. It is said that the temperature of the milk, while it is being churned, should be between 50° and 60° Fahr., and that this is all-important to success.

Cheese.—"The separation of the whey from the cheese may be effected by rennet, or by bitartrate of potash, or tamarinds, or alum, or various acids and acid wines and fruit juices." (Dr. Weber.)

Eggs may be dried at a gentle heat; then pounded and

preserved. This is a convenient plan of making a store of portable food out of the eggs of sea-birds, or those of ostriches.

Fish-roe is another kind of portable food. The chemists declare its composition to be nearly identical with that of ordinary eggs. (Pereira.) Caviare is made out of any kind of fish-roe; but the *recherché* sort, only from that of the sturgeon. Long narrow bags of strong linen, and a strong brine, are prepared. The bags are half-filled with the roe, and are then quite filled with the brine, which is allowed to ooze through slowly. This being done, the men wring the bags strongly with their hands, and the roe is allowed to dry. Roe-broth is a good dish.

Honey, to find, when Bees are seen.—Dredge as many bees as you can, with flour from a pepper-box; or else catch one of them, tie a feather or a straw to his leg, which can easily be done (natives thrust it up into his body), throw him into the air, and follow him as he flies slowly to his hive; or catch two bees, and turning them loose at some distance apart, search the place towards which their flights converge. But if bees are too scarce for either of these methods, choose an open place, and lay in it a plate of syrup as a bait for the bees; after one has fed and flown away again, remove the plate 200 yards in the direction in which he flew; and proceed in the same sort of way, until the nest is found.

Honey-bird.—The instinct of the honey-bird is well-known, which induces him to lead men to hives, that he may share in the plunder. The stories that are told of the apparent malice of the bird, in sometimes tricking a man, and leading him to the lair of wild animals, instead of to the bees' nest, are well authenticated.

Revolting Food, that may save the Lives of Starving Men.— *Suspicion of Poison.*—If any meat that you may find, or if the water of any pool at which you encamp, is under suspicion of being poisoned, let one of your dogs eat or drink before you do, and wait an hour to watch the effects of it upon him.

Carrion is not noxious to Starving Men.—In reading the accounts of travellers who have suffered severely from want of food, a striking fact is common to all, namely, that, under those circumstances, carrion and garbage of every kind can be eaten without the stomach rejecting it. Life can certainly be maintained on a revolting diet, that would cause a dangerous illness to a man who was not compelled to adopt it by the pangs of hunger. There is, moreover, a great difference in the power that different people possess of eating rank food without being made ill by it. It appears that no flesh, and very few fish, are poisonous to man; but vegetables are frequently poisonous.

Dead Animals, to find.—The converging flight of crows, and gorged vultures sitting on trees, show where dead game is lying; but it is often very difficult to find the carcase; for animals usually crawl under some bush or other hiding-place, to die. Jackal-tracks, &c., are often the only guide. It may be advisable, after an unsuccessful search, to remove to some distance, and watch patiently throughout the day, until the birds return to their food, and mark them down.

Rank Birds.—When rank birds are shot, they should be skinned, not plucked; for much of the rankness lies in their skin; or, if unskinned, they should be buried for some hours, because earth absorbs the oil that makes them rank. Their breast and wings are the least objectionable parts, and, if there be abundance of food, should alone be cooked. Rank sea-birds, when caught, put in a coop, and fed with corn, were found by Captain Bligh to become fat and well-tasted.

Skins.—All old hides or skins of any kind that are not tanned are fit and good for food; they improve soup by being mixed with it; or they may be toasted and hammered. Long boiling would make glue or gelatine of them. Many a hungry person has cooked and eaten his sandals or skin clothing.

Bones contain a great deal of nourishment, which is got at by boiling them, pounding their ends between two stones, and sucking them. There is a revolting account in French history, of a besieged garrison of Sancerre, in the time of Charles IX., and again subsequently at Paris, and it may be elsewhere, digging up the graveyards for bones as sustenance.

Blood from Live Animals.—The Aliab tribe, who have great herds of cattle on the White Nile, "not only milk their cows, but they bleed their cattle periodically, and boil the blood for food. Driving a lance into a vein in the neck, they bleed the animal copiously, which operation is repeated about once a month." (Sir S. Baker.)

Flesh from Live Animals.—The truth of Bruce's well-known tale of the Abyssinians and others occasionally slicing out a piece of a live ox for food is sufficiently confirmed. Thus Dr. Beke observes, "There could be no doubt of the fact. He had questioned hundreds of natives on the subject, and though at first they positively declared the statement to be a lie, many, on being more closely questioned, admitted the possibility of its truth, for they could not deny that cattle are frequently attacked by hyænas, whose practice is to leap on the animals from behind and at once begin devouring the hind quarters; and yet, if driven off in time, the cattle have still lived."—*Times*, Jan. 16, 1867.

It is reasonable enough that a small worn-out party should adopt this plan, when they are travelling in a desert where the absence of water makes it impossible to delay, and when they are sinking for want of food. If the ox were killed outright there would be material for one meal only, because a worn-out party would be incapable of carrying a load of flesh. By the Abyssinian plan the wounded beast continues to travel with the party, carrying his carcase that is destined to be turned into butcher's meat for their use at a further stage. Of course the idea is very revolting, for the animal must suffer as much as the average of the tens or hundreds of wounded hares and pheasants that are always left among the bushes after an ordinary English battue. To be sure, the Abyssinian plan should only be adopted to save human life.

When I travelled in South-West Africa, at one part of my journey a plague of bush-ticks attacked the roots of my oxen's tails. Their bites made festering sores, which ended in some of the tails dropping bodily off. I heard such accidents were not at all uncommon. The animals did not travel the worse for it. Now ox-tail soup is proverbially nutritious.

Insects.—Most kinds of creeping things are eatable, and are used by the Chinese. Locusts and grasshoppers are not at all bad. To prepare them, pull off the legs and wings and roast them with a little grease in an iron dish, like coffee. Even the gnats that swarm on the Shiré River are collected by the natives and pressed into cakes.

Wholesome and Poisonous Plants.—No certain rule can be given to distinguish wholesome plants from poisonous ones; but it has been observed that much the same thing suits the digestion of a bird that suits that of a man; and, therefore, that a traveller, who otherwise would make trials at haphazard, ought to examine the contents of those birds' crops that he may catch or shoot, to give a clue to his experiments. The rule has notable exceptions, but in the absence of any other guide it is a very useful one.

The only general rules that botany can give are vague and full of exceptions: they are, that a great many wholesome plants are found among the *Cruciferæ*, or those whose petals are arranged like a Maltese cross, and that many poisonous ones are found amongst the *Umbelliferæ*.

Nettle and Fern.—There are two moderately nutritious plants—nettle and fern—that are found wild in very many countries: and, therefore, the following extract from Messrs. Huc and Gabet's 'Travels in Thibet' may be of service:—
" When the young stems of ferns are gathered, quite tender, before they are covered with down, and while the first leaves are bent and rolled up in themselves, you have only to boil them in pure water to realise a dish of delicious asparagus. We would also recommend the nettle, which, in our opinion, might be made an advantageous substitute for spinach; indeed more than once we proved this by our own experience. The nettle should be gathered quite young, when the leaves are perfectly tender. The plant should be pulled up whole, with a portion of the root. In order to preserve your hands from the sharp biting liquid which issues from the points, you should wrap them in linen of close texture. When once the nettle is boiled, it is perfectly innocuous; and this vegetable, so rough in its exterior, becomes a very delicate dish. We were able to enjoy this delightful variety of esculents for more than a month. Then the little tubercles of the fern became hollow and horny, and the stems themselves grew as hard as wood while the nettle, armed with a long white beard,

presented only a menacing and awful aspect." The roots of many kinds of ferns, perhaps of all of them, are edible. Our poor in England will eat neither fern nor nettle: they say the first is innutritious, and the second acrid. I like them both.

Seaweed.—Several kinds of seaweed, such as Laver and Irish moss, are eatable.

Cooking Utensils.—*Cookery books.*—A book on cooking is of no use at all in the rougher kinds of travel, for all its recipes consist of phrases such as "Take a pound of so-and-so, half a pound of something else, a pinch of this, and a handful of that." Now in the bush a man has probably none of these things— he certainly has not all of them—and, therefore, the recipe is worthless.

Pots and Kettles.—Cooking apparatus of any degree of complexity, and of very portable shapes, can be bought at all military outfitters'; but for the bush, and travelling roughly, nothing is better than a light roomy iron pot and a large strong tin kettle. It is disagreeable to make tea in the same pot that meat is boiled in; besides, if you have only one vessel, it takes a longer time to prepare meals. If possible, take a second small tin kettle, both as a reserve against accidents and for the convenience of the thing. An iron pot, whose lid is the size of the crown of a hat, cooks amply enough for three persons at a time, and can, without much inconvenience, be made to do double duty; and, therefore, the above articles would do for six men. An iron pot should have very short legs, or some blow will break one of them off and leave a hole. Iron kettles far outwear tin ones, but the comparative difficulty of making them boil, and their great weight, are very objectionable. A good tin kettle, carefully cherished (and it is the interest of the whole party to watch over its safety), lasts many months in the bush. Copper is dangerous; but the recipe is given, further on, for tinning copper vessels when they require it. Have the handle of the kettle notched or bored near the place where it joins the body of the kettle, so as to give a holding by which the lid may be tied tightly down; then, if you stuff a wisp of grass into the spout, the kettle will carry water for a journey.

Damaged Pots.—A pot or kettle with a large hole in its

bottom, filled up with a piece of wood, has been made to boil water by burying it a little way in the earth and making the fire round it. A hole in the side of a pot can be botched up with clay or wood, so as not to leave it altogether useless.

Substitutes for Pots and Kettles.—It is possible to boil water over a slow fire in many kinds of vessels that would be destroyed by a greater degree of heat. In bark, wooden, skin, and even paper vessels, it is quite possible to boil water. The ruder tribes of the Indian Archipelago use a bamboo to boil their rice: "The green cane resisting the fire sufficiently long for the cooking of one mass of rice." (Crawfurd.) If, however, you have no vessel that you choose to expose to the risk of burning, you must heat stones and drop them into the water it contains; but sandstones, especially, are apt to shiver and make grit. The Dacota Indians, and very probably other tribes also, used to boil animals in their own hide. The description runs thus: "They stuck four stakes in the ground, and tied the four corners of the hide up to them, leaving a hollow in the middle; three or four gallons of water, and the meat cut up very fine, were then put in; three or four hot stones, each the size of a 6-lb. cannon-shot, cooked the whole into a good soup." To a fastidious palate, the soot, dirt, and ashes that are usually mixed up with the soup, are objectionable; but these may be avoided by a careful cook, who dusts and wipes the stones before dropping them in. The specific heat of stone is much less than that of water, so that the heating power of a measure of stone is only about one-half of that of an equal measure of equally hot water.

Graters are wanted to grate jerked meat. A piece of tin, punched through with holes, then bent a little, and nailed to a piece of wood, makes a good one.

Sieves.—Stretch parchment (*which see*) on a wooden hoop, exactly as on a drum-head; let it dry, and prick it with a red-hot iron, else punch it full of small holes.

Plates, to carry.—I have travelled much with plates, knives, forks, &c., for three persons, carried in a flat leather case like a portfolio, which hung from the side of the cook's saddle, and I found it very convenient. It was simply a square piece of leather, with a large pocket for the metal plates, and other smaller ones for the rest of the things; it had a flap to tie over it, which was kept down with a button.

Cups.—Each of the men, on a riding expedition, should carry his own tin mug, either tied to his waist or to his saddle. A wooden bowl is the best vessel for tea, and even for soup, if you have means of frequently washing it: tin mugs burn the lips too much. Wooden bowls are always used in Thibet; they are cut out of the knots that are found in timber.

Spoons.—It is easy to replace a lost spoon by cutting a new one out of hard wood, or by making one of horn. (See "Horn.")

Fireplaces for Cooking.—The most elementary fireplace consists of three stones in a triangle, to support the pot. If stones are not procurable, three piles of mud, or three stakes of green-wood driven into the earth, are an equivalent. Small recesses neatly cut in a bank, one for each fireplace, are much used, when the fuel is dry and well prepared.

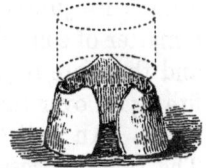

A more elaborate plan is to excavate a shallow saucer-like hole in the ground, a foot or eighteen inches in diameter, and kneading the soil so excavated into a circular wall, with a doorway in the windward side: the upper surface is curved, so as to leave three pointed turrets, upon which the cooking-vessel rests, as in the sketch. Thus the wind enters at the doorway, and the flames issue through the curved depressions at the top, and lick round the cooking-vessel placed above. The wall is sometimes built of stones.

Trenches and Holes.—In cooking for a large party with a small supply of fuel, either dig a narrow trench, above which all the pots and kettles may stand in a row, and in which the fire is made,—the mouth being open to the wind, and a small chimney built at the other end;—or else dig a round hole, one foot deep, and place the pots in a ring on its edge, half resting on the earth, and half overlapping the hole. A space will remain in the middle of them, and through this the fire must be fed.

Esquimaux Lamp.—The cooking of the Esquimaux is wholly

effected by stone lamps, with wicks made of moss, which are so carefully arranged that the flame gives little or no smoke. Their lamps vary in size from one foot and a half long to six inches. Each of the bits of moss gives a small but very bright flame. This lamp is all in all to the Esquimaux; it dries their clothes, and melts the snow for their drinking-water; its construction is very ingenious; without it they could not have inhabited the Arctic regions.

Ovens.—*Bedouin Oven.*—Dig a hole in the ground; wall and roof it with stones, leaving small apertures in the top. Then make a roaring fire in and about the oven (the roof having been temporarily removed for the purpose), and when the stones (including those of the roof) have become very hot, sweep away the ashes and strew the inside of the oven with grass, or leaves, taking care that whatever is used, has no disagreeable taste, else it would be communicated to the flesh. Then put in the meat: it is a common plan to sew it up in its own skin, which shields it from dust and at the same time retains its juices from evaporating. Now replace the roof, a matter of some difficulty, on account of the stones being hot, and therefore requiring previous rehearsal. Lastly, rake the fire again over the oven and let the baking continue for some hours. An entire sheep can be baked easily in this way. The same process is used for baking vegetables, except with the addition of pouring occasionally boiling water upon them, through the roof.

Gold-digger's Oven.—The figure represents a section of the oven. A hole or deep notch is dug into the side of a bank,

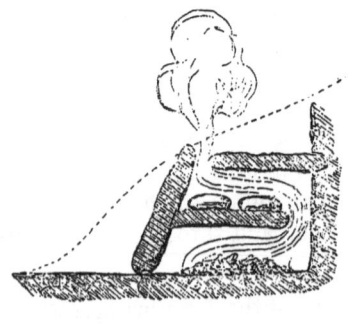

and two flat stones are slid horizontally, like shelves, into grooves made in the sides of the hole, as shown in the figure; where it will be observed that the uppermost stone does not quite reach to the face of the bank, and that the lowermost stone does not quite reach to the back of the hole. A fire of red-hot embers is placed on the floor of the hole; and the bread about to be baked is laid upon the lowermost stone. Lastly, another flat stone is used to close the mouth of the oven: it is set with its edge on the floor of the hole: it leans forward with the middle of its face resting against the front edge of the lowermost stone, a narrow interval being left between its top and the edge of the uppermost stone. This interval serves as a vent to the hot air from the embers, which takes the course shown in the figure. The oven should be thoroughly heated before the bread is put in.

Baking between two stones.—For baking slices of meat or thin cakes, it is sufficient to lay one large stone above another with a few pebbles between, to prevent them from touching. Next make a large fire about the stones until they are thoroughly hot; then sweep away the embers, and insert the slices.

Ant hills as Ovens.—Where there are no stones of which ovens may be built, and where there are old white-ant hills, the natives commonly dig holes in the sides of the ant hills and use them for that purpose.

Clay Ovens.—I have heard of a very neat construction, built with clay, in which grass had been kneaded. A fire was lit inside, to dry the work as it progressed; while the builder placed rings of clay, in tiers, one above the other, until a complete dome was made without mould or framework. Time was allowed for each ring to dry sufficiently, before the next one was added.

Baking beneath a camp fire.—A small piece of meat, enough for four or five people, can be baked by simply scraping a tolerably deep hole under the bivouac fire; putting in the meat rolled in the skin to which it is attached, and covering it with earth and fire. It is a slow process of cooking, for it requires many hours; but the meat, when done, is soft and juicy, and the skin gelatinous and excellent.

"Meat, previously wrapped up in paper or cloth, may be baked in a clay case, in any sort of pit or oven, well covered over, and with good economy." ('Handbook of Field Service.')

Baking in Pots.—A capital oven is improvised by means of two earthen or metal cooking-pots, of which one is placed on the fire, and in it the article to be baked; the other pot is put upon its top, as a cover, and in it a shovelful of red-hot embers.

Bush Cookery.—*Tough Meat.*—Hammer it well between two stones before putting it on the fire, and again when it is half cooked, to separate the fibres. I have often seen people save themselves much painful mastication, by hammering at each separate piece of meat, before putting it in their mouths.

Rank Meat.—I have spoken of this in another section, p. 200.

Kabobs.—Broil the rib-bones, or skewer your iron ramrod through a dozen small lumps of meat and roast them. This is the promptest way of cooking meat; but men on hard work are not satisfied with a diet of nothing else but tough roasted flesh, they crave for succulent food, such as boiled or baked meat.

Salt Meat, to prepare hurriedly.—Warm it slightly on both sides—this makes the salt draw to the outside—then rinse it well in a pannikin of water. This process extracts a large part of the salt, and leaves the meat more fit for cooking.

Haggis.—Hearne, the North American traveller, recommends a "haggis made with blood, a good quantity of fat shred small, some of the tenderest of the flesh, together with the heart and lungs, cut or torn into small skivers; all of which is put into the stomach, and roasted by being suspended before the fire with a string. Care must be taken that it does not get too much heat at first, or it will burst. It is a most delicious morsel, even without pepper, salt, or any seasoning."

Theory of Tea-making.—I have made a number of experiments on the art of making good tea. We constantly hear that some people are good and others bad tea-makers; that it takes a long time to understand the behaviour of a new teapot, and so forth; and, lastly, that good tea cannot be made except with boiling water. Now, this latter assertion is assuredly untrue, because, if tea be actually boiled in water, an emetic and partly poisonous drink is the certain result. I had a tin lid made to my teapot, a short tube passed through the lid, and in the tube was a cork, through a hole in which a thermometer was fitted, that enabled me to learn the temperature of the water in the teapot, at each moment. Thus provided, I continued to make my tea as usual, and to note down what I observed. In the first place, after warming the teapot in the ordinary way, the fresh boiling water that was poured into it, sank invariably to under 200° Fahr. It was usually 180°, so great was the amount of heat abstracted by the teapot. I also found that my teapot—it was a crockery one—allowed the water within it to cool down at the rate of about 2° per minute. When the pot was filled afresh, of course the temperature of its contents rose afresh, and by the addition of water two or three times repeated, I obtained a perfect mastery over the temperature of the pot, within reasonable limits. Now, after numerous days in which I made tea according to my usual method, but measuring strictly the quantity of leaves, and recording the times and the temperature, and noting the character of tea produced; then, taking as my type of excellence, tea that was full bodied, full tasted, and in no way bitter or flat, I found that this was only produced when the water in the teapot had remained between 180° and 190° Fahr., and had stood eight minutes on the leaves. It was only necessary for me to add water *once* to the tea, to ensure this temperature. Bitterness was the certain result of greater heat or of longer standing, and flatness was the result of colder water. If the tea did not stand for so long a time as eight minutes, it was not ripe; it was not full bodied enough. The palate becomes far less fastidious about the quality of the second cup. Other people may like tea of a different character from that which I do myself; but, be that as it may, all people can, I maintain, ensure uniformity of good tea, such as they best like, by attending to the principle of making it,—that is to say, to time, and quantities, and temperature. There is no other mystery in the teapot.

Tea made in the kettle.—Where there are no cups or teapot put the leaves in the pot or kettle, and drink through a reed with a wisp of grass in it, as they do in Paraguay. If there are cups and no teapot, the leaves may be put into the pot, previously enclosed in a loose gauze or muslin bag to prevent their floating about. A contrivance is sold in the shops for this purpose; it is made of metal gauze, and shaped like an egg. A purse made of metal rings would be better, for it would pack flat; but the advantage of muslin over metal apparatus is that you may throw away bag and all, and avoid the trouble of cleaning.

Tea made in tin mugs.—A correspondent assures me that he considers the Australian plan of making tea to be preferable to any other, for travellers and explorers; as it secures that the tea shall be made both well and quickly, and without the necessity of carrying kettles on horseback. Each person has

a common tin quart pot and a pint pot, slung to his saddle; the tea and sugar are carried in small bags. The quart pot requires very little fire to make it boil. When it begins to boil, it is taken from the fire, the tea is dropped in, and the pint pot is placed on its top as a cover. When the tea is ready, the sugar is dropped into the pint, and the tea is poured from one pot to the other till it is mixed. The pint is always kept clean for drinking out of, but not the quart, for the blacker it is, the sooner will the water boil.

Tea made over night.—To prepare tea for a very early breakfast, make it over night, and pour it away from the tea-leaves, into another vessel. It will keep perfectly well, for it is by long standing with the tea-leaves that it becomes bitter. In the morning, simply warm it up. Tea is drunk at a temperature of 140° Fahr., or 90° above an average night temperature of 50°. It is more than twice as easy to raise the temperature up to 140° than to 212°, letting alone the trouble of tea-making.

Extract of Tea and Coffee.—Dr. Rae speaks very highly of the convenience of extract of tea. Any scientific chemist could make it, but he should be begged to use first-rate tea. The extract from first-rate tea makes a very drinkable infusion, but that from second-rate tea is not good, the drink made from the extract being always a grade inferior to that made directly from the leaves. By pouring a small quantity of the extract into warm water, the tea is made; and, though inferior in taste to properly made tea, it has an equally good effect on the digestion.

Extract of coffee is well known. I believe it can be made of very good quality, but what is usually sold seems to me to be very much the contrary and not to be wholesome.

Tea and Coffee, without hot water.—In Unyoro, Sir S. Baker says, they have no idea of using coffee as a drink, but simply chew it raw as a stimulant. In Chinese Tartary, travellers who have no means of making a cup of tea, will chew the leaves as a substitute. Mr. Atkinson told me how very grateful he had found this makeshift.

WATER FOR DRINKING.

General Remarks.—In most of those countries where travelling is arduous, it is the daily care of an explorer to obtain water, for his own use and for that of his caravan. Should he be travelling in regions that are for the most part arid and rarely visited by showers, he must look for his supplies in ponds made by the drainage of a large extent of country, or in those left here and there along the beds of partly dried-up water-courses, or in fountains. If he be unsuccessful in his search, or when the dry season of the year has advanced, and all water has disappeared from the surface of the land, there remains no alternative for him but to dig wells where there are marks to show that pools formerly lay, or where there are other signs that well-water may be obtained.

Short Stages.—I may here remark that it is a good general rule for an explorer of an arid country, when he happens to come to water, after not less than three hours' travelling, to stop and encamp by it; it is better for him to avail himself of his good fortune and be content with his day's work, than to risk the uncertainty of another supply.

Purity of Watering-places.—Make no litter by the side of watering-places; and encourage among your party the Mahomedan feeling of respect for preserving the purity of drinking-water. Old travellers commonly encamp at a distance from the watering-place, and fetch the water to their camp.

Signs of the Neighbourhood of Water.—The quick intelligence with which experienced travellers discover watering-places, is so great that it might almost be mistaken for an instinct.

Intelligence of Dogs and Cattle.—Dogs are particularly clever in finding water, and the fact of a dog looking refreshed, and it may be wet, has often and often drawn attention to a pond that would otherwise have been overlooked and passed by. Cattle are very uncertain in their intelligence. Sometimes oxen go for miles and miles across a country unknown to them, straight to a pond of water; at other times they are most obtuse: Dr. Leichhardt, the Australian traveller, was quite astonished at their stupidity in this respect.

Trees and ordinary vegetation are not of much help in directing a traveller to water, for they thrive on dew or on occasional rain; but it is otherwise when the vegetation is unusually green or luxuriant, or when those trees are remarked, that are seldom seen to grow except near water in the particular country visited, as the blackthorn-tree in South Africa.

Birds.—Some species of birds (as water-fowl, parrots, and the diamond bird) or animals (as baboons) afford surer promise; but the converging flight of birds, or the converging fresh tracks of animals, is the most satisfactory sign of all. It is about nightfall that desert birds usually drink, and hence it often happens that the exhausted traveller, abandoning all hope as the shades of evening close in, has his attention arrested by flights of birds, that give him new life and tell him where to go.

Tracks.—In tropical countries that have rainy and dry seasons, it must be recollected that old paths of men or wild animals only mislead; they go to dry ponds that were full at the time they were trodden, but have since been abandoned on becoming exhausted.

Other Signs.—Well-water may be sought where the earth is still moist, though arid all around; or, failing that, where birds and wild animals have lately been scratching, or where gnats hover in swarms.

To find the Spring.—From the number of birds, tracks, and other signs, travellers are often pretty sure that they are near water, but cannot find the spring itself. In this case the party should at once be spread out as skirmishers, and the dogs cheered on.

To probe for Well-water.—It is usual, when no damp earth can be seen, but where the place appears likely to yield well-water, to force an iron ramrod deep into the soil; and, if it bring up any grains that are moist, to dig.

Pools of Water.—For many days after there has been rain, water is sure to be found among mountains, however desert may be their appearance; for not only does more wet fall upon them, but the drainage is more perfect; long after the ravines and stream-beds are quite dry, puddles and cupfuls of water will be found here and there, along their courses, in holes and chinks and under great stones, which together form a sufficiency. A sponge tied to the end of a stick will do good service in lapping these up.

The sandy Beds of Watercourses in arid countries frequently contain pools of stagnant water; but the places where these pools are to be found are not necessarily those where they have been found in preceding years. The conditions necessary for the existence of a pool are not alone those of the rocky substratum of the river-bed, but, more especially, the stratifications of mud and clay left after each flooding. For instance, an extensive bed of sand, enclosed between two layers of clay, would remain moist, and supply well-water during the dry season; but a trivial variation in the force and amount of the current, in different years, might materially affect the place and the character of the deposition of these clay strata.

In searching the beds of partly dried-up watercourses, the fact must never be forgotten, that it is especially in little tributaries at the point where they fall into the main one, that most water is to be found; and the most insignificant of these should never be overlooked. I presume that the bar, which always accumulates in front of tributaries, and is formed of numerous layers of alluvial deposit, parallel to the bed of the great stream, is very likely to have one, at least, of its layers of an impervious character. If so, the bar would shut in the wet sand of the tributary, like a wall, and prevent it from draining itself dry.

When a river-bed has been long followed by a traveller, and a frequent supply of water found along it, in pools or even in wells, say at every 5 or 10 miles—then, should this river-bed appear to lose itself in a plain that is arid, there is no reason why the traveller should be disheartened; for, on travelling further, the water will be sure to be found again, those plains being always green and grassy where the water in such river-beds entirely disappears.

By Sea-shore.—Fresh water is frequently to be found under the very sands of the sea-shore, whither it has oozed underground from the upper country, and where it overlies the denser salt water; or else abuts against it, if the compactness of the sand resists free percolation. In very many places along the skirt of the great African desert, fresh water is to be found by digging two or three feet.

Fountains.—Fountains in arid lands are as godsends. They are far more numerous and abundant in limestone districts than in any others, owing to the frequent fissures of those rocks: therefore, whenever limestone crops out in the midst of sand deserts, a careful search should be made for water. In granite, and other primary rocks, many, but small springs, are usually seen.

The theory of ordinary fountains is simple enough, and affords help in discovering them. In a few words, it is as follows:—All the water that runs from them has originally

Water for Drinking. 215

been supplied by rain, dew, or fog-damp, falling on the face of the land and sinking into it. But the subsoil and rocks below, are far from being of a uniform character: they are full of layers of every imaginable degree of sponginess. Strata of clay wholly impenetrable by water, often divide beds of gravel that imbibe it freely. There are also cracks that make continuous channels and dislocations that cause them to end abruptly; and there are rents, filled with various materials, that may either give a free passage or entirely bar the underground course of water. Hence, when water has sunk into the earth, it does not by any means soak through it in an equable degree. It is an easier matter for it to ooze many miles, along a layer of gravel, than to penetrate six inches into a layer of clay that may bound the gravel. Therefore, whenever a porous earth or a fissured rock crops out to the light of day, there is, in ignorance of all other facts, some chance of a spring being discovered in the lowest part of its outcrop. A favourable condition for the existence of a large and permanent fountain, is where a porous stratum spreads over a broad area at a high level, and is prolonged, by a gradually narrowing course, to an outlet at a lower one. The broad upper part of the stratum catches plenty of water during the wet season, which sinks into its depths as into a reservoir, and oozes out in a regular stream at its lower outlet. A fissured rock makes a still easier channel for the water.

As examples of ordinary cases of fountains, we will take those represented in the following figures. Fig. 1 is a moun-

Fig. 1. Fig. 2.

tain. Fig. 2 is a model, made to explain more clearly the conditions represented in fig. 1. It will be observed that there is a ravine, R, in front; a line of fault, L, M, N, on its left side, supposed to be filled with water-tight rock; and a valley, V (fig. 1), on the extreme right. The upper part of the mountain is supposed to be much more porous than its base, and the plane which divides the porous from the non-porous rock, to cut the surface of the mountain along the line, A, N, M, B, C, D, E, F. The highest point of the plane is F, and the lowest point A. The effect of rain upon the model fig. 2 would be, to wet its upper half: water would ooze out along the whole of the lines A, N, and M, B, C, D, E, F; and there would be a small fountain at A, and a large one at M. But in the actual mountain, fig. 1, we should not expect to find the same regularity as in the model. The rind of the earth, with its vegetation and weather-impacted surface, forms a comparatively impermeable envelope to the mountain, not likely to be broken through, except at a few places. But ravines, such as r, would be probably denuded of their rind, and there we should find a line of minute fountains at the base of the porous rock. If there be no actual fountains, there would at least be some vegetation that indicated dripping water: thus the appearance is well known and often described, of a ravine utterly bare of verdure above, but clothed with vegetation below a sharply defined line, whence the moisture proceeds that irrigates all beneath. We should also be almost certain of finding a spring breaking forth near m or even near a. But in the valley V we should only see a few signs of former moisture, along e, f; such as bunches of vegetation upon the arid cliff, or an efflorescence of salts. Whenever a traveller remarks these signs, he should observe the inclination of the strata, by which he would learn the position of m, where the probability of finding water is the greatest. In a very arid country, the anatomy of the land is so manifest, from the absence of mould, that geological indications are peculiarly easy to follow.

Wells.—*Digging Wells.*—In default of spades, water is to be dug for with a sharp-pointed stick. Take it in both hands, and, holding it upright like a dagger, stab and dig it in the ground, as in fig. 1; then clear out the loose earth with the hand, as in fig. 2. Continue thus working with the stick and hand alternately, and a hole as deep as the arm is easily made. In digging a large hole or well, the earth

Water for Drinking. 217

must be loosened in precisely the same manner, handed up to the surface and carried off by means of a bucket or bag, in default of a shovel and wheelbarrow.

Fig. 1.

Fig. 2.

After digging deeply, the sand will often be found just moist, no water actually lying in the well; but do not, therefore, be disheartened; wait a while, and the water will collect. After it has once begun to ooze through the sides of the well, it will continue to do so much more freely. Therefore, on arriving at night, with thirsty cattle, at a well of doubtful character, deepen it at once, by torch-light, that the water may have time to collect; then the cattle may be watered in the early morning, and sent to feed before the sun is hot.

It often happens, when digging wells in sandy watercourses, that a little water is found, and that below it is a stratum of clay. Now if the digging be continued deeper, in hopes of more water, the result is often most unfortunate; for the clay stratum may prove extremely thin, in which case the digging will pierce it: then the water that had been seen will drain rapidly and wholly away, to the utter discomfiture of the traveller.

Kerkari.—I am indebted to correspondents for an account of a method employed in the plains of the Sikhim Himalaya, and in Assam, where it is called a "Kerkari," also in lower Bengal, for digging deep holes. The natives take a *freshly cut* bamboo, say three inches in diameter: they cut it just

above one of the knots, and then split the wood as far as to the next joint, in about a dozen places, and point the pieces somewhat. The other end of the instrument should be cut slantingly, to thrust into the earth to loosen it; in order to give it strength, the cut should be made obliquely through a joint and not beyond it, as in the figure. The grass is then torn away from the ground, the cut end of the bamboo is well stabbed into the earth, and its other end is afterwards worked vertically with both hands. The soft soil is thus forced into the hollow of the bamboo, and spreads out its blades, as is intended to be shown in the figure. The bamboo is next withdrawn and the plug of earth is shaken out: it is then reintroduced and worked up and down as before. It is usual to drive a stake in the ground to act as a toothed comb, to comb out the plug of earth. Mr. Peal writes from Assam :—

"I have just had 4 holes dug in the course of ordinary work, in hard earth. Two men dug the holes in 1½ hour; they were 3 feet 6 inches deep and 6 inches in diameter. I weighed the clay raised at each stroke. In 4 consecutive strokes the weights were 1¼ lbs., 1¾ lbs., 1¾ lbs., 2 lbs. Another trial gave 7 lbs. lifted, after 5 or 6 strokes." According to the above data, an Assamese workman makes a hole, 1 foot deep and 6 inches in diameter, in 6 minutes. Holes 10 feet deep and 6 inches wide can be made, as I am informed, by this contrivance.

Protecting Wells.—The following extract from Bishop Heber, though hardly within the scope of the 'Art of Travel,' is very suggestive. "The wells of this country (Bhurtpoor, India), some of which are very deep, are made in a singular manner. They build a tower of masonry of the diameter required, and 20 or 30 feet high from the surface of the ground. This they allow to stand a year or more, till its masonry is rendered firm and compact by time; then they gradually undermine it, and promote its sinking into the sandy soil, which it does without difficulty, and altogether. When level with the surface, they raise its walls higher; and so go on, throwing out the sand and raising the wall, till they have reached the water. If they adopted our method, the soil is so light that it would fall on them before they could possibly raise the wall from the bottom; nor, without the wall, could they sink to any considerable depth." A stout square frame of wood scantling, boarded like a sentry-box, and of about the same size and shape, but without top or bottom, is used in making wells in America. The sides of a well in sandy soil are so liable to fall in, that travellers often sink a cask or some equivalent into the water, when they are encamped for any length of time in its vicinity.

Scanty wells in hot climates should be brushed over, when not in actual use, to check their evaporation.

Snow-water.—It is impossible for men to sustain life by eating snow or ice, instead of drinking water. They only aggravate the raging torments of thirst, instead of assuaging them, and hasten death. Among dogs, the Esquimaux is the only breed that can subsist on snow, as an equivalent for water. The Arctic animals, generally, have the same power.

But, as regards mankind, some means of melting snow into water, for the purposes of drinking, is an essential condition of life in the Arctic regions. Without the ingenious Esquimaux lamp (p. 205), which consists of a circle of moss wicks, fed by train-oil, and chiefly used for melting snow, the Esquimaux could not exist throughout the year, in the countries which they now inhabit.

That eating large quantities of snow should seriously disturb the animal system is credible enough, when we consider the very large amount of heat that must be abstracted from the stomach, in order to melt it. A mouthful of snow at 32° Fahr., that is to say, no colder than is necessary for it to be snow at all, robs as much heat from the stomach, as if the mouthful had been of water 143° colder than ice-cold water, if such a fluid may, for the moment, be imagined to exist. For the "latent heat" of water is 143° Fahr. In other words, it takes the same quantity of heat to convert a mass of snow of 32° into water of 32°, as it does to raise the same mass of water from 32° to 141° + 32° = 175° Fahr. It takes in practice about as long to melt snow of a low temperature into water, as it does to cause that same water to boil. Thus to raise snow of 5° below zero Fahr. to 32°, takes 37° of heat, and it requires 143° more, or 180° altogether, to melt it into water, Also it requires 180° to convert water of 32° into water of 212°, in other words, into boiling water.

Distilled Water.—It will take six or seven times as long to convert a kettle full of boiling-water into steam, as it did to make that kettle boil. For the "latent heat" of steam is 967° Fahr.; therefore, if the water that was put into the kettle was 60°, it would require to be raised through (212°− 60°=) 152° of temperature in order to make it begin to boil; and it would require a further quantity of heat, to the extent of 967° (=about 6½ times 152°), to boil it all away. Hence, it is of no use to attempt to distil, until you have provided abundance of good firewood of a fit size to burn quickly, and have built an efficient fireplace on which to set the kettle. Unfortunately, fuel is commonly deficient in those places where there is a lack of fresh water.

Rate of Distillation.—A drop per second is fully equivalent to an imperial pint of water in three hours, or to an imperial gallon in an entire day and night.

The simplest way to distil, but a very imperfect one, is to light a fire among stones, near a hollow in a rock, that is filled, or can be filled, with salt-water. When the stones are red-hot, drop them one by one into it: the water will hiss and give out clouds of vapour, some of which may be collected in a cloth, and wrung or sucked out of it. In the same way a pot on the fire may have a cloth stretched over it to catch the steam.

Still made with a Kettle and Gun-barrel.—There is an account of the crew of the 'Levant' packet, which was wrecked near the Cosmoledo Islands, who supplied themselves with fresh water by means of distillation alone, and whose Still was contrived with an iron pot and a gun-barrel, found on the spot where they were wrecked, They procured,

on the average, sixty bottles, or ten gallons, of distilled water in each twenty-four hours. "The iron pot was converted into a boiler to contain salt water; a lid was fitted to it out of the root of a tree, leaving a hole of sufficient size to receive the muzzle of the gun-barrel, which was to act as a steam-pipe; the barrel was run through the stump of a tree, hollowed out in the middle, and kept full of cold water for the purpose of condensation; and the water so distilled escaped at the nipple of the gun-barrel, and was conducted into a bottle placed to receive it." The accompanying sketch is taken from a model which I made, with a soldier's mess-tin for a boiler, and a tin tube in the place of a gun barrel. The knob represents the breech; and the projection, through which the water is dropping, the nipple. I may remark that there is nothing in the arrangement which would hurt the most highly-finished gun-barrel; and that the trough which holds the condensing water may be made with canvas, or even dispensed with altogether.

Condensing Pipe.—In default of other tubes, a reed may be used: one of the long bones of an animal, or of a wading bird, will be an indifferent substitute for a condensing pipe.

Still, made with Earthen Pots and a Metal Basin.—A very simple distilling apparatus is used in Bhootan; the sketch

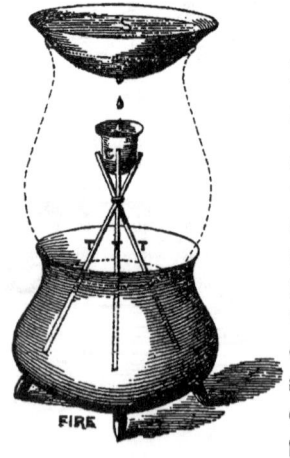

will show the principle on which it is constructed. Salt water is placed in a pot, set over the fire. Another vessel, but without top or bottom, which, for the convenience of illustration, I have indicated in the sketch by nothing more than a dotted line, is made to stand upon the pot. It serves as a support for a metal basin, s, which is filled with salt water, and acts as a condenser. When the pot boils, the steam ascends and condenses itself on the under surface of the basin s, whence it drops down and is collected in a cup, C, that is supported by a rude tripod of sticks, T, standing in the inside of the iron pot.

Occasional Means of Quenching Thirst.—*A Shower of Rain* will yield a good supply. The clothes may be stripped off and spread out, and the rain-water sucked from them. Or, when a storm is approaching, a cloth or blanket may be made fast by its four corners, and a quantity of bullets thrown in the middle of it; they will cause the water that it receives, to drain to one point and trickle through the cloth, into a cup or bucket set below. A reversed umbrella will catch water; but the first drippings from it, or from clothes that have been long unwashed, as from a macintosh cloak, are intolerably nauseous and very unwholesome. It must be remembered, that thirst is greatly relieved by the skin being wetted, and therefore it is well for a man suffering from thirst, to strip to the rain. Rain-water is lodged for some days in the huge pitcher-like corollas of many tropical flowers.

Sea-water.—Lives of sailors have more than once been saved when turned adrift in a boat, by bathing frequently and keeping their clothes damp with salt-water. However, after some days, the nauseous taste of the salt-water is very perceptible in the saliva, and at last becomes unbearable; such, at least, was the experience of the surgeon of the wrecked 'Pandora.'

Dew-water is abundant near the sea-shore, and may be collected in the same way as rain-water. The storehouse at Angra Pequeña, in S.W. Africa, in 1850, was entirely supplied by the dew-water deposited on its roof. The Australians who live near the sea, go among the wet bushes with a great piece of bark, and brush into it the dew-drops from the leaves with a wisp of grass; collecting in this way large quantities of water. Eyre used a sponge for the same purpose, and appears to have saved his life by its use.

Animal Fluids are resorted to in emergencies; such as the contents of the paunch of an animal that has been shot; its taste is like sweet-wort. Mr. Darwin writes of people who, catching turtles, drank the water that was found in their pericardia; it was pure and sweet. Blood will stand in the stead of solid food, but it is of no avail in the stead of water, on account of its saline qualities.

Vegetable Fluids.—Many roots exist, from which both natives and animals obtain a sufficiency of sap and pulp, to take the place of water. The traveller should inquire of the natives, and otherwise acquaint himself with those peculiar to the country that he visits; such as the roots which the eland eats, the bitter water-melon, &c.

To purify water that is muddy or putrid.—With muddy water, the remedy is to filter, and to use alum, if you have it. With putrid, to boil, to mix with charcoal, or expose to the sun and air; or what is best, to use all three methods at the same time. When the water is salt or brackish, nothing avails but distillation. (See "Distilled Water," p. 218.)

To filter Muddy Water.—When, at the watering-place, there is little else but a mess of mud and filth, take a good handful of grass or rushes, and tie it roughly together in the form of a cone, 6 or 8 inches long; then dipping the broad end into the puddle, and turning it up, a streamlet of fluid will trickle down through the small end. This excellent plan is used by the Northern Bushmen—at their wells quantities of these bundles are found lying about. (Andersson.) Otherwise suck water through your handkerchief by putting it over the mouth of your mug, or by throwing it on the gritty mess as it lies in the puddle. For obtaining a copious supply, the most perfect plan, if you have means, is to bore a cask full of auger holes, and put another small one, that has had the bottom knocked out, inside it; and then to fill the space between the two, with grass, moss, &c. Sink the whole in the midst of the pond; the water will run through the auger-holes, filter through the moss, and rise in the inner cask clear of weeds and sand. If you have only a single cask, holes may be bored in the lower part of its sides, and alternate layers of sand and grass thrown in, till they cover the holes; through these layers, the water will strain. Or any coarse bag, kept open with hoops made on the spot, may be moored in the mud, by placing a heavy stone inside; it will act on the same principle, but less efficiently than the casks. Sand, charcoal, sponge, and wool, are the substances most commonly used in properly constructed filters: peat charcoal is excellent. Charcoal acts not only as a mechanical filter for solid impurities, but it has the further advantage of absorbing putrid gases. (See below, "Putrid Water.") Snow is also used as a filter in the Arctic regions. Dr. Rae used to lay it on the water, until it was considerably higher than its level, and then to suck the water through the snow.

Alum.—Turbid water is also, in some way as yet insufficiently explained, made clear by the Indian plan of putting a piece of alum into it. The alum appears to unite with the mud, and to form a clayey deposit. Independently of this action, it has an astringent effect upon organic matters: it hardens them, and they subside to the bottom of the vessel, instead of being diffused in a glairy, viscous state, throughout the water. No taste of alum remains in the water, unless it has been used in great excess. Three thimblefuls of alum will clarify a bucketful of turbid water.

Putrid Water should always be purified by boiling it together with charcoal or charred sticks, as low fevers and dysenteries too often are the consequences of drinking it. The mere addition of charcoal largely disinfects it. Bitter herbs, if steeped in putrid water, or even rubbed well about the cup, are said to render it less unwholesome. The Indians plunge hot iron into putrid water.

Thirst, to relieve.—Thirst is a fever of the palate, which may be somewhat relieved by other means than drinking fluids.

By exciting Saliva.—The mouth is kept moist, and thirst is mitigated, by exciting the saliva to flow. This can be done by chewing something, as a leaf; or by keeping in the mouth a bullet, or a smooth, non-absorbent stone, such as a quartz pebble.

By Fat or Butter.—In Australia, Africa, and N. America, it is a frequent custom to carry a small quantity of fat or butter, and to eat a spoonful at a time, when the thirst is severe.

These act on the irritated membranes of the mouth and throat, just as cold cream upon chapped hands.

By Salt Water.—People may live long without drinking, if they have means of keeping their skin constantly wet with water, even though it be salt or otherwise undrinkable. A traveller may tie a handkerchief wetted with salt water round his neck. See p. 223.

By checking Evaporation.—The Arabs keep their mouths covered with a cloth, in order to prevent the sense of thirst caused by the lips being parched.

By Diet.—Drink well before starting, and make a habit of drinking only at long intervals, and then, plenty at a time.

On giving Water to Persons nearly dead from Thirst.—Give a little at a time, let them take it in spoonfuls; for the large draughts that their disordered instincts suggest, disarrange the weakened stomach: they do serious harm, and no corresponding good. Keep the whole body wet.

Small Water Vessels.—*General Remarks on Carrying Water.*—People drink excessively in hot dry climates, as the evaporation from the skin is enormous, and must be counterbalanced. Under these circumstances the daily ration of a European is at least two quarts. To make an exploring expedition in such countries efficient, there should be means of carrying at least one gallon of water for each white man; and in unknown lands this quantity should be carried on from every wateringplace, so long as means can possibly be obtained for carrying it, and should be served out thus:—two quarts the first day, in addition to whatever private store the men may have chosen to carry for themselves; a quart and a half during the second day; and half a quart on the morning of the third, which will carry them through that day without distress. Besides watervessels sufficient for carrying what I have mentioned, there ought to be others for the purpose of leaving water buried in the ground, as a store for the return of a reconnoitring expedition; also each man should be furnished with a small watervessel of some kind or other for his own use, and should be made to take care of it.

Water for Drinking.

Fill the Water-vessels.—" Never mind what the natives may tell you concerning the existence of water on the road, believe nothing, but resolutely determine to fill the girbas (water-vessels)." (Baker.)

Small Water-vessels.—No expedition should start without being fully supplied with these; for no bushman however ingenious, can make anything so efficient as casks, tin vessels or macintosh bags. A tin vessel of the shape shown in the sketch, and large enough to hold a quart, is, I believe, the easiest to carry, the cleanest, and the most durable of small water-vessels. The curve in its shape  is to allow of its accommodating itself to the back of the man who carries it. The tin loops at its sides are to admit the strap by which it is to be slung, and which passes through the loops underneath the bottom of the vessel, so that the weight may rest directly upon the strap. Lastly, the vessel has a pipette for drinking through, and a larger hole by which it is to be filled, and which at other times is stopped with a cork or wooden plug. When drinking out of the pipette, the cork must be loosened in order to admit air, like a vent hole. Macintosh bags, for wine or water, are very convenient to carry, and they will remain water-tight for a long period when fairly used. (*Mem.*—Oil and grease are as fatal to macintosh as they are to iron rust.) But the taste that these vessels impart to their contents is abominable, not only at first but for a very long time; in two-thirds of them it is never to be got rid of. Never believe shopkeepers in an india-rubber shop, in their assurances to the contrary; they are incompetent to judge aright, for their senses seem vitiated by the air they live in. The best shape for a small macintosh water-vessel has yet to be determined. Several alpine men use them; and their most recent patterns may probably best be seen at Carter's, Alpine Outfitter, 295, Oxford Street. A flask of dressed hide (pig, goat, or dog) with a wooden nozzle, and a wooden plug to fit into it, is very good. Canvas bags, smeared with grease on the outside, will become nearly waterproof after a short soaking. A strong glass flask may be made out of a soda-water bottle; it should have raw hide shrunk upon it to preserve it from sharp taps.

likely to make a crack. Calabashes and other gourds, cocoa-nuts and ostrich eggs, are all of them excellent for flasks. The Bushmen of South Africa make great use of ostrich shells as water-vessels. They have stations at many places in the desert, where they bury these shells filled with water, corked with grass, and occasionally waxed over. They thus go without hesitation over wide tracts, for their sense of locality is so strong that they never fear to forget the spot in which they have dug their hiding-place.

When a Dutchman or a Namaqua wants to carry a load of ostrich eggs to or from the watering-place, or when he robs a nest, he takes off his trousers, ties up the ankles, puts the eggs in the legs, and carries off his load slung round his neck. Nay, I have seen a half-civilised Hottentot carry water in his leather breeches, tied up and slung in the way I have just described, but without the intervention of ostrich eggs; the water squirted through the seams, but plenty remained after he had carried it to its destination, which was a couple of miles from the watering-place. In an emergency, water-flasks can be improvised from the raw or dry skins of animals, which should be greased down the back; or from the paunch, the heart-bag (pericardium), the intestines, or the bladder. These should have a wooden skewer run in and out along one side of their mouths, by which they can be carried, and a lashing under the skewer to make all tight (fig. below). The Bush-

men do this. The water oozes through the membrane, and by its evaporation the contents are kept very cool. Another plan is, after having tied a length of intestine at both ends, to roll it up in a handkerchief and wear it as a belt round the waist. The fault of these membranous bags, besides their disgusting character and want of strength is, that they become putrid after a few days' use.

Vessels for Cooling Water may be made that shall also act efficiently as flasks. Porous earthen jars are too brittle for long use, and their pores choke up if slimy water be put inside them. But the Arabs use a porous leather flask, called a Zemsemiyah, which is hung on the shady side of the camel, and by evaporation keeps the water deliciously cool: it is a rather wasteful way of carrying water. Canvas bags are equally effective.

Open Buckets, for carrying water for short distances, or for storing it in camp, may be made of the bark of a tree, either taken off in an entire cylinder, and having a bottom fitted on, or else of a knot or excrescence that has been cut off the outside of a tree, and its woody interior scooped out; or of birch bark sewed or pegged at the corners, and having its seams coated with the gum or resin of the pine-tree. Baskets with oiled cloth inside, make efficient water-vessels: they are in use in France as firemen's buckets. Water-tight pots are made on the Snake river by winding long tough roots in a spiral manner, and lashing the coils to one another, just as is done in making a beehive. Earthenware jars are excellent, when they can be obtained.

To prevent Splashing.—When carrying water in buckets, put a wreath of grass, or something else that will float, on the water, to prevent it from splashing; and also make a hoop, inside which the porter may walk, while his laden hands rest on its rim: the hoop keeps his hands wide from his body, and prevents the buckets from knocking against his legs.

Mending Leather Water-vessels.—If a water-vessel becomes leaky, the hole should be caulked by stuffing a rag, a wedge of wood, a tuft of grass, or anything else into it, as shown in the upper figure and also in the left side of the lower one (p. 230), nd then greasing or waxing it over. A larger rent must be seized upon, the lips of the wound pinched up, a thorn or other spike run through the lips, and lastly a piece of twine lashed firmly round, underneath the thorn; the thorn keeps

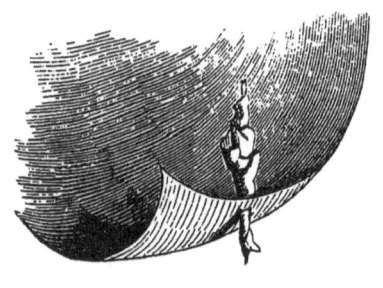

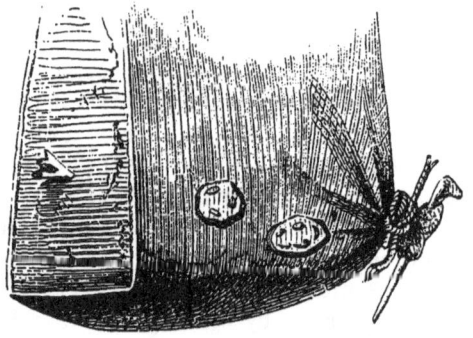

the string from slipping off. (See the right-hand corner of the lower figure.) When there is an opportunity, the bag must be patched, as is also shown in the lower figure.

Repairing a battered Metal Flask.—Fill it with dry seed, such as peas or mustard-seed; then pour in water and put the stopper into it. After a period varying from 1 to 3 or 4 hours, according to the nature of the seeds, they will begin to swell and to force the sides of the flask outwards into their original shape. The swelling proceeds rather rapidly after it has once commenced, so the operation requires watching, lest it should be overdone and the flask should burst.

Corks and Stoppers.—Thrust a cork tightly into the mouth of the flask, cut a hole through the cork and plug the hole, which will henceforth form the outlet of the flask—with a stopper of wood, bone, or other hard substance. Thread, wound round a slightly conical plug that has been sufficiently notched to retain it in its place, makes it nearly watertight as a stopper. It is of less importance that the stopper should fit closely, if the flask be so slung that its mouth shall be always uppermost: a very imperfect cork will then be sufficient to check evaporation and splashing, and to prevent the loss of more than a few drops from occasional upsets.

Drinking, when riding or walking.—It is an awkward matter to drink when jolting on wheels, on horseback, or on foot. I adopted the plan of carrying a piece of small india-rubber tubing 6 or 8 inches long, and when I wished to drink, I removed the stopper and inserted the tube, just as an insect might let down its proboscis, and sucked the contents. Sir S. Baker says of the people of Unyoro, " During a journey, a pretty, bottle-shaped, long-necked gourd is carried with a store of plantain-cider; the mouth of the bottle is stopped with a bundle of the white rush shreds, through which a reed is inserted that reaches to the bottom: thus the drink can be sucked up during the march, without the necessity of halting; nor is it possible to spill it by the movement of walking."

Kegs and Tanks.—*Kegs for Pack-saddles.*—Small barrels, flattened equally on both sides, so that their tops and bottoms shall be of an oval and not a circular shape, are the most convenient vessels, notwithstanding their weight, for carrying water on pack-saddles across a broken country. They are exceedingly strong, and require no particular attention, while bags of leather or macintosh suffer from thorns, and natives secretly prick them during the march, that they may suck a draught of water. These kegs should not exceed 22 inches in length, 10 in extreme breadth, and 7 in extreme width; a cask of these measurements would hold about 40 lbs. weight of water, and its own weight might be 15 lbs. As the water is expended, it is easy to replace the diminished weight by putting on a bag from one of the other packs. Before starting away into the bush, these kegs should be satisfactorily fitted and adjusted to the pack-saddle that is intended to carry them, in such a way that they may be packed on to it with the least possible trouble. A couple of leather or iron loops fixed to each keg, and made to catch on to hooks which are let flush into the sides of the pack-saddle, will effect this. The sketch represents a section of the pack-saddle, at the place where one of the hooks is situated on either side, but

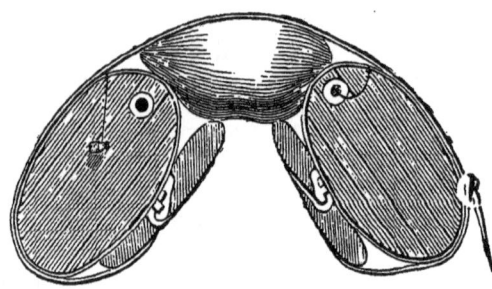

the front of the kegs themselves, and not their section, is given. Above and between the kegs lies a bag, and a strap passing from the near side of the saddle goes over the whole burden, and is buckled to a similar short strap on the other side. It is of importance that the bung-hole should be placed even nearer to the rim than where it is drawn, for it is necessary that it should be convenient to pour out of and to pour into, and that it should be placed on the highest part of the keg, both when on the beast's back and also when it stands on the ground, lest water should leak and be lost. According to the above plan, when water is ladled into it, the rim keeps it from spilling; and in pouring out water, the rim acts as a spout. In making the bung-hole, a metal plate, with a screw-hole in it, is firmly fixed in the face of the cask; into this a wooden stopper, bound with iron, is made to screw (natives would probably steal a metal one). The stopper has a small head and a deeply-cut neck, by which it is tied to the cask, and its body has a large hole bored in it, which admits of a stick being put through, to prize it round, if it should become jammed. A spigot, to screw into the bung-hole on arriving at camp, might be really useful; but if used, a gimlet-hole must be bored in the cask to act as an air-vent. A large tundish is very convenient, and a spare plug might be taken; but a traveller, with a little painstaking, could soon cut a plug with his own knife, sufficiently well made to allow of its being firmly screwed in, and of retaining the water, if it had a bit of rag wrapped round it. A piece of rag rolled tightly, will suffice to plug a hole.

Siphons.—A flexible tube of some kind, whether of indiarubber, gutta-percha, or, still better, of macintosh, strained over rings, would be very valuable as a siphon: both for filling large kegs out of buckets and for emptying them again. Vulcanised india-rubber becomes rotten after short use, and gutta-percha will stand no extremes of temperature.

Tanks for Wagons.—There still remain many large districts in Asia, Africa, and Australia which may be explored in wagons, but, so far as I am aware, no particular pattern of a water-tank, suitable for carriage on wheels, has yet been adopted by travellers. I believe kegs are generally used, but they are far too heavy for the requirements of a wagon. Probably the tins used for sending milk by cart and railway to towns, would be very serviceable for carrying water on expeditions. They are invariably made of the same shape, and only of few different sizes. Therefore experience must have shown that their pattern is better than any other yet devised. Their mouths can be padlocked, which is an important matter.

Macintosh Bags.—I would also recommend a trial of square bags of strong macintosh—say 18 inches deep and 10 inches square, in which case they would hold 60 lbs. of water—fitting into square compartments, in large panniers, like those in a bottle-basket. I have made some experiments upon this arrangement. The basket-work gives protection against blows and the jolting together of packages, and it yields without harm to a strain, and the bags yield also. Moreover, water is less churned in half-empty bags than in half-empty barrels. No unusual strength of materials would be required in making these bags: their mouths should be funnel-shaped, and corked at the neck of the funnel. The funnels should be wide at their mouths, for convenience in filling them; and a string to secure the cork should be tied round the neck of the funnel. The bags should have loops on their sides, through which a strap, passing underneath, might run, in order to give a good hold for lifting them up. They could easily be filled as they lay in their compartments, and would only require to be lifted out in order to empty them; there is, therefore, no objection to their holding as much as 60 lbs. weight of water. An india-rubber tube as a siphon, and with a common spigot at the end of it, would be particularly useful. A pannier not much exceeding 30 inches long, by 20 broad, and 18 deep, would hold six of these bags, or 360 lbs. weight of water in all; and two such panniers would be ample for exploring purposes. I had a pannier and two bags made for a trial, which were quite satisfactory, and I found that the weight of the panniers and bags together was at the rate of 6 lbs. for each compartment; therefore the weight of these water-vessels is not more than 10 per cent. of that of the water which they carry. It might be well to vary the contents of some of the compartments; putting, for instance, two or even three small bags into one, and tin cases into a few of the others, instead of the large bags. These panniers, with the bags inflated, and connected together by a stage, would form an excellent and powerful raft. If secured within a wagon about to cross a deep river, they would have enough power, in all ordinary cases, to cause it to float and not to sink to the bottom. I trust some explorer will try this plan. I may add that the macintosh water-bags cost me about 1*l*. each.

Raw Hide Bays.—Captain Sturt, when he explored in Australia, took a tank in his cart, which burst, and, besides that, he carried casks of water. By these he was enabled to face a desert country with a degree of success to which no traveller before had ever attained. For instance, when returning homewards, the water was found to be drying up on all sides of him. He was encamped by a pool where he was safe, whence the next stage was 118 miles, or 4 days' journey, but it was a matter of considerable doubt whether there remained any water at the end of the stage. It was absolutely necessary to reconnoitre, and, in order to do so, he had first to provide the messenger with means of returning, should the watering-place be found dry. He killed a bullock, skinned it, and filling the skin with water (which held 150 gallons), sent it by an ox-dray 30 miles, with orders to bury it and to return. Shortly after he despatched a light one-horse cart, carrying 36 gallons of water; the horse and man were to drink at the hide, and then to go on. Thus they had 36 gallons to supply them for a journey of 176 miles, or 6 days, at 30 miles a day, at the close of which they would return to the ox-hide—sleeping, in fact, 5 nights on 36 gallons of water. This a hardy, well-driven horse could do, even in the hottest climate.

To raise Water from Wells for Cattle.—*By hand.*—Let one man stand in the water, or just above it; another 5 feet higher; and again another higher still, if the depth of the well requires it. Then let the lowermost man dip a bucket in the water, and pass it from hand to hand, upwards; the top man pours the water into a trough, out of which the cattle drink. This trough may be simply a ditch scratched in the ground; a piece of canvas should be thrown over it, if the soil be sandy, to keep the water from being lost before the cattle have time to drink it. Thus Eyre speaks of watering his horse, out of his black servant's duck frock. Light gutta-percha buckets are very useful in temperate climates; and so are baskets, with oilcloth inside them.

The drove of cattle should be brought up to 60 yards from the watering-place; then three or four should be driven out —they will run at once to the water. After they have drunk, drive them to one side, and let another three or four take their place, and so on; keeping the two droves quite distinct —those that have drunk, and those that are waiting to drink. They will drink at the rate of one per minute; sheep and goats drink very much faster. Never let the cattle go in a rush to the well, else they will stamp it in, most of them will get no water, and they will all do a great deal of damage.

By horse power.—It does not fall within the scope of this book to describe water-wheels worked by cattle, or elaborate mechanism of any kind; I therefore only mention under this head, that the Tartars sometimes draw water from their wells, of 150 feet deep and upwards, by a rider harnessing the bucket-rope to his horse, and galloping him off to a mark that tells the proper distance. Their ropes are of twisted hair,

236   Art of Travel.

and are made to run over a smoothed stone, or a log of wood.

A pole and bucket is a very convenient way of raising water from 4 to 12 feet. The bucket may be made of canvas, basket-work, leather, wood, or almost any other material; leakage, though considerable, is of little consequence, because the action of the apparatus is so quick, that there is not time for much water to be lost. This contrivance is used over almost the whole globe—less in England than elsewhere; it is very common where long poles can easily be obtained, as in fir forests.

Pump.—An excellent and very simple pump is used by the Arabs in Algeria. A piece of leather or waxed canvas, is stretched round one or more hoops; it forms a hollow cylinder, that admits of being shut flat like an accordion. The top and bottom of the cylinder are secured round the edges of two discs of wood. Holes are bored in these discs and leather valves are fitted to them. The lower disc is nailed to the bottom of a tub; the hole in it corresponds with the feed-pipe, and the valve that covers the hole opens upwards. The upper disc

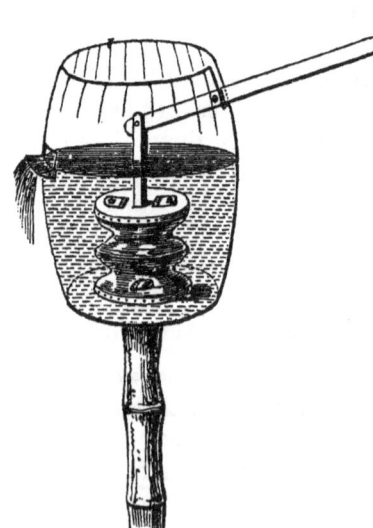

is attached to the pump handle; the valves that cover the holes in this disc, open upwards also. When the leather-pump barrel is pressed flat, water flows through the upper valves into the barrel around it; when it is pulled out, water is sucked up through the feed-pipe, and an equal quantity is displaced from the barrel. This flows out into the trough. A bag would do as well as a tub, to hold the water which surrounds the pump-barrel; but, without the water which it is the object of either the one or the other to contain, the pump-barrel must be air-proof as well as water-proof. The action of this pump is marvellously perfect. It attracted much attention in the French Exhibition of 1855.

GUNS AND RIFLES.

General Remarks.—*Breech-loaders.*—At the present time when the merits of different kinds of breech-loader are so hotly discussed, when all that have yet been invented have some faults, and every month brings to light some new invention, it would be foolish in me to write anything about them; it would be obsolete before the great majority of my readers should have seen this book. Therefore omitting breech-loaders altogether from the present edition, I will confine myself to repeating what I have said before upon muzzle-loaders, with additions and alterations.

Size of Gun.—American bushrangers advocate a long heavy pea-rifle, on the plea of its accurate shooting, and the enormous saving in weight of ammunition when bullets of a small size are used. The objections to small-bored rifles are, insufficiency against large game (even with conical bullets), and a tendency to become foul after a few shots. A short light rifle, whether with a large or a small bore, is, I believe, utterly worthless. In the hands of a man trembling with running and with exhaustion, it shakes like a wand: the shorter the rifle, the more quickly does it oscillate, and of course, in the same proportion, is it difficult to catch the exact moment when the sights cover the object.

For the larger kinds of game, such as elephants and buffaloes, experienced sportsmen mostly prefer guns of immense bore, carrying round bullets that weigh a quarter of a pound. The recoil is tremendous, and would injure the shoulder if the sportsman did not use a pad against which he rests the gun. The guns must be strong, because very large charges of powder are invariably used where great power of penetration is required. African sportsmen found this out experimentally long before the idea occurred to artillerists.

Sights.—The hind sight should be far from the eye, even though it be placed half-way down the barrel: else it becomes out of focus and indistinct, when the eye is firmly set on the object aimed at; this drawback is never compensated by the advantage of having the front and hind sights far asunder.

Ramrod.—The guns of servants and indeed those of their masters, should have thin soft-iron ramrods; the elasticity of these when slightly bent, will retain them in the ramrod-tubes; both ends of the ramrod must be forged broad.

Screw to secure the Cock.—In common guns, this screw is very liable to get loose, fall out and be lost; it is therefore desirable to have one or more spare screws.

Water-proof Cover should not be forgotten.

Rust, to prevent.—Paraffine and mercurial ointment are perhaps the two best things to keep rust off iron, in sea voyages or in boat-shooting. Before embarking for a voyage, it is convenient to enclose the guns in a leaden case, which, on arrival, can be melted up into bullets. It is remarkable how much better dirty guns withstand rust than clean ones.

Olive oil, to purify.—Put a piece of lead in the glass bottle that contains the oil, and expose to the sun; a quantity of cloudy matter will separate after a few days, then the refined oil may be decanted.

The small of the stock is the weakest part of a gun: it is constantly broken by falls in travel. Sir Samuel Baker justly recommends that "all guns made for sport in wild countries and rough riding, should have steel instead of iron from the breech-socket, extending far back to within six inches of the shoulder plate; the trigger-guard should likewise be steel, and should be carried back to an equal distance with the above rib; the steel should be of extra thickness, and screwed through to the upper piece; thus the two being connected by screws above and below, no fall could break the stock."

Injuries to Guns, to repair.—*Ramrod tubes* often break off, and it is a very troublesome accident when they do so. I know of no contrivance to fasten them on again, except by using soft solder, the application of which will not in the least hurt the gun: ashes, at a dull red heat, must be heaped over the barrel to warm it sufficiently, before applying the solder. If the ramrod tubes have been lost, others made of tin may replace them.

The Sight of a Gun, if it falls out and is lost, can easily be replaced by a substitute. A groove must be cut with a file across the substance of the barrel, if the gun be a single one, or across the midrib, if double-barrelled; into this, a piece of iron, ivory, bone, horn, or hard wood, with a projection carved in the middle for the sight, must be pushed, then the metal on either side must be battered down over it, with a hammer or stone, to keep it firm.

A broken Stock, however much it may be smashed, can be well mended by raw hide (see "Hides"). Blacksmith's work and carpentering are seldom sufficient for the purpose. It is within the power of a rough workman to make a gun-stock, but it is a work of great labour.

A Ramrod may be replaced by cutting a stick from a tree, straightening it in the fire, and then seasoning it. (See "Green Wood.")

Guns to hang up, to carry, and to clean.—*Hanging Guns to a Wall.*—Fix a loop of leather for the muzzle, and a strap and buckle for the stock, with a piece of sheepskin or canvas nailed so as to hang over it, as in fig. 1. A more complete way is to sew a long pocket with a flap to it, which is tied up on to a stick or bar, as in fig. 2: the gun has simply to be lifted out and in. The pocket must be made baggy at the part which corresponds to the cocks of the gun.

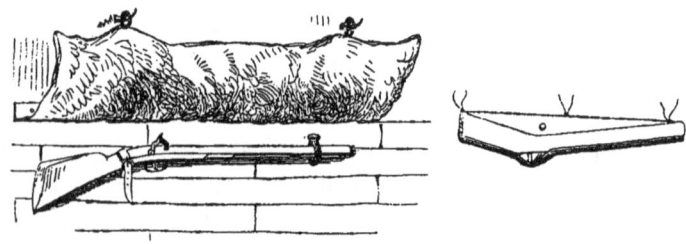

Fig. 1.   Fig. 2.

Carrying Guns on a Journey.—"Look at the gun, but never let the gun look at you, or at your companions," is a golden rule; for among the chances of death to which a traveller is exposed, that of being shot by an attendant's gun going off accidentally, ranks high. Servants should carry their guns

with the cock down on a piece of rag, that covers the cap: take it all in all, it is the best plan for them. A sportsman will find great convenience in having a third nick cut in the tumbler of his lock, so as to give an additional low half-cock, at which the cock just clears the nipple; it will prevent the cap from falling off or receiving a blow. I have long used this plan, and find no objections to it: many pistols are furnished with this contrivance. Careless gun-makers sometimes make this catch so low, that when the cock is lifted a little back from it, and let go, it strikes the cap by reason of the elasticity of its metal, and lets off the gun: the traveller should beware of this fault of workmanship.

As this book may fall into the hands of persons ignorant of the danger of carrying a gun with the cock down on the nipple (to which cause I find that three-fourths of gun accidents are owing, having once kept a list of those that were reported in the newspapers), I will remark that when the cock is down, a heavy blow on its back, nay, even the jar caused by the gun falling on the ground, will cause the cap to explode. Again, if the cock catch against the dress, or against a twig, it is liable to be lifted, when, on being released, it will snap down upon the cap. When a gun is at half-cock, the first of these accidents obviously cannot occur; and, as to the second, if the cock be pulled back and let drop, it falls, not down upon the cap, but to half-cock again, except only in the case where the trigger is also pressed back. The objections to carrying a gun at half-cock are, that careless people occasionally leave it on full-cock without perceiving the difference, and that there is a probability of weakening the main-spring, if day after day it be kept on the strain.

Carrying Guns when Stalking Game.—In creeping after game, the gun is always troublesome; there is no better plan than pushing it as far as the arm can reach, then creeping up to it, and again pushing it forwards.

Carrying Guns on Horseback.—Allow me very strongly to recommend a trial of the following plan, even for a shooting-pony in Scotland. It is the invention of the Namaquas. I and all my party in South Africa used it for a year and a half, and many persons have adopted the plan in England since I first published a description of it. Sew a bag of canvas, leather, or hide, of such a size as to admit the butt of the gun pretty freely. The straps that support the bag, buckle through a ring in the pommel; the thongs by which the slope of the bag is adjusted, are fastened round the girth, below. The exact adjustments may not be hit upon, by an unpractised person, for some little time; but, when they are once ascertained, the thongs need never be shifted. The gun is perfectly safe: it never comes below the armpit, even in taking a drop leap: it is pulled out in an instant by bringing the elbow forwards in front of the gun and then backwards, pressing it against the side; by this manœuvre, the gun is thrown to the outside of the arm: then, lowering the hand, catch the gun as near the trigger-guard as you can, and lift it out of the bag; (it is a bungling way to take out the gun whilst its barrel lies between the arm and the body). Any sized gun can be carried in this fashion, and it offers no obstacle to mounting or dismounting.

I hear that some sportsmen, who were probably unacquainted with this method, have used a bag or pocket of stiff leather attached to the side of the saddle, just behind the right leg; into this, when tired of carrying the gun, they

push the butt. It is said to lie there securely and to give no trouble, the barrel passes forwards under the right arm, and the muzzle is in front of the rider.

The French dragoons carry a gun in a way that is convenient for military purposes, because it does not interfere with the immense housings that cavalry soldiers require; but it is not so handy, it does not lie so freely as the above, nor is it as well suited to a traveller or a sportsman. The gun is placed butt downwards, as in the Namaqua method, and leans backwards in the same way; but the under side of the gun, instead of being backwards, or towards the horse's tail, is towards his head. The butt lies in a shallow bucket, secured by two straps fixed to the front of the saddle; another strap, leading from the pommel, and passing over the right thigh of the rider, is hitched round the barrel of the gun, and has to be unbuckled and cast off when the gun is taken out.

All ways of carrying the gun with its muzzle downwards, are very objectionable; since the jolting tends to dislodge the charge; if it be considerably dislodged, the gun will probably burst, on being fired. Also, a very little shaking, when the muzzle is downwards, will shake the powder out of the nipple, and, therefore, a gun, so carried, will constantly miss fire.

At Night, to dispose of Guns.—A gun is a very awkward thing to dispose of at night. It has occurred more than once that a native servant has crept up, drawn away the gun of his sleeping master, and shot him dead. The following appears to me an excellent plan:—" When getting sleepy, you return your rifle between your legs, roll over, and go to sleep. Some people may think this is a queer place for a rifle; but, on the contrary, it is the position of all others where utility and comfort are most combined. The butt rests on the arm, and serves as a pillow for the head; the muzzle points between the knees, and the arms encircle the lock and breech, so that you have a smooth pillow, and are always prepared to start

up armed at a moment's notice." (Parkyns' 'Abyssinia.') The longer the gun, the more secure is the sleeper from accident. The sketch is not quite accurate, for, in practice, the weight of the gun is never allowed to rest so entirely on the arm, as it is here represented: if it did so, the arm would soon be numbed. The gun-stock may be a little bolstered up if desired, to avoid any troublesome pressure on the arm.

Cleaning Guns.—A bit of rag does as well as tow, and can be used over and over again. A top furnished with a sponge, to screw to the cleaning-rod, is convenient. "A leaded barrel must be cleaned with fine sand." (Hawker.) Quicksilver, if it be at hand, will dissolve out the lead at once.

GUN-FITTINGS AND AMMUNITION.

Powder-flask.—The flask that is carried in the pocket may be small, if roomy; a large one, in reserve, being kept in a bag, at the front of the saddle.

To reduce bulges in a metal powder-flask, fill it up with Indian corn, or dry peas, or any other sort of hard grain; then pour water into it, and screw down the lid tightly. The grain will swell, at first slowly and then very rapidly, and the flask will resume its former dimensions, or burst if it is not watched. Peas do not begin to swell for a couple of hours or more.

Powder-horn, to make.—Saw off the required length from an ox's horn, flatten it somewhat by heat (see "Horn"), fit a wooden bottom into it, caulk it well, and sew raw hide round the edge to keep all tight. The mouth must be secured by a plug, which may be hollowed to make a charger. Pieces of cane of large diameter, and old gunpowder canisters, sewn up in hide, make useful powder-flasks.

Percussion Caps.—*Caps may be carried* very conveniently by means of a ring, with two dozen nipple-shaped beads, made of some metal, strung upon it; each bead being intended to be covered by a percussion-cap. The beads are cleft down the middle, which gives them a slight springiness, that more effectually secures the caps that are placed upon them: the ring is tied by a thong to the belt or button-hole. It is very difficult, without this contrivance, to keep caps free from sand, crumbs, and dirt, yet always at hand when required. I can confidently recommend it, though as it is old-fashioned and not well suited for sportsmen in England, it is rarely to be met with. Spring cap holders are, I am sure, too delicate for rough travel.

To protect Caps from the Rain.—Before stalking, or watching at night in rainy weather, wax or grease the edge of the cap as it rests on the nipple: it will thus become proof against water and damp air. Some persons carry a piece of grease with them, when shooting in wet weather, and with it they smear the top of the nipple after each loading, before putting on the fresh cap. It is said that the grease does not prevent the full action of the cap upon the powder. A sportsman has recommended to me a couple of well-marked caps, into the heads of which small wads of cork have been fitted; he uses them for loaded guns that are to be laid by for some hours or days. A broad leaf wrapped loosely round the lock of a gun, will protect it during a heavy shower.

Substitute for Caps.—When the revolution in Spain in 1854 began, "there was a great want of percussion caps; this the insurgents supplied by cutting off the heads of lucifer-matches and sticking them into the nipples. The plan was found to answer perfectly." (*Times*, July 31.)

Gun-pricker.—I am indebted for the following plan, both for clearing the touchhole, and also for the rather awkward operation of pricking down fresh gunpowder into it, to an old sportsman in the Orkney Island of Sanday. He takes a quill, and cuts off a broad ring from the large end of it; this is pushed over the small end of the quill, and lies securely there. Next, he cuts a wooden plug to fit the quill; into the plug, the pricker is fixed. The whole affair goes safely in the pocket; the  quill acting as a sheath to the sharp pricker. Now, when powder has to be pricked down the nipple, the "broad ring" is slipped off the quill and put on the nipple, which it fits; powder is poured into it, and the required operation is easily completed. This little contrivance, which *is so simple and* light, lasts for months, and is perfectly effective. I have tried metal holders, but I much prefer the simple quill, on account of its elasticity and lightness. A little binding with waxed thread, may be put on, as shown in the sketch, to prevent the quill from splitting.

Wadding.—The bush affords few materials from which wadding can be made; some birds' nests are excellent for the purpose. I am told that a dry hide will *not* serve as materials for wads.

Flints.—According to Ure's Dictionary, the best stones to choose for making gun-flints are those that are not irregular in shape; they should have, when broken, a greasy lustre, and be particularly smooth and fine-grained; the colour is of no importance, but it should be uniform in the same lump; and the more transparent the stones the better. Gun-flints are made with a hammer, and a chisel of steel that is not hardened. The stone is chipped by the hammer alone into pieces of the required thickness, which are fashioned by being laid upon the fixed chisel, and hammered against it. It takes nearly a minute for a practised workman to make one gun-flint.

Gunpowder.—*To carry Gunpowder.* Wrap it up in flannel or leather, not in paper, cotton, or linen; because these will catch fire, or smoulder like tinder, whilst the former will do neither the one nor the other. Gunpowder carried in a goat-skin bag, travels very safely. Mr. Gregory carried his in the middle of his flour; each flour-bag (see p. 69), during his North Australian expedition, had a tin of gunpowder in the middle of it.

To make Gunpowder.—It is difficult to make good gunpowder, but there is no skill required in making powder that will shoot and kill. Many of the negroes of Africa, make it for themselves,—burning the charcoal, gathering saltpetre from salt-pans, and buying the sulphur from trading caravans: they grind the materials on a stone. In Chinese Tartary and Thibet, every peasant manufactures it for himself.

To make 8 lbs. of gunpowder, take 1 lb. of charcoal, 1 lb. of sulphur, and 6 lbs. of saltpetre. These proportions should be followed as accurately as possible. Each of the three materials must be pounded into powder separately, and then all mixed together most thoroughly. The mixture must have a little water added to it, enough to make it bind into a stiff paste (about one-tenth part, by measure, of water is sufficient; that is to say, one cupful of water to ten cupfuls of the mixed powder). This paste must be well kneaded together, with one stone on another, just as travellers usually make meal or grind coffee. It should then be wrapped up in a piece of canvas, or a skin, and pressed, with as heavy a pressure as can be obtained, to condense it. Next, the cake is squeezed and worked against a sieve made of parchment, in which the holes have been burnt with a red-hot wire, and through which the cake is squeezed in grains. These grains are now put into a box, which is well shaken about, and in this way the grains rub each other smooth. The fine dust that is then found mixed with the grains, must be winnowed away; lastly, the grains are dried.

Recapitulation.—1. Pound the ingredients separately. 2. Mix them. 3. Add a little water, and knead the mass. 4. Press it. 5. Rub the mass through a sieve. 6. Shake up the grains in a box. 7. Get rid of the dust. 8. Dry the grains.

The ingredients should be used as pure as they can be obtained. For making a few charges of coarse powder, the sieve may be dispensed with: in this case, roll the dough into long pieces of the thickness of a pin; lay several of these side by side, and mince the whole into small grains; dust with powder, to prevent their sticking together: and then proceed as already described.

To procure good Charcoal.—Light woods that give a porous charcoal, are the best;—as poplar, alder, lime, horse-chestnut, willow, hazel-nut, and elder. It should be made with the greatest care, and used as soon as possible afterwards: it is the most important ingredient in gunpowder.

Sulphur.—The lumps must be melted over a gentle fire; the pot should then be put in a heap of hot sand, to give the impurities time to settle, before it cools into a mass. When this has taken place, the bottom part must be broken off and put aside as unfit for making gunpowder, and the top part alone used. Flower of sulphur is quite pure.

Saltpetre.—Dissolve the saltpetre that you wish to purify, in an equal measure of boiling water; a cupful of one to a cupful of the other. Strain this solution, and, letting it cool gradually, somewhat less than three-fourths of the nitre will separate in regular crystals. Saltpetre exists in the ashes of many plants, of which tobacco is one; it is also found copiously on the ground in many places, in saltpans, or simply as an efflorescence. Rubbish, such as old mud huts, and mortar, generally abounds with it. (It is made by the action of the air on the potash contained in the earths.) The taste, which is that of gunpowder, is the best test of its presence. To extract it, pour hot water on the mass, then evaporate and purify, as mentioned above.

Rocket Composition consists of gunpowder 16 parts, by

weight; charcoal, 3 parts. Or, in other words, of nitre, 16 parts; charcoal 7 parts; sulphur, 4 parts. It must not be forgotten, that when rockets are charged with the composition, a hollow tube must be left down their middle.

Blue Fire.—4 parts gunpowder meal; 2 parts nitre; 3 parts sulphur; 3 parts zinc.

Bengal Fire.—7 parts nitre; 2 parts sulphur; 1 part antimony.

Bullets.—Sportsmen, fresh from England, and acknowledged as good shots at home, begin by shooting vilely with balls at large game. They must not be discouraged at what is a general rule, but be satisfied that they will soon do themselves justice.

Alloy.—Common bullets of lead, whether round or conical, are far inferior to those of hard alloy; for the latter penetrate much more deeply, and break bones, instead of flattening against them. A mixture of very little tin, or pewter (which is lead and tin), with lead, hardens it: we read of sportsmen melting up their spoons and dishes for this purpose. A little quicksilver has the same effect. Sir Samuel Baker, who is one of the most experienced of sportsmen both in Ceylon and in Africa, latterly used a mixture of nine-tenths lead and one-tenth quicksilver for his bullets. He says, " This is superior to all [other] mixtures for that purpose, as it combines hardness with extra weight; the lead must be melted in a pot by itself to a red heat, and the proportion of quicksilver must be added a ladleful at a time, and stirred quickly with a piece of iron just in sufficient quantity to make three or four bullets. If the quicksilver is subjected to red heat in the large leadpot, it will evaporate." Proper alloy, or spelter, had best be ordered at a gun-maker's shop, and taken from England instead of lead: different alloys of spelter vary considerably in their degree of hardness, and therefore more than one specimen should be tried.

Shape of Bullets.—Round iron bullets are worthless, except at very close quarters, on account of the lightness of the metal: for the resistance of the air checks their force extremely. Whether elongated iron bullets would succeed, remains to be tried. Some savages—as, for instance, those of Timor—when in want of bullets, use stones two or three inches long. Some good sportsmen insist on the advantage, for shooting at very close quarters, of cleaving a conical bullet nearly down to its base, into four parts; these partly separate, and make a fearful wound. I suppose that the bullet leaves the gun with the same force as if it were entire; and that it traverses too short a distance for its altered form to tell seriously upon its speed: when it strikes, it acts like chain-shot.

Bullets, to carry.—Bullets should be carried sewn up in their patches, for the convenience of loading, and they should not fit too tight: a few may be carried bare, for the sake of rapid loading.

Recovering Bullets.—When ammunition is scarce, make a practice of recovering the bullets that may have been shot into a beast; if they are of spelter, they will be found to have been very little knocked out of shape, and may often be used again, without recasting.

Shot and Slugs.—Travellers frequently omit to take enough shot, which is a great mistake, as birds are always to be found, while large game is uncertain: besides this, shot gives amusement; and ducks, quails, and partridges are much better eating than antelopes and buffaloes. It must be borne in mind, that a rifle will carry shot quite well enough, on an emergency. Probably No. 7 is the most convenient size for shot, as the birds are likely to be tame; and also because a traveller can often fire into a covey or dense flight of birds—and the more pellets, the more execution. If birds are to be killed for stuffing, dust-shot will also be wanted; otherwise, it is undoubtedly better to take only one size of shot.

Shot is made in manufactories, as follows:—Arsenic is added to the lead, in the proportion of from 3 lbs. to 8 lbs. of arsenic to 1000 lbs. of lead. The melted lead is poured through cullenders drilled with *very fine* holes, and drops many feet down, into a tub of water; 100 feet fall is necessary for manufactories in which No. 4 shot is made; 150, for larger sorts. If the shot turns out to be lens-shaped, there has been too much arsenic; if hollow, flattened, or tailed, there has been too little. Pewter or tin is bad, as it makes tailed shot. The shot are sorted by sieves; bad shot are weeded out, by letting the shot roll over a slightly-inclined board, then the shot that are not quite round roll off to the side. Lastly, the shot is smoothed by being shaken up in a barrel with a little black-lead.

Slugs are wanted both for night-shooting and also in case of a hostile attack. They can be made by running melted lead into reeds, and chopping the reeds into short lengths; or by casting the lead in tubes made by rolling paper round a smooth stick: whether reeds or paper be used, they should be planted in the ground before the lead is poured in. The temperature of the lead is regulated by taking care that a small quantity of it remains unmelted in the ladle, at the moment of pouring out: if it be too hot it will burn the paper. (See "Lead.")

HINTS ON SHOOTING.

When lying down.—*Loading.*—Put in the powder as you best can, and ram the bullet home, lying flat on your back, with the barrel of the gun athwart your breast. It is easy to load in this way with cartridges.

On Horseback.—*Loading.*—Empty the charge of powder from the flask into the left hand, and pour it down the gun; then take a bullet, wet out of your mouth, and drop it into the barrel, using no ramrod; the wet will cake the bullet pretty firmly in its right place.

Firing.—"In firing, do not bring the gun to your shoulder; but present it across the pommel of the saddle, calculating the angle with your eye, and steadying yourself momentarily by standing in the stirrups, as you take aim." (Palliser.) In each bound of the horse, the moment when his fore legs strike the ground is one of comparative steadiness, and is therefore the proper instant for pulling the trigger.

On Water.—*Boat-shooting.*—A landing-net should be taken in the boat, as Colonel Hawker well advises, to pick up the dead birds as they float on the water, while the boat passes quickly by them.

Shooting over Water.—When shooting from a river-bank without boat or dog, take a long light string with a stick tied to one end of it, the other being held in the hand: by throwing the stick beyond the floating bird, it can gradually be drawn in. The stick should be 1½ or 2 feet long, 2 inches in diameter, and notched at either end, and attached to the hand-line by a couple of strings, each 6 feet long, tied round either notch. Thus, the hand-line terminates in a triangle (see the figure I have given, of a rude *Stirrup*), the two sides of which are of string, with the stick for a base. A stout stick of this kind can be thrown to a great distance; either it may be "heaved," as a sailor's Deep-sea Lead, or it may be whirled round the head, and then let fly.

Night-shooting.—Tie a band of white paper round the muzzle of the gun, behind the sight. Mr. Andersson, who has had very great experience, ties the paper, not round the smooth barrel, but over the sight and all; and, if the sight does not happen to be a large one, he ties a piece of thick string round the barrel, or uses other similar contrivance, to tilt up the fore end of the paper. By this means, the paper is not entirely lost sight of at the moment when the aim is being taken. Mr. Andersson also pinches the paper into a ridge along the middle of the gun, to ensure a more defined foresight.

Nocturnal Animals.—There are a large number of night-feeding animals, upon whose flesh a traveller might easily support himself, but of whose existence he would have few indications by daylight observation only. The following remarks of Professor Owen, in respect to Australia are very suggestive:—"All the marsupial animals—and it is one of their curious peculiarities—are nocturnal. Even the kangaroo, which is the least so, is scarcely ever seen feeding out on the plains in broad daylight: it prefers the early morning dawn, or the short twilight; and, above all, the bright moonlight nights. With regard to most of the other Australian forms of marsupial animals, they are most strictly nocturnal; so that, if a traveller were not aware of that peculiarity, he might fancy himself traversing a country destitute of the mammalian grade of animal life. If, however, after a weary day's journey, he could be awakened, and were to look out about the moonlight glade or scrub, or if he were to set traps by night, he would probably be surprised to find how great a number of interesting forms of mammalian animals were to be met with, in places where there was not the slightest appearance of them in the daytime."

Battues.—In Sweden, where hundreds of people are marshalled, each man has a number, and the number is *chalked* upon his hat.

Scarecrows.—A string with feathers tied to it at intervals, like the tail of a boy's kite, will scare most animals of the deer tribe, by their fluttering; and, in want of a sufficient force of men, passes may be closed by this contrivance. The Swedes use "lappar," viz. pieces of canvas, of half the height of a man, painted in glaring colours and left to flutter from a line.

Mr. Lloyd tells us of a peasant who, when walking without a gun, saw a glutton up in a tree. He at once took off his hat and coat and rigged out a scarecrow, the counterpart of himself, which he fixed close by, for the purpose of frightening the beast from coming down; he then went leisurely home, to fetch his gun: this notable expedient succeeded perfectly.

Stalking-horses.—*Artificial.*—A stalking-horse, or cow, is made by cutting out a piece of strong canvas into the shape of the animal, and painting it properly. Loops are sewn in different places, through which sticks are passed, to stretch the curves into shape: a stake, planted in the ground serves as a buttress to support the apparatus: at a proper height, there is a loophole to fire through. It packs up into a roll of canvas and a bundle of five or six sticks.

Bushes are used much in the same way. Colonel Hawker made a contrivance upon wheels which he pushed before him. The Esquimaux shoot seals by pushing a white screen before them over the ice, on a sledge. See figure.—(Kane.)

Real.—Both horses and oxen can be trained to shield a sportsman: they are said to enter into the spirit of the thing; and to show wonderful craft, walking round and round the object in narrowing circles, and stopping to graze unconcernedly, on witnessing the least sign of alarm. Oxen are taught to obey a touch on the horn: the common but cruel way of training them is to hammer and batter the horns for hours together, and on many days successively: they then become inflamed at the root and are highly sensitive.

Pan-hunting (used at salt-licks).—" Pan-hunting is a method of hunting deer at night. An iron pan attached to a long stick, serving as a handle, is carried in the left hand over the left shoulder; near where the hand grasps the handle, is a small projecting stick, forming a fork on which to rest the rifle, when firing. The pan is filled with burning pine-knots, which, being saturated with turpentine, shed a brilliant and constant light all around; shining into the eyes of any deer that may come in that direction, and making them look like two balls of fire. The effect is most curious to those unaccustomed to it. The distance between the eyes of the deer as he approaches, appears gradually to increase, reminding one of the lamps of a travelling carriage." (Palliser.)

The rush of an enraged Animal is far more easily avoided than is usually supposed. The way the Spanish bull-fighters play with the bull, is well known: any man can avoid a mere headlong charge. Even the speed of a racer, which is undeniably far greater than any wild quadruped, does not exceed 30 miles an hour or four times the speed of a man. The speed of an ordinary horse is not more than 24 miles an hour: now even the fastest wild beast is unable to catch an ordinary horse, except by crawling unobserved close to his side, and springing upon him; therefore I am convinced that the rush of no wild animal exceeds 24 miles an hour, or three times the speed of a man. (See Measurements of the rate of an animal's gallop, p. 37.) It is perfectly easy for a person who is cool, to avoid an animal, by dodging to one side or other of a bush. Few animals turn, if the rush be unsuccessful. The buffalo is an exception; he regularly hunts a man, and is therefore peculiarly dangerous. Unthinking persons talk of the fearful rapidity of a lion or tiger's spring. It is not rapid at all: it is a slow movement, as must be evident from the following consideration. No wild animal can leap ten yards, and they all make a high trajectory in their leaps. Now, think of the speed of a ball thrown, or rather pitched, with just sufficient force to be caught by a person ten yards off: it is a mere nothing. The catcher can play with it as he likes; he has even time to turn after it, if thrown wide. But the speed of a springing animal is undeniably the same as that of a ball, thrown so as to make a flight of equal length and height in the air. The corollary to all this is, that, if charged, you must keep cool and watchful, and your chance of escape is far greater than non-sportsmen would imagine. The blow of the free paw is far swifter than the bound.

Dogs kept at bay.—A correspondent assures me that "a dog flying at a man may be successfully repelled by means of a stout stick held *horizontally*, a hand at each end, and used to thrust the dog backwards over, by meeting him across the throat or breast. If followed by a blow on the nose, as the brute is falling, the result will be sooner attained."

A watch-dog usually desists from flying at a stranger when he seats himself quietly on the ground, like Ulysses. The dog then contents himself with barking and keeping guard until his master arrives.

Hiding Game.—In hiding game from birds of prey, bush it over, and they will seldom find it out; birds cannot smell well, but they have keen eyes. The meat should be hung from an overhanging bough; then, if the birds find it out, there will be no place for them to stand on and tear it. Leaving a handkerchief or a shirt to flutter from a tree, will scare animals of prey for a short time. (See "Scarecrows.")

Tying up your Horse.—You may tie your horse, on a bare plain, to the horns of an animal that you have shot, while you are skinning him, but it is better to hobble the horse with a stirrup-leather. (See "Shooting-horse.")

Division of Game.—Some rules are necessary in these matters, to avoid disputes, especially between whites and natives; and therefore the custom of the country must be attended to. But it is a very general and convenient rule (though, like all fixed rules, often unfair) that the animal should belong to the man who first wounded him, however slight the wound might have been; but that he or they who actually killed the animal, should have a right to a slice of the meat: it must however, be understood, that the man who gave the first wound should not thenceforward withdraw from the chase; if he does so, his claim is lost. In America the skin belongs to the first shot, the carcase is divided equally among the whole party. Whaling crews are bound by similar customs, in which nice distinctions are made, and which have all the force of laws.

Duck-shooting.—Wooden ducks, ballasted with lead, and painted, may be used at night as decoy-ducks; or the skins of birds already shot, may be stuffed and employed for the same purpose. They should be anchored in the water, or made fast to a frame attached to the shooting-punt, and dressed with sedge. It is convenient to sink a large barrel into the flat marsh or mud, as a dry place to stand or sit in, when waiting for the birds to come. A lady suggests to me, that if the sportsman took a bottle of hot water to put under his feet, it would be a great comfort to him, and in this I quite agree; I would take a keg of hot water, when about it. If real ducks be used as decoy-birds, the males should be tied in one place and the females in another, to induce them to quack. An artificial island may be made to attract ducks, when there is no real one.

Crocodile-shooting.—Mr. Gilby says, speaking of Egypt, " I killed several crocodiles by digging pits on the sand-islands and sleeping a part of the night in them; a dry shred of palm-branch, the colour of the sand, round the hole, formed a screen to put the gun through. Their flesh was most *excellent eating* —half-way between meat and fish: I had it several times. The difficulty of shooting them was, that the falcons and spurwing-plovers would hover round the pit, when the crocodiles invariably took to the water. Their sight and hearing were good, but their scent indifferent. I generally got a shot or two at daybreak after sleeping in the pit."

Tracks.—When the neighbourhood of a drinking-place is trodden down with tracks, " describe a circle a little distance from it, to ascertain if it be much frequented. This is the manner in which spoor should at all times be sought for." (Cumming's 'Life in South Africa.') To know if a burrow be tenanted, go to work on the same principle; but, if the ground be hard, sprinkle sand over it, in order to show the tracks more clearly. It is related in the Apocrypha, that the prophet Daniel did this, when he wished to learn who it really was who every night consumed the meat which was placed before the idol of Bel, and which the idol itself was supposed to eat: he thus discovered that the priests and their families had a secret door by which they entered the temple; and convinced the king of the matter, by showing him their footprints.

Carrying Game.—*To carry small Game, as Fallow Deer.*—Make a long slit with your knife between the back sinew and the bone of both of the hind-legs. Cut a thick pole of wood and a stout wooden skewer 8 inches long. Now thrust the right fore-leg through the slit in the left hind one, and then the left fore-leg through the slit in the right hind one, and holding these firmly in their places, push the skewer right through the left fore-leg, so as to peg it from drawing back. Lastly run the pole between the animal's legs and its body, and let two men carry it on their shoulders, one at each end of the pole; or, if a beast of burden be at hand, the carcase is in a very convenient shape for being packed. In animals whose back sinew is not very prominent, it is best to cross the legs as above, and to lash them together. Always take the bowels out of game, before carrying it; *it is so much weight saved.* "I rode out accompanied by an after-rider, and shot two springboks, which we bore to camp secured on our horses behind our saddles, by passing the buckles of the girths on each side through the fore and hind legs of the antelopes, having first performed an incision between the bone and the sinews with the *couteau de chasse*, according to colonial usage." (Cumming's 'Life in South Africa.') "After he had skinned and gutted the animal, he cut away the flesh from the bones, in one piece, without separating the limbs, so as to leave suspended from the tree merely the skeleton of the deer. This, it appeared, was the Turkish fashion in use upon long journeys, in order to relieve travellers from the useless burden of bones." (Huc's 'Tartary.') See also the section on "Heavy weights, to raise and carry," especially Mr. Wyndham's plan.

To float carcases of Game across a river.—Sir S. Baker recommends stripping off the skin of the animal, as though it were intended to make a water-skin of it: putting a stone behind each bullet-hole and tying it tightly in: also tying up the neck end of the skin; thus forming a water-tight sack, open at one end only. All the flesh is now to be cut off the bones, and packed into the sack; which is then to be inflated, and secured by tying up the open end. The skin of a large antelope thus inflated, will not only float the whole of the flesh, but will also support several swimmers.

" *To carry Ivory* on pack-animals, the North African traders use nets, slinging two large teeth on each side of an ass. Small teeth are wrapped up in skins and secured with rope." (Mungo Park.)

Setting a gun as a spring-gun.—*General Remarks.*—The string that goes across the pathway should be dark coloured, and so fine that, if the beast struggles against it, it should break rather than cause injury to the gun. I must however, add, that in the numerous cases in which I have witnessed or heard of guns being set with success, for large beasts of prey, I have never known of injury occurring to the gun. The height of the muzzle should be properly arranged with regard to the height of the expected animal; thus, the heart of a hyena is the height of a man's knee above the ground; that of a lion, is a span higher. The string should not be tight, but hang in a bow, or the animal will cause the gun to go off on first touching the string, and will only receive a flesh-wound across the front of his chest.

1*st Method.*—The annexed sketch (p. 258) explains the method I have described in previous editions of this book. The stock is firmly lashed to a tree, and the muzzle to a stake planted in the ground. A " lever-stick," 8 inches long, is bound across the grip of the gun so as to stand upright; but it is not bound so tightly as to prevent a slight degree of movement. The bottom of the " lever-stick " is tied to the trigger, and the top of it to a long, fine, dark-coloured string, which is passed through the empty ramrod tubes, and is fixed to a tree on the

other side of the pathway. It is evident that when a beast breasts this string, the trigger of the gun will be pulled.

2nd *Method*.—I have, however, been subsequently informed

of a better plan of adapting the "lever-stick." It is shown in the accompanying diagram (below). The fault of the previous plan, is the trouble of tying the string to the trigger; since its curvature is usually such as to make it a matter of some painstaking to fix it securely. A, B, C, is the "lever-stick." Notch it deeply at A, where it is to receive the trigger; notch it also at B, half an inch from A; and at C, 5 inches or so from B. In lashing B to the grip of the stock at D, the firmer you make the lashing, the better. If D admit of any yielding movement, on C being pulled, the gun will not go off, either readily or surely; as will easily be seen, on making experiment.

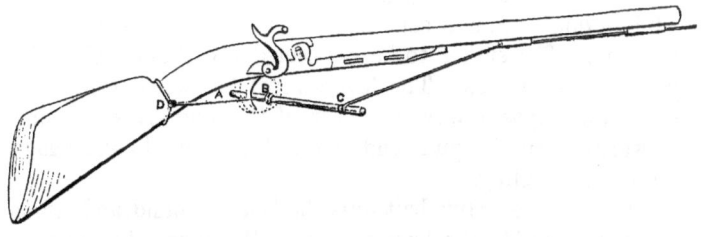

3rd Method.—I am indebted to Captain J. Meaden for the following account of the plan used in Ceylon for setting a spring gun for leopards:—

"Remove the sear, or tie up the trigger. Load the gun, and secure it at the proper height from the ground. Opposite the muzzle of the gun, or at such distance to the right, or left, as may be required, fasten the end of a black string, or line made of horsehair or fibre, and pass it across the path to the gun. Fasten the other end to a stake, long enough to stand higher than the hammer. Stick the end of the stake *slightly* in the ground, and let it rest upright against the lock projection, the black line being fastened nearly at that height. Pass round the small of the stock a loop of single or double string. Take a piece of stick 6 or 8 inches long, pass through the loop, and twist tourniquet fashion until the loop is reduced to the required length. Raise the hammer carefully, and pass the short end of the lever-stick, from the inner to the outer side, over the comb, and let the long end of the lever rest against the stake: the pressure of the hammer will keep the lever steady against the stake. To prevent the lower end of the stake flying out, from the pressure of the lever on the upper part, place a log or stone against the foot.

"An animal pushing against the black string, draws the upper end of the stake towards the muzzle, until the lever is disengaged and releases the hammer.

"In laying the long arm of the lever against the stake sufficient play must be allowed for the contraction of the black string, when wet by dew or rain.

"If a double gun is set, two stakes and two levers will be required. The stakes to be connected above and below the gun, by cross sticks. The levers must be passed round the combs the opposite way, to allow of the long arms pressing outwards from the gun, and enable the levers to disengage without entangling.

"The carcase or live bait must be hedged round, and means adopted to guide the leopard across the string, by running out a short hedge on one side. In this case the black line to be set taut, and some 4 inches from the line of fire. The breast then catches the string, and the push releases the hammer when the muzzle is in line with the chest.

"On this principle, two or more guns can be set, slightly varying in elevation, to allow of one barrel at least being effective."

Bow and Arrow set for Beasts.—The Chinese have some equivalent contrivance with bows and arrows. M. Huc tells us that a simply constructed machine is sold in the shops, by which, when sprung, a number of poisoned arrows are fired off in succession. These machines are planted in caves of sepulture, to guard them from pillage. They use spring-guns, and used to have spring-bows in Sweden, and in many other countries.

Knives.—*Hunting-knife.*—A great hunting-knife is a useless encumbrance: no old sportsman or traveller cares to encumber himself with one; but a butcher's knife, carried in a sheath, is excellent, both from its efficient shape, the soft quality of the steel, its lightness, and the strong way in which the blade is set in the haft.

Pocket-knife.—If a traveller wants a pocket-knife full of all kinds of tools, he had best order a very light one of 2¾ inches long, in a tortoise-shell handle, without the usual turnscrew at the end. It should have a light " picker" to shut over its back; this will act as a strike-light, and a file also, if its under surface be properly roughened. Underneath the picker, there should be a small triangular borer, for making holes in leather, and a gimlet. The front of the knife should contain a long, narrow pen-blade of *soft* steel; a cobbler's awl, slightly bent; and a packing-needle with a large eye, to push thongs and twine through holes in leather. Between the tortoise-shell part of the handle and the metal frame of the knife, should be a space to contain three flat thin pieces of steel, turning on the same pivot. The ends of these are to be ground to form turnscrews of different sizes, two of them being small, for the screws of brass instruments: when this excellent contrivance is used, it must be opened out like the letter T, the foot of which represents the turnscrew in use and the horizontal part represents the other two turnscrews, which serve as the handle. It may be thought advisable to add a button-hook, a corkscrew, and a large blade; but that is not my recommendation, because it increases the size of the knife and makes it heavy; now a heavy knife is apt to be laid by, and not to be at hand when wanted, while a light knife is a constant pocket companion.

Sheath Knives, to carry.—They are easily carried by half-naked, pocketless savages, by attaching the sheaths to a leather-loop, through which the left forearm and elbow are to be passed. A swimmer can easily carry a knife in this way; otherwise he holds it between his teeth.

Substitutes for Knives.—Steel is no doubt vastly better than iron, but it is not essential for the ordinary purposes of life; indeed, most ancient civilized nations had nothing better than iron. Any bit of good iron may be heated as hot as the camp-fire admits; hammered flat, lashed into a handle, and sharpened on a stone. A fragment of flint or obsidian may be made fast to a handle, to be used as a carpenter cuts paper with a chisel; namely, by holding it dagger-fashion, and drawing it over the skin or flesh which he wishes to cut. Shells are sometimes employed as substitutes for knives, also thin strips of bamboo, the sharp edges of which cut meat easily. (See " Sharpening Tools.")

Night-glass.—Opera-glasses are invaluable as night-glasses, for, by their aid, the sight of man is raised nearly to a par with that of night-roving animals; therefore, a sportsman would find them of great service when watching for game at night. A small and inexpensive glass is as useful for this purpose as a large one; but there is a considerable difference between the clearness of different opera-glasses.

OTHER MEANS OF CAPTURING GAME.

General Remarks.—A trapper will never succeed, unless he thoroughly enters into the habits of life and mind of wild animals. He must ever bear in mind how suspicious they are; how quickly their eye is caught by unusual traces; and, lastly, how strong and enduring a taint is left by the human touch. Our own senses do not make us aware of what it is disagreeable enough to acknowledge, that the whole species of man yields a powerful and wide-spreading emanation, that is utterly disgusting and repulsive to every animal in its wild state. It requires some experience to realise this fact: a man must frequently have watched the heads of a herd of far-distant animals, tossed up in alarm the moment that they catch his wind; he must have observed the tracks of animals—how, when they crossed his path of the preceding day, the beast that made the tracks has stopped, scrutinised, and shunned it—before he can believe what a Yahoo he is among the brute creation. No cleanliness of the individual seems to diminish this remarkable odour: indeed, the more civilised the man, the more subtle does it appear to be; the touch of a gamekeeper scares less than that of the master, and the touch of a negro or bushman less than that of a traveller from Europe.

If a novice thinks he will trap successfully by such artless endeavours as putting a bait on the plate of a trap that is covered over with moss, or by digging a pitfall in the middle of a wild beast's track, he is utterly mistaken. The bait should be thrown on the ground, and the trap placed on the way to it; then the animal's mind, being fixed on the meat, takes less heed of the footpath. Or a pitfall should be made near the main path; this being subsequently stopped by boughs, causes the animal to walk in the bushes, and to tumble into the covered hole. The slightest thing diverts an animal's step: watch a wild beast's path across a forest—little twigs and tufts of grass will be seen to have changed its course, and caused it to curve. It is in trifles of this sort that the trapper should look for auxiliaries. After setting traps, Mr. St. John recommends the use of a small branch of a tree; first, to smooth the ground, and then, having dipped it in water, to sprinkle the place: this entirely obliterates all foot-marks.

Springes.—*General Remarks.*—Harden the wood of which the mechanism has to be made, by means of fire; either baking it in hot sand or ashes, or otherwise applying heat to a degree just short of charring its surface. The mechanism will then retain the sharpness of its edges under a continuance of pressure, and during many hours of wet weather. The slighter the strain on the springe, the more delicately can its mechanism be set.

Nooses.—Catgut (which *see*) makes better nooses than string, because it is stiff enough to keep in shape when set: brass wire that has been heated red-hot, is excellent; for it has no tendency whatever to twist, and yet is perfectly pliable. Fish-hooks are sometimes attached to springes; sometimes a tree is bent down and a strong cord is used for the noose, by which large animals are strangled up in the air, as leopards are in Abyssinia. A noose may be set in any place where there is a run; it can be kept spread out, by thin rushes or twigs set crosswise in it. If the animal it is set for can gnaw, a heavy stone should be loosely propped up, which the animal in its struggles may set free, and by the weight of which it may be hung up and strangled. It is a very convenient plan for a traveller who has not time to look for runs, to make little hedges across a creek, or at right angles to a clump of trees, and to set his snares in gaps left in these artificial hedges. On the same principle, artificial islands of piles and faggots

Javelins.—Heavy poisoned javelins, hung over elephant and hippopotamus paths, and dropped on a catch being touched, after the manner of a springe, are used generally in Africa. They sometimes consist of a "sharp little assegai, or spike, most thoroughly poisoned, and stuck firmly into the end of a heavy block of thornwood, about four feet long and five inches in diameter. This formidable affair is suspended over the centre of a sea-cow path, at about thirty feet from the ground, by a bark cord, which passes over a high branch of a tree, and thence, by a peg, on one side of a path beneath." (Gordon Cumming.)

Trigger.—Where a trigger has to release a strong spring, an arrangement on the principle of a figure of 4 trap is, I believe, the most delicate: the standard may be a branch or the stock of a tree; and the other pieces should be hardened by fire.

Pitfalls.—Very small pitfalls, with sharpened stakes, planted inside them, that have been baked hard by the fire and well poisoned, are easily to be set, but they are very dangerous to man and beast. In preparing a pitfall for animals of prey, it is usual to ascertain whether they are deep enough, by putting in a large dog; if he cannot get out, it is very unlikely that any wild beast can. (See "Trous de loup," p. 312.)

Pitfalls are often dug in great numbers, near frequented watering-places, to which numerous intersecting paths lead: by stopping up particular paths, the pitfalls can be brought separately into use; therefore, those pitfalls need never be employed in which animals have been freshly killed, and where the smell of blood would scare the game. It is difficult to prevent the covers of pitfalls becoming hollow: the only way is to build the roofs in somewhat of an arch, so as to allow room for subsidence. If a herd of animals be driven over pitfalls, some are sure to be pushed in, as the crush makes it impossible for the beasts, however wary, to pick their way.

Uganda Thorn-wreath.—Captain Grant found a very ingenious contrivance in use in Uganda, in Africa. Two small stout hoops of equal diameter, made of wood fully an inch in thickness, were lashed one above the other; long acacia thorns were interposed, forming the spokes of a wheel of which the hoops formed the rim. The bases of the thorns were nipped between the hoops; and their points radiated towards the centre. A great many thorns were used, so that the appearance was that of a wheel without a nave, whose spokes were so close together that they touched each other, and, as thorns taper from base to point, the spokes touched one another along their whole length, from circumference to centre. This apparatus is always made with great neatness. It is laid over a hole 18 inches deep, dug in the beast's path, and the noose of a cord, of which the other end is secured to a log, is laid closely within the upper hoop. When the beast treads on the apparatus, he crashes through the thorns, but, on withdrawing his foot from the hole, the wreath clings to his fetlock like a ruff, and prevents the noose from slipping off. Thus there is time for the noose to become firmly jammed during the struggles of the beast. Of course, the trapper artfully bushes the path, so as to induce him to step full upon the trap. He sets a great many of them, and they require no looking after. The diameter of the hoops is made proportionate to the size of the beast for which they are intended. Six inches interior diameter was the size used for buffalo and hartebeest.

Traps.—Steel traps should never be tied fast, or the captured animal may struggle loose, or even gnaw off his leg. It is best to cut small bushes, and merely to secure the traps to their cut ends. Steel traps are of but little use to a traveller.

Hawks are trapped by selecting a bare tree, that stands in an open space: its top is sawn off level, and a trap is put upon it: the bait is laid somewhere near, on the ground: the bird is sure to visit the pole, either before or after he has fed.

Poison.—Savages frequently poison the water of drinking-places, and follow, capture, and eat the poisoned animals. Nux vomica or strychnine is a very dangerous poison to use, but it affords the best means of ridding a neighbourhood of noxious beasts and birds: if employed to kill beasts, put it in the belly; if, birds, in the eye, of the bait. Meat for killing beasts should be set after nightfall; else the crows and other birds will be sure to find it out, and eat it up before the beasts have time to discover it. It would be unsafe to eat an animal killed with strychnine, on account of the deadliness of the poison.

The Swedes put fulminating-powder in a raw shankbone, and throw it down to the wolves; when one of these gnaws and crunches it, it blows his head to atoms.

Poisoned Bullets.—I take the following extract from 'Galignani's Messenger:'—" A new method of catching whales is now being tried with considerable success, science having contributed to its discovery. Our readers are well aware of the deadly effects of the Indian poison called wurare, or woorali, concerning which we have often had occasion to record the most interesting experiments, especially in mentioning the attempts made to use it as a specific for lockjaw, its peculiar action consisting in relaxing the muscular system. Strychnine is a poison producing the contrary effect, the excessive contraction of that system, or, in other words, tetanus, or lockjaw. It is a curious fact that by the conjunction of these two agents, so diametrically opposite in their effects, a poison is obtained that will kill almost instantly if only administered in the dose of half a milligramme per kilogramme of the animal to be subjected to its action, provided its weight do not exceed ten kilogrammes. If larger, the dose must be proportionally increased. M. Thiercelin, the inventor of this poison, composes it by mixing a salt of strychnine with one-twentieth of woorali. To apply it to whale fishing, he makes the compound up into cartridges of thirty grammes (an ounce) each, which is enough to kill an animal of 60,000 kilogrammes weight. Each cartridge is imbedded in the gunpowder contained in an explosive shell which is fired off on the whale. In a late whaling voyage ten whales received such missiles, and all died within from four to eighteen minutes after the infliction of the wound. Out of these ten whales, six were cut up for their blubber and whalebone. Their remains were handled by careless men, who frequently had scratches and sores on their skin, and yet not one of them suffered the slightest injury, a circumstance which shows that the poison cannot be transmitted from the fish to the men. Its poisonous action on the whale is, however, so great that practically the dose will have to be diminished, so that the death of the creature may not be so sudden. We should not forget to state that two out of the ten whales above mentioned were lost by one of the many accidents incident to whaling, and that two others were of a kind that is not worth fishing for."

Poisoned Arrows.—Arrows are most readily poisoned by steeping a thread in the juice, and wrapping it round the barbs. Serpents' venom may always be used with effect.

Bird-lime can be made from the middle bark of most parasitic plants, that is to say, those that grow like mistletoe, out of the boughs of other trees. Holly and young elder shoots also afford it. The bark is boiled for seven or eight hours, till quite soft, and is then drained of its water and laid in heaps, in pits dug in the ground, where it is covered with stones and left for two or three weeks to ferment; but less time is required, if the weather be hot. It is watered from time to time, if necessary. In this way, it passes into a mucilaginous state; and is then pounded into a paste, washed in running water, and kneaded till it is free from dirt and chips. Lastly, it is left for four or five days in earthen vessels, to ferment and purify itself, when it becomes fit for use. It ought to be greenish, sour, gluey, stringy, and sticky. It becomes brittle when dry, and may be powdered; but, on being wetted, it becomes sticky again. (Ure's Dictionary.)

Vast flocks of birds frequent the scattered watering-places of dry countries at nightfall and at daybreak: by liming the sedges and bushes that grow about them, numbers of birds could be caught.

Crows may be killed by twisting up a piece of paper like an extinguisher, dropping a piece of meat in it, and smearing its sides with bird-lime. When the bird pokes his head in, his eyes are gummed up and blinded; and he towers upwards in the air, whence he soon falls down exhausted, and, it may be, dead with fright. (Lloyd.) Fish-hooks, baited with meat, are good to catch these sorts of birds.

Catching with the Hand.—*Ducks.*—We hear of Hindoos who, taking advantage of the many gourds floating on their waters, put one of them on their heads, and wade in among wild ducks; they pull them down, one after another, by their legs, under water; wring their necks, and tie them to their girdle. But in Australia, a swimmer binds grass and rushes, or weeds, round his head; and takes a long fishing-rod, with a slip noose working over the pliant twig that forms the last joint of the rod. When he comes near, he gently raises the end, and, putting the noose over the head of the bird, draws it under water to him. He thus catches one after another, and tucks the caught ones in his belt. A windy day is generally chosen, because the water is ruffled. (Eyre.)

Condors and Vultures are caught by spreading a raw ox-hide, under which a man creeps, with a piece of string in his hand, while one or two other men are posted in ambush close by, to give assistance at the proper moment. When the bird flies down upon the bait, his legs are seized by the man underneath the skin, and are tied within it, as in a bag. All his flapping is then useless; he cannot do mischief with his claws, and he is easily overpowered.

Bolas.—The bolas consists of three balls, composed either of lead or stone; two of them are heavy, but the third is rather lighter: they are fastened to long elastic strings, made of twisted sinews, and the ends of the strings are all tied together. The Indian holds the lightest of the three balls in his hand, and swings the two others in a wide circle above his head; then taking his aim, at the distance of about fifteen or twenty paces, he lets go the hand-ball; all the three balls whirl in a circle, and twine round the object aimed at. The aim is usually taken at the hind-legs of the animals, and, the cords twisting round them, they become firmly bound. It requires great skill and long practice to throw the bolas dexterously, especially when on horseback. A novice in the art incurs the risk of dangerously hurting either himself or his horse, by not giving the balls the proper swing, or by letting go the hand-ball too soon. (Tschudi's 'Peru.')

Lasso.—It is useless that I should enter into details about making and wielding the lasso, for it is impossible to become moderately adept in its use, without months of instruction and practice.

Hamstringing.—Animals are hamstrung by riding at them, armed with a sort of spear; the blade of which is fixed at right angles to the shaft, and has a cutting edge.

Hawking is a disappointing pursuit, owing to the frequent loss of hawks; and can hardly be carried on except in a hawking country, where the sportsman has a better chance than elsewhere, both of recovering and replacing them; it is impracticable except where the land is open and bare; and it is quite a science. There are some amateurs who will not hear a word of disparagement about their hawks, but the decided impression that I bear away with me from all I have learnt, is, that the birds are rarely affectionate or intelligent.

FISHING.

Fishing-tackle.—*Fish-hooks* are made of iron, not steel, wire. While the piece of wire is straight, it is laid along a little groove in a block of wood, and there barbed by the stroke of a chisel, slantwise across it. The other end is flattened by a tap of the hammer, or roughened, that it may be held by the whipping; then the point is sharpened by a file, and finished on a stone. The proper curvature is next given, and then the hook is case-hardened (see "Case-hardening"); lastly, the proper temper is given, by heating the hook red-hot, and quenching it in grease.

A traveller should always take a few hooks with him: they should be of the very small and also of the middling-sized sorts; he might have a dozen of each sort whipped on to gut; and at least a couple of casting-lines, with which to use them: also several dozens of tinned iron fish-hooks, of various sizes, such as are used at sea; and plenty of line.

Fishing-lines.—Twisted sinews will make a fishing-line. To make a strong fine line, unravel a good silk handkerchief, and twist the threads into a whipcord. (See also "Substitutes for String.")

Gut is made from silkworms; but the scrapings of the membrane in the manufacture of catgut (see "Sinew-thread") make a fine, strong, and somewhat transparent thread: twisted horsehair can almost always be obtained: and boiling this in soap-lees, takes away its oiliness.

Shoemakers' Wax is made by boiling together common resin and any kind of soft grease, which does not contain salt, such as oil or butter. A sixth or seventh part of pitch makes it more tough, but it is not absolutely necessary for making the wax. Try if the quantity of grease is sufficient by dipping the stick with which the wax is stirred, into water to cool it. When the wax is supposed to be successfully made, pour it into water, then taking it out while yet soft, pull it and stretch it with your wet hands as much as it will bear; do this over and over again, after dipping it in lukewarm water, till it is quite tough. Wax is used of different degrees of hardness, according as the weather is warm or cold.

Reel.—If you have no reel, make a couple of gimlet-holes, six inches apart, in the butt of your rod, at the place where

Fig. 1.

the reel is usually clamped; drive wooden pegs into these, and wind your spare line round them, as in fig. 1. The pegs should not be quite square with the butt, but should slope a little, each away from the other, that the line may be better retained

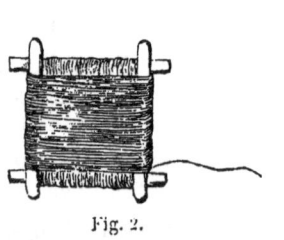

Fig. 2.

Fig. 3.

on them. A long line is conveniently wound on a square frame, as shown in the annexed sketch (fig. 2); and a shorter line, as in fig. 3.

If you have no equivalent for a reel, and if your tackle is slight, and the fish likely to be large, provide yourself with a bladder or other float; tie it to the line, and cast the whole adrift.

Trimmers are well known, and are a convenient way of fishing the middle of a pool, with only a short line. Anything will do for the float—a bladder or a bottle is very good.

To recover a lost Line, make a drag of a small bushy tree with plenty of branches, that are so lopped off as to leave spikes on the trunk. This is to be weighted with a stone, and dragged along the bottom.

Otters.—What is called "an otter" is useful to a person on the shore of a wide river or lake which he has no other means of fishing: it is very successful at first, but soon scares the fish; therefore it is better suited to a traveller than to an ordinary sportsman. It is made as follows:—A board of light wood, fourteen inches long and eight inches high, or thereabouts, is heavily weighted along its lower edge, so as to float upright in the water; a string like the bellyband of a kite, and for the same purpose, is fastened to it; and to this belly-band the end of a line, furnished with a dozen hooks at intervals, is tied. As the fisherman walks along the bank, the otter runs away from him, and carries his line and hooks far out into the stream. It is very convenient to have a large hand-reel to wind and unwind the line upon; but a forked stick will do very well.

Boat fishing.—In fishing with a long ground-line and many hooks, it is of importance to avoid entanglements; make a box in which to coil the line, and a great many deep saw-cuts across the sides, into which the thin short lines, to which the hooks are whipped, may be jammed.

Fishermen who do not use oars, but paddles, tie a loop to their line: they put their thumb through the loop, and fish while they paddle.

To see Things deep under Water, such as dead seals, use a long box or tube with a piece of glass at the lower end; this removes entirely the glare of the water and the effects of a rippled surface. Mr. Campbell, of Islay, suggests that a small glass window might be let into the bottom of the boat:

plate-glass would be amply strong enough. (See "Water-spectacles.")

Nets.—A small square net may be best turned to account by sinking it in holes and other parts of a river which fish frequent; throwing in bait to attract them over it; and then hauling up suddenly. The arrangement shown in the figure is very common. A seine net may be furnished with bladder

for floats, or else with pieces of light wood charred to make them more buoyant. The hauling-ropes may be made of bark steeped for three weeks, till the inner bark separates from the outer, when the latter is twisted into a rope. (Lloyd.) Wherever small fish are swimming in shoals near the surface, there the water is sure to be rippled.

Spearing Fish.—The weapon used (sometimes called the "grains") is identical with Neptune's or Britannia's trident, only the prongs should be more numerous and be placed nearer together, in order to catch small fish: the length of the handle gives steadiness to the blow. In spearing by torchlight, a broad oval piece of bark is coated with wet mud, and in it a blazing fire is lighted. It is fixed on a stage, or it is held in the bow of the boat, so high as to be above the spearman's eyes. He can see everything by its light, especially if the water be not above four feet deep, and the bottom sandy. But there are not many kinds of wood that will burn with a sufficiently bright flame; the dry bark of some resinous tree is often used. If tarred rope can be obtained, it may simply be wound round a pole fixed in the bow of the boat, and lighted. Fish can also be shot with a bow and a barbed arrow, to which a string is attached.

Intoxicating Fish.—Lime thrown into a pond will kill the fish; and the similar but far more energetic properties of *Cocculus Indicus* are well known. Throughout tropical Africa and in South America, the natives catch fish by poisoning them. Dams are made, which, when the river is very low, enclose deep pools of water with no current; into these the poison is thrown: it intoxicates the fish, which float and are taken by the hand.

Otters, Cormorants, and Dogs.—Both otters and cormorants are trained to catch fish for their masters; and dogs are trained by the Patagonians to drive fish into the nets, and to frighten them from breaking loose when the net is being hauled in. Cormorants, in China, fish during the winter from October to May, working from 10 A.M. to 5 P.M., at which hour their dinner is given to them. When they fish, a straw tie is put round their necks, to keep them from swallowing the fish, but not so tight as to slip down and choke them. A boat takes out ten or twelve of these birds. They obey the voice: if they are disobedient, the water near them is struck with the back of the oar; as soon as one of them has caught a fish, he is called to the boat, and the oar is held out for him to step upon. It requires caution to train a cormorant, because the bird has a habit, when angry, of striking with its beak at its instructor's eye with an exceedingly rapid and sure stroke.

SIGNALS.

Colomb and Bolton's flashing signals, adopted in our Army and Navy, and used in many other countries as well, are eminently suited to the wants of an expedition. Anything may be used for signalling, that appears and disappears, like a lantern, or an opened and closed umbrella, or that moves, as a waved flag or a person walking to and fro on the crest of a hill against the sky. Sound also can be employed, as long and short whistles. Their use can be thoroughly taught in two hours, and however small the practice of the operators, communication, though slow, is fairly accurate, while in practised hands its rapidity is astonishing. The proportion of time occupied by the flashes and intervals is as follows. (I extract all the rest of the article from the pamphlet published by the inventors of the system.)

Flashing Signals, with Flags.—Supposing the short flash to be half a second in duration, the long flash should be fully a second and a half. The interval between the flashes forming a figure should be equal to a short flash, and the interval between two figures should be equal to a long flash. After the last figure of the signal is finished, there should be a pause equal to at least one-third of the time taken up by the figures. After this pause, the signal should be again repeated with the same measured flashes and intervals, and so continued until answered by all to whom it is addressed.

Exam.: ▄▄ ▄ ▄▄▄▄ ▄ ▄▄▄ ▄▄ ▄▄▄   ▄▄▄ ▄▄ ▄▄▄▄ ▄ ▄▄▄
      3   6   7   9   Pause 3   6   7
▄▄ ▄▄▄   ▄▄▄ ▄▄ ▄▄▄▄ ▄ ▄▄▄ ▄▄ ▄▄▄, &c.
 9   Pause 3   6   7   9   Pause, &c.

Care must be taken never to commence a fresh signal before the answers to the last have ceased; and signals are never to be answered until their repetitions have been observed a sufficient number of times to make an error impossible.

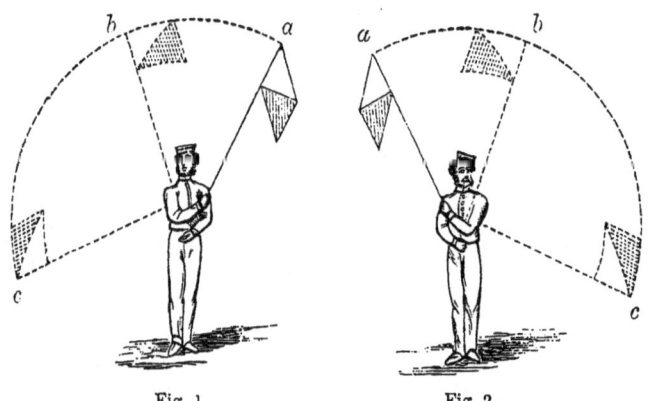

Fig. 1.   Fig. 2.

The signalman may work from left to right, or from right to left, as shown in figs. 1 and 2, according to convenience and the direction of the wind. To make a short flash, the flag is waved from *a* to *b*, and back to the normal position *a*. To make a long flash, the flag is waved from *a* to *c*, and back to the normal position *a*.

The numerals 1 to 5 are, therefore, denoted by one to five waves of the flag from *a* to *b*, recovering to *a*.

The numeral 6 by a wave from *a* to *c*, recovering to *a*. The

Signals. 275

numeral 7 by a wave from a to b, back to a, and then to c, recovering to the normal position a. The numeral 8 is denoted by a wave from a to c, back to a, and then to b, recovering to the normal position a. The numeral 9 is denoted by two waves from a to b, and one from a to c. The numeral 0 by one wave from a to c, recovering again to a, and then two waves from a to b. The other signs are made in the same manner, so that a short motion shall always represent a short flash, and a long motion a long flash.

On the completion of the motions required for each sign, the flag must always be brought to the position a. When the word, or group of figures, is completed, the flag may be lowered in front of the body.

In receiving a message, the flag should always be kept in the position a, except when answering.

In waving the flag, the point of the staff should be made to describe a figure of 8 in the air to keep the flag clear.

Each signal party must consist of not less than two men, whose duties will be as follows:—

In receiving messages :

No. 1 works the flag for answering, &c., and refers to the code for the interpretation of the numbers received, and calls out the words to No. 2.

No. 2 fixes the telescope and reads from the distant station, calling out the numbers as they are made for the information of No. 1, and writes down the numbers and meaning thereof.

Suppose station " A " in communication with station " B ":—

No. 1 at " A " on being told by No. 2 that " B " is about to send a message, takes up his position at attention, holding the flag over the left arm and under the right, or *vice versâ* across his body, according to the wind, with the code book in his hand. No. 2 fixes his eyes on the glass, and on receiving the numbers from " B " calls them out to No. 1, who ascertains their meaning from the code, and gives the words to No. 2, who writes them down in his book, and then placing his eye to the glass, tells No. 1 to make the answer. No. 2 does not, however, direct the answer to be made until he is sure of the correctness of the signal received.

Flashing Alphabet, for Use without a Code.—The following alphabet, &c., can be used under circumstances when it is not convenient or possible to have recourse to the Signal Book, and forms in itself a perfect *telegraphic* system, necessarily somewhat slow in its application, but having the great advantage of requiring very little previous knowledge and practice to work with correctness. The symbols and numbers expressing the alphabet are identical with those forming the alphabet in the Signal Book.

```
        Preparative  ▬▬▬▬▬▬▬▬▬▬▬
        Spelling Prefix  ▪ ▬▬▬ ▬▬▬ ▪
    1  ▪                       6  ▬▬▬
    2  ▪ ▪                     7  ▪ ▬▬▬
    3  ▪ ▪ ▪                   8  ▬▬▬ ▪
    4  ▪ ▪ ▪ ▪                 9  ▪ ▪ ▬▬▬
    5  ▪ ▪ ▪ ▪ ▪               0  ▬▬▬ ▪ ▪
```

1 Understood. ▪	2 Not understood. ▪ ▪	A 5 ▪ ▪ ▪ ▪ ▪	3 Numeral. ▪ ▪ ▪	4 Wait. ▪ ▪ ▪ ▪
B 6 ▬▬▬	C 7 ▪ ▬▬▬	D 8 ▬▬▬ ▪	E 9 ▪ ▪ ▬▬▬	F 10 ▪ ▬▬▬ ▪ ▪
G 11 ▪ ▪	H 12 ▪ ▪ ▪	I 13 ▪ ▬▬▬ ▪	J 14 ▪ ▪ ▪ ▪	K 15 ▪ ▪ ▪ ▪ ▪
L 16 ▪ ▬▬▬	M 17 ▪ ▬▬▬ ▪	N 18 ▪ ▬▬▬ ▪	O 19 ▪ ▪ ▬▬▬	P 20 ▪ ▪ ▬▬▬ ▪ ▪
Q 21 ▪ ▪ ▬▬▬ ▪	R 22 ▪ ▪ ▬▬▬ ▪ ▪	S 23 ▪ ▪ ▪ ▬▬▬	T 24 ▪ ▪ ▪ ▪ ▬▬▬	U 25 ▪ ▪ ▪ ▪ ▪ ▬▬▬
V 26 ▪ ▪ ▬▬▬	W 27 ▪ ▪ ▬▬▬ ▪	X 28 ▪ ▪ ▬▬▬ ▪	Y 29 ▪ ▪ ▬▬▬ ▪	Z 30 ▪ ▪ ▪ ▬▬▬ ▪ ▪

Stop or end of word — ,— — —, &c.

NOTE.—This signal is repeated twice at end of message.

All particulars as to the machines and lanterns used in the Service, for making these flashing signals, and the code, can be procured at W. Nunn & Co.'s Army and Navy Lamp and Signal Works, 65, George Street East, London, E.

Reflecting the Sun with a Mirror.—To attract the notice of a division of your party, five or even ten miles off, glitter a bit of looking-glass in the sun, throwing its flash towards where you expect them to be. It is quite astonishing at how great a distance the gleam of the glass will catch the sharp eyes of a bushman who has learnt to know what it is. It is now a common signal in the North American prairies. (Sullivan.) It should be recollected that a passing flash has far less brilliancy than one that dwells for an appreciable time on the retina of the observer; therefore the signaller should do all he can to steady his aim. I find the steadiest way of holding the mirror is to rest the hand firmly against the forehead, and to keep the eyes continually fixed upon the same distant object. The glare of the sun that is reflected from each point of the surface of a mirror forms a cone of light whose vertical angle is constant, and equal to that subtended by the sun. Hence when a flash is sent to a distant place, the size of the mirror is of no appreciable importance in affecting the size of the area over which the flash is visible. That area is the section of the fasciculus of cones that proceed from each point of the mirror, which, in the case we have supposed, differs immaterially from the cone reflected from a single point. Hence, if a man watches the play of the flash from his mirror upon a very near object, it will appear to him of the shape and size of the mirror; but as he retreats from the object, the edges of the flash become rounded, and very soon the flash appears a perfect circle, of precisely the same apparent diameter as the disc of the sun: it will, in short, look just like a very faint sun. The signaller has to cause this disc of light to cover the person whose notice he wishes to attract. I will proceed to show how he can do so; but in the mean time it will be evident that a pretty careful aim is requisite, or he will fail in his object. The steadiness of his aim must be just twice as accurate, neither more nor less, as would suffice to point a rifle at the sun when it was sufficiently obscured by a cloud to bear being looked at: for the object of the aim is of the same apparent size, but a movement of a mirror causes the ray reflected from it to move through a double angle.

The power of these sun-signals is extraordinarily great. The result of several experiments that I made in England showed that the smallest mirror visible under atmospheric conditions such that the signaller's station was discernible, but dim, subtended an angle of only one-tenth of a second of a degree. It is very important that the mirror should be of truly plane and parallel glass, such as instrument-makers procure; the index glass of a full-sized sextant is very suitable for this purpose: there is a loss of power when there is any imperfection in the glass. A plane mirror only three inches across, reflects as much of the sun as a globe of 120 feet diameter; it looks like a dazzling star at ten miles' distance.

To direct the flash of the Mirror.—There are makeshift ways of directing the flash of the mirror; as, by observing its play on an object some paces off, nearly in a line with the station it is wished to communicate with. In doing this, two cautions are requisite: first, the distance of the object must be so large compared to the diameter of the mirror that the play of the flash shall appear truly circular and exactly like a faint sun (see preceding paragraph): secondly, be careful to bring the eye to the very edge of the mirror; there should be as little "dispart" as possible, as artillerymen would say. Unless these cautions be attended to very strictly, the flash will never

be seen at the distant station. An object, in reality of a white colour but apparently dark, owing to its being shaded, shows the play of a mirror's flash better than any other. The play of a flash, sent through an open window, on the walls of a room, can be seen at upwards of 100 yards. It is a good object by which to adjust my hand heliostat, which I describe below. Two bits of paper and a couple of sticks, arranged as in the drawing, serve pretty well to direct a flash. Sight the distant object through the holes in the two bits of paper, A and B, at the ends of the horizontal stick; and when you are satisfied that the stick is properly adjusted and quite steady, take your mirror and throw the shadow of A upon B, and further endeavour to throw the white speck in the shadow of A, corresponding to its pin-hole in it, through the centre of the hole in B. Every now and then lay the mirror aside, and bend down to see that A B continues to be properly adjusted.

Hand Heliostat.—Some years ago, I took great pains to contrive a convenient pocket instrument, by which a traveller should be able to signal with the sun, and direct his flash with certainty, in whatever direction he desired. I did so in the belief that a signalling power of extraordinary intensity could thus be made use of; and, I am glad to say, I succeeded in my attempt. I at last obtained a pretty pocket instrument, the design of which I placed in the hands of Messrs. Troughton and Simms; and upon the earlier models of which I read a paper before the British Association in 1858. I called it a "hand heliostat." I always carry one when I travel, for it is a continual source of amusement. The instrument is shown in fig. 1 (p. 280), and its principle is illustrated by fig. 2. The scale is about $\frac{2}{3}$.

E is the eye of the signaller; M the mirror; and L, S, fig. 2, a tube, containing at one end, L, a lens, and at the other, S, a screen of white porcelain or *unpolished* ivory, placed at the exact solar focus of L: a shade, K, with two holes in it, is placed before L. Let R, r, be portions of a large pencil of parallel rays, proceeding from any *one point* on the sun's surface, and reflected from the mirror, as R' r' (fig. 2). r' impinges upon the lens, L, through one of the holes in K, and R' goes free toward some distant point, O. Those that impinge on the lens will be brought to a focus on S, where a bright speck of light might be seen. This speck radiates light in all direction; some of the rays, proceeding from it, impinge on the lens at the other hole in the shade K, as shown in fig. 2, and are reduced by its agency to *parallelism* with r′ and R′, that is, with the rays that originally left the mirror: consequently E, looking partly at the edge of the lens, and

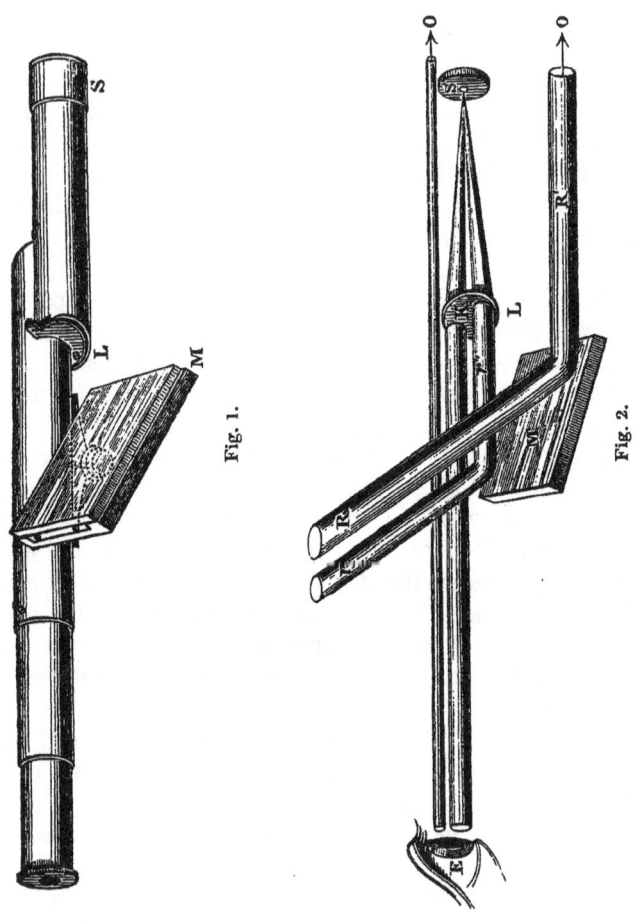

partly into space, sees a bright speck of light in the former, coincident with the point o in the latter. What is true for one point in the sun's disc, is true for every point in it. Accordingly, the signaller sees an image of the sun, and not a mere speck of light, in the lens; and the part of the landscape which that image appears to overlay, is precisely that part of it over which the flash from his mirror extends; or, in other words, it is that from any point of which a distant spectator may see some part or other of the sun's disc reflected in the mirror. There is no difficulty in signalling when the sun is far behind the back, if the eye-tubes are made to pull out to a total length of five inches, otherwise the shadow of the head interferes. For want of space, the drawing represents the tubes as only partly drawn out. The instrument is perfectly easy to manage, and letters can be signalled by flashes. Its power is perfectly marvellous. On a day so hazy that colours on the largest scale—such as green fields and white houses—are barely distinguishable at seven miles' distance, a looking-glass no larger than the finger-nail transmits signals clearly visible to the naked eye.

I have made a makeshift arrangement on the principle of my heliostat, using the object glass of an opera-glass for the lens, and an ordinary looking-glass: the great size and short focus of the object glass is a great convenience when using a mirror with a wide frame.

Professor W. H. Miller, the Foreign Secretary of the Royal Society, has since invented a yet more compact method of directing the flash, which he has described in the Proceedings of the Royal Society for 1865. It consists of a plate of silvered glass, one of whose rectangular corners is accurately ground and polished. On looking into the corner when the glass is properly held an image of the sun is seen, which overlays the actual flash. Beautifully simple as this instrument is, I do not like it so much as my own, for the very fact of its requiring no "setting" is its drawback. With mine, when the image of the sun is lost it is immediately found again by simply rotating the instrument on its axis; but with Professor Miller's the image must be felt for wholly anew.

Fire Signals.—Fire-beacons, hanging up a lantern, or setting fire to an old nest high up in a tree, serve as night-signals; but they are never to be depended on without previous concert, as bushes and undulations of the ground will often hide them entirely. The sparks from a well-struck flint and steel can be seen for much more than a mile.

Smoke Signals.—The smoke of fires is seen very far by day;

and green wood and rotten wood make the most smoke. It is best to make two fires 100 yards apart, lest your signalling should be mistaken for an ordinary fire in the bush. These double fires are a very common signal to vessels in the offing, on the African coast.

Other Signals.—*By Sight.*—A common signal for a distant scout is, that he should ride or walk round and round in a circle from right to left, or else in one from left to right.

Mr. Parkyns, speaking of Abyssinia, describes the habits of a caste of robbers in the following words:—" At other times they will lie concealed near a road, with scouts in every direction on the look-out; yet no one venturing to speak, but only making known by signs what he may have to communicate to his companions or leader. Thus he will point to his ear and foot on hearing footsteps, to his eyes on seeing persons approach, or to his tongue if voices be audible; and will also indicate on his fingers the numbers of those coming, describing also many particulars as to how many porters, beasts of burden or for riding, there may be with the party."

A kite has been suggested as a day signal; and also a kite with some kind of squib, let off by a slow-light and attached to its tail, as one by night. (Colonel Jackson.)

Sound.—Whistling through the fingers can be heard at considerable distances: the accomplishment should be learnt. Cooing in the Australian fashion, or jödling in that of the Swiss, are both of them heard a long way. The united holloa of many voices, is heard much further than separate cries. The cracking of a whip has a very penetrating sound.

Smells.—An abominable smell arrests the attention at night.

Letters carried by Animals.—In short reconnoitring expeditions made by a small detachment from a party, the cattle or dogs are often wild, and run home to their comrades on the first opportunity; in the event of not being able to watch them, owing to accident or other cause, advantage may be taken of their restlessness, by tying a note to one of their necks, and letting them go and serve as postmen, or rather as carrier-pigeons.

BEARINGS BY COMPASS, SUN, ETC.

Pocket Compass.—A pocket compass should not be too small; if one of the little toy compasses be carried in the pocket, it should be as a reserve, and not for regular use. A toy compass will of course tell N. from N.N.E., and the like; and that may be very useful information, but the traveller will find that he constantly needs more precise directions. He doubts the identity of some hill or the destination of some path, and finds on referring to his map, that the difference of bearing upon which he must base his conclusion, is small: he therefore requires a good sized compass, to determine the bearing with certainty. One from 1½ to 2 inches in diameter is practically the best. It should have plenty of depth, so that the card may traverse freely, even when the instrument is inclined: it should be light in weight, that it may not be easily jarred by a blow: the catch that relieves the card, when the instrument is closed, should be self-acting and should act well: lastly the movements of the needle should be quick; one that makes slow oscillations should be peremptorily refused, whatever its other merits may be: the graduation of the degrees on the card should be from 0° to 360°, North being 0° and East 90°. I wish some optician would make aluminium cards. The material can be procured as foil, like tinfoil. It can then be stamped and embossed, in which case it retains its shape perfectly, but I cannot satisfy myself as to a good pattern, nor do I see how to make the North and South halves of the disc sufficiently different in appearance.

Compass for use at night.—The great majority of compasses are well-nigh useless in the dark, that is, when it is most important to be able to consult them. They are rarely so constructed, that the difference between the north and south sides is visible by moonlight or by the light of a cigar or piece of tinder. The more modern contrivances are very effective; in these the southern half of the compass card is painted black, the northern being left white. With a very faint light, this difference can be appreciated. In compasses consisting simply of a needle, the north end of the needle should have a conspicuous arrow-head. It is extraordinary how much the power of seeing a compass or a watch at night is increased by looking nearly at it through a magnifying-glass. Thus, young people who can focus their vision through a wide range may be observed poring with their eyes close to their books when the light wanes. So again, at night-time, a placard, even in large type, is illegible at a short distance, but easily read on approaching it. It seems, in order that a faint image on the retina should be appreciated by the nerves of sight, that image must have considerable extent.

Moonlight or the light of a cigar may be condensed on the compass by a burning glass, or other substitute for it. (See "Burning Glass.")

True and Magnetic Bearings.—The confusion between true and magnetic bearings is a continual trouble, even to the most experienced travellers. Sir Thomas Mitchell's exploring party very nearly sustained a loss by mistaking the one for the other. I recommend that the points of the compass, viz. North, N.N.E., &c., should be solely used for the traveller for his true bearings; and the degrees, as 25° (or N. 25° E.), for his magnetic. There would then be no reason why the two nomenclatures should interfere with one another, for a traveller's recollection of the lay of a country depends entirely upon true bearings—or sunrise, sunset, and the stars—and is expressed by North, N.N.E, &c.; but his surveying data, which find no place in his memory, but are simply consigned to his note-book, are necessarily registered in degrees. To give every facility for carrying out this principle, a round of paper should be pasted in the middle of the traveller's pocket-compass card, just large enough to hide the ordinary rhumbs, but leaving uncovered the degrees round its rim. On this disc of paper the points of the compass (true bearings) should be marked so as to be as exact as possible for the country about to be visited.

Errors in Magnetic Bearings.—The compass-needle is often found to be disturbed, and sometimes apparently bewitched, when laid upon hill-tops; even when they consist of bare masses of granite. The disturbance is easily accounted for by the hornblende in the granite, or by other iron-bearing rocks. Explorers naturally select hills as their points of triangulation; but compass observations on hill-tops, if unchecked by a sextant observation of the sun's bearings, are never so reliable as those taken on a plain.

Bearings by Sun and Stars.—It requires very great practice to steer well by stars, for, on an average, they change their bearings even faster than they change their altitudes. In tropical countries, the zodiacal stars—as Orion and Antares—give excellent east and west points. The Great Bear is useful when the North Pole cannot be seen, for you may calculate

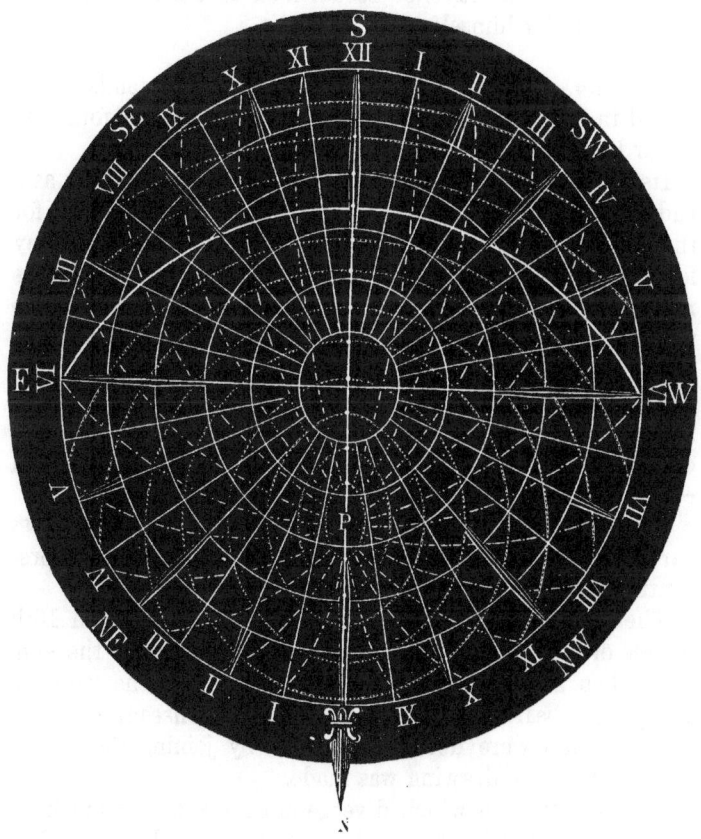

by the eye whereabout it would be in the heavens when its "pointers" were vertical, or due north; and the Southern Cross is available in precisely the same way. The true North Pole is about 1½ degree or 3 diameters of the full moon, apart from the Pole star; and its place is on a line between the Pole Star and the Great Bear. An almanac, calculated to show the bearing, and the times of moonrise and moonset, for the country to be travelled over, as well as those of sunrise and sunset, would be a very great convenience; it would be worth while for a traveller accustomed to such calculations to make one for himself.

Diagram.—The diagram (preceding page) is intended to be traced in lines of different colours, when it will be found to be far less confused than at present.

Its object is to enable a traveller to use the sun, both as a rude watch and as a compass. The diagram is calculated for the latitude of London, but will do with more or less accuracy for the whole of England. A traveller going to other countries may easily draw up one for himself, and on a larger scale if he prefers it, by using the Azimuth tables and the Horary tables of Lynn.

The diagram represents, 1st, circles of equal altitudes; 2ndly, the path of sun, stars, &c., for each 10th degree of declination; 3rdly, the hour angles, all projected down upon —4thly—the level compass card.

Thus, six circles are drawn round the centre of the compass card at equal distances apart, each ring between them representing a space of 15° in altitude.

The following angles were then calculated for each 10th degree of declination in turns, viz. :—The height of the sun, &c., when above the horizon at each point of the compass. 2ndly, the bearing of the sun at each consecutive hour. These points were dotted out; and, by joining the several sets of them, the drawing was made.

The broken lines which diverge in curves from P are hour lines; those which surround P in more or less complete ovals, are the paths of the sun and stars, for each 10th degree of declination; the prominent line running from E. round to W. being its path when on the Equator.

The diagram, when it is traced out for use, should have the names of the months written in coloured ink on either side of the south line at places corresponding to the declination of the sun during those months; viz.:—

January	S. 23°	to	S. 17°	July	N. 23°	to	N. 18°
February	S. 17	„	S. 8	August	N. 18	„	N. 8
March	S. 7	„	N. 4	September	N. 8	„	S. 3
April	N. 5	„	N. 15	October	S. 3	„	S. 14
May	N. 15	„	N. 22	November	S. 15	„	S. 22
June	N. 22	„	N. 23	December	S. 22	„	S. 23

To use the card.—Draw a broad pencil line, which may afterwards be rubbed out, corresponding to the date of travel, and there will be no further confusion.

Then, to know what o'clock it is, "span out" (see "Spanning") roughly the altitude of the sun. The point in the diagram where the altitude so obtained crosses the pencil mark, corresponds to the position of the sun. The hour is then read off; and the compass bearings on the diagram are adjusted by holding it level, and turning it round until a line, drawn from its centre through the point in question, points towards the sun. As to the moon or a star, if its declination be unknown, but its bearing and altitude being given, its declination and path may be found, and therefore the time since its rising or before its setting; a most useful piece of information to a traveller. Watches break, and compasses cannot be used on horseback without stopping, and therefore a diagram of this description, of which any number of copies can be traced out, may be of use for rough purposes.

Other Signs of Direction.—*Bearings by the Growth of Trees.*— In exposed situations and near the sea, the growth of trees is rarely symmetrical; they betray by their bent heads and stunted branches the direction of the prevalent influences most adverse to their growth. This direction is constant over wide districts in a flat country, but cannot be equally relied upon in a hilly one, where the mountains and valleys affect the conditions of shade and shelter, and deflect the course of the wind.

Moss grows best where there is continuous damp, therefore it prefers that side of a tree which affords the most suitable combination of exposure to damp winds and shelter from the sun. When the winds do not differ materially in dampness, the north side of the forest trees are the most thickly covered with moss.

Bearings by the shape of Ant-hills.—That most accurate observer, Pierre Huber, writes as follows concerning the nests of the yellow ants, which are abundantly to be found in the Swiss Alps and in some other mountainous countries. It must be recollected, in reading his statement, that the chief occupation of ants is to move their eggs and larvæ from one part of the nest to another, to ensure them a warm and equable temperature; therefore, it is reasonable to expect that the nests of ants should be built on a uniform principle as regards their shape and aspect. Huber says " they serve as a compass to mountaineers when they are surrounded by thick mists, or have lost their way during the night; they do so in the following manner:—The ant-hills (of the yellow ants), which are by far more numerous and more high in the mountains than anywhere else, are longer than they are broad, and are of a similar pattern in other respects. Their direction is invariably from east to west. Their highest point and their steepest side are turned towards the point of sunrise in the winter-time (*au levant d'hiver*), and they descend with a gradual slope in the opposite direction. I have verified these experiences of the shepherds upon thousands of ant-hills, and have found a very small number of exceptions; these occurred only in the case where the ant-hills had been disturbed by men or animals. The ant-hills do not maintain the constancy of their form in the lowlands, where they are more exposed to such accidents."

Ripple-marks on Snow or Sand.—The Siberians travel guided by the ripples in the snow, which run in a pretty fixed direction, owing to the prevalence of a particular wind. The ripples in a desert of sand are equally good as guides; or the wind itself, if it happens to be blowing, especially to a person pushing through a tangled belt of forest. Before leaving a well-known track, and striking out at night into the broad open plain, notice well which way the wind blows as regards the course you are about to pursue.

Flight of Birds.—I have read somewhere that in the old

days coasting sailors occasionally took pigeons with them, and when they had lost their bearings they let one fly, which it did at once to the land.

To follow a Track at Night.—Where the track is well marked, showers of sparks, ably struck with a flint and steel, are sufficient to show it, without taking the pains of making a flame.

Smell of an Old Track.—The earth of an old and well-trodden road has a perceptible smell, from the dung and trampling of animals passing over it, especially near to encampments. It is usual at night, when a guide doubts whether or no he is in the track, to take up handfuls of dirt and smell it. It is notorious that cattle can smell out a road.

MARKS FOR THE WAY-SIDE.

Marks on Trees—*Cutting Marks.*—A very excellent "tree-line" is made by cutting deep notches in a line of trees, starting from some conspicuous object, so that the notches will face the men that are to be guided by it: the trees must be so selected that three, or at least two of them, are in sight at once. The notch or sliced bark of a tree is called a "blaze" in bush language. These blazed trees are of much use as finger-posts on a dark night. They are best made by two persons; one chipping the trees on his right, and the other those on his left. If the axes are quite sharp, they only need to be dropped against the tree in order to make the chip. Doing so, hardly retards a person in his walking. Another way more suitable to some kinds of forests, is to strike the knife into the left side of the tree, to tear down a foot of bark, and to leave the bark hanging, for a double extent of white surface is shown in this way. Also, to break down tops of saplings and leave them hanging: the under sides of the leaves being paler than the upper, and the different lines of the reversed foliage make a broken bush to look unnatural among healthy trees, and it quickly arrests the attention. If you want a tree to be well-scored or slashed, so as to draw attention to it without fail, fire bullets into it, as into a mark, and let the natives cut them out in their own way, for the sake of the lead. They will effect your purpose admirably, without suspecting it.

Stamping Marks on Trees.—The keepers of some of the communal forests in Switzerland are provided with small axes, having the back of the axe-head worked into a large and sharp die, the impression of the die being some letter or cipher indicating the commune. When these foresters wish to mark a tree, they give it first a slice with the edge of the axe, and then (turning the axe) they deal it a heavy blow with the back of the axe-head. By the first operation they prepare a clean surface for their mark; and, by the second, they stamp their cipher deeply into the wood.

Branding Trees.—Some explorers take branding irons, and use them to mark each of their camping-places with its number. This is especially useful in Australian travel, where the country is monotonous, and there are few natives to tell the names of places.

Faggot hung to a Tree.—A bundle of grass or twigs about 2 feet long, slung by its middle athwart a small tree, at the level of the eye, by the side of a path, is well calculated to catch the attention. Its lines are so different to those seen elsewhere in the forest, that it would be scarcely possible to overlook it.

Boat or Canoe Routes through lakes well studded with islands, can be well marked by trimming conspicuous trees until only a tuft of branches is left at the top. This is called, in the parlance of the " Far West," a " lopstick."

Fig. 1.

Wooden Crosses.—A simple structure like fig. 1 is put together with a single nail or any kind of lashing. It catches the attention immediately.

Marks with Stones.—*Marks cut on Stone.*—I have observed a very simple and conspicuous permanent mark used in forest-roads, as represented in fig. 2. The stone is 8 inches above ground, 3½ wide, 8 inches long: the mark is

black and deeply cut. An arrow-head may be chiselled in
the face of a rock and filled with melted
lead. With a small "cold" chisel, 3
inches long and ¼ inch wide, a great deal
of stone carving may readily be effected.

Fig. 2.

Piles of Stones.—Piles of stones are
used by the Arabs in their deserts, and in
most mountain-tracts. "An immense length of the road,
both in the government of the Don Cossacks and in that
of Tambov, is marked out on a
gigantic scale by heaps of stones,
varying from 4 to 6 feet high. These
are visible from a great distance;
and it is very striking to see the

double row of them indicating the line of route over the
Great Steppe—undulations which often present no other trace
of the hand of man." (Spottiswoode.)

Gipsy Marks.—When gipsies travel, the party that goes in
advance leaves marks at cross-roads, in order to guide those
who follow. These marks are called "patterans;" there are
three patterans in common use. One is to pluck three large
handfuls of grass and to throw them on the ground, at a short
distance from one another, in the direction taken; another is,
to draw a cross on the ground, with one arm much longer
than the rest, as a pointer—a cross is better than any other
simple mark, for it catches many different lights. (In marking a road, do not be content with marking the dust—an
hour's breeze or a shower will efface it; but take a tent-peg,
or sharpened stick, and fairly break into the surface, and your
mark will be surprisingly durable.) The third of the gipsy
patterans is of especial use in the dark: a cleft stick is
planted by the road-side, close to the hedge, and, in the cleft,
is an arm like a signpost. The gipsies feel for this at cross-
roads, searching for it on the left-hand side. (Borrow's
'Zincali.') A twig, stripped bare, with the exception of two
or three leaves at its end, is sometimes laid on the road, with
its bared end pointing forwards.

Other similar marks of direction and locality, in use in

various parts of the world are as follows:—Knotting twigs; breaking boughs, and letting them dangle down; a bit of white paper in a cleft stick; spilling water, or liquid of any kind, on the pathway; a litter made of paper torn into small shreds, or of a stick cut into chips, or of feathers of a bird; a string, with papers knotted to it, like the tail of a boy's kite,—tie a stone to the end of it, and throw it high among the branches of a tree.

Paint.—*Whitewash* (which *see*), when mixed with salt, or grease, or glue size, will stand the weather for a year or more. It can be painted on a tree or rock: the rougher the surface on which it is painted, the longer will some sign of it remain.

Black for Inscriptions is made by mixing lamp-black (which *see*) with some kind of size, grease, wax, or tar. Dr. Kane, having no other material at hand, once burnt a large **K** with gunpowder on the side of a rock. It proved to be a durable and efficient mark. When letters are chiselled in a rock, they should be filled with black to make them more conspicuous.

Blood leaves a mark of a dingy hue, that remains long upon a light-coloured, absorbent surface, as upon the face of sandy rocks.

ON FINDING THE WAY.

Recollection of a Path.—It is difficult to estimate, by recollection only, the true distances between different points in a road that has been once travelled over. There are many circumstances which may mislead, such as the accidental tedium of one part, or the pleasure of another; but besides these, there is always the fact, that, in a long day's journey, a man's faculties of observation are more fresh and active on starting than later in the day, when, from the effect of weariness, even peculiar objects will fail to arrest his attention. Now, as a man's recollection of an interval of time is, as we all know, mainly derived from the number of impressions that his memory has received while it was passing, it follows that, so far as this cause alone is concerned, the earlier part of his day's journey will always seem to have been disproportionately long compared to the latter. It is remarkable, on taking a long half-day's walk, and subsequently returning, after resting some hours, how long a time the earlier part of the return journey seems to occupy, and how rapidly different well-remembered points seem to succeed each other, as the traveller draws homewards. In this case, the same cause acts in opposite directions in the two journeys.

To Walk in a Straight Line through Forests.—Every man who has had frequent occasion to find his way from one place to another in a forest, can do so without straining his attention. Thus, in the account of Lord Milton's travels, we read of some North American Indians who were incapable of understanding the white man's difficulty in keeping a straight line; but no man who has not had practice can walk through trees in a straight line, even with the utmost circumspection.

After making several experiments, I think the explanation of the difficulty and the way of overcoming it are as follows:—If a man walks on a level surface, guided by a single conspicuous mark, he is almost sure not to travel towards it in a straight line; his muscular sense is not delicate enough to guard him from making small deviations. If, therefore, after walking some hundred yards towards a single mark, on ground that preserves his track, the traveller should turn round, he will probably be astonished to see how sinuous his course has been. However, if he take note of a second mark and endeavour to keep it strictly in a line with the first, he will easily keep a perfectly straight course. But if he cannot find a second mark, it will not be difficult for him to use the tufts of grass, the stones, or the other accidents of the soil, in its place; they need not be precisely in the same line with the mark, but some may be on the right and some on the left of it, in which case, as he walks on, the perspective of their change of position will be symmetrical. Lastly, if he has not even one definite mark, but is walking among a throng of forest trees, he may learn to depend wholly on the symmetry of the changes of perspective of the trees as a guide to his path. He will keep his point of sight unchanged and will walk in its direction, and if he deviates from that direction, the want of symmetry in the change of perspective on either side of the point on which he wishes to walk, will warn him of his error. The appreciation of this optical effect grows easily into a habit. When the more distant view happens to be shut out, the traveller must regain his line under guidance similar to that by which a sailor steers who only looks at his compass at intervals—I mean by the aspect of the sky, the direction of the wind, and the appearance of the forest, when it has any peculiarity of growth dependent on direction. The chance of his judgment being erroneous to a small extent is the same on the right hand as on the left, consequently his errors tend to compensate each other. I wish some scientific traveller would rigidly test the powers of good bushmen and find their "probable" angular deviation from the true course under different circumstances. Their line should be given to them, and they should be told to make smokes at intervals. The position of these smokes could be easily mapped out by the traveller.

The art of walking in a straight line is possessed in an eminent degree by good ploughmen. They always look ahead, and let the plough take care of itself.

To find the way down a Hill-side.—If on arriving at the steep edge of a ridge, you have to take the caravan down into the plain, and it appears that a difficulty may arise in finding a good way for it; descend first yourself, as well as you can, and seek for a road as you climb back again. It is far more easy to succeed in doing this as you ascend, than as you descend: because when at the bottom of a hill, its bold bluffs and precipices face you, and you can at once see and avoid them: whereas at the top, these are precisely the parts that you overlook and cannot see.

Blind Paths.—Faintly-marked paths over grass (blind paths) are best seen from a distance.

Lost in a Fog.—Napoleon, when riding with his staff across a shallow arm of the Gulf of Suez, was caught in a fog: he utterly lost his way, and found himself in danger. He thereupon ordered his staff to ride from him, in radiating lines, in all directions, and that such of them as should find the water to become more shallow, should shout out.

Mirage.—When it is excessive, it is most bewildering: a man will often mistake a tuft of grass, or a tree, or other most dissimilar object, for his companion, or his horse, or game. An old traveller is rarely deceived by mirage. If he doubts, he can in many cases adopt the following hint given by Dr. Kane: "Refraction will baffle a novice, on the ice; but we have learned to baffle refraction. By sighting the suspected object with your rifle at rest, you soon detect motion."

Lost Path.—If you fairly lose your way in the dark, do not go on blundering hither and thither till you are exhausted; but make as comfortable bivouac as you can, and start at daybreak fresh on your search.

The bank of a watercourse, which is the best of clues, affords the worst of paths, and is quite unfit to be followed at night. The ground is always more broken in the neighbourhood of a river than far away from it; and the vegetation is more tangled. Explorers travel most easily by keeping far away from the banks of streams; because then they have fewer broad tributaries and deep ravines to cross.

If in the daytime you find that you have quite lost your way, set systematically to work to find it. At all events, do not make the matter doubly perplexing by wandering further. Mark the place very distinctly where you discover yourself at fault, that it may be the centre of your search. Be careful to ride in such places as will preserve your tracks. Break twigs if you are lost in a woodland: if in the open country, drag a stick to make a clear trail. Marks scratched on the ground to tell the hour and day that you passed by, will guide a relieving party. A great smoke is useful for the same purpose and is visible for a long distance. (See "Signals.")

A man who loses himself, especially in a desert, is sadly apt to find his presence of mind forsake him, the sense of desolation is so strange and overpowering; but he may console himself with the statistics of his chance of safety—viz., that travellers, though constantly losing their party, have hardly ever been known to perish unrelieved.

When the lost traveller is dead beat with fatigue, let him

exert a strong control over himself, for if he gives way to terror, and wanders wildly about hither and thither, he will do no good and exhaust his vital powers much sooner. He should erect some signal—as conspicuous a one as he can—with something fluttering upon it, sit down in the shade, and, listening keenly for any sound of succour, bear his fate like a man. His ultimate safety is merely a question of time, for he is sure to be searched for; and, if he can keep alive for two or three days, he will, in all probability, be found and saved. (To relieve thirst, p. 223; hunger, p. 197, 17.)

Theory.—When you discover you are lost, ask yourself the following three questions: they comprise the A B C of the art of pathfinding, and I will therefore distinguish them by the letters A, B, and C respectively:—

A. What is the least distance that I can with certainty specify, within which the caravan-path, the river, or the sea-shore, that I wish to regain, lies?

B. What is the direction, in a vague general way, towards which the path or river runs, or the sea-coast tends?

C. When I last left the path, did I turn to the left or to the right.

As regards A, calculate coolly how long you have been riding or walking, and at what pace, since you left your party; subtract for stoppages and well-recollected zigzags; allow a mile and a half per hour for the pace when you have been loitering on foot, and three and a half when you have been walking fast. Bear in mind that occasional running makes an almost inappreciable difference; and that a man is always much nearer to the lost path, than he is inclined to fear.

As regards B, if the man knows the course of the path to within eight points of the compass (or one-fourth of the whole horizon), it is a great gain; or even if he knows B to within twelve points, say 120°, or one-third of the whole horizon, his knowledge is available. For instance, let us suppose a man's general idea of the run of the path to be, that it goes in a northerly and southerly direction: then if he is also positive that the path does not deviate more than to the N.E. on the one side of that direction, or to the N.W. on the other, he knows the direction to within eight points. Similarly, he is sure to twelve points, if his limits, on either hand, are E.N.E. and W.N.W. respectively.

C requires no further explanation.

Now, if a man can answer all three questions, A, B, to within eight points of the compass, and C, he is four and a half times as well off as if he could only answer A; as will be seen by the following considerations. A knowledge of B in addition to A, is of only one-third the use that it would be if C also were known.

1. Let P (fig. 1) be the point where the traveller finds himself at fault, and let P D be a distance within which the path certainly lies; then the circle, E D F, somewhere cuts the path, and the traveller starting from P must first go to D, and then make the entire circuit, D E H F D, before he has exhausted his search. This distance of P D + D E H F D = P D + 6 P D nearly, = 7 P D altogether, which gives the length of road that the man must be prepared to travel over who can answer no other than the question A. Of course, P D may cut the path, but I am speaking of the *extreme* distance which the lost man may have to travel.

2. Supposing that question B can be answered as well as

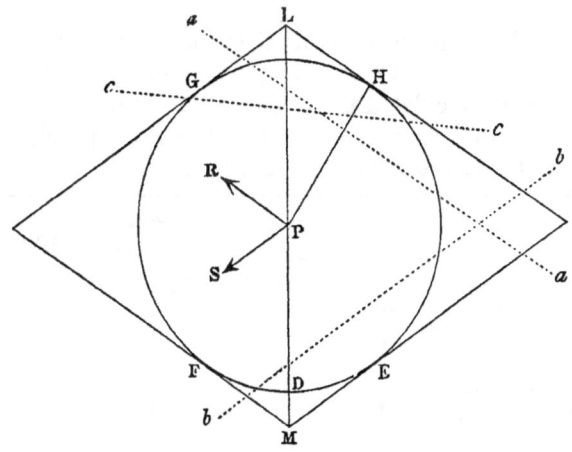

Fig. 1.

question A, and that the direction of the line of road lies

certainly within the points of the compass, P S and P R. Draw the circumscribing parallelogram, G L H E M, whose sides are respectively parallel to P S and P R. Join L M. By the conditions of this problem, the path must somewhere cut the circle E D F; and since L M cuts L H, which is a tangent to it, it is clear it must cut every path—such as *a a*, parallel to L H, or to P R—that cuts the circle. Similarly, the same line, L M, must cut every path parallel to P S, such as *b b*. Now, if L M cuts every path that is parallel to either of the extreme directions, P R or P S, it is obvious that it must also cut every path that is parallel to an intermediate direction, such as *c c*, but

$$P L = \frac{PH}{\cos HPL} = \frac{PD}{\cos \frac{1}{2} RPS;}$$

the consequence of which is that P L exceeds P D by one-sixth, one-half as much again, or twice as much again, according as R P S = 60°, 90°, 120°, or 140.°

The traveller who can only answer the questions A and B, but not C, must be prepared to travel from P to L, and back again through P to M, a distance equal to 3 P L. If, however, he can answer the question C, he knows at once whether to travel towards L or towards M, and he has no return journey to fear. At the worst, he has simply to travel the distance P L.

The *probable* distance, as distinguished from the utmost possible distance that a man may have to travel in the three cases, can be calculated mathematically. It would be out of place here to give the working of the little problem, but I append the rough numerical results in a table.

	Extreme length of Road it may be necessary to travel.	Probable length of Road it will be necessary to travel.
Knows A, alone	7 times the "least distance." *	2 times the "least distance."
Knows A; and B to within 8 points. Not C.	4½ ,, ,,	2¼ ,, ,,
Knows A; and B to within 12 points. Not C.	7¼ ,, ,,	3¾ ,, ,,
Knows A and C; and B to within 8 points	1½ ,, ,,	¾ ,, ,,
Knows A and C; and B to within 12 points	2¼ ,, ,,	1¼ ,, ,,
Knows A and C; and B to within 13 points	3½ ,, ,,	1¾ ,, ,,

* The words "least distance," mean the least distance that the traveller can specify with absolute confidence, as that within which the path, &c., he wishes to regain, is situated.

The epitome of the whole is this:—1. If you can only answer the question A, you must seek for the lost path by the tedious circle plan; or, what is the same, and a more manageable way of setting to work, by travelling in an octagon, each

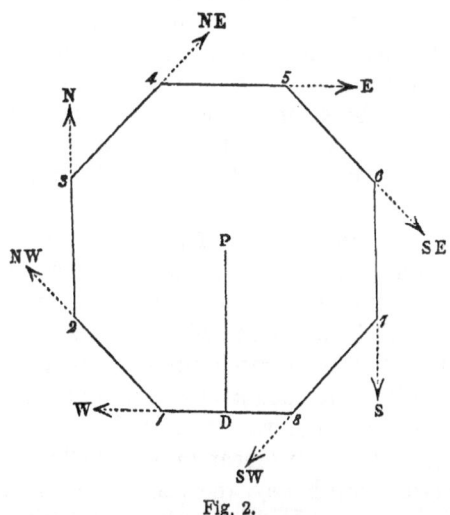

Fig. 2.

side of which must be equal to four-fifths of P D. (See fig. 2.) That is to say, look at your compass and start in any direction you please; we will say to the south, as represented in the drawing. Travel for a distance, P D; then, supposing you have not crossed the path, turn at right angles, and start afresh,—we will suppose your present direction to be west,— travel for a distance $\frac{4}{10}$ of P D, which will take you to 1; then turn to the N.W. and travel for a distance $\frac{8}{10}$ of P D, which will take you to 2; then to the N. for a similar distance, which will take you to 3; and so on, till the octagon has been completed. If you know B to eight points, and not C, adopt the L M system; also, if you know A and C, and B to within thirteen points (out of the sixteen that form the semicircle), you may still adopt the L M system; but not otherwise. A rough diagram scratched on the ground with a stick would suffice to recall the above remarks to a traveller's recollection.

CACHES AND DEPÔTS.

Caches.—It is easy enough to choose a spot, which you yourself shall again recognise, for digging a hole, where stores of all kinds may be buried against your return: neither is it difficult to choose one, so that you may indicate its position to others, or else leave it to a party who are travelling in concert, to find it out for themselves. But excessive caution in the mode of *depositing* the stores is, in every case, required, as hungry and thieving natives keep watch on all the movements of a party; they follow their tracks and hunt over their old camping-places, in search of anything there may be to pick up. And hyenas, wolves, wild dogs, and all kinds of prowling animals, guided by their sharp scent, will soon scratch up any provisions that are buried carelessly, or in such a way as to taint the earth.

The natives in Ceylon, when they wish to make a depôt of game, jerk it, put the dry meat into the hollow of a tree, fill up the reservoir with honey, and plaster it over with clay.

Some dried plants of M. Bourgeau, the botanist attached to Captain Palliser's expedition to the Rocky Mountains, remained underground for ten months without injury.

Newly disturbed Ground sinks when Wetted.—If a *cache* be made in dry weather, and the ground be simply levelled over it, the first heavy rain will cause the earth to sink, and will proclaim the hidden store to an observant eye. Soldiers, in sacking a town, find out hastily-buried treasures by throwing a pailful of water over any suspected spot: if the ground sinks, it has surely been recently disturbed.

Best place for a Cache.—The best position to choose for a *câche* is in a sandy or gravelly soil, on account of its dryness and the facility of digging. Old burrows, or the gigantic but abandoned hills of white ants, may be thought of, if the stores are enclosed in cases of painted tin: also clefts in rocks: some things can be conveniently buried under water. The place must be chosen under circumstances that admit of your effacing all signs of the ground having been disturbed. A good plan is to set up your tent and to dig a deep hole in the floor, depositing what you have to bury wrapped in an oilcloth, in an earthen jar, or in a wooden vessel, according to what you are able to get. It must be secure against the attacks of the insects of the place: avoid the use of skins, for animals will smell and dig them out. Continue to inhabit the tent for at least a day, well stamping and smoothing down the soil at leisure. After this, change the position of the tent, shifting the tethering-place or kraal of your cattle to where it stood. They will speedily efface any marks that may be left. Travellers often make their fires over the holes where their stores are buried; but natives are so accustomed to suspect fireplaces, that this plan does not prove to be safe. During summer travel, in countries pestered with gnats, a smoke fire for the horses (that is, a fire for keeping off flies), made near the place, will attract the horses and cause them to trample all about. This is an excellent way of obliterating marks left about the *cache*.

Hiding Small Things.—It is easy to make a small *cache* by bending down a young tree, tying your bundle to the top, and letting it spring up again. A spruce-tree gives excellent shelter to anything placed in its branches. (See also what is said on "Burying Letters," p. 303.)

Hiding Large Things.—Large things, as a wagon or boat, must either be pushed into thick bushes or reeds and left to chance, or they may be buried in a sand drift or in a sandy deposit by a river side. A small reedy island is a convenient place for such *caches*.

Double Caches.—Some persons, when they know that their intentions are suspected, make two *caches*: the one with a few things buried in it, and concealed with little care; the other, containing those that are really valuable, and very artfully made. Thieves are sure to discover the first, and are likely enough to omit a further search.

To find your Store again, you should have ascertained the distance and bearing, by compass, of the hole from some marked place—as a tree—about which you are sure not to be mistaken; or from the centre of the place where your fire was made, which is a mark that years will not entirely efface. If there be anything in the ground itself to indicate the position of the hole, you have made a clumsy *cache*. It is not a bad plan, after the things are buried, and before the tent is removed, to scratch a furrow a couple of inches deep, and three or four feet long, and picking up any bits of stick, reeds, or straw, that may be found at hand lying upon the ground, to place them end to end in it. These will be easy enough to find again by making a cross furrow, and when found will lead you straight above the depôt. They would never excite suspicion, even if a native got hold of them; for they would appear to have been dropped or blown on the ground by chance, not seen, and trampled in. Mr. Atkinson mentions an ingenious way by which the boundaries of valuable mining property are marked in the Ural, a modification of which might serve for indicating *caches*. A trench is dug and filled with charcoal beat small, and then covered over. The charcoal lasts for ever, and cannot be tampered with without leaving an unmistakable mark.

Secreting Jewels.—Before going to a rich but imperfectly civilised country, travellers sometimes buy jewels and bury them in their flesh. They make a gash, put the jewels in, and allow the flesh to grow over them as it would over a bullet. The operation is more sure to succeed if the jewels are put into a silver tube with rounded ends, for silver does not irritate. If the jewels are buried without the tube, they must have no sharp edges. The best place for burying them is in the left arm, at the spot chosen for vaccination. A traveller who was thus provided would always have a small capital to fall back upon, though robbed of everything he wore.

A Chain of gold is sometimes carried by Arabs, who sew it in dirty leather under their belt. They cut off and sell a link at a time. (Burton.)

The gun-stock is a good receptacle for small valuables. Unscrew the heel-plate and bore recesses; insert what you desire, after wrapping it tightly in cloth and plugging it in; then replace the heel-plate. (Peal.)

Depositing Letters.—*To direct Attention to the Place of Deposit.*
—When you make a *cache* in an inhabited land, for the use of a travelling party who are ignorant of your purpose, there is of course some difficulty in ensuring that their attention should be directed to the place, but that the natives should have no clue to it. If you have means of gashing, painting or burning characters, something of this sort (see fig.), they

> **LETTER BURIED**
>
> 50 yards N.N.E.

will explain themselves. Savages, however, take such pains to efface any mark they may find left by white men, entertaining thoughts like those of Morgiana in the 'Arabian Nights'' tale of the Forty Thieves, that it would be most imprudent to trust to a single mark. A relief party should therefore be provided with a branding-iron and moveable letters, and with paints, and they should mark the tree in many places. A couple of hours spent in doing this would leave more marks than the desultory efforts of roving savages would be likely to efface. A good sign to show that Europeans have visited a spot is a saw mark (no savages use saws): it catches the eye directly.

A system occasionally employed by Arctic expeditions, of making a *cache* 10 feet *true* north (and not *magnetic* north) from the cairn or mark, deserves to be generally employed, at least with modifications. Let me therefore suggest, that persons who find a cairn built or a tree marked, so as to attract notice, and who are searching blindly in all directions for further clue, should *invariably* dig out and examine that particular spot. The notice deposited there may consist of no more than a single sentence, to indicate some distant point as the place where the longer letter is buried. I hope it will be understood, that the precaution of always burying a notice 10 feet true north of the cairn mark is proposed as *additional to* and not in the place of other contrivances for giving information. There will often arise some doubt as to the exact point in the circumference of the cairn or mark whence the 10 feet measurement should be made. This is due to the irregularity of the bases of all such marks. Therefore, when searching for letters, a short trench, running to the north, will frequently have to be dug, and not a mere hole. I should propose that the short notice be punched or pricked on a thin sheet of lead, made by pouring two or three melted bullets on a flat stone, and that the plate so made and inscribed should be rolled up and pushed into a hole bored or burnt through the head of a large tent peg. The peg could be driven deeply in the ground, quite out of sight, without disturbing the surrounding earth. It might even suffice to pick up a common stone and to scratch or paint upon it what you had to say, and to leave it on the ground, with its written face downwards, at the place in question.

To secure Buried Letters from Damp.—They may be wrapped in waxed cloth or paper, if there be no fear of the ravages of insects. Lead plate is far more safe: it can be made easily enough by a traveller out of his bullets. (See "Lead.") A glass bottle (with something that insects cannot eat, such as lead-plate, sealing-wax, or clay, put carefully over the cork) or an earthen jar may be used. The quill of a large feather will hold a long letter, if it is written in very small handwriting and on thin paper, and it will preserve it from the wet. After the letter has been rolled up and inserted in the quill, the open end of the latter may be squeezed flat between two stones, heated sufficiently to soften the quill (see "Horn") but not so hot as to burn it, and then, for greater security against wet, the end of the quill should be twisted tight. Wax affords another easy means of closing the quill.

Picture-writing.—As very many excellent bushrangers are unable to read, rude picture-writing is often used by them, especially in America. The figure of a man with a spear or bow, drawn as a child would draw, stands for a savage; one with a hat or gun for a European; horses, oxen, and sheep are equally to be drawn; lines represent numbers, and arrowheads direction. Even without more conventional symbols, vast deal may be expressed by rude picture-writing.

Caches and Depôts.

Reconnoitring Barren Countries by help of Porters and Caches.—The distance to which an explorer can attain in barren countries depends on the number of days' provisions that he can carry with him. Half of his load supports him on his way out, the other half on his way home. But if he start in company with a laden porter, he may reserve his own store and supply both himself and the porter from the pack carried by the latter. When half of this is consumed, the other half may be divided into two equal portions. The one is retained by the porter who makes his way back to camp, consuming it as he goes, and the other is cached (see " Caches ") for the sustenance of the traveller on his return journey. This being arranged, the traveller can start from the *cache* with his own load of provisions untouched, just as he would have started from the camp if he had had no porter to assist him. It is evident a process of this description might be frequently repeated ; that a large party of porters might start, and by a system of successive subdivisions, they could enable the traveller to reach a position many days' journey distant from his camp, with his own load of provisions and with other food placed in a succession of *caches*, for the supply of his wants all the way home again. The principle by which this may be effected without waste, is to send back at each successive step the *smallest detachment* competent to travel alone, and to do this as soon as *one half* of their load of food has been consumed by the *whole party*. Then, the other half is to be divided into two portions ; one consisting of rations to supply the detachment back to the previous *cache*, whence their journey home has been provided for, the other portion to be buried, to supply rations for the remainder of the party, when they shall have returned (either all together or else in separate and successive detachments) back to the previous *cache*, whence their journey home has also been provided for. An inspection of the Table which I annex (p. 307) makes details unnecessary. The dotted lines show how the porters who first return may be dispatched afresh as relief parties. I give, in the table, a schedule of the three most important cases. In these the regular supply of two meals per diem, and a morning and an afternoon journey, are supposed. I wrote a paper on this subject, which is published in the ' Royal Geographical Society's

Proceedings,' vol. ii., to which I refer those who care to inquire further into the matter. Cases where each man or horse carries a number of rations intermediate to those specified in the Table, are, perhaps, too complicated for use without much previous practice. It would be easy for a leader to satisfy himself that he was making no mistake, and to drill his men to any one of the tabulated cases, by planting a row of sticks, 50 yards apart, to represent the successive halting-places of his intended journey, and by making his men go through a sham rehearsal of what they would severally have to do. Then each man's duties could be written down in a schedule and all possibility of mistake be avoided.

The Table represents the proceedings of four men (or horses and men), who leave camp. Two turn back at P_1, one more turns back at P_2, and the remaining man pushes on to P_3. Food has been cached for him both at P_2 and P_1; but to make matters doubly sure, a relief party, as shown by the dotted line, can be sent to meet him at P_2.

In Case A, each man carries 1¼ day's rations.
 „ B,   „   (or horse) „ 3¼ days' rations for himself (and drivers).
 „ C,   „   „   „ 5¼   „   „   „

We will take the case C as an example. The figures that refer to it are in the lines adjacent to the letter C in the Table. They are those in the uppermost line, and also those in the line up the left-hand side of the diagram, and they stand for days' journey and for days respectively. P_1 is reached after 1½ day's travel, P_2 after 3 days, P_3 after 6 days from camp. The entire party might consist of 5 men, 2 carts (one a very light one), and four horses, together with one saddle and bridle. The heavier cart and 2 men and 2 horses would turn back at P_1. One of the two horses of the second cart would be saddled and ridden back by a third man from P_2; and, finally, the remaining cart, single horse, and 2 men, would turn back, after 6 days, from P_3.—The relief party would originally consist of the first cart and 3 horses. On arriving at P_1, a horse and man would be sent back. At P_2 it would have more than enough spare rations to admit of its waiting two whole days for the exploring cart, if it were necessary to do so.

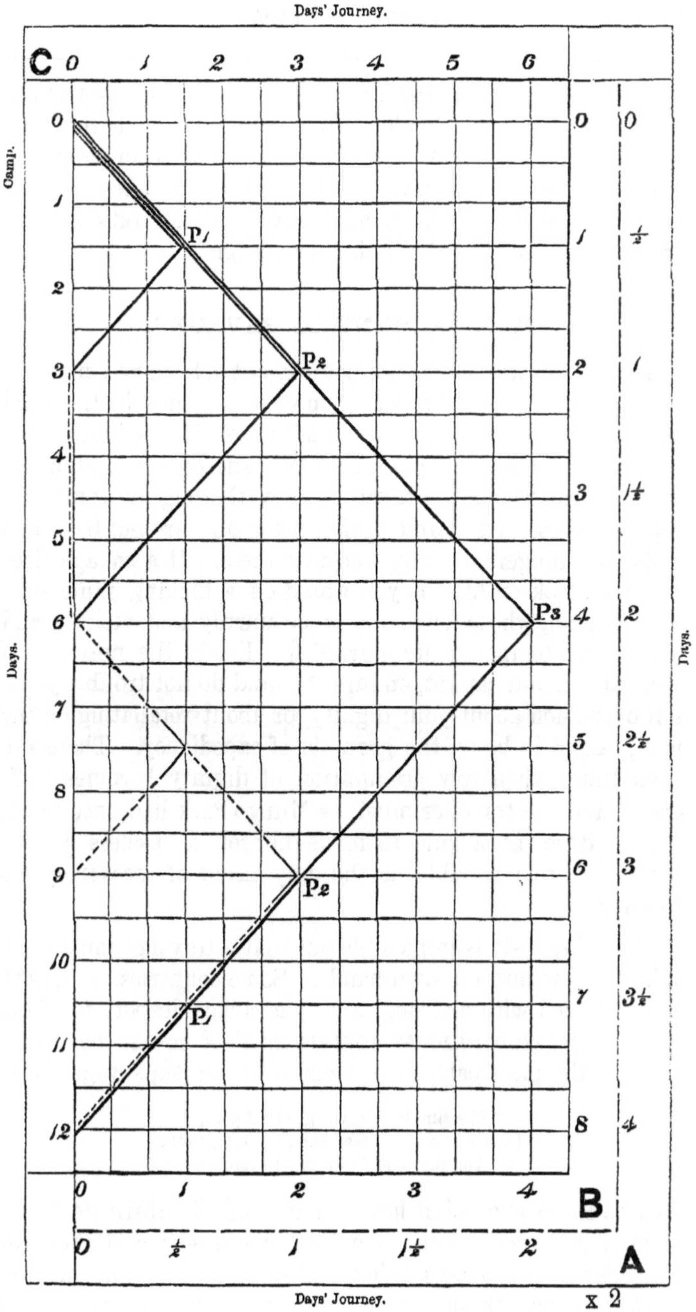
Days' Journey.
C
0 1 2 3 4 5 6
Camp.
Days.
0 1 2 3 4 5 6 7 8 9 10 11 12
P1
P2
P3
P2
P1
0 1 2 3 4 5 6 7 8
0 ½ 1 1½ 2 2½ 3 3½ 4
Days.
0 1 2 3 4
B
0 ½ 1 1½ 2
A
Days' Journey.
x 2

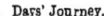

It will be seen from the Table that as 6 days' journey is the limit to which C can explore, so 4 days' journey is the limit for B, and 2 days for A. But where abundance of provision is secured at P_2 by means of a relief party, the explorers might well make an effort and travel on half rations to a greater distance than the limits here assigned.

MANAGEMENT OF SAVAGES.

General Remarks.—A frank, joking, but determined manner, joined with an air of showing more confidence in the good faith of the natives than you really feel, is the best, It is observed, that a sea-captain generally succeeds in making an excellent impression on savages: they thoroughly appreciate common sense, truth, and uprightness; and are not half such fools as strangers usually account them. If a savage does mischief, look on him as you would on a kicking mule, or a wild animal, whose nature is to be unruly and vicious, and keep your temper quite unruffled. Evade the mischief, if you can: if you cannot, endure it; and do not trouble yourself overmuch about your dignity, or about retaliating on the man, except it be on the grounds of expediency. There are even times when any assumption of dignity becomes ludicrous, and the traveller must, as Mungo Park had once to do, "lay it down as a rule to make himself as useless and as insignificant as possible, as the only means of recovering his liberty."

Bush Law.—It is impossible but that a traveller must often take the law into his own hands. Some countries, no doubt, are governed with a strong arm by a savage despot; to whom or to whose subordinates appeals must of course be made; but, for the most part, the system of life among savages is—

> "The simple rule, the good old plan,—
> That they should take, who have the power;
> And they should keep, who can."

Where there is no civil law, or any kind of substitute for it, each man is, as it were, a nation in himself; and then the traveller ought to be guided in his actions by the motives that influence nations, whether to make war or to abstain from it, rather than by the criminal code of civilised countries. The traveller must settle in his own mind what his scale of punishments should be; and it will be found a convenient principle that a culprit should be punished in proportion to the quantity of harm that he has done, rather than according to the presumed wickedness of the offence. Thus, if two men were caught, one of whom had stolen an ox, and the other a sheep, it would be best to flog the first much more heavily than the second; it is a measure of punishment more intelligible to savages than ours. The principle of double or treble restitution, to which they are well used, is of the same nature. If all theft be punished, your administration will be a reign of terror; for every savage, even your best friends, will pilfer little things from you, whenever they have a good opportunity. Be very severe if any of your own party steal trifles from natives: order double or treble restitution, if the man does not know better; and, if he does, a flogging besides, and not in place of it.

Seizing Food.—On arriving at an encampment, the natives commonly run away in fright. If you are hungry, or in serious need of anything that they have, go boldly into their huts, take just what you want, and leave fully adequate payment. It is absurd to be over-scrupulous in these cases.

Feast-Days.—Interrupt the monotony of travel, by marked days, on which you give extra tobacco and sugar to the servants. Avoid constant good feeding, but rather have frequent slight fasts to ensure occasional good feasts; and let those occasions when marked stages of your journey have been reached, be great gala-days. Recollect that a savage cannot endure the steady labour that we Anglo-Saxons have been bred to support. His nature is adapted to alternations of laziness and of severe exertion. Promote merriment, singing, fiddling, and so forth, with all your power. Autolycus says, in 'A Winter's Tale,'—

> "Jog on, jog on, the foot-path way,
> Merrily bent the stile-a:
> A merry heart goes all the day,
> Your sad tires in a mile-a."

Flogging.—Different tribes have very different customs in

the matter of corporal punishment : there are some who fancy it a disgrace and a serious insult. A young traveller must therefore be discriminating and cautious in the licence he allows to his stick, or he may fall into sad trouble.

Kindliness of Women.—Wherever you go, you will find kindheartedness amongst women. Mungo Park is fond of recording his experiences of this; but I must add, that he seems to have been an especial favourite with the sex. The gentler of the two sexes is a " *teterrima causa belli.*"

When you wish a Savage to keep count, give him a string of beads. The boxes and parcels that are sent by the overland route are, or were, counted in this way by an Arab overseer. He was described as having a cord with great beads strung on it, and the end of the cord was thrown over his shoulder. As each box passed him, he jerked a bead from the fore part of the cord to the back part of it, over his shoulder.

Drawing Lots.—It is often necessary to distribute things by lot. Do it by what children call " soldiering : " one stands with his back to the rest; another, pointing to the portions in succession, calls out " Who is to have this ? " To which the first one replies by naming somebody, who at once takes possession.

HOSTILITIES.

To Fortify a Camp.—*Forts at opposite Corners.*—Explorers have frequent occasion to form a depôt: either a few men are left in charge of the heavy luggage, while the rest of the party ride on a distant reconnoitring expedition; or else the whole party may encamp for weeks, until the state of the season, or other cause, permits further travel. In either case, a little forethought and labour will vastly increase the security of the depôt against hostile attempts. For instance, it should be placed at least 200 yards from any cover, or commanding heights; if the ground on which it stands have any features of strength about it, as being near the side of a stream, or being on a hill, so much the better; the neighbourhood of shingle prevents persons from stealing across unheard; and, finally, the camp should be fortified. Now the principle of fortification best suited to a small party, is to form the camp into a square, and to have two projecting enclosures at opposite corners, where all the men who have guns may place themselves to fire on the assailants. It will be seen by the sketch, how completely the guns in each enclosure can sweep the edges as well as the whole of the environs of the camp. A square is better than a round for the projecting enclosures, as it allows more men to use their guns at the same time on the same point; but it is so convenient to make the walls of the enclosure serve as sidings for the tents, that it is perhaps best to allow the size and shape of the tent to determine

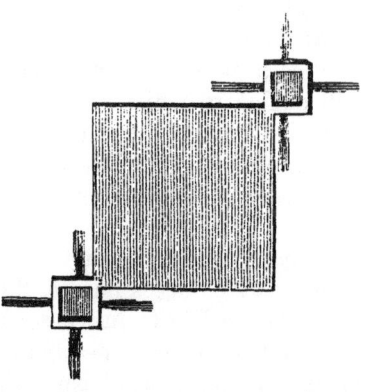

those of the enclosures. A square of nine or ten feet, inside measurement, is amply sufficient for three guns or archers. The parapets can be built of large stones. A travelling party rarely carries spades, but when they have them, the parapet may be formed of the earth thrown up by digging a trench outside it; the common calculation is, that, with good tools, a labourer can dig one cubic yard of earth an-hour, and can continue working for eight hours in the day. The parapet should be raised four feet above the ground, as that is the most convenient height to fire from when standing; and it is high enough to shield a person kneeling down to load. Upon this parapet, large stones should be laid, having loopholes between them, and above the stones the tent may be pitched; its pole being lengthened by lashing a piece of wood to it, or by cutting a fresh pole altogether. It will make a high roof to the enclosure, and will complete a comfortable abode. We have thus a square enclosed camp for the cattle, the wagons, and the natives of the party; and, at opposite corners of it, two fortified houses: one of which would naturally be inhabited by the leaders of the party; and the other, either by the storekeeper, or by the white servants generally.

Trous de Loup are holes, with a sharp stake driven in the bottom of each of them (see "Pitfalls," p. 264) with the pointed end upwards. The South Sea Islanders use them in multitudes to prevent the possibility of an enemy's approach at night, otherwise than along the narrow paths that lead to their villages: if a man deviates from a path, he is sure to stumble into one of these contrivances, and to be lamed. The holes need not exceed one foot in diameter; and the stake may be a stick no thicker than the little finger, and yet it will suffice to maim an ill-shod man, if its point be baked hard. A traveller could only use these pitfalls where, from the circumstances of the case, there was no risk of his own men, cattle, or dogs falling into them.

Weapons, to resist an Attack.—Unless your ammunition is so kept as to be accessible in the confusion of an attack, the fortifications I have just described would be of little service. If the guns are all, or nearly all, of the same bore, it is simple enough to have small bags filled with cartridges, and also papers with a dozen caps in each. Buck-shot and slugs are better than bullets, for the purposes of which we are speaking. Bows and arrows might render good service. The Chinese, in their junks, when they expect a piratical attack, bring up baskets filled with stones from the ballast of the ship, and put them on deck ready at hand. They throw them with great force and precision: the idea is not a bad one. Boiling water and hot sand, if circumstances happened to permit their use, are worth bearing in mind, as they tell well on the bodies of naked assailants. In close quarters, thrust, do not strike; and recollect that it is not the slightest use to hit a negro on the head with a stick, as it is a fact that his skull endures a blow better than any other part of his person. In picking out the chiefs, do not select the men that are the most showily ornamented, for they are not the chiefs; but the biggest and the busiest. A good horseman will find a powerful weapon at hand by unhitching his stirrup leather and attached stirrup from the saddle. I know of a case where this idea saved the rider.

Rockets.—Of all European inventions, nothing so impresses

and terrifies savages as fireworks, especially rockets. I cannot account for the remarkable effect they produce, but in every land it appears to be the same. A rocket, judiciously sent up, is very likely to frighten off an intended attack and save bloodshed. If a traveller is supplied with any of these, he should never make playthings of them, but keep them for great emergencies.

Natives forbidden to throng the Camp.—Have a standing rule that many natives should never be allowed to go inside your camp at the same time: for it is everywhere a common practice among them, to collect quietly in a friendly way, and at a signal to rise *en masse* and overpower their hosts. Even when they profess to have left their arms behind, do not be too confident: they are often deposited close at hand. Captain Sturt says, that he has known Australian savages to trail their spears between their toes, as they lounged towards him through the grass, professedly unarmed.

Keeping Watch.—*Head near the ground.*—When you think you hear anything astir, lie down and lay your ear on the ground. To see to the best advantage, take the same position; you thus bring low objects in bold relief against the sky. Besides this, in a wooded country, it is often easy to see far between the bare stems of the trees, while their spreading tops shut out all objects more than a few yards off. Thus, a dog or other small animal usually sees a man's legs long before he sees his face.

Opera-glass.—An opera-glass is an excellent night-glass, and at least doubles the clearness of vision in the dark (p. 284).

Ear-trumpet.—I should be glad to hear that a fair trial had been also given by a traveller to an ear-trumpet.

Watchfulness of Cattle.—Cattle keep guard very well: a stranger can hardly approach a herd of oxen, without their finding him out; for several of them are always sure to be awake and watchful. The habits of bush life make a traveller, though otherwise sound asleep, start up directly at a very slight rustle of alarm among his cattle.

Of Wild Birds and Beasts.—Scared birds and beasts often give useful warning.

Smell of Negro.—A skulking negro may sometimes be smelt out like a fox.

Dahoman Night-watch.—The Dahomans, the famous military nation of N.W. Africa, have an odd method of dividing their watches by night, but "which is generally managed very correctly. At each gate of a stockaded town, is posted a sentry, who is provided with a pile of stones, the exact number of which has been previously ascertained. The night is divided into four watches; during each watch the sentry removes the pile of stones, one by one, at a measured pace, from one gate to another, calling out at each tenth removal: when all are removed, the watch is relieved."—*Forbes*.

Setting a common Gun as an Alarm-gun.—The gun may be loaded with bullet, or simply with powder, or only with a cap: even the click of the hammer may suffice to awaken attention. For the ways of setting it, *see* p. 257.

Prairie set on Fire.—This is often done as a means of offence. But when the grass is short (lower than the knee), the strip of it on fire, at the same moment, does not exceed 12 feet in width; therefore if a belt of grass of 12 feet in width be destroyed in advance of the line of fire, the conflagration will be arrested as soon as it reaches that belt. The fire will be incapable of traversing the interval, narrow though it be, where there is a total absence of fuel to feed it. Travellers avail themselves of this fact in a very happy manner, when a fire in the prairie is advancing towards them, by burning a strip of grass, to the windward of their camp, of 12 feet in breadth; beating down the blaze with their blankets wherever it would otherwise extend too widely. Behind this easily constructed line of defence, the camp rests in security, and the adjacent grass remains uninjured for the use of the cattle. If, however, the wind is high and sparks are drifted for some distance beyond the belt of fire, this method is insufficient: two lines of defence should then be constructed.

Tricks upon Robbers.—It is perhaps just worth while to

mention a trick that has been practised in most countries, from England to Peru. A traveller is threatened by a robber with a gun, and ordered to throw himself on the ground, or he will be fired at. The traveller taking a pistol from his belt, shouts out, "If this were loaded you should not treat me thus!" and throws himself on the ground as the robber bids him. There he lies till the robber, in his triumph, comes up for his booty; when the intended victim takes a quick aim and shoots him dead—the pistol being really loaded all the time. I have also heard of an incident in the days of Shooter's Hill, in England, where a ruffian waylaid and sprang upon a traveller, and, holding a pistol to his breast, summoned him for the contents of his pocket. The traveller dived his hand into one of them, and, silently cocking a small pistol that lay in it, shot the robber dead, firing out through the side of the pocket.

Passing through a Hostile Country.—*How to encamp.*—A small party has often occasion to try to steal through a belt of hostile country without being observed. At such times, it is a rule never to encamp until long after sun-down, in order that people on your track may be unable to pursue it with ease. If you are pursuing a beaten path, turn sharp out of it, when you intend to encamp, selecting a place for doing so where the ground is too hard to show footprints; then travel away for a quarter of an hour, at least. Lastly, look out for a hollow place, in the midst of an open flat. Never allow hammering of any kind in your camp, nor loud talking; but there is no danger in lighting a small fire, if reasonable precautions be taken, as a flame cannot be seen far through bushes. Keep a strict watch all night: the watchers should be 100 yards out from camp, and should relieve one another, every two hours at least. Enough animals for riding, one for each man, should always be tied up, in readiness for instant use.

When riding alone.—A person who is riding a journey for his life, sleeps most safely with his horse's head tied short up to his wrist. The horse, if he hears anything, tosses his head and jerks the rider's arm. The horse is a careful animal, and there appears to be little danger of his treading on his sleeping master. The Indians of South America habitually adopt this plan, when circumstances require extreme caution (*see* fig.)

To prevent your Horse from neighing.—If a troop of horse-

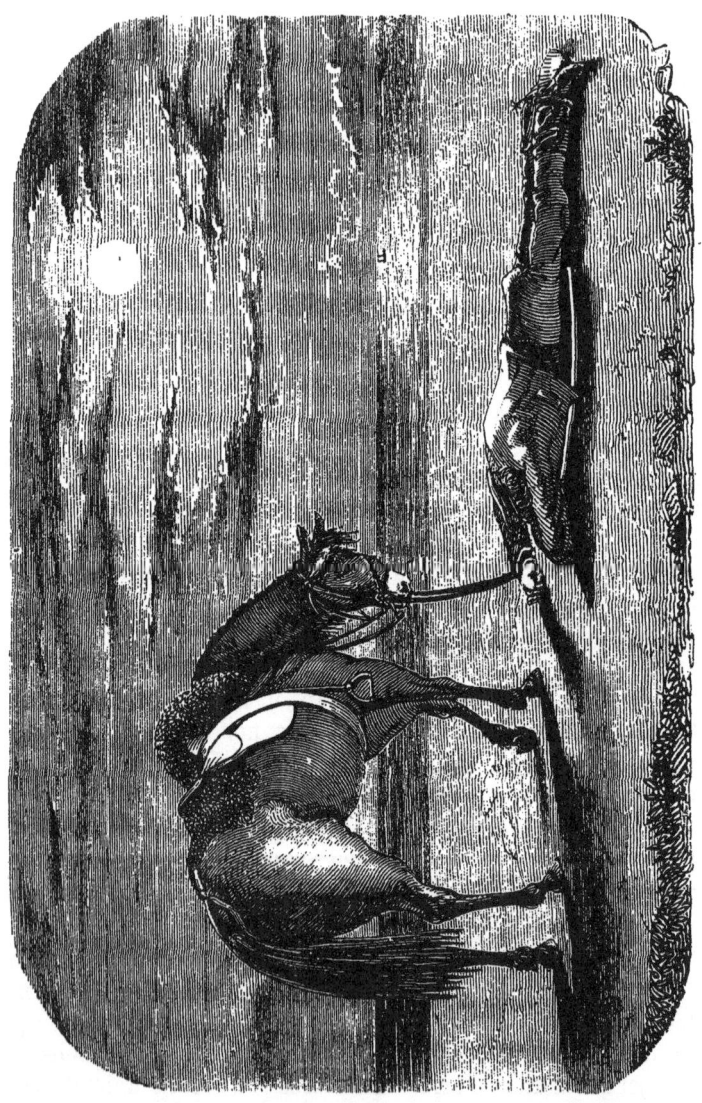

men pass near your hiding-place, it may be necessary to

clutch your steed's muzzle with both hands, to prevent his neighing.

Hurried retreat of a Party.—When a party, partly of horsemen and partly of footmen, are running away from danger as hard as they can, the footmen lay hold of the stirrup-leathers of the riders, to assist them. (See " Litters for the Wounded," p. 23.)

Securing Prisoners.—*To take a strong man Prisoner* single-handed, threaten him with your gun, and compel him to throw all his arms away; then, marching him before you some little distance, make him lie flat on his face and put his hands behind him. Of course he will be in a dreadful fright, and require reassuring. Next take your knife, put it between your teeth, and, standing over him, take the caps off your gun, and lay it down by your side. Then handcuff him, in whatever way you best can. The reason of setting to work in this way is, that a quick supple savage, while you are fumbling with your strings, and bothered with a loaded gun, might easily spring round, seize hold of it, and quite turn the tables against you. But if the gun had no caps on, it would be of little use in his hands, except as a club; and also, if you had a knife between your teeth, it would be impossible for him to free himself by struggling, without exposing himself to a thrust from it.

Cord to be well stretched.—It is an imperfect security to tie an ingenious active man, whose hands and feet are small, unless the cord or whatever else you may use, has been thoroughly well stretched. Many people have exhibited themselves for money, who allowed themselves to be tied hand and foot and then to be put into a sack, whence they emerged after a few minutes, with the cords in a neat coil in their hands. The brothers Davenport were notorious for possessing this skill. They did not show themselves for halfpence at country fairs; but, by implying that they were set free by supranatural agencies, they held fashionable séances in London and created an immense sensation a few years ago. Two of these exhibitors were tied, face to face in a cupboard, respectively by two persons selected by the audience. The latter inspected one another's knots as well as they could, and on their expressing themselves satisfied, the doors of the cupboard were closed, the lights of the room were kept low for 5 or 10 minutes, until a signal was made by the exhibitors from within the cupboard; then in a blaze of gas light the doors were opened from within and out walked the two men, leaving the ropes behind them. After this, they tied themselves in their own knots; and under those easy conditions a number of so-called spiritual manifestations took place, which I need not here describe; the real curiosity of the exhibition being that which I have just explained. These exhibitions continued for months; but at length two nautical gentlemen insisted on using their own cord, which they had previously well stretched, and this proceeding utterly baffled the Davenports. Thenceforward wherever the Davenports showed themselves, the nautical gentlemen appeared also, appealing to the audience to elect them to tie the hands of the exhibitors. In this way, they fairly exposed the pretensions of the Davenports, and drove them from England. Once I was proposed by an audience to tie the hands. I did my best, and I also scrutinised my colleague's knot, as well as the confined place in which the exhibitors were tied, permitted. The cord we had to use was perhaps a little too thick, but it was supple and strong, and I was greatly surprised at the ease with which the Davenports disembarrassed themselves. They were not more than 10 minutes in getting free. Of course if either of the exhibitors could struggle loose, he would assist his colleague. It therefore struck me as an exceedingly ingenious idea of the Davenports, to have two persons, and not one person, to tie them. I considered it was very improbable that a person taken at hap-hazard should be capable of tying his man securely; and it was evident that the improbability would be increased in a duplicate ratio, that both persons should be capable. Thus if it be 20 to 1 against any one person's having sufficient skill, it is (20 by 20 or) 400 to 1 against both the persons, who might be selected to tie the Davenports, being able to do so effectively. As I have already said, the opportunity that was afforded to each of scrutinising the work of the other, was worth very little, because of the dark and confined space in which the exhibitors sat.

Tying the Hands.—To tie a man's hands behind his back, take a handkerchief, it is the best thing; failing that, a thin cord. It is necessary that its length should not be less than 2 feet, but 2 feet 6 inches is the right length; for a *double* tie, it should be 3 feet 6 inches. Compel him to lay his hands as in the sketch, and, wrapping the cord once (or twice if it be long enough) round the arms, pretty tightly, pass the longest end in between the arms as shown in the figure, and tie quite tightly. If you are quick in tying the common "tom-fool's knot," well known 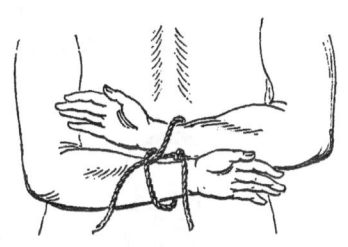 to every sailor, it is still better for the purpose. Put the prisoner's hands one within each loop, then draw tightly the running ends, and knot them together.

Tying the Thumbs.—To secure a prisoner with the least amount of string, place his hands back to back, behind him, then tie the thumbs together, and also the little fingers. Two bits of thin string, each a foot long, will thoroughly do this. But, if you have not any string at hand, cut a thong from his leathern apron, or tear a strip from your own linen.

Strait-Waistcoats.—A strait-waistcoat is the least inconvenient mode of confinement, as the joints of the prisoner are not cut by cords. A makeshift for one is soon stitched together, by stitching a piece of canvas into the shape of a sleeve, and sewing one end of this to one cuff of a strong jacket, and the other end to the other cuff; so that, instead of the jacket having two sleeves, it has but one long one. The jacket is then put on in the usual way, and buttoned and sewn in front. In a proper strait-waistcoat, the opening is behind and the sleeves in front; it laces up behind.

Tying up a Prisoner for the night.—If a man has to be kept prisoner all night, it is not sufficient to tie his hands, as he will be sure to watch his time and run away. It is therefore necessary to tie them round a standing tree, or a heavy log of wood. A convenient plan is to fell a large forked bough, and to make the man's arms fast round one of the branches. It is thus impossible for him to slip away, as the fork on one side, and the bushy top of the branch on the other, prevent his doing so; and, notwithstanding his cramped position, it is quite possible for him to get sleep.

Files of Prisoners.—When several men have to be made fast and marched away, the usual method of securing them is to tie them, one behind another, to a long pole or rope.

In marching off a Culprit, make him walk between two of your men, while a third, carrying a gun, walks behind him.

If riding alone, tie the prisoner's hands together, and, taking your off-stirrup leather (for want of a cord), pass it round his left arm, and round your horse's girth, and buckle it. The off-stirrup leather is the least inconvenient one to part with, on account of mounting, and the prisoner is under your right hand.

Tying on Horseback.—In cases where a prisoner has to be secured and galloped off, there are but two ways: either putting him in the saddle and strapping his ankles together under the horse's belly—in which case, if he be mad with rage, and attempts to throw himself off, the saddle must turn with him; or else securing him Mazeppa-fashion—when four loops are passed, one round each leg of the horse, and to each of these is tied one limb of the prisoner, as he lies with his back against that of the horse; a surcingle is also passed round both horse and man. It is, of course, a barbarous method, but circumstances might arise when it would be of use.

Proceedings in case of Death.—If a man of the party dies, write down a detailed account of the matter, and have it attested by the others, especially if accident be the cause of his death. If a man be lost, before you turn away and abandon him to his fate, call the party formally together, and ask them if they are satisfied that you have done all that was possible to save him, and record their answers. After death, it is well to follow the custom at sea,—*i. e.* to sell by auction all the dead man's effects among his comrades, deducting the money they fetch from the pay of the buyers, to be handed over to his relatives on the return of the expedition. The things will probably be sold at a much higher price than they would elsewhere fetch, and the carriage of useless lumber is saved. Any trinkets he may have had, should of course be sealed up and put aside, and not included in the sale: they should be collected in presence of the whole party, a list made of them, and the articles at once packed up. In committing the body to the earth, choose a well-marked situation, dig a deep grave, bush it with thorns, and weight it well over with heavy stones, as a defence against animals of prey.

MECHANICAL APPLIANCES.

To Raise and Move a Heavy Body.—*On Land.*—Lever up its ends alternately, and build underneath them when they are lifted up. After a sufficient height has been gained, build a sloping causeway down to the place to which the mass has to be moved, and along which it may be dragged, with the assistance of rollers and grease. If the mass be too awkwardly shaped to admit of this, burrow below it; pass poles underneath it, and raise the ends of the poles alternately. Mr. Williams, the well-known missionary of the South Sea Islands, relates how his schooner of from seventy to eighty tons had been driven by a violent hurricane and rising of the sea, on one of the islands near which she was anchored, and was lodged several hundred yards inland; and thus describes how he got her back:—" The method by which we contrived to raise the vessel was exceedingly simple, and by it we were enabled to accomplish the task with great ease. Long levers were passed under her keel, with the fulcrum so fixed as to give them an elevation of about forty-five degrees. The ends of these were then fastened together with several cross-beams, upon which a quantity of stones were placed; the weight of which gradually elevated one end of the vessel, until the levers reached the ground. Propping up the bow thus raised, we shifted our levers to the stern, which was in like manner elevated; and, by repeating this process three or four times, we lifted her in one day entirely out of the hole (which she had worked for herself, and which was about four feet deep). The bog that lay between her and the sea was then filled up with stones, logs of wood were laid across it, rollers were placed under the vessel, the chain cable passed round her; and, by the united strength of about 2000 people, she was compelled to take a short voyage upon the land, before she floated in her pride on the sea."

In some cases, the body of a cart may be taken down, and deep ruts having been dug on each side of the mass, the vehicle can be backed, till the axletree comes across it; then, after lashing and making fast, the sand can be shovelled from below the mass, which will hang suspended from the axletree, and may be carted away. Or a sledge may be built beneath the mass by burrowing below it and thrusting the poles beneath it. Then the remainder of the intervening sand can be shovelled away, and the mass, now resting directly upon the sledge, can be dragged away by a team of cattle.

A sarcophagus of immense weight was raised from out of a deep recess into which it had been fitted pretty closely, at the end of a long narrow gallery in an Egyptian tomb, where there was no room for the application of tackle or other machinery, by the simple expedient of slightly disturbing it in its place and sifting sand into the narrow interval between its sides and the recess. This process was repeated continually: the sand settled below the bottom of the sarcophagus, which gradually rose out of the hole in which it had lain. The principle of this piece of engineering was borrowed, I suppose, from observing that whenever a mass of sand and stones is shaken together, the stones invariably rise out of the sand, the biggest of them always forming the highest layer.

Expansive Power of Wetted Seeds.—Admiral Sir E. Belcher read a curious paper before the British Association in 1866, showing the remarkable power to be obtained by filling tubes with peas or other seed, allowing the weight to rest upon the surface of the peas through the medium of a rude piston. When the peas were wetted they swelled upwards with considerable force. A pint of peas placed in a tube of a diameter that was not expressed in the newspaper report, from which I take this account, lifted 60 lbs. through a height of one inch in twenty-four hours. The Admiral proposed to fix a number of tubes side by side in a frame below the mass to be lifted, preferring to use zinc tubes of from two or three inches in diameter, and of about one foot high. Thus, in the small space of a cubic foot, a large number of tubes (thirty-six in the one case, sixteen in the other) could be made to act simultaneously; the force of the stroke could be increased by arranging a number of frames side by side, or the length of the stroke could be increased by building the frames in a series one above the other. I have elsewhere described how wetted seeds may be used to restore the shape of a battered flask either for holding water or gunpowder (pp. 230, 244).

Parbuckling.—A round log or a barrel should be rolled, not dragged; and many irregularly-shaped objects may have bundles of faggots lashed round them, by which they become barrel-shaped and fit to be rolled. In these cases, parbuckling doubles the ease of rolling them; one or more ropes have one of each of their ends made fast in the direction to which the log has to be rolled, while the other is carried underneath the log, round it, and back again. By pulling at these free ends, the log will be rolled on. An equivalent plan, and in some

cases a more practicable one, is to make fast one end of the rope to the log itself; then, winding the rope two or three times round it, like cotton on a reel, to haul at the free end as before. Horses can be used, as well as men, for this work.

Accumulation of Efforts.—South American Indians are said to avail themselves of their forest trees, and of the creepers which stretch from branch to branch, in moving very heavy weights, as in lifting a log of timber up on a stage to be sawn, in the following ingenious manner. The labourer gets hold of one of these creepers that runs from the top boughs of a tree in the direction in which he wants to move his log, and pulling this creeper home with all his force, bending down the bough, he attaches it to the log; then he goes to another creeper and does the same with that; and so on until he has the accumulated strain of many bent boughs, urging the log forward and of sufficient power to move it.

Short cords of india-rubber with a hook at either end, are sold under the name of "accumulators." It is proposed that each of these should be stretched and hooked by one of its ends to a fixed ring, and by the other, to the body to be moved; by applying a number of these, in succession, an immense accumulation of force can be obtained.

Levers.—A piece of green wood has insufficient strength to be used as a crowbar; it must first be seasoned. (See " Green Wood, to season.")

Other Means of Raising Weights.—I do not propose to take space by describing jacks, ordinary pulleys, differential pulleys, Chinese windlasses, and the like. It is sufficient that I should recall them by name to the traveller's recollection; for if he has access to any of these things he is probably either a sailor or engineer and knows all about them, or he is in a land where mechanical appliances are understood.

To raise Weights out of Water.—If the mass should lie below water, a boat may be brought over it and sunk to its gunwales; then, after making fast to it, the boat can be baled and the thing floated away. A raft weighted with stones will serve the same purpose. In some cases a raft may be built round the mass during low water; then the returning tide or the next flush of the stream will float it away.

"Although from its bulk several men might be puzzled to lift a cow-fish from the water when dead, yet one single Indian will stow the largest in his montaria without assistance. The boat is sunk under the body, and rising, the difficult feat is accomplished." (Edwards' 'Amazon.')

The huge blocks of marble quarried at Carrara are shipped in the small vessels of the country, as follows:—at low water the vessel is buried bodily in the sand, and a temporary railway laid down from the quarry to withinside of it. Along this the blocks are conveyed, and, when deposited in the vessel, the sand is dug away from under them, and they settle down in its hold, and the ship floats away at the returning tide.

KNOTS.

Elementary Knots.—The three elementary knots which every one should know are here represented,—viz., the Timber-hitch, the Bowline, and the Clove-hitch. (See also "Knots," p. 49; "Malay hitch," p. 147.)

Timber-hitch.—The virtues of the timber-hitch (fig. 1, p. 326) are, that, so long as the strain upon it is kept up, it will hold fast; when the strain is taken off, it can be cast loose immediately. A timber-hitch had better have the loose end twisted more than once, if the rope be stiff.

Bowline.—The bowline (fig. 2) makes a knot difficult to undo; with it the ends of two strings are tied together, or a loop made at the end of a single piece of string, as in the drawing. For slip nooses, use the bowline to make the draw-loop. When tying a bowline, or any other knot for temporary purposes, insert a stick into the knot before pulling

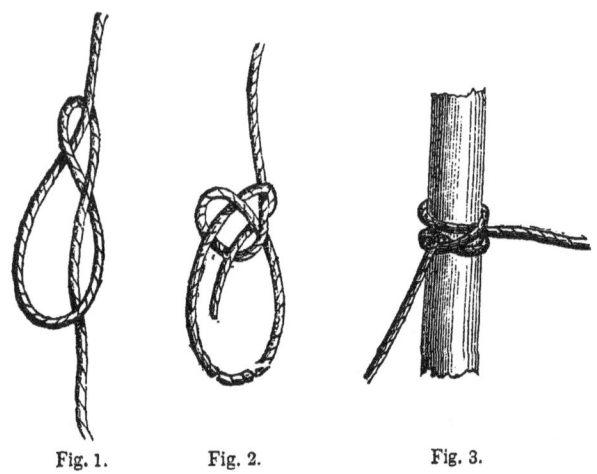

Fig. 1. Fig. 2. Fig. 3.

tight. The stick will enable you, at will, to untie the knot—to break its back, as the sailors say—with little difficulty. A bowline is firmer, if doubled; that is, if the free end of the cord be made to wrap round a second time.

Clove-hitch.—The clove-hitch (fig. 3) binds with excessive force, and by it, and it alone, can a weight be hung to a perfectly smooth pole, as to a tent-pole. A kind of double clove-hitch is generally used, but the simple one suffices, and is more easily recollected. A double clove-hitch is firmer than a single one; that is, the rope should make two turns, instead of one turn, round the pole beneath the lowest end of the cord in the figure. (See "Tent-poles, to tie things to.")

Knots at End of Rope.—To make a large knot at the end of a piece of string, to prevent it from pulling through a hole, turn the end of the string back upon itself, so as to make it double, and then tie a common knot. The string may be quadrupled instead of doubled, if required.

Toggle and Strop.—This is a tourniquet. A single or a double band is made to enclose the two pieces of wood it is desired to lash together; then a stick is pushed into the band and forcibly twisted round. The band should be of soft material, such as the strands of a rope that has been picked to pieces for that purpose: the strands must, each of them, be untwisted and well rubbed with a stick to take the kink out of them, and finally twisted in a direction opposite to their original one.

To sling a Jar.—Put it in a handkerchief or a net.

To tie a Parcel on the back, like a Knapsack.—Take a cord 10 feet long, double it, and lay the loop end upon a rock or other convenient elevation; then place the object to be carried upon the cord, taking care that the loop is so spread out as to admit of its ultimately enclosing the object with a good hold and balance. Next pass the free ends of the cord over the object and through the loop; then, bringing your shoulder to a level with the package, draw the free ends of the cords over your right shoulder: the cords will by this time have assumed the appearance shown in the sketch.

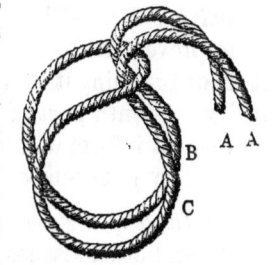

Now pass the left arm between the left-hand cord and the package at B, and the right arm between the right-hand cord and the package at C. Lastly, draw the cords tight, and the object will be found to be fastened on to your back like a knapsack. A gun may be passed between the cords and the top of the object. This is a capital method of carrying a load of game over a broken country, where at least one hand is required to be free. I am indebted to Mr. F. M. Wyndham for a knowledge of it: he found it frequently in use in Norway. In hot countries the plan would not be so convenient, as the heat of a soft package strapped closely to the back is very oppressive.

WRITING MATERIALS.

Paper. — *Its Numerous Applications.* — Captain Sherard Osborn, in writing of the Japanese, says:—"It was wonderful to see the thousand useful as well as ornamental purposes to which paper was applicable in the hands of these industrious and tasteful people. Our papier-mâché manufacturers, as well as the Continental ones, should go to Yeddo to learn what can be done with paper. With the aid of lacker varnish and skilful painting, paper made excellent trunks, tobacco bags, cigar cases, saddles, telescope cases, the frames of microscopes; and we even saw and used excellent waterproof coats made of simple paper, which *did* keep out the rain, and were as supple as the best macintosh . . . . . The inner walls of many a Japanese apartment are formed of paper, being nothing more than painted screens; their windows are covered with a fine translucent description of the same material; it enters largely into the manufacture of nearly everything in a Japanese household, and we saw what seemed balls of twine, which were nothing but long shreds of tough paper rolled up. . . . . In short, without paper, all Japan would come to a dead lock."

Sizing Paper.—The coarsest foreign paper can be sized, so as to prevent its blotting when written on, by simply dipping it in, or brushing it well over with, milk and water, and letting it dry. A tenth part of milk is amply sufficient. Messrs. Huc and Gabet inform us that this is the regular process of sizing, as used by paper-makers in Thibet.

Substitutes for Paper are chips of wood, inner bark of trees, calico and other tissues, lead plates, and slaty stone. I knew an eminent engineer who habitually jotted his pencil memoranda on the well-starched wristband of his left shirt-sleeve, pushing back the cuff of his coat in order to expose it. The natives in some parts of Bengal, when in the jungle, write on any large smooth leaf with the broken-off moist end of a leaf-stalk or twig of any milky sap-producing tree. They then throw dust upon it, which makes the writing legible. If the leaf be so written upon, the writing is imperceptible until the dust is sprinkled. This plan might, therefore, be of use for concealed writing. A person could write on the leaf without detaching it from the tree. (See "Sympathetic Ink.")

Prepared Paper, for use with pencils of metallic lead (see "Pencils"), is made by rubbing a paste of weak glue and bones burnt to whiteness and pounded, on the surface of the paper.

Waxed Paper is an excellent substitute for tin-foil, for excluding the air and damp from parcels. It is made by spreading a sheet of writing-paper on a hot plate or stone and smearing it with wax. A hot flat-iron is convenient for making it.

Carbonised Paper, for tracing or for manifold writing, is made by rubbing a mixture of soap, lampblack, and a little water on the paper, and, when dry, wiping off as much as possible with a cloth.

Tracing Designs.—Transparent tracing-paper can hardly be made by a traveller, unless he contents himself with the use of waxed paper; but he may prick out the leading points of his map or other design, and laying the map on a sheet of clean paper, charcoal or other powder that will leave a stain, it can be rubbed through.

Book-binding.—Travellers' unbound books become so terribly dilapidated, that I think it well to give a detailed description of a method of book-binding which a relative of mine has adopted for many years with remarkable success, and to a great extent. The books are not tidy-looking, but they open flat and never fall to pieces. Take a cup of paste; a piece of calico or other cloth, large enough to cover the back and sides of the book; a strip of strong linen—if you can get it, if not, of calico—to cover the back; and abundance of stout cotton or thread. 1st. Paste the strip of linen down the back, and leave the book in the sun or near a fire—but not too near it—to dry, which it will do in half a day. 2ndly. Open the book and look for the place where the stiching is to be seen down the middle of the pages, or, in other words, for the middle of the sheets; if it be an 8vo. book it will be at every 16th page, if a 12mo. at every 24th page, and so on: it is a mere matter of semi-mechanical reckoning to know where each succeeding stitching is to be found; in this volume the stitching is at pages 216, 232, 248, &c., the interval being 16 pages. Next take the cotton and wind it in between the pages where the stitching is, and over the back round and round, beginning with the first sheet, and going on sheet after sheet until you have reached the last one. 3rdly. Lay the book on the table back upwards, daub it thoroughly with paste, put on the calico cover as neatly as you can, and set it to dry as before; when dry it is complete.

Other Materials for Writing.—*Quills and other Pens.*—Any feather that is large enough, can be at once made into a good writing-quill. It has only to be dipped in hot sand, which causes the membrane inside the quill to shrivel up, and the outside membrane to split and peel off: a few instants are sufficient to do this. The proper temperature of the sand is about 340°. The operation may be repeated with advantage two or three times. Reeds are in universal use throughout the East for writing with ink. Flat fish-bones make decent pens.

Pencils.—Lead pencils were literally made of the metal lead in former days; and there are some parts of the world, as in Arabia, where they are still to be met with. A piece of lead may be cast into a serviceable shape in the method described under "Lead," and will make a legible mark upon ordinary paper. Lead is the best material for writing in note-books of "Prepared Paper" (which *see*). A better sort of pencil for general use is made by sawing charcoal into narrow strips, and laying them in melted wax to drench for a couple of days, they are then ready for use.

Paint brushes.—Wash the bit of tail or skin, whence the hair is to be taken, in ox-gall, till it is quite free from grease. Then snip off the hairs close to the skin, put them points downwards resting in a box, and pick out the long hairs. After a sufficient quantity have been obtained of about the same length, a piece of string is knotted tightly round them, and pulled firm with the aid of two sticks. Then a quill, that has been soaked in water for a day in order to soften it, is taken, and the pinch of hair is put into the large end of the quill, points forward, and pushed right through to the other end with a bit of stick, and so the brush is made. The Chinese paint-brush is a feather—a woodcock's feather is often used. Feather, like hairs, must be washed in ox-gall.

Ink.—Excellent writing-ink may be made in the bush. The readiest way of making it is to blacken sticks in the fire and to rub them well in a spoonful of milk till the milk becomes quite black. Gunpowder or lamp-soot will do as well as the burnt stick; and water, with the addition of a very little gum, glue, or fish-glue (isinglass) is better than the milk, as it will not so soon turn sour. Indian ink is simply lamp-soot and some kind of glue: it is one of the best of inks. If pure water be used, instead of gum or glue and water, the writing will rub out very easily when dry, the use of the milk, gum, or glue being to *fix* it: anything else that is glutinous will serve as well as these. Strong coffee, and many other vegetable products, such as the bark of trees boiled in water, make a mark which is very legible and will not rub. Blood is an indifferent substitute for ink. To make 12 gallons of good common writing-ink, use 12 lbs. of nut-galls, 5 lbs. of green sulphate of iron, 5 lbs. of gum, and 12 gallons of water. (Ure.)

Lampblack.—Hold a piece of metal, or even a stone, over a flaring wick in a cup of oil, and plenty of soot will collect.

Sympathetic Ink.—Nothing is better or handier than milk. The writing is invisible until the paper is almost toasted in the fire, when it turns a rich brown. The juice of lemons and many other fruits may also be used. (See "Substitutes for Paper.")

Gall of Animals, or Ox-gall to purify.—To make ink or paint take upon greasy paper, a very little ox-gall should be mixed with it. It is very important to know this simple remedy, and I therefore extract the following information from Ure's 'Dictionary.' I have often practised it. "Take it from the newly-killed animal, let it settle for 12 or 15 hours in a basin, pour the liquid off the sediment into an earthenware pot, and set the pot into a pan of water kept boiling until the gall-liquid becomes somewhat thick. Then spread it on a dish and place it before the fire till nearly dry. In this state it may be kept, without any looking after, for years. When wanted, a piece the size of a pea should be dissolved in water. Ox-gall removes all grease-spots from clothes, &c."

Wafers, Paste, and Gum.—*Wafers.*—The common wafers are punched out of a sheet made of a paste of flour and water that has suddenly been baked hard. Gum wafers are punched out of a sheet made of thick gum and water poured on a slightly-greased surface (a looking-glass for example), another greased glass having been put on the top of the gum to make it dry even.

Paste should be made like arrowroot, by mixing the flour in a minimum of cold water, and then pouring a flush of absolutely boiling water upon it. It is made a trifle thicker and more secure from insects by the addition of alum. Corrosive sublimate is a more powerful protection against insects, but is by no means an absolute safeguard, and it is dangerous to use.

Gum.—The white of eggs forms a substitute for gum. Some sea-weeds yield gum. (See also "Glue," "Isinglass," and "Sealing-wax Varnish.")

Signets.—Many excellent and worthy bushmen have the misfortune of not knowing how to write: should any such be placed in a post of confidence by an explorer, it might be well that he should cut for himself a signet out of soft stone —such as the Europeans of bygone generations, and the Turks of the last one, very generally employed. A device is cut on the seal; before using it, the paper is moistened with a wet finger, and the ink is dabbed over the ring with another; the impression is then made, using the ball of the thumb for a pad.

Sealing-wax Varnish.—Black or red sealing-wax, dissolved in spirits of wine, makes a very effective stiff and waterproof varnish, epecially for boxes of paper or cardboard. It might be useful in keeping some iron things from rust: it is the same material that is used to cover toy magnets. When made stiff it is an excellent cement for small articles. Opticians employ it for many of these purposes. I have also used it as a paint for marking initials on luggage, cutting out the letters in paper and dabbing the red stuff through.

Small Boxes for Specimens.—Cut the side of a cigar-box, or a strip of pasteboard, half through in three places, add two smaller pieces, like wings, one on each side, by means of a piece of gummed paper overlapping them, as in the picture. Any number of these may be carried like the leaves of a book, and when a box is wanted they may be bent into shape, and by the adherence of the moistened gum-paper, can be made into a box at a moment's notice. The shaded bor-

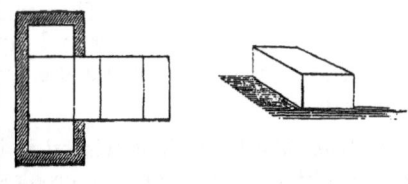

der of the figure represents the gummed paper. Quills make convenient receptacles for minute specimens. They should be dressed (see "Quills"), and may be corked with a plug of wood or wax, or, for greater security, a small quill may be pushed, mouth forward, into a larger one, as into a sheath.

TIMBER.

Green Wood.—*To season Wood.*—Green wood cannot be employed in carpentry, as it is very weak; it also warps, cracks, and becomes rotten: wood dried with too great a heat loses its toughness as well as its pliability: it becomes hard and brittle. Green wood is seasoned by washing out the sap, and then drying it thoroughly. The traveller's way of doing this by one rapid operation, is to dig a long trench and make a roaring fire in it; when the ground is burning hot, sweep the ashes away, deluge the trench with boiling water; and in the middle of the clouds of steam that arise, throw in the log of wood, shovel hot earth over it, and leave it to steam and bake. A log thick enough to make an axletree may thus be somewhat seasoned in a single night. The log would be seasoned more thoroughly if it were saturated with boiling water before putting it into the trench; that can be done by laying it in a deep narrow puddle, and shovelling hot stones into the water. All crowbars, wagon-lifters, &c., should be roughly seasoned, as green wood is far too weak for such uses. The regular way of seasoning is to leave the timber to soak for a long time in water, that the juices may be washed out. Fresh water is better for this purpose than salt; but a mineral spring, if it is warm, is better than cold fresh water. Parties travelling with a wagon ought to fell a little timber on their outward journey, and leave it to season against their return, in readiness to replace strained axletrees, broken poles, and the like. They might, at all events, cut a ring round through the bark and sap-wood of the tree, and leave it to discharge its juices, die, and become half-seasoned as it stands.

To bend Wood.—If it is wished to bend a rod of wood, or to straighten it if originally crooked, it must be steamed, or at least be submitted to hot water. Thus a rod of green wood may be passed through the ashes of a smouldering fire and, when hot, bent and shaped with the hand; but if the wood be dry it must first be thoroughly soaked in a pond or puddle. If the puddle is made to boil by shovelling in hot stones, as described in the last paragraph, the stick will bend more easily. The long straight spears of savages are often made of exceedingly crooked sticks, straightened in the ashes of their camp fires. A thick piece of wood may be well swabbed with hot water, forcibly bent, as far as can be safely done, tied in position and steamed, as if for the purpose of seasoning (see last paragraph), in a trench; after a quarter of an hour it must be taken out, damped afresh if necessary, bent further, and again returned to steam—the process being repeated till the wood has attained the shape required; it should then be left in the trench to season thoroughly. The heads of dog-sledges, and the pieces of wood used for the outsides of snow-shoes, are all bent by this process.

Carpenters' Tools.—Tools of too hard steel should not be taken on a journey; they splinter against the dense wood of tropical countries, and they are very troublesome to sharpen. The remedy for over-hardness is to heat them red-hot; retempering them by quenching in grease. A small iron axe, with a file to sharpen it, and a few awls, are (if nothing else can be taken) a very useful outfit.

As much carpentry as a traveller is likely to want, can be effected by means of a small axe with a hammer-head, a very small single-handed adze, a mortise-chisel, a strong gouge, a couple of medium-sized gimlets, a few awls, a small Turkey-hone, and a whetstone. If a saw be taken, it should be of a sort intended for green wood. In addition to these, a small tin box full of tools, all of which fit into a single handle, is very valuable; many travellers have found them extremely convenient. There is a tool-shop near the bottom of the Haymarket and another in the Strand near the Lowther Arcade, where they can be bought; probably also at Holtzapfel's in Trafalgar Square. The box that contains them is about six inches long by four broad and one deep; the cost is from 20s. to 30s. Lastly, a saw for metals, a few drills, and small files, may be added with advantage. It is advisable to see that the tools are ground and set before starting. A small "hard chisel" of the best steel, three inches long, a quarter of an inch wide, and three-eighths thick—which any blacksmith can make—will cut iron, will chisel marks on rocks, and be useful in numerous emergencies.

Sharpening Tools.—A man will get through most work with his tools, if he stops from time to time to sharpen them up. The son of Sirach says, speaking of a carpenter,—" If the iron be blunt, and he do not whet the edge, then must he put to more strength; but wisdom is profitable to direct."—*Ecclesiasticus*. A small fine file is very effectual in giving an edge to tools of soft steel. It is a common error to suppose that the best edge is given by grinding the sides of the tool until they meet at an exceedingly acute angle. Such an edge would have no strength, and would chip or bend directly. The proper way of sharpening a tool, is to grind it until it is sufficiently thin, and then to give it an edge whose sides are inclined to one another, about as much as those of the letter **V**. The edge of a chisel is an obvious case in point; so also is the edge of a butcher's knife, which is given by applying it to the steel at a considerable inclination. A razor has only to cut hairs, and will splinter if used to mend a pen, yet even a razor is shaped like a wedge, that it may not receive too fine an edge when stropped with its face flat upon the hone.

Nails, Substitutes for.—Lashings of raw hide supersede nails for almost every purpose. It is perfectly marvellous how a gunstock, that has been shattered into splinters, can be made as strong again as ever, by means of raw hide sewn round it and left to dry; or by drawing the skin of an ox's leg like a stocking over it. It is well to treat your bit of skin as though parchment (which *see*) were to be made of it, burying the skin and scraping off the hair, before sewing it on, that it may make no eyesore. Tendons, or stout fish-skin such as shagreen, may also be used on the same principle. An axle-tree, cracked lengthwise, can easily be mended with raw hide; even a broken wheel-tire may be replaced with rhinoceros or other thick hide; if the country to be travelled over be dry.

Lathes may be wanted by a traveller, because the pulleys necessary for a large sailing-boat, and the screw of a car-

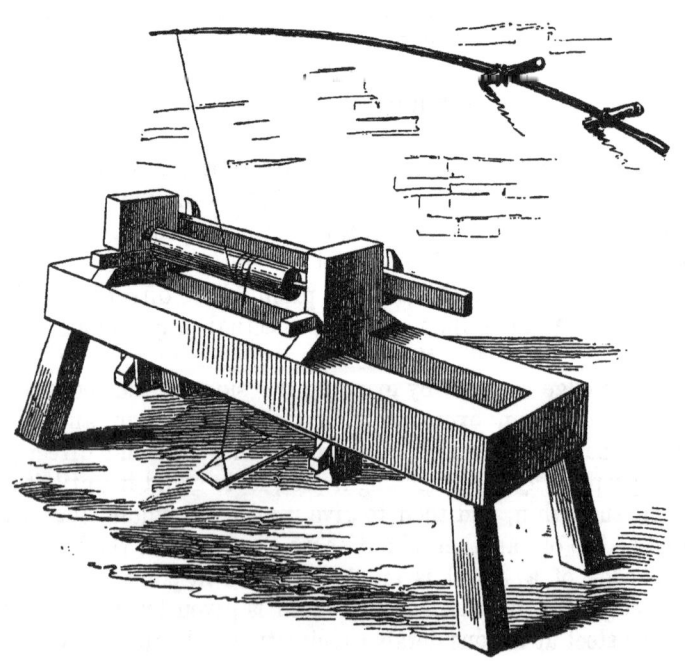

penter's bench, cannot be made without one. The sketch will recall to mind the orginal machine, now almost forgotten in England, but still in common use on the Continent. It is obvious that makeshift contrivances can be set up on this principle, two steady points being the main things wanted. A forked bough suffices for a treadle. A very common Indian lathe consists of two tent-pegs, two nails for the points; a leather thong, and some makeshift hand-rest; neither pole nor treadle is used, but an assistant takes one end of the thong in one hand, and the other end in the other hand, and hauls away in a see-saw fashion. For turning hollows, a long spike is used instead of a short point: then, a hole is bored into the wood to the depth of the intended hollow, and the spike is pushed forward until it abuts against the bottom of the hole. One form of lathe is simplicity itself: two thick stakes are driven in the ground, so far apart as to include the object to be turned; a cross piece is lashed to them (by a creeper cut out of the jungle), for the double purpose of holding them together, and of serving as a rest for the gouge. The object is turned with a thong, as already described.

Charcoal, Tar, and Pitch.—*Charcoal.*—Dig a hole in the earth, or choose some gigantic burrow, or old well, and fill it with piles of wood, arranging them so as to leave a kind of chimney down the centre: the top of the hole is now to be covered over with sods excepting the chimney, down which a brand is dropped to set fire to the wood. The burning should be governed by opening or shutting the chimney-top with a flat stone; it should proceed very gradually, for the wood ought to smoulder, and never attain to a bright red heat: the operation will require from two days to a week. The tarry products of the wood drain to the bottom of the well.

Tar is made by burning larch, fir, or pine, as though charcoal had to be made; dead or withered trees, and especially their roots, yield tar most copiously. A vast deal is easily obtained. It collects at the bottom of the pit, and a hole with smooth sides should be dug there, into which it may drain. For making tar on a smaller scale:—ram an iron pot full of pine wood; reverse it and lay it upon a board pierced with a hole one inch in diameter; then prop the board over another pot buried in the earth. Make all air-tight with wet clay round the upper pot and board, covering the board, but exposing the bottom of the reversed pot. Make a grand fire above and round the latter, and the tar will freely drop. It will be thin and not very pure tar, but clean, and it will thicken on exposure to the air.

Pitch is tar boiled down.

Turpentine and Resin.—*Turpentine* is the juice secreted by the pine, fir, or larch tree, in blisters under the bark; the trees are tapped for the purpose of obtaining it. *Resin* is turpentine boiled down.

METALS.

Fuel for Forge.—Dry fuel gives out far more heat than that which is damp. As a comparison of the heating powers of different sorts of fuel, it may be reckoned that 1 lb. of dry charcoal will raise 73 lbs. of water from freezing to boiling; 1 lb. of pit coal, about 60 lbs.; and 1 lb. of peat, about 30 lbs. Some kinds of manure-fuel give intense heat, and are excellent for blacksmith's purposes: that of goats and sheep is the best; camels' dung is next best, but is not nearly so good; then that of oxen: the dung of horses is of little use, except as tinder in lighting a fire.

Bellows.—It is of no use attempting to do blacksmith's work, if you have not a pair of bellows. These can be made of a single goat-skin, of sufficient power, in skilful hands, to raise small bars of iron to a welding heat. The goat's head is cut off close under the chin, his legs at the knee-joint, and a slit is made between the hind legs, through which the carcase is entirely extracted. After dressing the hide, two strongish pieces of wood are sewn along the slit, one at each side, just like the ironwork on each side of the mouth of a carpet-bag, and for the same purpose, *i.e.* to strengthen it: a nozzle is inserted at the neck. To use this apparatus, its mouth is opened, and pulled out; then it is suddenly shut, by which means the bellows are made to enclose a bagful of air; this, by pushing the mouth flat home, is ejected through the nozzle. These bellows require no valve, and are the simplest that can be made: they are in use throughout India. The nozzle or tube to convey the blast may be made of a plaster of clay or loam, mixed with grass, and moulded round a smooth pole.

Metals, to work.—*Iron Ore* is more easily reduced than the ore of any other metal: it is usually sufficient to throw the ore into a charcoal-fire and keep it there for a day or more, when the pure metal will begin to appear.

Welding Composition for iron or steel, is made of borax 10 parts, sal ammoniac 1 part; to be melted, run out on an iron plate, and, when cold, pounded for use.

Cast Steel.—A mixture of 100 parts of soft iron, and two of lamp-soot, melts as easily as ordinary steel—more easily than iron. This is a ready way of making cast-steel where great heat cannot be obtained.

Case-hardening is the name given to a simple process, by which the outside of iron may be turned into steel. Small tools, fish-hooks, and keys, &c., are usually made of iron; they are fashioned first, and case-hardened afterwards. There are good reasons for this: first, because it is the cheapest way of making them; and secondly, because while steel is hard, iron is tough; and anything made of iron and coated with steel, combines some of the advantages of both metals. The civilised method of case-hardening, is to brighten up the iron and to cover it with prussiate of potash, either powdered or made into a paste. The iron is then heated, until the prussiate of potash has burned away: this operation is repeated three or four times. Finally, the iron, now covered with a thin layer of steel, is hardened by quenching it in water. In default of prussiate of potash, animal or even vegetable charcoal may be used, but the latter is a very imperfect substitute. To make animal charcoal, take a scrap of leather, hide, hoof, horn, flesh, blood—anything, in fact, that has animal matter in it; dry it into hard chips like charcoal, before a fire, and powder it. Put the iron that is to be case-hardened, with some of this charcoal round it, into the midst of a lump of loam. This is first placed near the fire to harden, and then quite into it, where it should be allowed to slowly attain a blood-red heat, but no higher. Then, break open the lump, take out the iron, and drop it into water to harden.

Lead is very useful to a traveller, for he always has bullets, which furnish the supply of the metal, and it is so fusible that he can readily melt and cast it into any required shape; using wood, or paper, partly buried in the earth, for his mould. If a small portion of the lead remain unmelted in the ladle, the fluid is sure not to burn the mould. By attending to this, a wooden mould may be used scores of times.

Fig. 1 shows how to cast a leaden plate, which would be useful for inscriptions, or for notices to other parties. If

Fig. 1.   Fig. 2.   Fig. 3.

minced into squares, it would make a substitute for slugs. The figure represents two flat pieces of wood, enclosing a folded piece of paper, and partly buried in the earth; the lead is to be poured into the paper.

To make a mould for a pencil, or a rod which may be cut into short lengths for slugs, roll up a piece of paper as shown in fig. 2, and bury it in the earth: reeds, when they are to be obtained, make a stronger mould than paper.

To cast a lamp, a bottle, or other hollow article, use a cylinder of paper, buried in the ground, as in fig. 3, and hold a stick fast in the middle, while the lead is poured round.

Loose, shaky articles often admit of being set to rights, by warming the joints and pouring a little melted lead into the cracks.

Tin.—Solder for tin plates, is made of one or two parts of tin, and one of lead. Before soldering, the surfaces must be quite bright and close together; and the contact of air must be excluded during the operation, else the heat will tarnish the surface and prevent the adhesion of the solder: the borax and resin commonly in use, effect this. The best plan is to clean the surfaces with muriatic acid saturated with tin: this method is invariably adopted by watchmakers and opticians, who never use borax and resin. The point of the soldering-tool must be filed bright.

Copper, to tin.—Clean the copper well with sandstone; heat it, and rub it with sal-ammoniac till it is quite clean and bright; the tin, with some powdered resin, is now placed on the copper, which is made so hot as to melt the tin, and allow it to be spread over the surface with a bit of rag. A very little tin is used in this way: it is said that a piece as big as a pea, would tin a large saucepan; which is at the rate of twenty grains of tin to a square foot of copper.

LEATHER.

Raw Hides.—*Dressing Hides.*—Skins that have been dressed are essential to a traveller in an uncivilised country, for they make his packing-straps, his bags, his clothes, shoes, nails, and string, therefore no hide should be wasted. There is no clever secret in dressing skins: it is hard work that they want, either continual crumpling and stretching with the hands, or working and trampling with the feet. To dress a goat-skin will occupy one person for a whole day, to dress an ox-hide will give hard labour to two persons for a day and a half, or even for two days. It is best to begin to operate upon the skin half an hour after it has been flayed. If it has been allowed to dry during the process, it must be re-softened by damping, not with water—for it will never end by being supple, if water be used—but with whatever the natives generally employ: clotted milk and linseed-meal are used in Abyssinia; cow-dung by the Caffres and Bushmen. When a skin is put aside for the night, it must be rolled up, to prevent it from becoming dry by the morning. It is generally necessary to slightly grease the skin, when it is half-dressed, to make it thoroughly supple.

Smoking Hides.—Mr. Catlin, speaking of the skins used by the N. American Indians, says that the greater part of them "go through still another operation afterwards (besides dressing), which gives them a greater value, and renders them much more serviceable—that is, the process of smoking. For this, a small hole is dug in the ground, and a fire is built in it with rotten wood, which will produce a great quantity of smoke without much blaze, and several small poles of the proper length stuck in the ground around it, and drawn and fastened together at the top (making a cone), around which a skin is wrapped in form of a tent, and generally sewed together at the edges to secure the smoke within it: within this the skins to be smoked are placed, and in this condition the tent will stand a day or two, enclosing the heated smoke; and by some chemical process or other, which I do not understand, the skins thus acquire a quality which enables them, after being ever so many times wet, to dry soft and pliant as they were before, which secret I have never seen practised in my own country, and for the lack of which all our dressed skins, when once wet, are, I think, chiefly ruined." A single skin may conveniently be smoked by sewing the edges together, so as to make a tube of it: the lower end is tied round an iron pot with rotten wood burning inside, the upper end is kept open with a hoop, and slung to a triangle, as shown in the figure.

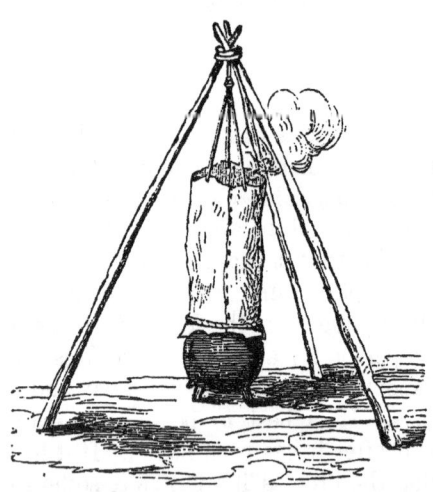

Tanning Hides.—Steep them in a strong solution of alum

and a little salt, for a period dependent on the thickness of the hide. The gradual change of the hide into tanned leather is visible, and should be watched. If desired, the hair may be removed before the operation, as described in "Parchment;" kid gloves are made of leather that has been prepared in this way.

Greasing Leather.—All leather articles should be occasionally well rubbed with fat, when used in hot, dry climates, or when they are often wetted and dried again: it makes a difference of many hundred per cent. in their wear. It is a great desideratum to be possessed of a supply of fat, but it is not easy to obtain it from antelopes and other sinewy game. The French troops adopt the following method, which Lord Lucan copied from them, when in the Crimea:—the marrowbones of the slaughtered animals are broken between stones; they are then well boiled, and the broth is skimmed when cold.

To preserve Hides in a dried State.—After the hide has been flayed from a beast, if it is not intended to "dress" it, it should be pegged out in the sun. If it be also rubbed over with wood-ashes, or better still with salt, it will keep longer. Most small furs that reach the hands of English furriers have been merely sun-dried; but large hides are usually salted, before being shipped for Europe to be tanned. A hide that has been salted is injured for dressing by the hand, but it is not entirely spoiled: and therefore the following extract from Mr. Dana's 'Two Years before the Mast' may be of service to travellers who have shot many head of game in one place, or to those who have lost a herd of goats by distemper.

Salting Hides.—" The first thing is to put the hides to soak. This is done by carrying them down at low tide, and making them fast in small piles by ropes, and letting the tide come up and cover them. Every day we put 25 in soak for each man, which with us make 150. There they lie 48 hours, when they are taken out and rolled up in wheelbarrows, and thrown into vats. These vats contain brine made very strong, being sea-water with great quantities of salt thrown in. This pickles the hides, and in this they lie 48 hours: the use of the sea-water into which they are first put being merely to soften and clean them.

"From these vats they are taken to lie on a platform 24 hours, and are then spread upon the ground and carefully stretched and staked out, so that they may dry smooth. After they were staked, and while yet wet and soft, we used to go upon them with our knives, and carefully cut off all the bad parts: the pieces of meat and fat, which would otherwise corrupt and affect the whole if stowed away in a vessel for months, the large flippers, the ears, and all other parts that prevent close stowage. This was the most difficult part of our duty, as it required much skill to take off everything necessary, and not to cut or injure the hides. It was also a long process, as six of us had to clean 150; most of which required a great deal to be done to them, as the Spaniards are very careless in skinning their cattle. Then, too, as we cleaned them while they were staked out, we were obliged to kneel down upon them, which always gives beginners the back-ache. The first day I was so slow and awkward that I only cleaned eight; at the end of a few days I doubled my number, and in a fortnight or three weeks could keep up with the others, and clean my proportion—twenty-five."

CORD, STRING, THREAD.

General Remarks.—I have spoken of the strength of different cords in "Alpine outfit," p. 48. All kinds of cord become exceedingly rotten in hot, dry countries: the fishermen of the Cape preserve their nets by steeping them occasionally in blood. Thread and twine should be waxed before using them for sewing, whenever there is reason to doubt their durability.

Substitutes.—The substitutes for thread, string, and cord, are as follows:—Thongs cut spirally, like a watch-spring, out of a piece of leather or hide, and made pliant by working them round a stick; sinew and catgut (pp. 346, 347); inner bark of trees—this is easily separated by long steeping in water, but chewing it is better; roots of trees, as the spruce-fir, split to the proper size; woodbines, runners, or pliant twigs twisted together. Some seaweeds—the only English one of which I have heard is the common olive-green weed called *Chorda Filum*; it looks like a whip-thong, and sometimes grows to a length of thirty or forty feet; when half-dried, the skin is taken off and twisted into fishing-lines, &c. Hay-bands; horsehair ropes, or even a few twisted hairs from the tail of a horse; the stems of numerous plants afford fibres that are more or less effective substitutes for hemp, those that are used by the natives of the country visited should be noticed; "Indian grass" is an animal substance attached to the ovaries of small sharks and some other fish of the same class.

In lashing things together with twigs, hay-bands, and the like, the way of securing the loose ends is *not* by means of a knot, which usually causes them to break, but by twisting the ends together until they "kink." All faggots and trusses are secured in this way.

Sewing.—*Sewing Materials.*—These are best carried in a linen bag; they consist of sail needles, packed in a long box with cork wads at the ends, to preserve their points; a sailor's palm; beeswax; twine; awls; bristles; cobbler's wax; large bodkin; packing-needle; ordinary sewing-needles; tailor's thimble; threads; cottons; silks; buttons; scissors; and pins.

Stitches.—The enthusiastic traveller should be thoroughly grounded by a tailor in the rudiments of sewing and the most useful stitches. They are as follows:—To make a knot at the end of the thread; to run; to stitch; to "sew;" to fell, or otherwise to make a double seam; to herring-bone (essential for flannels); to hem; to sew over; to bind; to sew on a button; to make a button-hole; to darn; and to fine-draw. He should also practise taking patterns of some articles of clothing in paper, cutting them out in common materials and putting them together. He should take a lesson or two from a saddler, and several, when on board ship, from a sail-maker.

Needles, to make.—The natives of Unyoro sew their beautifully prepared goat-skins in a wonderfully neat manner, with needles manufactured by themselves. "They make them not by boring the eye, but by sharpening the end into a fine point and turning it over, the extremity being hammered into a small cut in the body of the needle, to prevent it from catching."—Sir S. Baker.

MEMBRANE, SINEW, HORN.

Parchment.—The substance which is called parchment when made from sheep or goat skins, and vellum when from those of calves, kids, or dead-born lambs, can also be made from any other skin. The raw hide is buried for one or two days, till the hair comes off easily; then it is taken out and well scraped. Next, a skewer is run in and out along each of its four sides, and strings being made fast to these skewers, the skin is very tightly stretched; it is carefully scraped over as it lies on the stretch, by which means the water is squeezed out; then it is rubbed with rough stones, as pumice or sandstone, after which it is allowed to dry, the strings by which the skewers are secured being tightened from time to time. If this parchment be used for writing, it will be found rather greasy, but washing it with oxgall will probably remedy this fault. (See "Ox-gall," p. 331.) In the regular preparation of parchment, the skin is soaked for a short time in a lime-pit before taking off the hairs, to get rid of the grease.

Catgut.—Steep the intestines of any animal in water for a day, peel off the outer membrane, then turn the gut inside

out, which is easily to be done by turning a very short piece of it inside out, just as you would turn up the cuff of your sleeve; then, catching hold of the turned-up cuff, dip the whole into a bucket, and scoop up a little water between the cuff and the rest of the gut. The weight of this water will do what is wanted: it will bear down an additional length of previously unturned gut; and thus, by a few successive dippings, the entire length of any amount of intestine, however narrow it may be, can be turned inside out in a minute or two. Having turned the intestine inside out, scrape off the whole of its inner soft parts; what remains is a fine transparent tube, which, being twisted up tightly and stretched to dry, forms catgut.

Membrane Thread.—Steep the intestines of any animal in water for a day; then peel off the outer membrane, which will come off in long strips; these should be twisted up between the hands, and hung out to dry; they form excellent threads for sewing skins together, or indeed for any other purpose.

Sinews for Thread.—Any sinews will do for making thread if the fibres admit of being twisted or plaited together into pieces of sufficient length. The sinews lying alongside the backbone are the most convenient, on account of the length of their fibres. After the sinew is dried straight strips are torn off it of the proper size; they are wetted, and scraped into evenness by being drawn through the mouth and teeth; then, by one or two rubs between the hand and the thigh, they become twisted and their fibres are retained together. A piece of dried sinew is usually kept in reserve for making thread or string.

Glue is made by boiling down hides, or even tendons, hoofs, and horns, for a long time, taking care that they are not charred; then drawing off the fluid and letting it set.

Isinglass is made readily by steeping the stomach and intestines of fish in cold water, and then gently boiling them into a jelly: this is spread into sheets and allowed to dry. The air-bladder of the sturgeon makes the true isinglass. (See "Paste and Gum," p. 332.)

Horn, Tortoiseshell, and Whalebone.—Horn is so easily worked into shape that travellers, especially in pastoral countries, should be acquainted with its properties. By boiling, or exposing it to heat in hot sand, it is made quite soft, and can be moulded into whatever shape you will. Not only this, but it can also be welded by heating and pressing two edges together, which, however, must be quite clean and free from grease, even the touch of the hand taints them. Sheets of horn are a well-known substitute for glass, and are made as follows:—The horn is left to soak for a fortnight in a pond; then it is well washed, to separate the pith; next it is sawn lengthwise, and boiled till it can be easily split into sheets with a chisel; which sheets are again boiled, then scraped to a uniform thickness, and set into shape to dry. Tortoiseshell and whalebone can be softened and worked in the same way.

POTTERY.

To glaze Pottery.—Most savages have pottery, but few know how to glaze it. One way, and that which was the earliest known, of doing this, is to throw handfuls of salt upon the jar when red-hot in the kiln. The reader will doubtless call to mind the difficulties of Robinson Crusoe in making his earthenware water-tight.

Substitute for Clay.—In Damara land, where there is no natural material fitted for pottery, the savages procured mud from the interior of the white-ant hills, with which they made their pots. They were exceedingly brittle, but nevertheless were large and serviceable for storing provisions and even for holding water over the fire. I have seen them two feet high. What it was that caused the clay taken from the ant-hills to possess this property, I do not know.

Pots for Stores and Caches.—An earthen pot is excellent for a store of provisions or for a *cache*, because it keeps out moisture and insects, and animals cannot smell and therefore do not attack its contents.

CANDLES AND LAMPS.

Candles.—*Moulds for Candles.*—It is usual, on an expedition, to take tin moulds and a ball of wick for the purpose of making candles, from time to time, when fat happens to be abundant. The most convenient mould is of the shape shown in the figure. The tallow should be poured in, when its heat is so reduced that it hardly feels warm to the finger; that is, just before setting. If this be done over-night, the candles will come out in the morning without difficulty. But, if you are obliged to make many at a time, then, after the tallow has been poured in, the mould should be dipped in cold water to cool it : and then when the tallow has set, the mould should be dipped for a moment in hot water to melt the outside of the newly-made candle and enable it to be easily extracted. By this method, the candles are not made so neatly as by the other, though they are made more quickly. It is well to take, if not to make, a proper needle for putting the wicks into the moulds. It should be a hooked piece of wire, like a crochet needle, which catches the wick by its middle and pulls it doubled through the hole. A stick across the mouth of the mould secures the other end. When the tallow is setting, give an additional pull downwards. A gun-barrel, with a cork or wad put the required distance down the barrel, has been used for a mould. Pull the candle out by the wick after heating the barrel. Two wads might be used; the one strongly rammed in, to prevent the tallow from running too far, the other merely as a support for the wick. Perhaps, even paper moulds might be used; they could be made by gumming or pasting paper in a roll.

Dip Candles.—Candles that are made by "dipping," gutter and run much more than mould candles, if they have to be used as soon as made. The way of dipping them is to tie a number of wicks to the end of a wooden handle, so shaped that the whole affair looks much like a garden-rake—the wicks being represented by the teeth of the rake; then the wicks are dipped in the tallow, and each is rubbed and messed by the hand till it stands stiff and straight; after this they are dipped all together, several times in succession, allowing each fresh coat of tallow to dry before another dipping. Wax candles are always made by this process.

Substitute for Candles.—A strip of cotton, 1½ foot long, drenched in grease, and wound spirally round a wand, will burn for half an hour. A lump of beeswax, with a tatter of an old handkerchief run through it, makes a candle on an emergency.

Materials for Candles.—*Tallow.*—Mutton-suet mixed with ox-tallow is the best material for candles. Tallow should never be melted over a hot fire: it is best to melt it by putting the pot in hot sand. To procure fat, see " Greasing Leather," p. 343.

Wax.—Boil the comb for hours, together with a little water to keep it from burning, then press the melted mass through a cloth into a deep puddle of cold water. This makes beeswax. (See " Honey, to find," p. 199.)

Candlestick.—A hole cut with the knife in a sod of turf or a potato; 3, 4, or 5 nails hammered in a circle into a piece of wood, to act as a socket; a hollow bone; an empty bottle; a strap with the end passed the wrong way through the buckle and coiled inside; and a bayonet stuck in the ground, are all used as makeshift candlesticks. "In bygone days the broad feet, or rather legs, of the swan, after being stretched and dried, were converted into candlesticks."—Lloyd.

Lamps.—Lamps may be made of hard wood, hollowed out to receive the oil; also of lead. (See " Lead," p. 340.) The shed hoof of an ox or other beast is sometimes used.

Slush Lamp is simply a pannikin full of fat, with a rag wrapped round a small stick planted as a wick in the middle of it.

Lantern.—A wooden box, a native bucket, or a calabash, will make the frame, and a piece of greased calico stretched across a hole in its side, will take the place of glass.

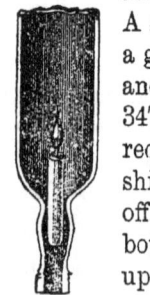

A small tin, such as a preserved-meat case, makes a good lantern, if a hole is broken into the bottom, and an opening in the side or front. Horn (see p. 347) is easily to be worked by a traveller into any required shape. A good and often a ready makeshift for a lantern, is a bottle with its end cracked off. This is best effected by putting water into the bottle to the depth of an inch, and then setting it upon hot embers. The bottle will crack all round at the level of the top of the water. It takes a strong wind to blow out a candle stuck into the neck inside the broken bottle. Alpine tourists often employ this contrivance when they start from their bivouac in the dark morning.

ON CONCLUDING THE JOURNEY.

Complete your Collections.—When your journey draws near its close, resist restless feelings; make every effort before it is too late to supplement deficiencies in your various collections; take stock of what you have gathered together, and think how the things will serve in England to illustrate your journey or your book. Keep whatever is pretty in itself, or is illustrative of your every-day life, or that of the savages, in the way of arms, utensils, and dresses. Make careful drawings of your encampment, your retinue, and whatever else you may in indolence have omitted to sketch, that will possess an after-interest. Look over your vocabularies for the last time, and complete them as far as possible. Make presents of all your travelling gear and old guns to your native attendants, for they will be mere litter in England, costly to house and attractive to moth and rust; while in the country where you have been travelling, they are of acknowledged value, and would be additionally acceptable as keepsakes.

Memoranda, to arrange.—Paste all loose slips of MSS. into the pages of a blank book; and stitch your memoranda books where they are torn; give them to a bookbinder, at the first opportunity, to re-bind and page them, adding an abundance of blank leaves. Write an index to the whole of your MSS.; put plenty of cross-references, insert necessary explanations, and supplement imperfect descriptions, while your memory of the events remains fresh. It appears impossible to a traveller, at the close of his journey, to believe he will ever forget its events, however trivial; for after long brooding on few facts, they will seem to be fairly branded into his memory. But this is not the case; for the crowds of new impressions, during a few months or years of civilised life, will efface the sharpness of the old ones. I have conversed with men of low mental power, servants and others, the greater part of whose experiences in savagedom had passed out of their memories like the events of a dream.

Alphabetical Lists.—Every explorer has frequent occasion to draw up long catalogues in alphabetical order, whether of words for vocabularies, or of things that he has in store: now, there is a right and a wrong way of setting to work to make them. The *wrong way* is to divide the paper into equal parts, and to assign one of them to each letter in order. The *right way* is to divide the paper into parts of a size proportionate to the number of words in the English language which begin with each particular letter. In the first case the paper will be overcrowded in some parts and utterly blank in others, in the second it will be equally overspread with writing; and an ordinary-sized sheet of paper, if closely and clearly written, will be sufficient for the drawing up of a very extended catalogue. A convenient way of carrying out the principle I have indicated is to take an English dictionary, and after having divided the paper into as many equal parts as there are leaves in the dictionary, to adopt the first word of each leaf as headings to them. It may save trouble to my reader if I give a list of headings appropriate to a small catalogue. We will suppose the paper to be divided into fifty-two spaces—*that is to say, into four columns and thirteen spaces in each column*—then the headings of these spaces, in order, will be as follows:—

A	dul	pul	son
adv	eve	per	sta
app	fin	ple	str
bal	gin	pre	sur
bil	hee	pro	tem
bre	imp	que	tos
cap	int	rec	tur
chi	k	reg	umb
col	lan	ris	une
com	mac	sab	ven
cra	mil	sca	wea
dec	nap	sha	wor
dis	off	siz	x y z

Verification of Instruments.—On arriving at the sea-level, make daily observations with your boiling-point thermometer, barometer, and aneroid, as they are all subject to changes in their index-errors. As soon as you have an opportunity, compare them with a standard barometer, compare also your ordinary thermometer and azimuth-compass with standard instruments, and finally, have them carefully re-verified at the Kew observatory on your return to England. A vast deal of labour has been wholly thrown away by travellers owing to their neglecting to ascertain the index-errors of these instruments at the close of their journey. A careful observer ought to have eliminated the effects of instrumental errors from his sextant observations; nevertheless it will be satisfactory to him, and it may clear up some apparent anomalies, to have his entire instrumental outfit re-verified at Kew.

Observations, to recalculate.—Send by post to England a complete copy (always preserve the originals) of all your astronomical observations, that they may be carefully re-calculated before your return, otherwise a long period may elapse before the longitudes are finally settled, and your book may be delayed through the consequent impossibility of preparing a correct map. The Royal Geographical Society has frequently procured the re-calculation of observations made on important journeys, at the Royal Greenwich Observatory and elsewhere. I presume that a well-known traveller would never find a difficulty in obtaining the calculations he might desire, through the medium of that Society, if it was distinctly understood that they were to be made at his own cost.

Lithograph Maps.—It may add greatly to the interest which a traveller will take in drawing up a large and graphic route-map of his journey, if he knows the extreme ease and cheapness with which copies of such a map may be multiplied to any extent by a well-known process in lithography: for these being distributed among persons interested in the country where he has travelled, will prevent his painstaking from being lost to the world. Sketches and bird's-eye views may be multiplied in the same manner. The method to which I refer is the so-called Anastatic process; the materials can be obtained, with full instructions, at any lithographer's shop, and consist of autographic ink and paper. The paper has been prepared by being glazed over with a composition, and the ink is in appearance something like Indian ink, and used in much the same way. With an ordinary pen, with this ink, and upon this paper, the traveller draws his map; they are neither more nor less difficult to employ than common stationery, and he may avail himself of tracing-paper without danger. He has one single precaution to guard against, which is, not to touch the paper overmuch with his bare hand, but to keep a bit of loose paper between it and the map as he draws. As soon as it is finished, the map is taken to a lithographer, who puts it face downwards on a stone, and passes it under his press, when every particle of ink leaves the surface of the paper and attaches itself to the surface of the stone, precisely as though it had originally been written there ; the glaze on the paper, which prevents the ink from soaking into it, makes this transference more easy and complete. The stone can now be worked with, just as a stone that has been regularly lithographed in the usual manner ; that is to say, printing ink may be rubbed over it and impressions may be taken off in any number. It will be observed that the writing on the paper is reversed upon the stone, and is re-reversed, or set right again, in the impressions that are taken from it. The lithographer's charges for furnishing autographic ink and paper, working the stone, striking off fifty copies of a folio size, and supplying the paper (common white paper) for the copies—in fact every expense included— need not exceed ten shillings, and may be much less. If before drawing his map the traveller were to go to some working lithographer and witness the process, and make two or three experiments in a small way, he would naturally succeed all the better. A map drawn on a large scale, though without any pretension to artistic skill, with abundance of profile views of prominent landmarks, and copious information upon the routes that were explored, written along their sides, would be of the utmost value to future travellers, and to geographers at home.

INDEX.

ACCUMULATORS.

Accumulators, 324.
Advantages of Travel, 2.
Agates for striking sparks, 174.
Agreement with Servants, 6.
Alarm gun, 314 257.
Alloy for bullets, 248.
Alkali, 121.
Almanack, (see "Diagram," 286).
Alpenstock, 52.
Alphabet, signal, 275.
Alpine tent, 160.
Amadou, 180.
Ammunition, 244 (see GUN FITTINGS and AMMUNITION).
Anastatic process, 353.
Anchors, 103.
Andersson, Mr., 12, 90, 224, 251.
Angareb (bedstead), 169.
Angles, to measure, 36; by means of chords, 37.
Animal heat, 125, 128.
Anthills of white ants, as ovens, 207; yellow ants, as signs of direction, 288.
Arctic, see "Snow," "Esquimaux," and "Climbing and Mountaineering."
Arms, weapons, 312.
Arrows, 312; set by a springe, 260; to poison, 267; to shoot fish, 272.
Artificial horizon, 25.
Ashes, for soap, 120, 121; for salt, 197; for saltpetre and touchpaper, 181; bivouac in, 138; in flooring, 149; dressing skins, 341.
Ass, 58; kicking, to check, 58; braying, 58.
Atkinson, Mr., 159, 302.
Austin, Mr., 6, 193.
Autographic ink, 353.
Awnings, to boat, 107; to litter, 23; to tents, 163.
Axe, for marking trees, 289; for ice, 49; to re-temper, 335.
Axletree, to mend, 336; to prepare wood for, 335.

Backs, sore, 67.
Bags for sleeping in, 150, 128, 140, 144; saddle-bags, 66; bags carried over saddle, 67; on packsaddle, 71; to tie the mouth of, 73.

BIRDS.

Baines, Mr., 68.
Baker, Sir S., 70, 112, 238, 248, 257, 346.
Baking, 207.
Ball (bullet), 248; poisoned, 266 (see "Lead").
Ballantyne, Mr , 195.
Bamboo rafts, 89; to dig with, 218; to cut meat, 262; to strike sparks, 174; to boil water in, 204; to hitch together, 147.
Barclay, Captain, of Ury, 19.
Bark, to strip, 146; for boats, 97, 95; for water vessels, 229; for string and cord, 344; for cloth, 112.
Barrels, as water vessels, 231; in digging wells, 219; to make filters, 224; as floats, 87 (see also "Gourd-floats," 84, 91).
Barth, Dr., 91, 164.
Basket-work boats, 94, 95 ; bucket, 229, 236; to protect water-bags, 232.
Bath, vapour, 15; bath-glove, 123.
Battues, marking beaters at, 252.
Beach, bivouac on, 138, 310 (see "Dáterám," 164).
Beacons, fire and smoke, 281.
Beads, for presents and payments, 12 ; as means of counting, 310.
Beale, Lieutenant, 57.
Bearings by Compass, Sun, &c., 283.—Pocket compass, 283; bearings by sun and stars, 285; other signs of direction, 287; to follow a track at night, 289.
Bedding, 123.—General remarks, 123; vital heat, 124; mattresses and their substitutes,125; preparing the ground for bed, 126; coverlets, 127; pillows, 129.
Bedstead, 169.
Bees, to find hive, 199.
Beke, Dr., 201.
Belcher, Admiral Sir E., 25, 323.
Bellows, 338.
Bells for cattle, 64; to strings (thieves), 168.
Belt, life, 84; for trousers, 116; bundle tied to, 115.
Bengal fire, 248.
Birds, flight of, shows water, 212; dead game, 200; direction of unseen coast,

BIRDLIME.

288. Food of birds wholesome to man, 202; rank birds, to prepare, for eating, 200; watchfulness of, 314, 255 (see "Feathers," "Quills," Shooting, and Game).
Birdlime, 267.
Biscuit, meat, 195.
Bivouac, 129.—General remarks on shelter, 130; various methods of bivouacking, 134; bivouac in special localities, 137; in hostile country, 315, 743; in unhealthy countries, 17; flies at night, 63.
Blacksmith's work 338 (see Metals).
Black paint, 292; lampblack, 331.
Bladder for carrying water, 228 (see "Floats," 83; Membrane, 346).
Blakiston, Captain, R.A., 26, 81.
Blanket stocking, 116.
Blaze (marked trees), 289; of fire in early morning, 189.
Bleeding, hæmorrhage, 20; blood-letting, 16.
Bligh, Captain, 120, 200.
Blisters, 19.
Blood, in making floors, 149; as food, 208, 200; as paint, 292; as ink, 331.
Blue fire, 248.
Boats, 92, 102, 105 (see Rafts and Boats). Boat fire-place, 189; routes, to mark, 290; shipping great weights, 325; moving them on land, 322; shooting from, 250; fishing from, 271.
Bogs, to cross, 108.
Bois de Vache (cattle-dung), 184.
Bolas, 268.
Bones, as fuel, 184; food, 200; to extract fat from, 343; broken bones, 21.
Books, for MS., 26; to bind, 329; on conclusion of journey, 351.
Boots, 52, 117.
Borrow, Mr., 291.
Bougeau, Mr., 300.
Bows set by a spring, 260 (see Arrows).
Box of card, to pack flat, 333.
Braces, for trousers, 116; for saddlery, 72; to weave, 147.
Brands, for trees, 290, 303; for cattle, 64.
Break to carriage wheels, 77.
Breakwater of floating spars, 106.
Bridges, of felled trees, 110; flying bridges, 110.
Bridles, 72.
Broken limbs, 21.
Brush, to make, 123; paint-brush, 330.
Buccaneer, 196.
Bucket, 229; pole and bucket at wells, 236.
Buckle, 72, 73.

CATTLE.

Bullet, 248; poisoned, 266 (see "Lead").
Buoys, 104.
Burning down trees, 145, 90; hollows in wood, 93.
Burning-glasses, 172.
Bush-costume, 118.
Bush-laws, 308, 254, 321.
Bushing a tent, 166.
Butcher, 197. Butcher's knife, 260.
Butter, 198; relieves thirst, 225.

Caches and Depôts, 300.—Caches, 300; hiding jewels, 302; depositing letters, 303; reconnoitring by help of porters, 305.
Cæsar, 7, 168.
Calabash floats, 84, 91; water vessels, 228.
Calculations, to procure, 353; blank forms, 30.
Calf stuffed with hay (Tulchan), 61.
Campbell, Mr. J., of Islay, 271.
Camel, 62.
Camp (see Bivouac, Hut, Tent), to fortify, 310; camp fire, 187; baking beneath, 207.
Candles and Lamps, 348.—Candles, 348; materials for candles, 349; candlesticks, 350; lamps, 350. To obtain a blaze in early morning, 189.
Canoe, of a log, 93; of three planks, 93; of reeds and fibre, 95; of bark, 92; of the Rob Roy pattern, 107; to carry on horseback, 103.
Canvas, life-belt, 84; water vessels, 227; boat, 94; painted, for sleeping rug, 125.
Cap (hat), 114; (percussion), 244; to obtain fire from, 174.
Carbon paper for tracing, 329.
Carcass (carrion), to find, 200; newly dead animal, warmth of, 138.
Card-boxes, to pack flat, 333.
Carpenters' tools, 334 (see "Burning down Trees," 145 90,.
Carrara, shipping heavy blocks, 325.
Carriages, 75.—Wagons, 75; drays, 76; tarring wheels, 77; breaks and drags, 77; sledges, 80; North American travel (trail), 81; palanquins, 81.
Carrion, 199.
Carross (fur), 127 (see 113).
Cartel (bedstead), 168.
Carter, Alpine Outfitter, 160, 227.
Case-hardening, 339.
Cask (see "Barrel").
Castings, of lead, 340, 304; cast-steel, 339.
Cats cannot endure high altitudes, 19.
Catgut, 346; for nooses, 263.
Cattle, 53.—Weights carried by cattle, 54; theory of loads and distances, 54;

CATTLE-DUNG.

horses, 55; mules, 56; asses, 58; oxen, 58; cows, 61; camels, 62; dogs, 63; goats and sheep, 63; management of horses and other cattle, 63; intelligence of, in finding water, 212; smell road, 289; keep guard, 313; will efface cache marks, 301; to water cattle, 235; to swim with, 87; to use as messengers, 282 (see 'Horse' in "Index").

Cattle-dung, as fuel, 184; as tinder, 183; in plastering huts, 145; in making floors, 149; in dressing skins, 342.

Catlin, Mr., 342.

Caulking boats, 105; leaky water vessels, 229.

Caviare, 199.

Cerate ointment, 15.

Chaff, to cut, with a sickle, 67.

Chairs, 170.

Chalk to mark hats of beaters, 252; whitewash, 149.

Charcoal, to make, 337, 189; for gunpowder, 247; in balls (gúlo), 184; fire-place for, 189; used in filters, 225; pencils made of, 330; powdered and buried as a mark, 302. Animal charcoal, 339.

Cheese, to make, 198.

Chill, radiation, 132 (see "Vital Heat," 124; "Wet Clothes," 118; and "Comfort in Travel").

Chisel, cold, for metals or stone, 334.

Chollet's dried vegetables, 196.

Chords, table of, 37; table for triangulation by, 41.

Christison, Dr., tables on diet, 190.

Chronometer (see "Watch-pocket," 115).

Clay for pottery, 348.

Cleanliness (see "Washing Clothes," 120; "Washing Oneself," 122; "Warmth of Dirt," 122).

Cliffs, to descend with ropes, 44.

Climbing and Mountaineering, 43.—Climbing, 43; descending cliffs with ropes, 44; leaping poles and ropes, 46; the art of climbing difficult places, 47; snow mountains, 47; ropes, 47; ice-axe, 49; alpenstock, 52; boots, spectacles, and masks, 53. —Climbing with a horse, 56; descending with wagons, 80, 294; rarefied air, effect of, 19; mountains, *coup d'air* on, 111; magnetism of, 284.

Clothing, 111.—Materials, 111; warmth of different kinds, 112; waterproofing and making incombustible, 113; sewing materials, 114; articles of dress (caps, coats, socks, &c.), 114; wet clothes, to dry, 118; to keep dry, 119; washing clothes, 120; soap, 121; washing flannels, 121; washing oneself, 122; warmth of dirt,

DEFENCE.

122; bath glove and brush, 123. Double clothing for sleeping in, 126.

Clove-hitch, 326.

Coat, 114; to carry, 114.

Cold 132 (see "Chill").

Collar, horse, 75; swimming-collar, 85.

Colomb and Bolton's signals, 273.

Comfort in travel, 123, 4; dry clothes, 129, 136.

Compass, 283.

Conclusion of the Journey, 351.— Completing collections, 351; memoranda, to arrange, 351; alphabetical lists, 351; observations re-calculated, 353; lithographical map, 353.

Concrete for floors, 149.

Condiments, 197.

Condors, to trap, 268.

Convergence of tracks aflight, to water, 212; to dead game, 200; of bees to hive, 199.

Cooking, 208; utensils, 203; fire-places, 205; ovens, 206; cook to be quick in making the fire, 185.

Cooper, Mr. W. M., 167.

Copper, to cover with tin, 341; copper boats, 102.

Cormorants, 273.

Corracles, 95.

Cord, String, Thread, 344.—Substitutes, 344; sewing, 345; needles, to make, 345 (see "Ropes").

Corks and stoppers, 230, 232.

Cot, 169.

Cotton, for clothing, 111; for tinder, 181.

Counting, as done by savages, 310.

Coverlets, 127.

Cows, 61.

Crawfurd, Mr. J., 204.

Cresswell, Lieut., R.N., 140.

Crocodiles, to shoot, 255.

Cross, as a mark for roads, 290.

Crowbar, 325.

Crows, to destroy, 267.

Crupper, 71.

Culprits, to secure, 317; punishment, 309.

Cumming, Mr. Gordon, 118, 136, 256, 262.

Cups, 205; to make tea in, 210.

Curing meat, 194, 196; hides, 345.

D's for saddle, 66.

Dahoman night-watch, 314.

Dalyell, Sir R., 110.

Dana, Mr., 343.

Dangers of travel, 1.

Darwin, Mr., 57, 184, 223.

Dáterám (for tent and picket ropes), 164.

Davenport brothers, 317.

Death of one of the party, 321.

Decoy-ducks, 255.

Defence, 310, 312.

DEPÔT.

Depôt, 300 (see CACHES and DEPÔTS).
Dew, to collect for drinking, 223.
Diagram of altitudes and bearings, 286.
Dial, sun, 42.
Diarrhœa, 17.
Diet, theory of, 191.
Digging, 216, 311.
Dirt, warmth of, 122.
Discipline, 308, 6.
Diseases, 16.
Distances, to measure, 38; travelled over day by day, 4; loads and distances, theory of, 54.
Distilling, 220.
Division of game, 254; by drawing lots, 310.
Dœbereiner and Œlsner, 113.
Dogs, in harness, 63, 81; in fishing, 273; in finding water, 212; as messengers, 282; to keep at bay, 254; eating snow, 219; sheep-dogs, 63.
Donkey 58 (see "Ass").
Douglas, Sir H., 110.
Down of plants as tinder, 182.
Drags and breaks, 77.
Drain to tents, 166.
Dray (wagon), 76.
Dress 111 (see CLOTHING); dressing-gown, 117.
Drinking, when riding, 231; from muddy puddles, 224.
Drowning, 21.
Drugs, 14.
Druitt, Mr., 21.
Dry, to keep, importance of, 129, 136; to dry clothes, 118; to keep clothes dry, 119; small packets, when swimming, 85, 83; tinder in wet weather, 183; buried letters, 304; dry fuel, to find, 186; to dry meat, 196; fish, 196; eggs, 198.
Duck shooting, 255, 266.
Dung, cattle, 184 (see "Cattle-dung").

Ear-trumpet, 313.
Ecclesiasticus, 335.
Echo, as a guide in steering, 106.
Edge of tools, 335.
Edgington, tents, 157.
Edwards, Mr., 325.
Eggs, to dry, 198; white of, as gum, 332.
Elephants, 62.
Emetics, 15.
Encampments, 129 (see BIVOUAC, HUT, TENT).
Enquiries, 1 (see PREPARATORY ENQUIRIES).
Esquimaux, lamp for cooking, 205; spectacles for snow, 53; raw meat for scurvy, 20; raw meat and fur bag, 14 (see "Snow").
Estimates, 9 (see OUTFIT).

FLOGGING.

Everest, Colonel Sir G., 39.
Expedition, 5 (see ORGANIZING AN EXPEDITION).
Extract, of meat, 194; of tea and coffee, 210.
Eyre, General, 223, 235, 268.

Faggot hung to tree, as a mark, 290.
Falconer, Mr., 153.
Fat, 343 (see "Grease").
Feast-days, 309.
Feathers, for bed, 128; for mark by road-side, 292; on string, to scare game, 252.
Felt, to make, 159.
Ferns as food, 202.
Ferry, African, of calabashes, 84; of reeds, 90; flying bridges, 110.
Fever, 16, 1.
Filters, 224.
Fire, 171.—General remarks, 171; to obtain fire from the sun (burning-glasses, reflectors), 172; by conversion of motion into heat (flint and steel, guns, lucifers, fire-sticks), 173; by chemical means (spontaneous combustion), 180; tinder, 180; tinder-boxes, 183; fuel, 184; small fuel for lighting the fire, 185; to kindle a spark into a flame, 186; camp fires, 187. Burning down trees, 145, 90; hollows in wood, 93; fire-beacons, 281; prairie on fire, 314; fires obliterate cache marks, 301; leave an enduring mark, 303; heating power of fuels, 338; blacksmithery, 338; wet clothes, to dry, 118; tent, to warm, 167; incombustible stuffs, 113 (see "Brands").
Fishing, 269.—Fishing-tackle, 269; to recover a lost line, 271; otters, 271; boat-fishing, 271; to see things under water, 271; nets, 272; spearing fish, 272; intoxicating fish, 272; otters, cormorants, and dogs, 273. Fish roe as food, 199; fish, dried and pounded, 196; fish skin (see "Skin"); fish-hook for springes, 263, 267.
Fitzroy, Admiral, 95.
Flags, for signals, 273.
Flannel, 111; to wash, 121.
Flash of sun from mirror, 277.
Flashing signals, 273.
——— alphabet, 275.
Flask, battered, to mend, 230, 244 (see 323).
Fleas, 18.
Flies, near cattle-kraals, 63.
Flints, 173; for gun, 246; sparks used as a signal, 281; as a light to show the road, 289; flint knives, 261.
Floats, 83; floating powers of wood, 89.
Flogging, 309.

FLOORS.

Floors, to make, 149.
Flour, nutritive value, 191; to carry, 69, 196.
Flying bridges, 110.
Food, 189.—Nutritive elements of food, 189; food suitable for stores, 193; condiments, 197; butcher, 197; storekeeping, 197; wholesome food procurable in bush, 198; revolting food, to save lives of starving men, 199; cooking utensils, 203; fire-places for cooking, 205; ovens, 206; bushcookery, 208.
Forbes, Captain, R.N., 314.
Forbes, Professor J., 26.
Fords and Bridges, 107.—Fords, 107; swamps, 108; passing things from hand to hand, 109; plank roads, 109; snow-drifts and weak ice, 110; bridges, 110; flying bridges, 110.
Forge, 338.
Forest as shelter, 137; log huts, 141; to travel in a straight line through forests, 293.
Form, for log-book, 28; calculations, 30, 31; for agreement with servants, 6.
Fortification of camp, 310.
Fountains, 214.
Fuel, 184; heating powers of various kinds, 338.
Fulminating powder in destroying wolves, 266; percussion caps, 244.
Furniture, 168.—Bed, 169; hammocks and cots, 169; mosquito-nets, 170; chairs, 170, 171; table, 171.—(See also, 168.)
Fusees, in making a fire, 172.

Gall (ox-gall), 331, 120; girth-galls, 68; blisters, 19.
Game, other means of Capturing (besides shooting), 262.—General remarks, 262; springes, 263; pitfalls, 264; traps, 265; poison, 265; birdlime, 267; catching with the hand, 268; bolas, 268; lasso, 262; hamstringing, 269; hawking, 269. To hide from animals of prey, 254; division of spoils, 254, 310; to float across a river, 257; to carry, 256, 327. Dead animals, to find, 200; water, in paunch of, 223.
Garibaldi, 111.
Gauze, for mosquito-curtains, 169, 163; to make incombustible, 113; stretched over mercurial horizon, 25.
Geographical Society, 1, 3.
Gilby, Mr., 104, 255.
Gipsy tent, 161; marks (patterans), 291.
Girths, 72, 147; girth-galls, 68.
Glass, to shape, 149, 350; substitute for,

HARNESS.

in mercurial horizon, 25; to silver, 25; substitute for glass, 149.
Glaisher, Mr., 133.
Glaze for pottery, 348.
Glove (bath-glove), 123.
Glue, 347.
Goats, 63.
Gold, to carry, 302.
Gourd float, 84; boat (mákara), 91.
Grains (for spearing fish), 272.
Grant, Captain, 264.
Grass shutters, 149.
Graters, 204.
Grease for leather, 75, 343; in dressing skins, 342; for wheels, 77; to procure from bones, 343; for relieving thirst, 225; oiling the person, 122; butter, 198; olive oil, to purify, 238.
Gregory, Mr., 68, 246.
Gûl (ball of charcoal), 185.
Gum, 332.
Gun-fittings and Ammunition, 244.—Powder-flask, 244; percussion-caps, 244; wadding, 246; flints, 246; gunpowder, 246; bullets, 248; shot and slug, 249.
Guns and Rifles, 237.—Breech-loading, 237, best size of gun, 237; sights, ramrod, &c., 238; rust, 238; olive-oil, to purify, 238; injuries to gun, to repair, 239; guns to hang up, 239; to carry on a journey, 240; on horseback, 241; to dispose of at night, 243; to clean, 244.—To procure fire, 174; to set an alarm-gun, 314, 257; to support tenting, 135.
Gunpowder, to make, 246; to carry, 246; mark on stone left by flash, 291; in lighting a fire, 174; in making touch-paper, 181; substitute for salt, 197; fulminating powder to kill beasts, 266; powder-flask, 244; battered, to mend, 244, 230 (see 323).
Gut, 266; catgut, 349.
Gutta percha, 125 (see "Macintosh").
Guy-rope in tenting), 164.

Hæmorrhage, 20.
Haggis, 208.
Hall, Dr. Marshall, 22.
Hammering, sound of, 315.
Hammock, 169.
Hamstringing, 269.
Handing things across a swamp, 109.
Handbook for Field Service, 91, 98.
Handkerchief, to sling a jar, 327; to tie the wrists, 319.
Hands of prisoner, to secure, 319.
Harness, 65.—Saddles for riding, 65; bags, 66; sore backs, 67; pack-saddles, 68; pack-bags, 68; art of packing, 71; girths, stirrups, bridles, &c., 72, 73; tethers, hobbles and knee-

HATS.

halters, 73; horse-collar, traces and trek-tows, 75.
Hats, 114.
Hawker, Colonel, 244.
Hawks for hawking, 269; to trap, 265.
Head, Sir F., 110.
Hearne, Mr., 7, 208.
Heat, vital, 124; heating power of different fuels, 338 (see FIRE).
Heather in bivouac, 139.
Heavy bodies, to move, 322.
Heber, Bishop, 219.
Heliostat, 279.
Helm, 104.
Hides, 343 (see "Skins;" also LEATHER).
Hiding-places, 300 (see CACHES and DEPÔTS).
Hills 43 (see CLIMBING, &c.).
Hitch, Malay, 147 (see KNOTS).
Hobbles, 73.
Holes, to dig, 216.
Honey, to find, 199; honey-bird, 199.
Hooker, Dr., 138.
Hooks, for walls of hut, 171; fish-hooks, 269; for springes, 263, 267.
Horizon, artificial, 25.
Horn, 347; substitute for glass, 150; powder-horn, 244.
Horse, 55; to check descent of wagon, 78; tied to sleeping master, 316; to horn of dead game, 254; picketted to a dáterám, 164; running by side of, 317; climbing with, 56; descending with, 294; in deep snow, 110; swimming with, 85; carrying a gun on, 241; loading on, 250; tying a prisoner on, 321; raising water from wells, 235; horseflesh, 193; hair for string, 345; collar, 75.
Hostilities, 310.—To fortify a camp, 310; weapons to resist an attack, 312; natives forbidden to throng the camp, 313; keeping watch, 313; prairie set on fire, 314; tricks upon robbers, 314; passing through a hostile country, 315; securing prisoners, 317; proceedings in case of death, 321.
Hours' journey, 32.
Huber, M., 288.
Huc and Gabet, MM., 18, 58, 61, 202, 257, 260, 328.
Hunger, 17, 199.
Huts, 141.—Log huts, 141; underground huts, 142; snow-houses, 143; wattle and daub, 144; palisades, 145; straw or reed walls, 145; bark, 146; mats, 147; Malay hitch, 147; tarpaulin, 148; whitewash, 149; roofs, floors, windows, 149.

Ice, weak, to cross, 110; axe, 49; burning lens, made of, 171.

LEAD.

Incombustible stuffs, 113.
Index, to make, 351.
India-rubber 125 (see "Macintosh").
Information, preparatory, to obtain, 2; through native women, 7.
Ink, 331; autographic, 353; sympathetic, 331.
Insects as food, 201; mosquitos, 169, 163; flies, 63; fleas, 18; lice, 18.
Instruments for surveying, 24; verification of, 352; porters for, 24; surgical instruments, 14.
Interpreters, 7.
Intestine to carry water, 228; as swimming-belt, 84; to make catgut from, 346; membrane thread, 347.
Iron, ore to reduce, 339; forge, 339; boats, 102.
Isinglass, 347.
Ivory, to sling on pack-saddle, 257.

Jar, to sling, 327.
Jackson, Colonel, 43, 282.
Javelins, set over beast paths, 264.
Jerked meat, 196.
Jewels, to secrete, 302.
Jourt, Kirghis, 157.

Kabobs, 208.
Kane, Dr., 5, 139, 252, 292.
Kegs for pack-saddles, 231.
Keels, 104.
Kerkari, 218.
Kettle, 203; used for distilling, 221.
Kite, as a signal, 282.
Knapsack sleeping-bag, 150; to carry heavy weights knapsack fashion, 327.
Knee-halter, 73.
Knife, 260.
Knots, 325. — See also "Knots in Alpine Ropes," 48; tying to tent-pole, 166; tent-pole, to mend, 165; knotting neck of a bag, 73; Malay hitch, 147; matting and weaving, 147; raft fastening, 89; leather vessels, to mend, 229; hide lashings, 336; rush chairs, 170. For a place to make fast to, see "Burning down Trees," 90, 145; "Digging Holes to plant them," 217; "Dáterám," 164.
Kraals, 63.

Ladder, 44.
Laird, M'Gregor, Mr., 102.
Lamp, 350; of lead, to cast, 340; Esquimaux, 205; lamp-black, 331.
Lantern, 350.
Lappar (to scare game), 252.
Lashings of raw hide, 336.
Lasso, 268.
Lathe, 336.
Laws of the bush, 308, 254, 321.
Lead, 340; to cast, 340.

LEAKS.

Leaks, to caulk, in boats, 105; in water vessels, 229, 232.
Leaping-ropes and poles, 46.
Leather, 341.—To dress hides, 341; to preserve them without dressing, 343; greasing leather, 343. Leather clothing, 111; tents, 154; lashings of raw hide, 336; leather vessels, to repair, 229; ropes, 46. (*See* "Skins.")
Leggings, 117.
Leichhardt, Dr., 196, 212.
Length, measurement of, 35.
Letters, to deposit, 303; carried by animals, 282; of alphabet, to stamp and to brand, 290.
Lever, 325.
Lice, 18.
Lime, to make, 292; to poison fish, 272; bird-lime, 267.
Linen clothing, 111.
Lines, for fishing, 269.
Lists, of stores, 9; of instruments, 24; alphabetical, to make, 351.
Lithographic map, to make, 353.
Litter for the wounded, 23; horse-litter, 81.
Livingstone, Dr., 5, 94.
Lloyd, Mr., 252, 267, 272, 350.
Loading guns, 250.
Loads and distances, theory of, 54.
Locusts, to cook, 201.
Log-book, 27; log for a boat's speed, 105; log-hut, 141.
Lopstick (to mark a road), 290.
Lost road, 295; articles in sand, 168; fishing-line, in water, 271; to see things lost under water, 271, 87.
Lots, how to draw, 310.
Lucan, Lord, 343.
Lucifer matches, 172, 175; for percussion caps, 244.
Lunars, 31.
Luxuries of tent-life, 168.
Lye (for soap), 120, 121.
Lynch, Lieutenant, 102.

McClintock, Captain Sir L., 143.
Macgregor, Mr., 103.
Macintosh for under bedding, 125; sleeping-bag, 153; inflatable boats, 94; water vessels, 233; gun-cover, 238; is spoilt by grease, 227.
Maclear, Sir Thos., 31, 115.
McWilliams, Dr., 16.
Madrina (of mules), 57.
Magnetic bearings, 284; magnetism of rocks, 284.
Makara (gourd-raft), 91.
Malaria fever, 16.
Malay hitch, 147.
Marks for the way-side, 289.—Marks in the forest, 289; for canoe

MURRAY.

routes, 290; marks with stones, 290; gipsy and other marks, 291; paint, 292. To mark cattle, 64 (*see* also "Caches," 300).
Mask for snow mountains, 53.
Mast, substitute for, 104.
Match, lucifer, 175; sulphur, 187.
Mats, 147; for tents, 154 (*see* "Reed huts," 143).
Mattresses, 125; feathers for, 128.
Meaden, Captain J., 259.
Measurements, 32.—Distance travelled, 32; of rate of movement, 32; tables for ditto, 34; natural units, 35; measurement of angles, 36; chords and [table of, 37; triangulation, 38; table for, on principle of chords, 39; time, measurement of, 42.
Meat biscuit, 195.
Mechanical appliances, 322.—On land, 322; by wetted seeds, 323; accumulation of efforts, 324; to raise weights out of water, 325.
Medicine, 14.—General remarks, 14; drugs and instruments, 14; bush remedies, 15; illnesses and accidents, 16; litter for the wounded, 23 (*see also* "Palanquin," 81).
Membrane, Sinew, Horn, 346.—Parchment, 346; cat-gut, 346; membrane thread, 347; sinews for thread, 347; glue, 347; isinglass, 347; horn, tortoise-shell and whalebone, 347.
Memoranda and Log-books, 26.—General remarks, 26; pocket MS.-book, 27; log-book, 27; calculation books, 30; *number of observations requiring record*, 30. Memoranda, to arrange, 351.
Metals, 338.—Fuel for forge, 338; bellows, 338; iron and steel, 339; case-hardening, 339; lead, to cast, 340; tin-plates, 341; copper, 341.
Mercury, to harden lead with, 248.
Metallic (prepared) paper, 329.
Miller, Professor W. H., 281.
Milk, to preserve, 198; sizing paper with, 328; used as sympathetic ink, 331; to milk wild cows, 13.
Milton, Lord, 293.
Mirage, 295.
Mirror, signalling with the sun, 277.
Mitchell, Sir Thomas, 284.
Moltke, 184.
Mosquito curtains, 169; tent of, 163.
Moss on trees, a sign of direction, 287.
Mould, for candles, 348.
Mountain 43 (*see* CLIMBING AND MOUNTAINEERING).
Muddy water, to filter, 224.
Muff, 116.
Mule, 56.
Murray, Admiral Hon. C., 186.

NAILS.

Nails, substitutes for, 336, 105.
Napoleon I., on bivouac, 130, 153.
Natives, 308 (see "Savages").
Navy (British) diet, 191.
Needles, 345, 114.
Neighing, 56, 316.
Nets, 272.
Nettle as food, 202.
Niger, expedition to, 16.
Night, to follow a track by, 289; shooting, 251; night-glass, 262; compass, 283.
Nocturnal animals, 251
Nooses, 263, 268.
Notes, to keep, 26.
Notices to another party, 303.
Number of a party, 5; to camps, 155.
Nunn, W. & Co., 277.
Nutritive elements of food, 189.

Oakum, for bedding, 126.
Observations, number required, 30; to procure calculation of, 353.
Occultations, telescopes for, 30.
Oil (olive) to refine, 238 (see "Grease").
Ointment, 15.
Opera glass as a night glass, 262, 313; supplies a burning lens, 172; and a lens to condense light, 281.
Ophthalmia, 17.
Organising an Expedition, 5.—Best size for party, 5; servants' engagement, 6; women, 7.
Osborn, Captain Sherard, R.N., 328.
Ostrich eggs, to carry, 228.
Oswell, Mr. W. C., 114.
Otter, 271; fishermen's board, 271.
Outfit, 9.—Stores for general use, 9; for individual use, 11; presents and articles for payment, 12; summary, 13; means of transport, 13.—Outfit of medicine, 14; Alpine gear, 47; sewing materials, 114.
Outline forms for calculations, 29; for the log-book, 28.
Outrigger, to balance canoes, 93; irons for oars, 104.
Ovampo camp-fires, 188.
Ovens, 206.
Owen, Professor, 251.
Ox, 58; for stalking, 252; ox-gall, 331, 120.

Paces, length of, 34; to measure rate of travel by, 32.
Pack saddles, 68; kegs for, 231; art of packing, 71.
Padlock to a buckled strap, 73.
Paillasse, 125.
Paint, 292; to paint cattle, 64; paint-brush, 330.
Palanquin, 81 (see "Litter," 23).
Palisades, 145, 90.

PREPARATORY.

Palliser, Captain J., 96, 120, 250, 253, 300.
Pan-hunting, 253.
Paper, 328; warmth of, in coverlet, 128.
Parbuckling, 324.
Parchment, 346.
Park, Mungo, 6, 56, 58, 257, 308, 310.
Parkyns, Mansfield, Mr., 21, 119, 244, 282.
Party, to organise, 5 (see ORGANISING AN EXPEDITION).
Paste, 332.
Patch to a water-bag, 229.
Path, lost, 295.
Patterans (gipsy marks by road), 291.
Paunch of dead animal, water in, 228.
Payment, articles of, 12.
Peal, Mr., 218.
Peat, 184.
Pegs, tent, 154; to secure tent ropes, 163; for hooks, 171.
Pemmican, 194.
Pencils, 330, 26, 27.
Pendulum, 42.
Pens, 330.
Percussion caps, 244.
Pereira, Dr., 199.
Picketting horses in sand, 74.
Picture writing, 304.
Pillow, 129.
Pitch, 338.
Pitching a tent, 163.
Pitfall, 264, 312.
Pith for tinder, 184; for hats, 112.
Plaids in bivouac in heather, 139; wetted, in wind, 127.
Planks, to sew together, 105 (see TIMBER); plank-roads, 109.
Poaching devices, 262 (see GAME, OTHER MEANS, &c.).
Poison, for beasts, 265; for fish, 272; for stakes in pitfalls, 264; for arrows, 267; for bullets, 266; snake bites, 21; suspicion of poison, 199; poisonous plants, 202; antidotes to poison, 18.
Pole for tent, 166; pole and bucket, 236; pole star, 42, 286.
Poncho, 117.
Portable food, 191-193.
Porters for instruments, 24; of provisions for depôts, 305.
Pottery, 348.—Glaze for, 348; clay, 348; pots for stores and caches, 348.—Pot for cooking, 203; to mend, 203; substitute for, 204; baking in, 208; distilling from, 222.
Powder, 245 (see "Gunpowder").
Prairie on fire, 314.
Precautions against poison, 199; malaria, 17; unwholesome water, 224; thieves, 168
Preparatory Inquiries, 1.—Qualifications for a traveller, 1; dangers of

PRESENTS.

travel, 1; advantages 2; to obtain information, 2; conditions of failure and success, 4; the leader, 4; servants, 5.
Presents for savages, 12.
Preserving food, 193, 198.
Pricker for gun-nipples, 245.
Prisoners, to secure, 317; punishment, 309.
Pulley, 325.
Pump, 236.
Puna (effect of high mountain air), 19.
Punishment, 309.
Punt of hide, 95; of tin, 99.
Putrid water, 225.
Pyrites, 174.

Qualifications for a traveller, 1.
Quicksilver, to harden lead, 248.
Quills, to prepare, 330; to carry letters, 304; to hold minute specimens, 333.
Quinine, 14, 16.

Radiation chill, 132.
Rae, Dr., 192, 225.
Rafts and boats, 88 —Rafts of wood, 88; of bamboo, 89; floating power of woods, 89; burning down trees, 90, 145; rafts of reeds, 90; of hide, 91; of gourds (Makára), 91; rude boats, 92; sailing, 92; log canoe, 93; of three planks, 93; inflatable india-rubber, 94; of basket, 94; of reed or fibre, 95; of hide, 95; corracle and skin punt, 95; bark boat and canoe, 97; tin boat, 99; boats, well built, of various materials, 102; boating gear, 103; boat building, 105; boat management, 105; awning, 107.—(See also "Boats.")
Rain, to catch, 223.
Ramrod, 238; to replace, 239; probing with, for water, 213; broken ramrod tubes, 239
Rank birds, to prepare for eating, 200.
Rarefied air, 19.
Rarey, Mr., 55.
Rate of movement, to measure, 32; of swimming, 82; theory of load, and rate of travel, 54.
Rations, 190, 14; of water, 226.
Raw meat, 201; as an antiscorbutic, 20.
Reconnoitring arid lands, 305.
Reeds, for rafts, 90; mats, 147; huts and fences, 142; to weave, 147; for pens, 330; as a cache, 301 (see "Bamboo").
Reel, substitutes for, 270.
Reflectors, to light tinder, 172; of sun for a signal, 277.
Remedies, 14.
Resin, 338.
Retreat, hurried, 317, 23.

SEEDS.

Richardson, Sir J., 194; Mr., 102.
Rifle, 237 (see GUNS and RIFLES).
Right angle, to lay out, 37.
Rings for saddle, 66, 73.
Rivers, to cross, 107 (see FORDS and BRIDGES); their banks are bad roads, 295.
Road, to mark, 289; plank-road, 109; lost road, 295.
Rob Roy canoe, 102.
Robbers, 168 (see "Thieves").
Robbiboo, 195.
Rock, a reservoir of heat at night, 138; magnetism of, 284.
Rockets, 247, 312.
Roe of fish, as food, 199.
Roofs, 133, 149.
Ropes, for descending cliffs, 44; Alpine, 47; of sheeting, 44; of bark, 344 (see CORD, STRING, THREAD); tying a prisoner, 317.
Rudder, 104.
Rumford, Count, 112.
Running, with horses, 317.
Rushes (see "Reeds"), for chairs, 170.
Rust, 238.

Sack, 153 (see "Bag").
Saddle, 65; packsaddle, 68; saddle as pillow, 129; saddle bags, 66; as screens against wind, 134.
Sails to raft, 92, 104; sail-tent, 107.
Salt, 197; given to cattle, 56, 61; salt-licks, 253; salt meat, 194; to make 194, 196; to salt hides, 343; to prepare salt meat for cooking, 208 (see "Sea-water").
Saltpetre, 181, 197; for gunpowder, 247.
Sand, sleeping in, 138; to pitch tents or picket horses in, 164; ripple marks on, give sign of direction, 288; used in raising a sarcophagus, 323.
Sarcophagus, raised by sand, 323.
Savages, management of, 308.— General remarks, 308; bush laws, 308; to enable a savage to keep count, 310; drawing lots, 310.
Saw mark, 303.
Scarecrow, 250, 254.
Scent of human touch, 262.
Schlagintweit, H., 20.
Science, preparatory information in, 2.
Scorpion sting, 21.
Scurvy, 20.
Sea-birds, as food, 200.—Sea-water, wetting with, a remedy for thirst, 222; a remedy for damp through rain, 120; to distil, 221.—Sea-weed as fuel, 184; as food, 203; as fodder, 65; as string, 344; to make gum, 332; its ashes, 120.
Seeds wetted, expansive force of, 323, 230, 244.

SEALING-WAX.

Sealing-wax varnish, 332.
Seamanship, 104.
Seasoning wood, 333.
Seidlitz powders, 15.
Servants, 5, 6.
Sewing, 345, 114.
Sextant, to learn the use of, 3; glasses to re-silver, 25.
Shavings for bedding, 126.
Sheep, 63; sheep dogs, 63.
Sheets used as ropes, 44.
Shelter from wind, 130; from sky, 133.
Shingle, bivouac on, 138, 310.
Shingles (wood tiles), 149.
Shirt sleeves, how to tuck up, 116; writing notes upon, 328.
Shoes, 52, 117; of untanned leather, eatable, 200; shoemakers' wax, 270.
Shooting, hints on, 250.—How to load, 250; shooting in water, 250; night shooting, 251; battues to mark the beaters, 252; scarecrows, 252; stalking horses, 252; pan-hunting, 253; the rush of an enraged animal, 253; hiding game, 254; tying up the shooting horse, 254; division of game, 254; duck shooting, 255; crocodile shooting, 255; tracks, 255; carrying game, 256; setting a gun as a spring-gun, 257; bow and arrows, 260; knives, 260; night-glass, 262.
Shot, 249; for defence, 312.
Shutters of grass, 149.
Sickness 16 (see "Medicine").
Sickle, in cutting chaff, 64.
Sights of a gun, 238; to replace, 239.
Signals, 273.—Flashing with flags, 273; reflecting the sun with a mirror, 277; fire and smoke, 281; other signals, 282; letters carried by animals, 282.
Signets, 332.
Sinew-thread, 347.
Size, for paper, 328.
Skins (see LEATHER), eatable when untanned, 200; salting animals in their own skins, 196; baking them, ditto, 206, 207; boiling, ditto, 204; skin rafts, 91; boats, 95; water bags, 228, 229; lashings of raw hide, 336; to make glue, 347.
Sky, shelter from, 133.
Sledge, 80.
Sleeping-bags, 150.—Knapsack bags, 150; Arctic bags, 152; peasants' sack, 153 (see also, 128, 140, 144).
Slippers, 117.
Slugs (shot), 249; to cast, 340.
Smell of road, 289; of water, 212; of human touch, 262; of a negro, 314; as an indication to stop, 282.
Smith, Archibald, Mr., 33.
Smith, Dr., 190.

STRAIT-WAISTCOAT.

Smith's work, 338.
Smoke signals, 281; smoking skins, 342;
Snake bites, 21; tree snakes, in boating, 107; poison for arrows, 267.
Snares, 263.
Snow, bivouac on, 139; huts of, 143; hearth on, 189; filter for muddy water, 224; snow does not satisfy thirst, 219; blindness and spectacles, 53; drifts to cross, 110; ripple marks, to steer by, 288; snowy mountains, to climb, 47.
Soap, 120, 121.
Socks, 115.
Solder for tin, 341.
Soldiering (lots), 310.
Sore backs to horses, 67.
Sound, velocity of, 38; signals by, 282.
Span, measure of length, 35; of angles, 36.
Sparks, 172; to strike, 183; to make a fire from, 186; struck as a signal, 281; to show the road by night, 289.
Spears, for fish, 272; set over beast paths, 264; trailed through grass by savages, 313; to straighten wood for, 334.
Specific gravities of wood, 89.
Spectacles for snow, 53; for seeing under water, 87.
Speke, Captain, 31, 117.
Spokeshave, 126.
Sponge, lapping up water from puddles, 213; dew from leaves, 223.
Spontaneous combustion, 180.
Spoons, 205.
Spring gun, 257, 314; bow, 260.
Springes, 263.
Squaring (right angles, to lay out), 37.
Stalking-horses and screens, 252; stalking game, 241.
Stars for bearings, 285.
Starving men, 17, 199.
Steels for flints, 174; steel tools, 334; cast steel, 339; case-hardening, 339.
Steering at night, by echoes, 106.
Sticks, small, for lighting fires, 185; for fire by rubbing, 176; for tenting purposes and substitutes, 135; to bend or straighten, 334.
Still (distilling), 220.
Sting of scorpions and wasps, 21.
Stirrups, 72.
Stitches, 345.
Stockings, 115.
Stones, heated, to make water boil, 204; as weapons of defence, 312; as marks by roadside, 290; to chisel marks upon, 335.
Stool, 170.
Stoppers, 230, 232.
Stores, lists of, 9; store-keeping, 197.
Strait-waistcoat, 320.

Straw, to work, 147; straw walls, 145.
Stretchers, 23.
String, 344.
Strychnine, 265, 266.
Stuffy bedding, 128.
Sturt, Captain, 234, 313.
Sulphur matches, 187, 172; for gunpowder, 247.
Sunrise and sunset, diagram, 285.
Sun signals, 277; solar bearings, 285.
Surveying Instruments, 24.
Swag, 67.
Swamps, 108.
Swimming, 82.—Rate of swimming, 82; learning to swim, 82; to support those who cannot swim, 83; landing through breakers, 83; floats, 83; African swimming ferry, 84; swimming with parcels, 85; with horses, 85; taking a wagon across a river, 87; water spectacles, 87;—Swimming with carcass of game, 256; with a sheath knife, 261.
Swivels for tether ropes, 74.
Sympathetic ink, 331.
Syphons, to empty water vessels, 233.

Tables and chairs, 171.
Tables, of diet, 191; of outfit, 9; for rate of movement, 34; of chords, 37; for triangulation by chords, 41.
Tallow for candles, 350 (see "Grease").
Tanks for wagons, 231, 233.
Tar, 337; tarpaulin, 148; tarring wheels, 77.
Tawing hides, 342.
Taylor, Mr., 58.
Tea, theory of making, 208.
Temper, good, 5.
Temper of steel, to reduce, 334.
Tents, 153.—General remarks, 153; materials for making them, 154; large tents, 154; small tents, 159; pitching tents, 163; tent poles, 165; tying things to them, 166; to warm tents, 167; permanent camp, 167; to search for things lost in the sand, 168; precautions against thieves, 168.—Awning, to litter, 23; to boat, 107; sail tent, 107; tent and sleeping bag, 153; gipsy tent, 162.
Tethers, 73.
Thatch, 149.
Theory of finding a lost path, 296; of fords, 108; of fountains, 214; of loads and distances, 54; of nutriment, 190; of reconnoitring by help of depôts, 305; of tea making, 208.
Thiercelin, M., 266.
Thieves, hedge round tent, 168; tricks upon, 314 (see HOSTILITIES).
Thirst, 17, 225 (see WATER FOR DRINKING).

Thorn-wreath in noosing animals, 254.
Thread, 344, 114.
Thumbs, to tie, 320.
Tiller, 104.
Timber, 333.—Green wood, to season, 333; to bend wood, 334; carpenters' tools, 334; sharpening tools, 335; nails, substitutes for, 336; lathe, 336; charcoal, tar, and pitch, 337; turpentine and resin, 338.—(See also "Trees.")
Timber-hitch (knot), 325.
Time, to measure, 42; journey measured by, 32.
Tin, 341; tin boat, 99.
Tinder, 180, 173; tinder-boxes, 183.
Toggle and strop, 327.
Toilet in travel, 122.
Tools, 334.
Toothache, 17.
Tortoiseshell, 347.
Touchwood, 182; touch-paper, 181.
Tourniquet, 20, 327.
Tow rope, to fix, 105.
Traces (harness), 75.
Tracing designs, 329.
Tracks, convergence of, towards water, 212; towards dead game, 200; to prepare ground to receive tracks, 255; to obliterate tracks, 301.
Transport, means of, 13, 54.
Trapping, 263, 265.
Travail (North America), 81, 80.
Travel, rate of, 32.
Trees (see TIMBER), as shelter, 132; to mark, 289; to fell with fire, 90, 145; to hollow with fire, 93; as signs of neighbouring water, 212; to climb, 43; to steer by, 287; to make caches in, 301; boughs bent as accumulators, 324; bark to strip, 146; tree-bridges, 110.
Trektows (traces), 75.
Triangulation, 38; table for, by chords 41.
Trenches, for cooking, 205.
Trimmers, 271.
Trous de loup, 312, 264.
Trowsers, 115.
Tschudi, Dr., 19, 268.
Tulchan bishops, 62.
Turf screen against wind, 132.
Turnscrew in pocket-knife, 261.
Turpentine, 338.
Turtle, water in its pericardium, 223.
Tylor, Mr., 173, 177.
Tyndall, Professor, 113.

Uganda thorn-wreath, 264.
Ulysses, 254.
Underground huts, 142.
Units of length, 35.
Ure's Dictionary, 246, 267, 331.

VAPOUR.

Vapour baths, 15.
Varnish of sealing-wax, 332.
Vavasour, Lady, 76.
Vegetables, Chollet's, 196.
Vegetation indicates water, 212.
Verification of instruments, 352.
Vermin on the person, 18.
Vessels to carry water, small, 226; large, 230.
Vice in horses, 56; in oxen, 60.
Virgil, 173.
Vital heat, 124, 128.
Vraic, 184 (see "Seaweed").
Vulture trapping, 268.

Wadding, 246.
Wafers, 332.
Wagons, 75; to take across a river, 87; axle-tree, to repair, 336, 334.
Waistcoat, 115; strait-waistcoat, 320.
Wakefulness, 6.
Walls, 132, 135, 137; of snow, 143; of straw or reeds, 146.
Washing, clothes, 120; oneself, 122.
Watch, pocket for, 115; watch-glass as a burning lens, 172; cover as a reflector, 172.
Watching, 313, 315.
Water for Drinking, 211.—General remarks, 211; signs of the neighbourhood of water, 212; pools of water, 213; fountains, 214; wells, 216; snow-water, 219; distilled water, 220; occasional means of quenching thirst, 223; to purify water that is muddy or putrid, 224; thirst, to relieve, 225; small water-vessels, 226; kegs and tanks, 231; to raise water from wells for cattle, 235.—To see things under water, 87, 271; shooting by waterside, 250; floating game across water, 257; raising heavy bodies out of water, 325; banks of watercourse a bad pathway, 295; bivouac by water, 138; water causes earth over caches to sink, 300; waterproofing 113.
Wattle and daub, 144.
Wax, bee-hives, to find, 199; waxed paper, 329; wax candles, 350; shoemakers' wax, 270.

ZEMSEMIYAH.

Way, to find, 292.—Recollection of a path, 292; to walk in a straight line through forest, 293; to find the best way down a hill-side, 294; blind paths, 294; lost in a fog, 294; mirage, 295; lost path, 295; theory, 296.
Weapons of defence, 312.
Weaving mats, 147; girths, 72.
Webbing, 72.
Weber, Dr., 198.
Weights drawn and carried by cattle, 13, 54; theory of, and distances, 54; heavy weights, to move, 322; to carry, 256.
Welding iron, 339.
Wells, 216; dry, used as sleeping places, 138.
Wet clothes, to dry, 118 (see "Dry").
Whalebone, 347.
Wheels, to tar and grease, 77; tire made of hide, 336.
Whistle, 282.
Whitewash, 149, 292.
Whymper, Mr., 160.
Williams, Rev. Mr., 322.
Wind, shelter from, 130; as a guide, 288.
Women, strength of, 7; kindliness of, 310.
Wood (see TIMBER and TREES) shavings for bed, 126; fire-wood, 184. Wooden cups for tea, 205; shingles for roof, 149.
Woolley, Mr., 44.
Wounded persons, to carry, 23.
Wrangel, Admiral, 63.
Writing Materials, 328.—Paper, 328; bookbinding, 329; pens and paint-brushes, 330; ink, 331; oxgall, 331; wafers, paste, and gum, 332; signets, 332; sealing-wax varnish, 332; small boxes for specimens, 333.—Letters, to deposit *en Cache*, 303; writing in the dark, 26; on horseback, 65.
Wyndham, Mr. F. M., 327.

Zemsemiyah, 229.

THE END.

Made in United States
Troutdale, OR
05/13/2024